Jean Froissart was born in Valenciennes (c. 1337) and came to England in 1361, where he joined the entourage of Edward III's Queen, Philippa of Hainaut. Whilst in England he journeyed to Scotland and the Welsh Marches and revisited the Continent several times. In 1368 he went in the wedding retinue of Lionel of Clarence to Italy – Chaucer was in the same party and it is possible that he at least glimpsed Petrarch. Coming back he received the news that Queen Philippa had died and so decided to remain in the Netherlands, where he enjoyed the patronage of Wenceslas of Bohemia, Robert of Namur, and Guy de Chântillon, under whose protection he took holy orders. He visited the brilliant court of Gaston Phébus, Count of Foix, in 1388, and in 1395 went back to England to be welcomed by Richard II. Five years later he recorded that monarch's downfall. His first book of the *Chroniques* was published in three versions, the second book was completed by 1388 and the third in 1390. He was revising the fourth when he died in c. 1410.

•

Geoffrey Brereton, born in 1906, took a first degree at Oxford in Modern Languages, and later received a *Doctorat d'Université* at the Sorbonne. He spent some twelve years teaching in schools and universities and concurrently practised journalism and other writing. As a young journalist he reported on the Spanish Civil war for the *New Statesman* and was later attached to General Eisenhower's North African H.Q. as press officer and director of allied broadcasts in French from Algiers.

Returning to the B.B.C., from which he had been seconded, he soon abandoned political journalism to concentrate on literature proper. His books include *A Short History of French Literature* (rev. ed., 1976), *An Introduction to the French Poets* (rev. ed., 1973), *Principles of Tragedy* (1969), *French Tragic Drama in the Sixteenth and Seventeenth Centuries* (1973), and *French Comic Drama from the Sixteenth to the Eighteenth Century* (1977). He translated or edited several modern dramatists, from Claudel to Sartre and Adamov, and also the poems in the 16th–18th–century section of *The Penguin Book of French Verse*. He was a Fellow of the Royal Society of Literature. Geoffrey Brereton died in 1979.

JEAN FROISSART

Chronicles

Selected, Translated and Edited by
GEOFFREY BRERETON

PENGUIN BOOKS

PENGUIN BOOKS

Published by the Penguin Group
Penguin Books Ltd, 80 Strand, London WC2R 0RL, England
Penguin Group (USA) Inc., 375 Hudson Street, New York, New York 10014, USA
Penguin Books Australia Ltd, 250 Camberwell Road, Camberwell, Victoria 3124, Australia
Penguin Books Canada Ltd, 10 Alcorn Avenue, Toronto, Ontario, Canada M4V 3B2
Penguin Books India (P) Ltd, 11 Community Centre, Panchsheel Park, New Delhi – 110 017, India
Penguin Books (NZ) Ltd, Cnr Rosedale and Airborne Roads, Albany, Aukland, New Zealand
Penguin Books (South Africa) (Pty) Ltd, 24 Sturdee Avenue, Rosebank 2196, South Africa

Penguin Books Ltd, Registered Offices: 80 Strand, London WC2R 0RL, England

www.penguin.com

This translation first published 1968
Reprinted with minor corrections 1978

047

Copyright © Geoffrey Brereton, 1968, 1978
All rights reserved

Printed and bound in Great Britain by Clays Ltd, Elcograf S.p.A.
Set in Monotype Garamond

ISBN-13: 978-0-140-44200-7

www.greenpenguin.co.uk

Contents

CONTENTS

BOOK TWO (1376-85)

BOOK THREE (1386-8)

BOOK FOUR (1389-1400)

CONTENTS

CONTENTS

Introduction

FROISSART, sometimes loosely described as the historian of the Hundred Years War (he was both more and less than that), was one of the greatest of the medieval European writers. In his own century, the fourteenth, it is not easy to see anyone who can be put beside him as a prose-writer. But the literary language of the day was still predominantly verse, and prose was still regarded as something of a utility medium. Because of this and because Froissart is known principally for his descriptions of warfare – an absorbing but ultimately limiting topic – it has not always been realized that he offers a range of interest not so greatly inferior to that of Chaucer, his almost exact contemporary, or that his *Chronicles* reveal the same kind of human and social curiosity which underlies the *Canterbury Tales*. Froissart also wrote verse, prolifically but not very memorably, but it is for the *Chronicles*, that vast work to which he devoted most of his life, that he is rightly read and remembered.

In one sense, Froissart was the first of the great war-reporters. To say this is to compare his work less to the day-to-day despatches filed for a newspaper deadline than to the books written afterwards by the best of modern correspondents, based on a combination of personal experience, reflection and research. If one described Froissart as the earliest great journalist, this would be no disparagement of his literary merits. It would simply mark the difference between a naturally extrovert writer and an introvert such as another of his contemporaries, Petrarch. Both produced 'literature', and the dedication and skill which went into a few pages of action description by Froissart were not less than Petrarch displayed in some analysis of emotion in a sonnet.

Jean Froissart was born, probably in 1337,[1] at Valenciennes,

1. Almost the whole of Froissart's biography is based on occasional statements in his own works, or on deductions drawn from them. There are no external references of any importance. He is sometimes inconsistent and his remarks suggest two different birth-dates, the other being 1333.

a prosperous town now in north-east France, but then in the independent County of Hainault. While his birthplace lay near to territory ruled by the Kings of France and his language was French, his nationality was not. What is known of his family indicates that they were local business-people, with a strong interest in money-lending, and that Froissart was expected to follow the same career. He gravitated instead towards court life, helped by his facility for writing verse, which would give him a place among the minstrels and clerks maintained by most of the great households. His first patron was quite possibly John of Hainault, the uncle of the ruling Count, though there is no certainty about these early years. In his twenties he went to the court of England, a fairly natural move for a citizen of the Netherlands. The two countries had close connexions based on common trading interests, alliances directed against France and dynastic marriages. Philippa of Hainault, who had become Queen of England by her early marriage to Edward III, took him into her service as one of her 'household clerks'.

According to his own statement,[1] Froissart reached England in 1361, the year after peace had been concluded between England and France and while the English were still riding on the crest of the wave thrown up by the great victory at Poitiers five years earlier. London was still full of unransomed French prisoners and hostages, including princes of the royal family, who were there to guarantee payment of the huge sum of three million francs agreed on for the release of King John. Froissart remained attached for a number of years to the English royal household, only quitting it definitely on the death of Queen Philippa in 1369. He became familiar with London and the royal residences in and around it: the Tower, Westminster Palace, Eltham, Leeds Castle, Windsor, Langley, Berkhamsted. In 1365 he made a six-month journey to Scotland and travelled as far as the Highlands, which he calls 'Wild Scotland', in the train of David II Bruce. On another occasion he visited the Welsh Marches, riding among the towns and castles of Severnside in the company of Edward Despenser, whose

1. See below, p. 470.

turbulent family had once possessed vast estates in the region. During that period he revisited the Continent several times, staying both in Valenciennes and Brussels, the capital of Brabant, and establishing or strengthening his connexions with the ruling houses of the Netherlands. Since there was then peace between France and England, he could also travel through French territory, at the risk only of falling in with the bandit soldiers of the Free Companies, and he went south to Avignon and west to Brittany. From Brittany he travelled, apparently overland, to Aquitaine, which the Black Prince was ruling as his father's viceroy. Froissart was present in Bordeaux, 'sitting at table', he says, when the future Richard II was born there at the beginning of 1367.

In the following year he was a member of the English party which went to Italy with Edward III's second son, Lionel of Clarence, for his marriage to Violante Visconti of Milan. Geoffrey Chaucer was in the same retinue. Petrarch, considerably senior to both of them in years and reputation, was an honoured guest at the feasts. There is no record that any of them exchanged a word or made the slightest personal impression on the others. Froissart mentions Petrarch nowhere and Chaucer only once, as a member of a diplomatic mission in 1376. Since court circles were restricted, he may well have been acquainted with him in 1368, but it would only have been as a young official. Neither had yet written their important works.

Froissart returned slowly from Milan, visiting Rome and Ferrara and hearing the news of Queen Philippa's death while he was in Brussels. No doubt realizing that there would be nothing for him in England, he did not go back, but stayed in the Netherlands for most of the remainder of his life. He was to have three great lords as his principal patrons: Robert of Namur, of the family of the Count of Flanders, Wenceslas of Bohemia, Duke of Luxembourg and Brabant, and Guy de Châtillon, Count of Blois, who was related to the French royal line and possessed extensive territories in the Netherlands. It was for Robert of Namur, according to his first Prologue, that Froissart began writing the *Chronicles*, either in 1369 or shortly after.

Although this was the earliest version of Book I of the *Chronicles* as we know them,[1] it can hardly have been his first attempt in the medium. He says in his prologue to Book IV, written many years later, that he had served Queen Philippa with 'fine ditties and writings on love', which no doubt meant sentimental poetry in the conventional verse-forms to be read aloud or, more usually, set to music and sung troubadour-fashion. But also, in the prologue to Book I (included in this selection), he speaks of a youthful work of a different nature which he had presented to the Queen on his first arrival in England. Although no trace of it remains, it can hardly have been other than a rhymed and partly romanced chronicle of a kind already in favour. Throughout his stay in England Froissart's duties, in part at least, bear the appearance of those of an accredited chronicler. His various journeys, particularly that to Scotland, seem to have been journeys in search of material, authorized, and perhaps subsidized, by his royal patron. There are other indications to bear this out, but the strongest is the remark which he records on the occasion of the birth of Richard of Bordeaux: 'At that hour Sir Richard de Pontchardon, who was Marshal of Aquitaine at the time, entered and said to me: "Froissart, write down and place on record that her Highness the Princess has been delivered of a fine boy ...".' That was in January 1367, and it carries the definite implication that Froissart was already regarded as an official recorder of public events.

One must therefore suppose that the chronicle which Froissart began writing for Robert of Namur was based in part at least on material gathered professionally during the previous ten years or so, and in part already written up in some form, though no manuscript survives as evidence of this. Perhaps it merely consisted of a running Diary of Events, of the kind classed as annals. When, however, he undertook the composition of a continuous and pleasantly readable narrative of 'the great wars of France and England' – to which were later added those of other countries – he had to go back in time to a

1. For fuller details of the various texts of the *Chronicles*, see below, p. 24 ff.

date well beyond his own birth and experience. His solution was to base the first part of his narrative on the Chronicle of a compatriot, Jean Le Bel. Le Bel, a knight and soldier – which Froissart was not – had been a fairly important member of the entourage of John of Hainault. He had taken part in some of the events he described, such as Edward III's campaign against the Scots in 1327. Though evidently not present at Crécy himself, he was closely acquainted with some who fought on the French side. In reading many of the earlier pages of Froissart's Book I, it must be remembered that the author one is reading is really Le Bel. Froissart takes long passages from him almost word for word, while fully acknowledging his debt to him in his prologue.

It has been well said that Froissart has absorbed Le Bel. For a long time the latter's chronicle lay forgotten and it survives only in a single anonymous manuscript.[1] But it was on that foundation that Froissart went on to build his own more colourful and adventurous work. After 1360–61, when Le Bel's chronicle ends, he is entirely on his own, but already before that date the independent descriptions begin. A notable example is the Battle of Poitiers, which Le Bel had recorded only in outline.

At about the time when he finished his long Book I in its first version, he took holy orders and became the parish priest of Estinnes-au-Mont in Brabant, which was in the gift of Guy de Châtillon. The protection of Robert of Namur seems to have ceased then and henceforward his principal patrons were Guy de Châtillon and Wenceslas of Bohemia. Whereas Robert of Namur was pro-English – he married a sister of Queen Philippa and commanded a ship in King Edward's fleet at the Battle of Winchelsea, as Froissart records – the other two supported the French. Wenceslas was the son of the blind King of Bohemia who fell at Crécy. These circumstances no doubt coloured the revised versions of Book I which Froissart went on to write and had some influence on the tone and content of the three subsequent Books. But it is possible to make too

1. Edited by J. Viard and E. Déprez (Société de l'Histoire de France, 1904).

much of Froissart's supposed swing from pro-Englishness to pro-Frenchness. For one thing, the concept of nationalism which it implies would be anachronistic in the society for which he wrote. Most of these ruling houses were interrelated and a change of side was sometimes a mere political gambit.[1] For another, Froissart was always striving to be impartial. In warfare he constantly looks for the outstanding deed and his praise goes to whoever produces it, no matter which side he is on. The main effect of his French connexions was that they changed and widened his horizon. He was able to travel more freely in French territory and to mingle with French person-alities, so that his account of the affairs of Western Europe became fuller and more balanced and contained in particular most interesting portraits of the Valois royal line.

For Wenceslas of Bohemia he wrote a long verse romance, *Meliador*, in which he managed to incorporate the short poems, *ballades* and *rondeaux*, composed by his patron, an aristocratic practitioner of the minstrel's art. When Wenceslas died in 1383, he became a chaplain to Guy de Blois, was appointed canon of Chimay, near Liège, and continued his work on the *Chronicles*.

During this whole period he seems to have remained in the Netherlands, apart from comparatively short visits to France. In his later years he made two notable journeys. The first, in 1388, was to Foix and Béarn, a small independent principality on the northern side of the Pyrenees, where he went to gather information on the wars in Spain and Portugal. He travelled there *via* Blois, carrying letters of introduction from his patron Guy and picking up en route two couples of greyhounds as a present for the Count of Foix. His stay in the south and the impression made on him by the somewhat enigmatic Gaston Phoebus of Foix provide one of the most intriguing sections of the *Chronicles* and are represented in this volume.

The second journey was to England – a sentimental one,

1. Even Robert de Namur changed sides temporarily, accepting a pension from Charles V in 1368, though by 1376 he was back in Edward III's pay. It is hazardous to say categorically which side he supported at the date when Froissart began the *Chronicles*.

apparently, to revisit the country he had last seen twenty-seven years before. He arrived at the court of Richard II in the last years of that unfortunate monarch, presented him with a book 'about love', and stayed in England for three months. When, only five years later, he wrote in Hainault the immediately topical story of Richard's downfall and the triumph of Boling-broke, he was at least familiar with some of the chief actors, if not with the exact progression of events.

The *Chronicles* end in 1400. Froissart is believed to have lived on until about 1410 and to have been buried at Chimay, where he held his canonry. But of his last years absolutely nothing definite is known.

THE CHRONICLES AND THEIR HISTORICITY

Froissart's aim in the *Chronicles* was to record all the important events which had occurred in Western Europe in his lifetime, and one or two decades before. These events were pre-dominantly military, but also political and social, as seen from the viewpoints of the courts in which he lived. They stemmed from the long rivalry between England and France, their wars, their negotiations, their defensive and offensive alliances, but there were many ramifications to that central theme. There were the internal affairs of the two countries. There were their separate wars, in Scotland, Flanders, Spain, Italy, Hungary, Barbary – sometimes, but not always, a by-product of their mutual rivalry – and besides that there were the independent developments in some of those countries. To cover this huge field, which today would occupy scores of correspondents, agencies and all the modern techniques of communication, Froissart relied mainly on his eyes and ears, his personal con-nexions, and a horse. No doubt he made some use of docu-mentary sources, in addition to Le Bel, but most of his material was collected in the way he describes: by being present when possible at official occasions, by going about asking questions, by skilfully conducted conversations with men who had fought in battles and particularly with heralds, one of whose duties was to record deeds of arms on the spot and to identify and list the casualties. Immediately afterwards, he made written notes on what he had been told.

The result was a new kind of chronicle, combining the virtues and defects of the individual eye-witness and the all-seeing eye. Partly because of the method of compilation and partly because of Froissart's literary skill, it differed from the many other chronicles composed to that date. These had been of three main kinds. Either they were personal accounts by men who had played a part in events, very valuable for their authenticity, but limited in scope and sometimes baldly written; or they were official records of the sort usually kept by religious communities, generally though not invariably trustworthy, but lacking in detail and life; or they were sagas, nearly always in verse, romancing the exploits of some legendary hero or attempting to create a legend for a modern one. These three basic but conflicting approaches to history and biography are endemic in all literature, and all can be seen in Froissart. His combination of them produced a fascinating work, but one which contains numerous puzzles and anomalies. His overriding preoccupation was undoubtedly to present the factual truth, but his talent – developing as he grew older – was for passages, long or short, of exciting and continuous narrative. This left little place for admissions of ignorance or reservations.[1]

The modern factual historian uses him with great circum-spection, not to say suspicion. Froissart has often been proved wrong on points of detail, places, dates and sometimes on larger questions. But even in those fields he is often right and one must always bear in mind that because of his contem-porary position he had access, or *may have had access*, to sources of information now lost. For the precise historian, this is the most irritating situation possible. He cannot – as was the tendency some fifty years ago – discard Froissart as altogether unreliable. He has to be patient and compare Froissart's version

1. Although he sometimes writes: 'According to my information . . .' or 'I do not know what became of him', such reservations usually bear on unimportant points. Also, one feels that he might have admitted doubt more often.

with other evidence, where it is available, concluding sometimes in favour of Froissart.

In outline, he is generally trustworthy. It is his detailed narrative – for example, when writing of events in England when he himself was in the Netherlands – which is often questionable. In this translation I have pointed out in footnotes or in other ways some of his more important errors, but many have been left unannotated. Rather than crowd these pages with what, on the whole, would be minor corrections and qualifications, it seemed preferable to leave his masterly accounts of such things as the Peasants' Revolt and the downfall of Richard II to speak for themselves. The latter has something of the grand sweep of Shakespeare's *Richard II*, though written two centuries earlier. Both, whether regarded as fact or fact-based fiction, have the great merit of presenting those happenings as a contemporary mind saw them.

THE VALUE OF THE CHRONICLES

One may be tempted into reading the *Chronicles* as romanced history, like the historical novel of a later age, and there seems no harm in yielding to the temptation. But there is much more to be had. When the military historian has retired in frustration and the political historian has gone back prudently to Rymer and the Record Office, the social historian still has a diamond mine in front of him. Even more – though this is not yet an academically defined branch of history – the student of social and moral attitudes. How people lived, how they reacted and perhaps why, what were the considerations which determined their behaviour and opinions. Much information on such things can be learnt or deduced from Froissart.

On the material aspects of life he is an invaluable guide: customs, dress, eating and drinking, housing, trade, ceremonial, warfare. He throws light on all these incidentally and is necessarily reliable. It may be that a particular battle, or even a tournament or a procession, did not go exactly as he describes it, but there can be no doubt that battles in general were fought in that way, tournaments were so conducted, processions so ordered. He was writing for a knowledgeable contemporary audience who would require his account to be realistic. On such matters he can be trusted implicitly.

He is deeply illuminating on the mental attitudes of his century, though the fact may not be so immediately apparent. The tone in which that hardened old captain of mercenaries, the Bascot de Mauléon, relates his experiences explains more than a whole treatise on the Free Companies. The conversation of Henry Crystede, as Froissart reports it, is a more enlightening comment on Anglo-Irish relations than anything that could be achieved by a formal analysis. Neither of these could have been invented. A conversation such as that of Thomas, Duke of Gloucester, talking in private to his confidant, may well have been: it could hardly be otherwise. But the kind of language which Froissart attributes to him is likely to have been characteristic. Only a year or two earlier the chronicler had been at the English court. He had met Gloucester and visited him at Pleshey, and he had been in circles where Gloucester's way of talking was well known and, it seems fair to assume, was regarded as something of a joke. So it may have been also at the court of Hainault, for which the account of it was written. By such typical and familiar touches Froissart brings us near to the feeling of his age. Sometimes the questions at issue are relatively trivial. Sometimes they touch the foundations of medieval society.

Froissart has always been regarded as an admirer of chivalry and as the spokesman to an over-exclusive degree of the ruling and knightly class. In a sense it was inevitable, for that was where his readers lay. He respects high rank, admires the knight for his fighting qualities in particular, and praises generosity in money and other matters. But the portrait is not all idealistic. Indeed, in reading Froissart with one's mind free of Victorian preoccupations with 'very perfect gentle knights' (who were Arthurian rather than Chaucerian), one's first impression is of crudely savage small wars and private feuds in emergent nations not far removed from tribalism. Over this brutal reality were pasted a few laudatory adjectives such as 'noble' and 'gallant' which deceived no one, though they may have made them feel better. On examination this too is an exaggeration, because the savagery of fourteenth-century Europe was tempered and sometimes controlled by a tradition of order and culture. Its guardians were precisely the same knightly class which on occasion massacred its prisoners and tortured its enemies in public.

For Froissart they were its only guardians, and who can say that he was wrong? He shows the Papacy in disarray, having lost much of its prestige, but still honestly striving, like some half-effective United Nations, to mediate without true sanctions. Though a priest, Froissart is not respectful towards Rome or Avignon, and in this he appears to reflect the outlook of the secular lords. The latter alone had effective power for good or evil, in which consisted both their significance for the chronicler and their interest for the writer. They possessed a code of behaviour – a caste code, certainly, founded largely on mutual self-interest, and in which money played a leading part – which it was the exception not to observe and whose imperatives were backed ultimately by force. 'My lord,' says Sir Walter Manny to Edward III, when the King is contemplating killing all the defenders of Calais, including the knights of the garrison, 'you are setting a bad example for us. Suppose one day you sent us to defend one of your fortresses, we should go less cheerfully if you have these people put to death, for then they would do the same to us if they had the chance.' At Crécy (as elsewhere), it is the pillagers and irregulars, 'Welshmen and Cornishmen armed with long knives', who slip about the battlefield slaughtering the wounded French knights, whereas the King would have liked to have had them spared to pay ransoms.

It is hardly cynical to say that this was chivalry in Froissart's day and eyes, an observance of rules among an international stratum of society through fear of the penalties of infringement. Of course it had its forms which were highly important because the image they helped to create promoted the knightly ideal. Men sometimes behaved 'chivalrously' or 'courteously' with no thought of self-interest: the blind King of Bohemia, King John the Good of France, the Black Prince after Poitiers, all in their different ways. This was the ideal pattern, rare enough to be singled out for special mention, and not of course without influence on lesser men. But its continued existence still depended on the power to enforce its moral imperatives.[1]

The common people had no such power, and therefore no such code. Froissart has often been criticized for his disregard of them, sharpening in several passages into contempt. One must first say that sympathy with them would have been exceptional in a writer of his century, long before there was a mystique of the proletariat. One can also say that, from the point of view of the whole of the gentry, especially in France, they belonged to a different, virtually a foreign, race. In Froissart's account of the *Jacquerie* the colonialist spirit is strikingly evident. First come the rising and the ghastly atrocity stories. The masters flee to a place of temporary safety and barricade themselves there. Help is ridden in from abroad by other masters equipped with the most advanced and costly armament of the day, armour impervious against sticks and knives, horses they have been trained to manipulate, lances and swords. They mow down the peasants in thousands, killing them 'like cattle', as they no doubt regarded them. But Froissart's most revealing phrase, underlining intentionally or not a physical difference between the races, is this: 'There they faced the villeins, *small and dark* and very poorly armed, confronting them with the banners of the Count of Foix and the Duke of Orléans . . .'.

For Froissart and many others the villeins were an unknown and dangerous quantity, who could unaccountably become that most detestable of all things – a mob. While a modern observer would condone a popular rising if he found it to be unpremeditated and unorganized, those are precisely its worst features in Froissart's eyes. 'Those wicked men,' he writes, 'who had come together *without leaders* and with no proper arms . . . When asked why they did these things, they replied that they did not know.' Leaderless, planless, weaponless,

1. For a further note on 'chivalry' the reader is referred to that word in the Glossary, p. 474.

these are cited not as proofs of innocence, but as the most
damning parts of the indictment. The *Jacquerie* was a negation
of Order, which for Froissart was paramount, combined with
Reason if possible, but if not possible, alone. The harshest
ruler was preferable to one who could not compel obedience
to a law. Everywhere in Froissart one meets this same preoccupation, whether the order is military – the trained soldier
observes it on purely practical grounds, the citizen army
usually lacks it – or whether it extends to the government of a
whole realm. The greatest evils were disorder and anarchy,
and in the context of the age this is understandable because the
worst sufferings came from such sources – from peasant revolts, civil wars and bands of unemployed mercenaries.
Froissart was too near to analyse the deeper causes of these –
that is his main limitation – but he saw and depicted their
effects.

He did evolve, however. His account of the Peasants' Revolt
in England is very different from his account of the *Jacquerie*,
which had occurred over twenty years earlier. He is aware of
such causes as taxation and serfdom. He divides the rebels into
'bad' and 'good', conceding that there were many of the
latter, who, after their perhaps not unreasonable demands had
been satisfied, were prepared to go quietly home. He para-
phrases John Ball's sermon in terms which put the peasants'
case movingly and effectively. He does not say that he agrees
with it – indeed, he condemns John Ball very strongly as a
trouble-maker – but at least he gives him a hearing. Whether
this was true ambivalence on Froissart's part, whether his
social conscience was clandestinely evolving, or whether, with
a romancer's instinct rather than an historian's, he was simply
writing what his imagination dictated to him, are probably
unanswerable questions. Their complexity at least suggests a
corresponding complexity in Froissart.

Although he had attached himself to the nobility, Froissart
was a product of the merchant middle class in a region where
it was especially powerful and militant. It is not easy to deter-
mine the part which this played in his work. His constant references to money-values reflect an obsession which was common

to both the bourgeoisie and the aristocracy, and to which only the very greatest (and not always they) were immune. He writes with a fuller understanding and warmth of the citizen-led revolts in the Netherlands than a purely aristocratic chronicler would have done, though generally careful to show that ultimately he is not on that side. Ethically, his conscience can be seen to be middle class, sentimental and not hierarchical – as, over the next three or four centuries, the whole conscience of Western Europe was to become. The germs of both protestantism and humanism are in his work, unrecognized naturally by himself, but detectable in retrospect.

His attitude towards the Papacy is detached and even mocking. When he speaks of the Church as an establishment, it is as a pillar of stability in the same way as the nobility, or else as a source and possessor of wealth in the form of estates and endowments. He records the deeds of priests most enthusiastically when they are performed in battle – when the man of God has become assimilated to the man-at-arms. Saints and their shrines he treats with respect, as is only to be expected, though how far this is conventional there is no means of telling. It is equally difficult to decide whether his invocations of God stem from customary piety or express a more personal feeling. 'May God have mercy on his soul!' he writes often enough, after recording the death of some usually admirable man. Whether heartfelt or a cliché, the exclamation does suppose an appeal from the harshness of this world to some absolute principle of justice and mercy such as the protestant spirit was about to attempt in its direct dialogue with God.

Very often he invokes pity, not always in a religious context. The word has become debased in modern English and, after a description of some particularly barbarous deed, it is impossible to translate literally Froissart's comment that 'It was a great pity'. But there are other ways of rendering it, and the comment and the concept are there. So, more rarely, are his references to 'humanity' and 'inhuman acts'. What all this amounts to is an emotional protest, religious perhaps in origin but not always in expression, against the barbarity and injustice which pursue the partly or wholly innocent. Froissart makes it explicitly when describing the massacre at Limoges, notwithstanding that it was ordered by his hero the Black Prince. There and elsewhere, he remarks that humble people, who were in no way guilty, suffered more than the great lords who were. Is this, contrary to what has been written above, a democratic impulse? In embryo perhaps, since it carries a condemnation of the great in certain rare circumstances. But it belongs more properly to the whole concept of the humanist conscience, just beginning to be outraged by the inflexibility of a gradually declining Order, and moved to spontaneous sympathy with its innocent victims.

FROISSART AS A WRITER

There is very much more in Froissart than descriptions of battles and pageantry, though those were no doubt his strongest single feature. He developed considerably in the thirty years during which he was composing the *Chronicles*, and the change of style will be noticeable in translation. Somewhat terse and stiff in the early part, when he is either reproducing or imitating Le Bel, he later grows more relaxed – more wordy, too – and in many passages his style becomes conversational. This follows in part from his technique of chatting with his informants and drawing them out until he had the whole story in their own words. He obviously had the gift of winning people's confidence and encouraging them to talk. Thus, some of his most successful chapters are simply records of conversations between Froissart and an informant. Or so they are presented, though no doubt a good deal of rearrangement and rewriting went into them.

But besides these passages of interview type, Froissart uses conversation as a method of narrative. There is dialogue in nearly every one of his stories, and sometimes it is used to tell practically the whole of them. This was altogether unprecedented in the chronicles of his century and was his great innovation as a writer. He uses dialogue, not only to heighten the immediacy of his reports, but as a means of characterization. While he commanded a lesser range of vocabulary than a modern writer,[1] within his limits he succeeded in conveying the differences in language and tone belonging to different speakers. They spoke as they lived, in person, class and circumstance: Gaunt speaking for the Throne in one idiom, the officers in the field in another, the populace in yet another. This characterization through dialogue, which would now be seen as a dramatist's quality, is a particular danger-sign for the historian. Froissart reports conversations which he could never have overheard and which are most unlikely to have been repeated to him. A similar reservation applies to his second great virtue as a narrator, his use of concrete detail. It is a method which carries conviction so long as the reader surrenders to the story-teller. Once adopted, it cannot be abandoned in mid-course, since a retreat into vagueness would break the illusion of omniscience. But a critical reader quickly realizes that many small touches have been introduced less for their factual truth than for verisimilitude. Froissart is relating what must have happened, rather than what did.

He thus uses, at a very early date, techniques of the historical novelist to write what purports to be history. Indeed it *is* history in many places, as far as is known or where there is no other good authority to check him by. This tantalizing area of doubt makes him endlessly explorable and debatable as a chronicler, though never negligible. As a popularizer of history, whose account of certain famous events is by now so deeply engraved on the West European mind as to be almost ineradicable, he is quite unrivalled. To that quality he has always owed the majority of his readers, and should continue to do so. But a not inconsiderable minority will study him as a representative mentality of the fourteenth century.

THE TEXT OF FROISSART

Of the four Books into which the *Chronicles* are divided, Book I is considerably the longest and presents the principal editorial

1. Thus, his one word *volontiers* can be translated as: 'Yes', 'Yes indeed', 'Of course', 'Certainly', 'Willingly', 'By all means', 'Right' and so on.

problems. Covering in its different forms the years 1322–78 (the first four years and the last five very sketchily), it exists in three main versions. The first of these was evidently written for the most part between 1369 and 1373, in the circumstances already described. It is preserved in about fifty manuscripts, complete or fragmentary, one group of which constitutes a 'revision'. It incorporates, virtually unchanged, long passages of Le Bel's chronicle. It is by very far the most popular and best known of the different versions and has been reproduced in all the printed editions, from Antoine Vérard's in the late fifteenth century until today.

A second version of Book I shows less reliance on Le Bel and contains interesting expansions in parts, though abridgements in others. It exists in a single complete manuscript, the *Amiens MS*.

A third version also exists in one manuscript only, the *Rome MS*. It is considerably fuller and more original than the preceding versions. Beginning to write it after 1400, near the end of his life, Froissart most probably intended it as the definitive version, superseding the others. But it cannot be used to replace them, since it runs only to 1350.

In contrast to Book I, Book II presents no great problems. There is only one version, preserved in some thirty manuscripts containing comparatively minor differences among them. Covering 1376–85, it slightly overlaps the end of Book I. It was probably begun in 1387 and completed by 1388. It incorporates, with certain abridgements and changes, a separate work of Froissart's, *The Chronicles of Flanders*, convincingly dated 1386.

Of Book III there are two main versions, but except for the specialized scholar, the differences between them are not great. The first (represented by for example the Besançon MS and the revised Breslau MS) was composed in 1390–1, the second probably in 1396. Here again, there is a backward overlap with previous books – a very considerable one if one counts the reminiscences extracted by Froissart from his interviewees – but the main period covered is 1386–8.

Book IV, covering 1389–1400, exists in only one version,

with minor variants among the manuscripts. It was begun some time after 1395 and completed by 1400.

The *Chronicles* were first printed in France soon after printing began there, but there is still no completely satisfactory edition of the whole work. In view of the complexity of the task and the almost superhuman labour involved, this is not really surprising. The most authoritative edition of the text is that of the Société de l'Histoire de France (*Chroniques*, 15 vols, 1869–1975, in progress), which so far, however, stops at the beginning of Book IV (1389). For the crucial Book I it prints a revision of the First Version as its main text, but gives all important variants from other versions in appendices.

The other monumental edition is that published in Brussels by Kervyn de Lettenhove, who edited the complete works of Froissart (*Œuvres*, 28 vols, 1867–77), in which the *Chronicles*, with much valuable editorial matter, occupy the first twenty-five volumes. This edition has been criticized by some scholars in France as somewhat slipshod, but its great merit is that it contains the whole of the *Chronicles* in all the principal versions, in addition to a mass of pertinent information to be found nowhere else.

Thirdly, there is J. A. C. Buchon: *Chroniques* (3 vols, Panthéon Littéraire, 1840), which contains a complete text, with some variants, in partly modernized spelling. Published before all the different Froissart manuscripts had been scientifically classified, it gives Book I in what is essentially the standard first version. While intended for a literate general public, as Froissart should be, it is a work of careful and devoted scholarship and its text is used in modern French partial editions, such as that of the Pléiade.

THIS TRANSLATION

On practical grounds Buchon's edition has been used as the basis of this translation. I have, however, made considerable use of the S.H.F. and K. de Lettenhove editions, consulting them in particular wherever Buchon's reading appeared

dubious or unsatisfactory. This has provided a certain number
of better readings and several interesting variants. In Book I,
I have occasionally preferred the text of the second or third
versions to that of the first, marking the fact in footnotes
(*Amiens MS* and *Rome MS*). I have had occasional recourse to
the early printed editions of the *Chroniques* in the British
Museum (IB. 41229) and the Bibliothèque Nationale (Vélin
743–6). I have also consulted with much profit Professor A. H.
Diverres's transcription of part of Book III from the Besançon
MS (*Voyage en Béarn*, Manchester University Press, 1953).

Whatever the aspirations of the great nineteenth-century
scholar-editors, it seemed to be the main duty of a modern
translator to present the most interesting and comprehensible
version possible without blurring the essential distinctions
drawn by rigorous scholarship. In aiming at this, I hope I
have not been entirely unsuccessful. Froissart is a great and
much-quoted writer who has suffered strangely from in-
accessibility.

To make a selection covering less than one-sixth of the total
length of the *Chronicles* was not the easiest part of the task.
Froissart is sometimes repetitive, sometimes he describes at
length military and other events which rate little space in the
history-books. But over all, and more and more as his writing
matures, he has a narrative stride and vigour which it seems a
pity to interrupt. I have been obliged, however, to do so,
maintaining coherence as far as possible by short editorial
summaries.

I have selected some of the traditional highlights – for
English readers Sluys, Crécy, Calais, Poitiers are unexpendable
– but have also tried to be as representative as possible of the
different theatres of activity covered in the *Chronicles* and of
Froissart's range as an observer and writer. Happenings in
England and France and the wars between them occupy the
chief place, as they did in the original, but something is preserved of Froissart's many pages on Scotland, Flanders and
Spain, and also on private life. More of these could have been
translated without tiring the reader and I decided with particular reluctance to omit altogether such curious chapters as

those on Barbary and the Turks, marginal though they are to the *Chronicles* as a whole. I hope, however, that this selection has a certain coherence of its own, beginning as it does with the deposition of Edward II and ending, as it must, with the downfall of Richard II and the accession of Bolingbroke.

Froissart is full of names – of people and places – a few of which seem impossible to identify. Apart from the known vagaries of fifteenth-century spelling, some of the scribes who produced the manuscripts, usually under dictation, were no better spellers than the rest of us, particularly of names foreign to them (e.g. 'Asquessufort' for 'Oxford'). Wherever they are recognizable, I have printed the modern forms. The place-names (some of which have changed altogether since Frois-sart's day) are those given on a modern map. Personal names, when they appear in the works quoted, I have standardized thus: for England and Scotland, on the *Dictionary of National Biography*, for the Netherlands, on the *Biographie Nationale de Belgique*, for France, on the *Dictionnaire de Biographie Française* as far as it extends (*A* to *Dreyfus* only at this date) and, beyond that, on the best authorities available, including in particular Kervyn de Lettenhove. Inevitably a number of minor names must remain unidentified or uncertain.

Another area of doubt concerns numerals. Froissart, or his scribes, often use precise numbers very loosely. Military historians, trying to assess the strength of armies in battles, will be sickeningly familiar with this feature. Sometimes the numbers are meant to be exact and perhaps they are. Some-times 'thirty thousand' or 'sixty thousand' are used con-ventionally for 'a great number'. They may have been further garbled by scribes who, using Roman numerals, miscounted the X's, or even the C's or the M's. Cognate with this is the computation of distances, which in general is reasonably accurate. Froissart's 'league' (on the Continent) I have con-sistently interpreted as three miles; his 'short league' or 'English league' as one mile. Wherever possible, the distance has been checked, occasionally corrected, or discussed in a footnote. One cannot always guarantee accuracy. Blackheath, for example, mentioned in the chapter on the Peasants' Revolt, is about six miles in a straight line from London Bridge. I do not know whether, in saying 'about twelve miles', Froissart was making a generous approximation, or whether it was indeed that distance by some wandering road in the fourteenth century.

These are puzzling but relatively minor points. A larger one is that of the idiom to be used in a translation. In a sense, nearly every English phrase one writes in the twentieth century is anachronistic in that the same thing would not have been put in quite that way in the fourteenth century. There is no help for this, but I have tried to avoid some of the more blatant anachronisms by preserving a few terms which may strike the reader as archaic, but which have to be kept because there is no satisfactory modern equivalent. Thus, 'minstrelsy', 'joust' – the second because the more familiar 'tilt' could not have been used by Froissart, since the tilt-barrier which supplied the word was not invented until the next century. For an explanation of such special terms, from 'lance' to 'rounsey', the reader is referred to the Glossary on p. 473, which is designed to replace repetitive footnotes.

The whole of Froissart has been translated twice, first in 1525 by Lord Berners, whose work, undertaken at the command of Henry VIII, remains as an admirable example of Tudor prose; secondly in 1805 by Thomas Johnes of Hafod, a wealthy connoisseur of Froissart who collected some of the manuscripts and also had the endurance to complete the entire work. His style, however, inclines to the false archaic and the over-genteel and is flat by both fourteenth-century and modern standards. I have tried to avoid at least those faults in the present translation, but have only once printed a six-letter word not specifically contained in the French, though I believe that the context justifies its use.

G. B.

January 1967

Acknowledgements

THIS translation was originally commissioned by Dr E. V. Rieu, for whose encouragement and patience during several years of waiting I owed a real debt. More lately, as the translation neared completion, I profited by the friendly counsels of the late Dr Robert Baldick.

It is a pleasure to acknowledge the help of Professor Armel Diverres, who generously gave me his advice on certain specific points of interpretation, and of Mr R. E. Oakeshott, who allowed me to draw on his expert knowledge of medieval weaponry.

Libraries are too often taken for granted. Although it may be true, on a long view, that without writers they would not exist, the great libraries repay their debt in full measure. I must therefore thank the authorities of the British Museum and the Bibliothèque Nationale for their unfailing kindness in making both printed books and manuscripts available to me; and the Librarians of Durham University, Nottingham University, and the City of Nottingham for lending me, through the National Central Library, valuable books which greatly faciliated this work.

The Chronological Background

1307	England: Edward II (1307–27) succeeds Edward I.
1309	Popes move from Rome to Avignon.
1314	France: Louis X (1314–16) succeeds Philip IV.
	Scots defeat English at Bannockburn.
1316	France: Philip V (1316–22).

<hr>

THE CHRONICLES BEGIN

<hr>

1322	France: Charles IV (1322–8).
	Thomas of Lancaster beheaded by Edward II.
1323–6	Unrest in England, culminating in Queen Isabella's return.
1327	England: Edward III (1327–77).
1328	France: Philip VI of Valois (1328–50).
	Treaty of Northampton confirms Scotland's independence.
1329	Scotland: Robert Bruce succeeded by David II (1329–71).
1333–4	English defeat Scots at Halidon Hill. Franco-Scottish alliance.
1337	Technical opening of Hundred Years War.
1337–45	James van Artevelde dominates Ghent.
1340	Battle of Sluys.
1346	Battle of Crécy.
	Battle of Neville's Cross. David Bruce captured.
1347	Fall of Calais.
1348–50	Black Death.
1350	France: John II (1350–64).
	Castile: Peter the Cruel (1350–69).
	Navarre: Charles the Bad (1350–87).
1356	Battle of Poitiers.
1356–8	Étienne Marcel leads the Third Estate.
1358	The *Jacquerie*.
1360	Treaties of Brétigny and Calais between England and France.

1361–6   Lionel of Clarence attempts to reassert English authority in Ireland.

1364   France: Charles V (1364–80).

1369   Spain: Peter the Cruel defeated at Montiel by Henry of Trastamara (1369–79).

1370   Direct fighting between England and France resumed. Du Guesclin appointed Constable of France.

1371   Scotland: Robert II Stewart (1371–90) succeeds David II Bruce.

1377   England: Richard II (1377–99).

1378   Beginning of papal Great Schism.

1379–82   Philip van Artevelde dominates Ghent.

1380   France: Charles VI (1380–1422).
           Edmund Mortimer in Ireland secures submission of chiefs.

1381   Peasants' Revolt in England.

1382   Battle of Roosebeke.

1385   Portuguese defeat Castilians at Aljubarrota.

1386–8   Unrest in England. The Merciless Parliament.

1388   Scots defeat English at Otterburn.

1389   Turks defeat Serbs at Kossovo.

1394–5   Richard II receives submission of Irish Kings.

1396   Turks defeat Hungarians and French at Nicopolis.
           Richard II marries Isabella of France. Truce between France and England.

1399   England: Henry IV (1399–1413) succeeds Richard II.

1400   Death of Richard II.

THE CHRONICLES END

1413   England: Henry V (1413–22).

1415   Battle of Agincourt.

BOOK ONE
(1322–77)

Prologue

IN order that the honourable enterprises, noble adventures and deeds of arms which took place during the wars waged by France and England should be fittingly related and preserved for posterity, so that brave men should be inspired thereby to follow such examples, I wish to place on record these matters of great renown.

But first of all, I beseech the Saviour of the whole world, who from nothing created all things, to fill me with such excellent sense and understanding that I may continue this book which I have begun in such a way that all who see it, read it or hear it read may take delight and pleasure in it, and that I may earn their regard.

It is said with truth that every building is constructed stone by stone and that all great rivers are made up from many springs and streams; so knowledge is extracted and compiled by many learned men, and what one of them knows is unknown to another, though nothing is unknown if one seeks far enough. Therefore, to enter upon the subject which I have undertaken – first trusting in the grace of God and of the Blessed Virgin Mary from whom all consolation and advancement come – I will base my work on the true chronicles formerly brought together by the wise and venerable Sir Jean Le Bel, canon of St Lambert of Liège, who took great pains over this matter and continued it during his whole life – and much did it cost him to obtain his material. But, whatever the expenses he incurred, he never regretted them. He was rich and powerful and could well support them; and then he was by nature a generous, honourable and chivalrous man, always ready to spend his wealth. Also, he was in his lifetime an intimate friend of the most noble and mighty Lord John of Hainault, whose deeds are rightly commemorated in this book, for he was the mover and leader of a number of fine exploits and a near counsellor of kings. Because of this, Sir

37

Jean Le Bel was able to witness or learn through him the truth of many of the incidents described in these pages.

I can say with truth that I, who have undertaken to compose this book, have been led by a constant inclination to seek the company of various nobles and great lords, either in France or in England, in Scotland, Brittany and other countries, and have been acquainted with them. Thus, I have always made inquiries to the best of my ability about the exact course of the wars and other events which have occurred, particularly since the great battle of Poitiers, in which the noble King John of France was taken prisoner, for before then I was very young in years and understanding. Yet in spite of that I undertook, perhaps rather boldly, when just out of school, to rhyme and indite the wars just mentioned and to take the finished book with me to England.[1] There I presented it to that most high and noble lady, Philippa of Hainault, who received it gladly and graciously and rewarded me well.

Now perhaps that book was not thought out and composed as scrupulously as such a subject demands – for deeds of arms, in which distinction is so dearly bought, should be faithfully credited to those whose valour has achieved them. Therefore, to discharge my debt to all, as is only proper, I have undertaken the writing of this history according to the method and foundation already mentioned, at the request of one of my dear patrons and masters, Robert of Namur, Lord of Beaufort, towards whom I gladly acknowledge my affection and allegiance. And may God assist me to write a work which will please him.

1. For this early, lost, chronicle, see Introduction, p. 12.

The Beginning of a Reign

DEPOSITION OF EDWARD II AND ACCESSION
OF EDWARD III

NOW first, as an introduction to the glorious and stirring
story of the noble King Edward of England, who was
crowned in London on Christmas Day, 1326, in the lifetime of
the King his father and his mother the Queen, one thing can
be said: it is commonly believed amongst the English – and
this has often been borne out since the time of good King
Arthur – that in between two brave and warlike kings there
has always reigned one less gifted in body and mind. This is
well illustrated by the parentage of the King Edward whom
I have just mentioned. His grandfather, Edward I, was a
brave, wise and resourceful ruler, enterprising and very
successful in war. He did much fighting against the Scots and
overcame them three or four times. They were never able to
beat him or stand up against him. But when he died he was
succeeded by his son by his first marriage (the father of the
noble King Edward) who was quite unlike him in wisdom and
courage and governed his realm very harshly on the advice of
others. This brought great misfortunes upon him, as you
shall hear. Soon after he had been crowned, Robert Bruce,
King of Scotland, who had given so much trouble to the
gallant King Edward I, reconquered the whole of Scotland
and the city of Berwick as well, twice burnt and ravaged a
large part of England stretching as far as four or five days' ride
beyond the border, and defeated this king and all the barons
of England at a place in Scotland called Stirling.[1] The pursuit
of the fugitives went on for two days and nights, while the
King of England fled back to London with a small remnant
of his men....

This King Edward II governed his kingdom so badly and

1. Battle of Bannockburn, 1314.

did such foolish things in the country because he was advised by an evil counsellor called Sir Hugh Despenser, who had been brought up with him from youth. Sir Hugh had managed things so well that he and his father, of the same name, had become the richest barons in England and were always the chief masters of the King's council, ambitious to overtop the other great barons of the realm. This had disastrous consequences for themselves and the country.

After the rout of Stirling there was great discontent among the English nobles and the King's council, directed in particular against Hugh Despenser, who was held responsible for their defeat and suspected of favouring the King of Scotland and encouraging the King of England to act negligently. The barons, of whom the greatest and most prominent was the King's cousin, Thomas, Earl of Lancaster, held several parliaments to discuss what they should do. Hugh Despenser became aware of this and of the compiaints made about him and his actions. He was much afraid that he would come to harm and he at once devised a very foul plot to prevent it.

Taking advantage of his nearness to the King, who placed more trust in his word alone than in that of all his other nobles together, Hugh Despenser told King Edward that the barons had formed an alliance against him and would remove him from the throne if he was not careful. Swayed by his subtle arguments, the King had all these barons seized at a parliament at which they were assembled. Twenty-two of the greatest of them were beheaded, immediately and without trial. Foremost among them was Thomas, Earl of Lancaster, a good and saintly man, at the place of whose execution a number of miracles afterwards occurred. By this action, Hugh Despenser earned the hatred of the whole country, and especially of the Queen and of the Earl of Kent, who was the King's brother.

When Hugh Despenser perceived that he was in disfavour with these two, he cunningly stirred up such discord between the King and Queen that the King refused either to receive the Queen or to visit her. This went on for some time, until the Queen and the Earl were secretly warned that some harm might soon befall them unless they took steps to protect themselves.

According to Froissart's account, Queen Isabella escaped secretly to France with her son Edward, the Earl of Kent, and Roger Mortimer. She appealed for help to her brother, Charles IV of France, but after receiving her sympathetically and preparing to support her, he and his council were bribed by Hugh Despenser and turned against her. The Pope was then persuaded, by the intrigues of Despenser, to order the return of Isabella to her lawful husband, upon which she was banished from France. Moving to Hainault (where the future Edward III was betrothed to the ruling Count's daughter, Philippa) she secured the support of John of Hainault, brother of the Count, who assembled a fighting force to accompany her and her son back to England, where they hoped to be joined by her partisans. Setting sail from Dordrecht, they were thrown off course by a storm, says Froissart, eventually landing on a deserted beach from which they moved inland to Bury St Edmunds.

News of their arrival spread through the country, until it reached those on whose invitation and promise of support the Queen had returned. These hastened to join her son, whom they wanted to have as their sovereign. The first of them, whose coming brought most reassurance to the prince's party, was Henry Earl of Lancaster, known as Wryneck, brother of the Thomas of Lancaster who had been beheaded and father of that Duke of Lancaster who was to become such a great and famous soldier, as you will hear later in these chronicles. Henry of Lancaster came with a powerful force of fighting men, and after him so many others, earls, barons, knights and squires, also accompanied by men-at-arms, that they now felt themselves out of all danger. Each day as they moved forward more men joined them. A council was held at which it was decided that they would lead their army straight to Bristol, a large, prosperous town and seaport, with good fortifications. It also had a strong castle, built above the sea which surrounds it. This was where the King was, with Hugh Despenser the elder, who was about ninety years of age, Hugh Despenser the younger, the King's evil counsellor, the Earl of Arundel, who had married the younger

Despenser's daughter, and a number of knights and squires who had followed the King as court-knights usually do.

The Queen and her whole company, with Sir John of Hainault and the English earls and barons and their men, advanced towards them by the shortest road. They were acclaimed in every town through which they passed and people continued to join them from all sides until they reached Bristol and laid siege to it in full military form. The King and the younger Despenser had chosen to remain in the castle; the elder Despenser and the Earl of Arundel, with a number of their supporters, were in the town.

The citizens of Bristol soon opened their gates to the Queen and handed over Arundel and the elder Despenser to be dealt with 'in whatever way she chose'. The two were indicted before an assembly of barons and sentenced to be drawn, beheaded and their bodies hanged. The execution took place outside the castle, in full view of the King and the younger Despenser.[1]

After this act of justice, the King and the younger Despenser, finding themselves so closely besieged, with no hope of relief from any quarter, embarked one morning behind the castle in a small boat with a few followers. Their plan was to escape to Wales if they could, but their sins weighed so heavily upon them that God would not permit it. An astonishing thing befell them, which caused them to remain for eleven whole days in that small boat. Though they made every effort to sail forward, they could never get so far but that a contrary wind drove them back once or twice daily to within less than a mile of the castle. Finally Sir Henry de Beaumont, son of the Viscount of Beaumont in England, boarded a barge with a few companions and went out towards them. They rowed so

1. This is inexact on several counts. Though the elder Despenser was executed at Bristol (27 October), Arundel was not caught and executed until later. The King and the younger Despenser had left Bristol before it surrendered to the Queen, and crossed the Severn to Chepstow. Storms prevented them from escaping from there by sea and they travelled overland to Glamorgan. Lancaster captured them at Neath Abbey on 16 November. The description which follows of their capture by Henry de Beaumont is therefore unhistorical. It may be read as an imaginative compression of a more complicated story.

fast and so strongly that the King's seamen could not escape them. Their boat was taken and those in it were brought back to Bristol and delivered up as prisoners to the Queen and her son, who were overjoyed by their capture. So were all the others, with good reason, for with God's help they had accomplished their desire in exactly the way they had hoped.

Thus the Queen reconquered the realm of England for her eldest son, with the guidance and support of Sir John of Hainault and his company. For this the Hainaulters were hailed as very gallant knights, who had carried out a famous enterprise. When they set sail from Dordrecht they had been only three hundred men-at-arms, yet for love of the Queen they had ventured across the sea in such small numbers for the conquest of a country such as England, in the teeth of the King himself and all his partisans. . . .

After the King and Sir Hugh Despenser had been brought back to Bristol by Henry de Beaumont, the King was sent, on the advice of all the barons and knights, to Berkeley Castle on the Severn. The keeper of Berkeley was urged to take good care of him, with orders to give him all honourable service and attention and to place court officials round him who were familiar with their duties, but never to allow him to leave the castle precincts[1]. Hugh Despenser was handed over to Lord Thomas Wake, Marshal of the army. When the Queen set out with her army for London, Lord Thomas had Hugh Despenser tightly bound to the smallest, thinnest and most weakly horse he could find, dressed him in a tunic blazoned with the arms he usually bore and led him in derision

[1]. Froissart's only mention of Edward II's death is in his last version of Book I (Rome MS): '. . . After the King had arrived at Berkeley, he did not live very long. And how should he have lived, when things were as I will tell you? For I, Jean Froissart, author of this chronicle, was at Berkeley Castle in September 1366 in the company of Edward Lord Despenser, the grandson of that Hugh Despenser of whom I will say more in a moment. We spent three days either in the castle or in amusements in the neighbourhood. In order to confirm my chronicle, I inquired about that king, asking what had become of him. An old squire told me that in the same year in which he was taken there he died, for they shortened his life for him. So ended that King of England and we shall speak no more of him . . .'.

to the sound of horns and trumpets through all the towns through which the Queen passed until they reached the city of Hereford. Here she celebrated the Feast of All Saints in great splendour for the sake of her son and the foreign nobles who were with him.

After the feast this same Sir Hugh, who was not loved in those parts, was brought before the Queen and the assembled nobles. All his deeds had been written down and were now read out to him, but he said nothing in reply. He was condemned by the unanimous verdict of the barons and knights to suffer the following punishment. First, he was dragged on a hurdle through all the streets of Hereford. to the sound of horns and trumpets, until he reached the main square of the town, where all the people were assembled. There he was tied to a long ladder, so that everyone could see him. A big fire had been lit in the square. When he had been tied up, his member and his testicles were first cut off, because he was a heretic and a sodomite, even, it was said, with the King, and this was why the King had driven away the Queen on his suggestion. When his private parts had been cut off they were thrown into the fire to burn, and afterwards his heart was torn from his body and thrown into the fire, because he was a false-hearted traitor, who by his treasonable advice and promptings had led the King to bring shame and misfortune upon his kingdom and to behead the greatest lords of England, by whom the kingdom ought to have been upheld and defended; and besides that, he had so worked upon the King that he, who should have been their consort and sire, had refused to see the Queen and his eldest son, but rather had expelled them from the realm of England, at the hazard of their lives.

After Sir Hugh Despenser had been cut up in the way described, his head was struck off and sent to the city of London. His body was divided into four quarters, which were sent to the four principal cities of England after London.

The Queen and her son proceeded to London, where they were met by rejoicing crowds. The majority of the Hainaulters returned home, after being suitably rewarded, though Sir John of Hainault was per-

suaded to remain at court for a time with a few companions. The English nobles also dispersed temporarily, under promise to return at Christmas.

When Christmas came the Queen held a great court, attended by all the earls, barons, knights and nobles of England, the prelates, and the councils of the towns. At this festivity and assembly it was decided – since the country could not long remain without a sovereign – to put down in writing all those things which the King, then in prison, had done under the influence of evil counsellors, all his habits and evil behaviour, and the way he had governed the country: to the end that it should be read out in open court before all the people, and that the wise men of the country should be enabled to reach an agreement upon how and by whom the realm should be governed in the future. When this had been done, and all the measures which the King had taken or authorized, together with his habitual conduct, had been published for all to hear, the barons and knights and the whole council of the realm went into consultation. They concluded by a large majority, both from what had been read out and from their own knowledge of the facts, that such a man was in no way worthy to wear a crown or to be called king. They further agreed that his eldest son, who was present among them and was the direct heir, should be crowned at once in his father's place, adding that he should be surrounded by wise and loyal counsellors to ensure that henceforth the realm should be better governed than in the past. The father was to be well guarded and honourably maintained in accordance with his rank for as long as he should live.

As a result of this decision, the young King Edward, who was to be so successful in war, was crowned king in the Palace of Westminster on Christmas Day, 1326. He would then be about sixteen.[1]

1. Edward III was crowned on 1 February 1327, at the age of fifteen. The events described in the last two paragraphs occurred in fact in January 1327 (N.S.).

The Scots Invade England (1327)

Now it happened that Robert King of Scotland, a great soldier who had suffered much from the English and had known many defeats in the time of Edward I, the young King Edward's grandfather, had grown old and was afflicted with leprosy, of which he was expected to die. When he heard of the events in England, the capture and deposition of its king and the execution of his counsellors, he decided to send a challenge to the young sovereign. Since the latter was so young and the English barons were at loggerheads (for so he thought, or perhaps had been given to understand by some of the Despensers' faction), it seemed a good opportunity to conquer a part of England. Towards Easter 1327, therefore, he issued a challenge to the young King Edward and the whole of England, threatening to invade their country and ravage and burn it as far southwards as he had done previously when he had inflicted such a crushing defeat on them at Stirling Castle.

To meet this threat, Edward leads an army north. He is joined by a force of the faithful Hainaulters, who have again been called upon for aid. Among them is Jean Le Bel, author of the chronicle on which this part of the Froissart is closely based. At York, fighting breaks out between the Hainaulters and the English archers, but eventually the whole army moves on past Durham and enters Northumberland, which the Scots are already ravaging.

The Scots are a bold, hardy people, very experienced in war. At that time they had little love or respect for the English, and the same is true today. When they cross the border they advance sixty to seventy miles in a day and night, which would seem astonishing to anyone ignorant of their customs. The explanation is that, on their expeditions into England, they all come on horseback, except the irregulars who follow on foot. The knights and squires are mounted on fine, strong horses and the commoners on small ponies. Because they have to pass over the wild hills of Northumberland, they bring no baggage-carts and so carry no supplies of bread or wine. So frugal are they that their practice in war is to subsist for a long time on underdone meat, without bread, and to drink river-water, without wine. This does away with the need for pots and pans, for they cook their meat in the hides of the cattle it is taken from, after skinning. Since they are sure to find plenty of cattle in the country they pass through, the only things they take with them are a large flat stone placed between the saddle and the saddle-cloth and a bag of oatmeal strapped behind. When they have lived so long on half-cooked meat that their stomachs feel weak and hollow, they lay these stones on a fire and, mixing a little of their oatmeal with water, they sprinkle the thin paste on the hot stone and make a small cake, rather like a wafer, which they eat to help their digestion. Hence it is not surprising that they can travel faster than other armies.

So the Scots had entered Northumberland. They ravaged and burnt it, finding more livestock than they knew what to do with. They were at least three thousand men in armour, knights and squires, mounted on good rounseys and coursers, and twenty thousand other brave and warlike men, armed each in his own fashion and riding those little ponies which they neither groom nor tether, but turn loose to graze freely wherever they dismount.

Their king, Robert Bruce, being too old and ill to go with them, had appointed as their leaders the Earl of Moray, whose arms were argent three oreillers gules, and Sir James Douglas, who bore for arms a shield azure on a chief argent three mullets gules. These two were the highest and most powerful lords of the kingdom of Scotland and the most famous for their feats of arms and great exploits.

When the English army saw the smoke of the burning villages, they knew that the Scots had entered their country. The alert was at once sounded and the order given to leave quarters and follow the banners. They all moved out into the country, armed and ready for immediate battle. They were formed into three large bodies of foot-soldiers, each with two wings consisting of five hundred men in armour who were to remain mounted. It was said that there were at least eight thousand knights and squires and thirty thousand other armed men, of whom half was mounted on small horses and the other half were foot-sergeants and light infantry. These had been raised and were paid by the loyal towns, each town contributing according to its rating. There were also a good twenty-four thousand foot-archers, without counting the irregulars.

Battle is not joined because the Scots slip away. The English follow all day, guided by the smoke of the fires, but are unable to contact the enemy. Concluding that they will eventually be obliged to re-cross the Tyne if they are not to remain trapped in England, they set out for that river next day in the hope of cutting them off. For faster movement, the supply-train has been left behind near Durham, but each man carries a loaf of bread behind his saddle in the Scottish fashion.

Before the battalions had been formed up in order, day had begun to break. They began to move forward very raggedly over heaths, hills and valleys and through difficult woodland, without a trace of level country. Among the mountains and valleys were great marshes and bogs which were so dangerous to cross that it was surprising that more men were not lost in them. For each man rode steadily forward, without waiting for his captain or his companions, and anyone who got stuck in those bogs would have been lucky to find help. Indeed, a large number of banners with the horses, as well as many pack-animals, did get left in them, never to be seen again.

Throughout the day there were many alerts, which made it appear that the foremost were engaging the enemy. Those behind urged on their horses over swamps and rocky ground, up hill and down dale, with their helmets on and their shields slung, their swords or lances in their hands, without waiting for father, brother or comrade. But when they had galloped a mile or so and reached the place from which the sounds came, they found that it was a false alarm. The cause was the herds of deer, or other animals, which abound on the moors of that wild country and which fled in panic before the banners and the advancing horsemen. These hulloa'd after them and their shouts were mistaken for battle-cries.

Young King Edward and his army rode all that day over those hills and desolate heaths, finding no towns, and following no road, with only the sun to guide them over those trackless wastes. By late afternoon they had reached the Tyne, which the Scots had crossed and would have to re-cross, or so the English supposed. Exhausted by the day's journey, they forded it with much difficulty because of the great stones which lay in it. When they gained the other side, each chose a piece of ground along the bank on which to spend the night, but before they had all found a pitch the sun was setting. Few of them had axes or any other tools to cut wood and build shelters and many had lost touch with their companions and had no idea where they were. The foot-soldiers in particular had been left far behind – though where they did not know nor how to get news of them – and all this filled them with anxiety. Some who claimed to know the country well said that they had covered twenty-eight miles in the day, riding hard as I have described, with no halts except to piss or retighten their horses' girths. Mounts and riders were tired out, yet the men had to sleep in full armour, holding their horses by the bridles since they had nothing to tie them to, having left their equipment in the carts which could not follow them over such country. For the same reason there were no oats or other fodder to give the horses and they themselves had nothing to eat all that day and night except the loaves which they had tied behind their saddles, and these were all soiled and sodden with the horses' sweat. They had nothing to drink but the water of the river, except for some of the commanders who had brought bottles of wine, which were a great comfort to them. They had no lights or fires and no means of kindling them, except that some knights could burn torches, having brought them on their pack-animals.

Having passed the night thus miserably, without taking off their armour or unsaddling their horses, they hoped for better things when day dawned. But as they were looking round for some prospect of food and shelter and for traces of the Scots, whom they eagerly wanted to fight in order to put an end to their own hardships, it began to rain. It continued so heavily and steadily all day that by noon already the river near which they were was too swollen to be re-crossed. No one could be sent to discover where they were or to find forage and bedding for their horses or bread, wine and other things for themselves. They had to fast all that day as well, while the horses ate earth, or heather, or moss or leaves. They cut down saplings with their swords to make stakes to tether them to, and also to build shelters for themselves.

Towards noon the next day some peasants were found. These told them that they were about forty-two miles from Newcastle and about thirty-three from Carlisle.[1] There were no nearer towns in which they could get provisions. The King and his commanders being informed of this, each sent out messengers with ponies and packhorses to fetch supplies. The King also sent a proclamation to the town of Newcastle saying that anyone who wanted to make money should bring out bread, wine, oats, poultry, cheese, eggs and other produce and he would be paid on the nail and given a safe-conduct as far as the army. It was also made known that they would not leave the district until they knew where the Scots had gone to.

Towards the middle of the next day the messengers returned, bringing what they could carry in the way of provisions. It was not much. With them came traders, driving small horses and little mules loaded with baskets of badly baked bread, large barrels of thin wine and other saleable goods, with which the army had to be satisfied. This was repeated each day during the rest of the week they remained by the river, among those mountains, awaiting the arrival of the Scots, who did not know the whereabouts of the English any more than the English knew theirs. In this way they had gone three days and nights without food, wine, fodder, candles and everything else; and in the next four days they were obliged to pay six pence for badly baked loaves worth

1. The original has '14 leagues' and '11 leagues'. No point on the Tyne exactly meets these requirements, but assuming they had really covered 28 miles ('English leagues') as the crow flies on the previous day, as noted above, their approximate position must have been near Hexham. They would thus be nearer to Newcastle than to Carlisle, and this seems supported by the fact that they went to Newcastle for provisions.

only a halfpenny, and twenty-four pence for a gallon of wine which should have cost only six.[1] Some were so famished that they snatched the food from their comrades' hands, which gave rise to serious brawls among the men. As an added misery, it never stopped raining the whole week and consequently their saddles, saddle-clothes and girths became sodden and most of the horses developed sores on their backs. They had nothing to cover them with, except their own surcoats, and no means of re-shoeing the horses which needed it. They themselves had nothing to keep out the wet and the cold except their tunics and their armour, and nothing to make fires with except green wood, which will not stay alight under rain.

The English commanders decide to move and the army is led back across the river at a different point. After several days the Scots are found in an unassailable position on the slopes above another river. The English establish themselves on their side of it and the two armies remain deadlocked.

They remained like that for three days, with the Scots on their mountain-slope opposite. There were, however, skirmishes every day, in which men were killed and prisoners taken. At nightfall the Scots always lit great fires and raised such a din by blowing on their horns and whooping in chorus that it sounded to the English as though all the devils in hell had been let loose. The intention of the English leaders, since they could not properly fight the Scots, was to keep them pinned down there and starve them out. They had learnt from prisoners that the Scots had no supplies of bread, wine or salt, though they had plenty of captured livestock. They could eat this boiled or roasted as they liked, without bread, as long as they had a little of the meal which they carry, as I described above. Some of the English do the same, when they go on long rides and it suits them.

1. The word translated as *pence* in each case is *estrelins* (probably: 1d. sterling) and as a *halfpenny* is *parisis* (probably: 1 sol parisis), but since there is some uncertainty about the interpretation, this cannot be taken as a precise guide to prices. There are also minor variants among the manuscripts.

On the morning of the fourth day after the English had arrived there, they looked at the slopes which the Scots had been holding and, to their great surprise, saw no one there; the Scots had slipped away in the night. Unable to guess where they had gone, they sent out scouts on horse and on foot, who found them that same morning on a still stronger hill situated near the same river. They had taken up positions in a wood, in order to be in shelter and to be able to come and go in greater secrecy.

The English follow the enemy and post themselves on another slope opposite, with the river still between. As before, the terrain is too unfavourable for a regular attack.

The first night that the English spent on this second hill, Sir James Douglas, who was a grand fighter and a daring leader, assembled some two hundred men in armour and led them across the river at a point far enough away from the army not to be noticed. He spurred into the English most gallantly, shouting 'Douglas! Douglas! Die, you English thieves!' He and his company killed more than three hundred in all. He spurred as far as the very tent of the King, still whooping and shouting: 'Douglas!' and cut two or three of the tent-cords before galloping away. He may well have lost a few men as he withdrew, but they were not many.

There were no more actions of this kind, but after that the English sent out strong patrols and established sentry-points and listening-posts, with orders to alert the army at the least sign or sound of movement. Most of the knights slept in their armour. Every day there were minor skirmishes, in which any who liked to took part. There were killed and wounded on both sides, as well as numerous prisoners.

On their twenty-second and last day in the field, the English captured a Scottish knight from whom they tried to find out his leaders' plans. He was questioned and interrogated until he told them, very unwillingly, that it had been decided that morning that all were to be armed by the evening in readiness to follow the banner of Sir James Douglas, wherever he might lead them, but that this was to be kept secret. Exactly what was in his leaders' minds the knight did not know.

The English interpret this as a preparation for a full-scale night attack upon them, and make their dispositions accordingly. But in the morning they find that the Scots have gone, this time finally. The English army stands down.

Upon this, some of the English got on their horses and crossed the river at great risk and went up the hill which the Scots had abandoned.[1] There they found the carcasses of five hundred fat cattle, which the Scots had killed because they were too heavy to run with them and they did not want to leave them alive for the English. Besides these they found over four hundred leather cauldrons, with the hair still on the hides, filled with meat and water, ready to be boiled over the fires; a thousand spits loaded with flesh for roasting; and more than five thousand worn-out shoes, made of untanned leather with the hair still on it, which the Scots had left behind. They also came upon five poor English prisoners whom the Scots had bound naked to the trees out of sheer spite, and two whose legs had been broken. They untied them and let them go and then went back to the army, which was just striking camp and getting ready for the return to England.

All that day they followed the unfurled banners of the marshals, halting at a late hour in some good pasture-land where they found badly needed fodder for their horses, which were so weak and hungry that they could hardly go farther. The next night they halted near an abbey some five miles from the city of Durham. The King took up his quarters in the great courtyard of the abbey, and the army in the meadows below. Here again there was plenty of forage, grass, vetches and corn. The army rested there quietly on the following day, while the King and his nobles went to Durham cathedral, where the bishop and chapter and also the citizens took their oath of fealty to him, since they had not done so before. In

1. Cf. Le Bel, *Chronique*: 'Immediately some of the companions, and I with them, mounted our horses and crossed the river . . .' His account of the Scots' leaving is almost identical to that given in Froissart, except that he or his copyist speaks of '10,000 old shoes'. He adds that they were unable to talk to the English prisoners whom they found, so implying that the whole of his party were Hainaulters.

the city they found their carts and carters with all the equipment which they had left in a neighbouring wood twenty-seven days previously. Finding them there, the citizens had taken them into the town at their own expense and put them in empty barns, each cart with its pennant to mark the owner. The nobles were highly pleased to recover their wagons and their gear. They rested for two days in the town with the army round it, since there was not room for them all to be quartered inside. The horses were re-shod and they then set out for York.

The inconclusive campaign was a greater setback for the English than this account suggests. The Treaty of Northampton in the following year conceded all the Scottish demands, including the recognition of Robert Bruce as King of an independent Scotland. At this price peace was established for a few years.

Edward III Does Homage to Philip VI (1329)

IN 1328, the year after Edward III's accession, Philip VI of Valois succeeded to the French throne. He required Edward to do homage for the Duchy of Guienne or Aquitaine, which the English kings had held almost continuously since 1152 as a fief under the French crown. Edward crossed to France.

It is hardly necessary to say that King Philip received the young King of England with all honour and dignity, and so did all the kings,[1] dukes and counts who were present there. All these great lords were assembled at Amiens, and there remained for a fortnight. Many discussions were held and arrangements proposed and I believe that King Edward paid homage with words and a kiss only, without putting his hands between the hands of the King of France, or of any other prince or prelate delegated by him. The King of England refused on that occasion, on the advice he was given, to proceed further with his homage without first returning to England to see and study the earlier charters which would throw light on the matter and show how and in what respect the King of England should declare himself the man of the King of France.

The King of France, seeing that his cousin the King of England was young, understood this reasoning perfectly and did not try to press him then. He knew quite well that he could repair the omission when he wanted to, and said: 'Cousin, we do not wish to mislead you and we are quite satisfied with what you have done now, until such time as you are in your country and have seen, from the documents signed by your predecessors, what it is you ought to do.'

The King of England and his counsellors replied: 'Dear lord, many thanks.'

1. Of Bohemia, Navarre and Majorca.

Back in England, there are long deliberations until, convinced by a study of the documents that he has no alternative, Edward writes letters doing liege homage without reservation for the fiefs of Aquitaine, Ponthieu and Montreuil.

Preliminaries of the Hundred Years War

DURING *the next few years, Edward grows rapidly in resolution and experience. The older generation are shaken off: his mother is 'retired' to pleasant country castles, her lover Mortimer executed with the same barbarity as the Younger Despenser. Edward's early marriage to Philippa of Hainault prospers and begins producing children. New, successful campaigns are undertaken against the Scots, with the result that their young King David Bruce takes refuge temporarily in France and a Franco-Scottish alliance is concluded. Edward has natural allies in the Low Countries – his father-in-law the Count of Hainault, the Duke of Brabant and the Count of Gelderland – with whom he begins negotiations. The Count of Flanders is loyal to Philip of France, but his subjects, led by the Ghent burgher James van Artevelde, revolt and virtually dispossess him. The Flemish burghers are pro-English, partly because of their dependence on wool imports from England. Matters come to a head in the autumn of 1337, after the return from Valenciennes of an English mission which has tried vainly to open negotiations with the French.*

At Michaelmas a great parliament was held at Westminster, outside London, which lasted three weeks. At it were all the greatest and wisest in England, prelates, earls, barons, knights and the councillors of the large towns. The two bishops of Lincoln and Durham and those barons and others who had been at Valenciennes made a report to the King on what they had done, waiting for the French delegation which never came. When the bishops had had their say, the King rose to his feet and asked to be advised as best befitted his honour and that of his kingdom. Those who were esteemed the wisest made reply that, after consideration of the requests, the proposals, the offers, the accommodations, the negotiations and the conversations which the King had suggested or put forward, and of which the French had taken no account, he could not delay revoking his homage to the King of France and making a declaration of war on him and all his adherents. This advice was approved and adopted and the Bishop of Lincoln was asked to go over to France with the declaration. At the request and on the instructions of the King and the lords in council, he readily agreed to do so.

It was further decided that, to assist the King to raise funds for his military expenses, a double tax should be imposed on each sack of wool for as long a period as the war lasted. Consideration was then given to the sum by which the King's share should be increased. Six burgesses, two from London, two from York and two from Coventry, proposed that his share of this duty should be raised by three hundred thousand nobles a year and that they would pay him in all six hundred thousand nobles yearly in three instalments.

It was next proposed and decreed that no one in the realm of England, on pain of decapitation, should practise any game or sport other than that of shooting with bow and arrows, and that all craftsmen making bows and arrows should be exempted from all debts.

It was also decreed that every knight, squire and fighting-man serving the King in his war should draw the King's pay but that each should maintain himself according to his standing for half the year out of his own funds, any prisoner or other war-gains which he might make remaining with him for his personal profit.

It was also decreed that in the coastal areas and islands, such as Cornwall, Guernsey, Wight, Hampshire and Sheppey, no men-at-arms or defence personnel should be moved away, regardless of any levy called by the King, but should guard their coasts and borders and should train their children in the use of arms and archery, in return for twopence each a day drawn from the duties on the wool within their districts.

It was also ordained and decreed that every lord, baron, knight and honest citizen of the larger towns should make every effort to instruct their children in the French language, in order that they should be more efficient and feel more at home in the wars.

It was further ordained that no horse was to be shipped

overseas from any part of England without the Chancellor's permission, on pain of incurring the King's displeasure.

It was also decided to send men-at-arms and archers to the Island of Cadsant[1] to fight the Flemings who were garrisoning it on behalf of the Count of Flanders. . . .

The parliament also ordained and confirmed the marriage of Sir William Montagu, who had loyally served the King in the Scottish wars. . . . To reward him for his services, the King gave him the young Countess of Salisbury, Madame Alys, whose estate he held in wardship. She was one of the most beautiful young ladies in the land.[2]

As agreed in parliament, the Bishop of Lincoln goes to France to deliver the 'challenge' to Philip, arriving in Paris at the beginning of November. He hands the parchment documents to the French King.

The King looked at them for a short time and then gave them to one of his secretaries to read out. Their content was as follows, or nearly so, as I have heard since from people who were in a position to know, and particularly the Lord of Saint-Venant, who was present.

'Edward, by the grace of God King of England and Ireland, writes to Philip of Valois: Since it falls out that, in succession to our beloved uncle the Lord Charles, King of France, we are heir to the realm and crown of France by a much closer degree of kinship than yourself, who have entered into possession of our heritage and are holding and desire to hold it by force, although we have several times pointed this out to you and have had it again pointed out by such worthy and eminent advisers as those of the Church and the Holy College of Rome, in agreement with the noble Emperor, head of all adjudications; to which matters and demands you have never been willing to listen, but have held and still hold to your unjustly founded opinion. Wherefore we give you notice that we shall claim and conquer our heritage of France by the armed force of us and ours, and from this day forward we and ours challenge you and yours, and we

1. An island at the mouth of the Scheldt, from which sea communications between England and the Low Countries were threatened.
2. From the Amiens MS.

rescind the pledge and homage which we gave you without good grounds; and we now place our domain of Ponthieu, together with our other heritage, under the protection of God, not under yours, since we consider you as our enemy and adversary. Given in our palace of Westminster, in the presence of our whole council, the nineteenth day of October.'

When King Philip had heard this letter read, he turned towards the Bishop of Lincoln and he did not seem to be greatly impressed, but began to smile and said: 'Bishop, you have discharged your mission admirably. This letter does not require an answer. You are at liberty to leave when you wish.' 'Sire,' replied the Bishop, 'I thank you.' He took his leave and went back to his lodging, where he remained all day. In the evening the King sent a safe-conduct for him and his followers, with which he travelled back across France unmolested. Returning to England, he reported on what he had done to the King and his barons. The English were highly pleased by it.[1]

Almost immediately an English landing-force takes the Island of Cadsant, so removing one threat to communications with Flanders, but there is no fighting of any importance. In the summer of 1338 Edward crosses to Antwerp with Queen Philippa and makes still inconclusive attempts to persuade his prospective allies to commit themselves to war with France. He is back there again in 1339, now with a sizeable army, and this time most of the Netherlands' lords and certain German princes who are involved agree to send declarations of war to Philip. It is again the Bishop of Lincoln who takes them to Paris, together with a renewed 'challenge' from Edward. This, rather than the earlier 'challenge', marks the effective opening of hostilities. Towns in French territory are attacked, while a French army, led by Philip's eldest son, the Duke of Normandy, marches to confront Edward, though there is no battle. At sea, the Norman and other freebooters, who have already been harassing the English coasts and attacking shipping, carry out a large-scale raid.

As soon as Sir Hugh Kieret and his companions on the seas heard that the challenges had been sent and war had opened between France and England, they were jubilant. They set

1. From the Amiens MS.

out with their fleet, which carried at least a thousand fighting-men of various kinds, and sailed for England, coming into Southampton[1] harbour one Sunday morning when the people were at mass. The Normans and Genoese entered the town and pillaged and looted it completely. They killed many people and raped a number of women and girls, which was a deplorable thing. They loaded their ships and vessels with the great plunder they found in the town, which was rich and well stocked, and then went back on board. When the tide was high again, they raised anchor and sailed with a good wind towards Normandy, putting in at Dieppe, where they shared out their booty.

In 1340 the fighting on land is intensified. William II, the new Count of Hainault, adds his declaration of war to the others and marches against the Duke of Normandy. Outside the besieged town of Thun-l'Évêque, near Cambrai, he is joined by a strong force of Flemings under the burghers' leader James van Artevelde. Meanwhile, Edward has adopted the title and arms of King of France — rather unwillingly, says Froissart, and pushed by van Artevelde, who insists on that condition. He installs his queen Philippa at Ghent, probably as a guarantee that he will not desert his allies, and returns briefly to England to attend to affairs of state. New complaints are made to him of the depredations of the Norman freebooters in the Channel and against the coastal towns. In June, he is ready to return.

1. Although, following all precedents, I have consistently rendered Froissart's *Hantonne* as 'Southampton' (or occasionally 'Hampshire'), it is virtually certain that in several passages it should be 'Portsmouth' or 'Portchester'. Here, for instance, a surprise attack up Southampton Water seems hardly possible.

Battle of Sluys (1340)

THE King of England put to sea with the intention of reaching Flanders and from there going to Hainault to aid his brother-in-law, the Count of Hainault, in his war against the French. On 22 June 1340, he set sail from the Thames Estuary with a large fleet of fine ships and steered straight towards Sluys. At the same time there lay between Blanken-berghe and Sluys a fleet commanded by Sir Hugh Kieret, Sir Peter Behuchet and Barbavara. It was made up of close on a hundred and fifty big ships, without counting the barges, and carried a good forty thousand men – Normans, light infantry, Genoese and Picards. This fleet was drawn up at anchor, on orders received from the King of France, to await the English, who they knew must pass that way, and prevent them from reaching the coast.

As the English sailed forward, they looked towards Sluys and saw such a huge number of ships that their masts resembled a forest. The King was greatly surprised and asked the commander of his fleet what this could be. He replied that he thought it must be the Norman navy which the King of France maintained at sea and which had done him great harm on various occasions, as when it had sacked and burnt South-ampton and when it had captured his great ship *Christopher*, with the slaughter of her soldiery and crew. When King Edward heard this, he said: 'I have long wanted to fight them. We will do so, if it pleases God and St George. They have inflicted so much damage on me that I mean to settle accounts with them if I can.'

The King then redisposed his whole fleet, putting his most powerful ships in the van and placing vessels filled with archers on all the sides, and between every two shiploads of archers there was one of men-at-arms. In addition, he detached a flanking squadron made up entirely of archers, which was to give support wherever needed to the most heavily engaged. With them were travelling a large number of English ladies, countesses, baronesses, knights' ladies and wives of London burgesses, who were on their way to visit the Queen of England at Ghent, where she had been without seeing them for a long time. The King took care to give them a strong guard, allotting three hundred men-at-arms to the task. Then he exhorted his men to fight well and stand up for his honour, which they all swore to do.

When King Edward and his Marshal had completed the disposition of their fleet, they had the sails hoisted to catch the wind on their starboard quarter, in order to avoid the glare of the sun, which was shining straight in their faces. Considering that this would be a disadvantage, they fell away a little and came round until they had all the wind they wanted. Seeing them turn away, the Normans wondered why they did so and said: 'They are afraid and are retreating, for they are not men enough to fight us.' They could tell from the banners that the King of England himself was there, at which they were delighted, since they were eager to fight him. They put their ships in readiness, like the skilled seamen and good fighters they were, and set the big ship *Christopher*, which they had taken from the English that same year, in the van with a big company of Genoese crossbowmen on board to defend it and harass the English. Then they sounded scores of trumpets, horns and other instruments and bore down on their enemies to engage them.

Fierce fighting broke out on every side, archers and crossbowmen shooting arrows and bolts at each other pell-mell, and men-at-arms struggling and striking in hand-to-hand combat. In order to come to closer quarters, they had great iron grappling-hooks fixed to chains, and these they hurled into each others' ships to draw them together and hold them fast while the men engaged. Many deadly blows were struck and gallant deeds performed, ships and men were battered, captured and recaptured. The great ship *Christopher* was recovered by the English at the beginning of the battle and all those on board were killed or taken prisoner. This capture took place in the midst of tremendous clamour and shouting, at which more English came to the scene and immediately re-manned her with a force made up entirely of archers, before sending her forward to confront the Genoese.

It was indeed a bloody and murderous battle. Sea-fights are always fiercer than fights on land, because retreat and flight are impossible. Every man is obliged to hazard his life and hope for success, relying on his own personal bravery and skill. There is no question that Sir Hugh Kieret was a good, courageous knight, and so were Sir Peter Behuchet and Barbavara, who in the past had wrought such havoc at sea and put an end to so many Englishmen. Thus the battle continued to rage furiously from early morning until afternoon, during which time there were many notable feats of arms and the English were hard put to it to hold their own, since they were opposed by hardened soldiers and seamen, who outnumbered them by four to one. . . .

But they performed with such courage that, thanks to a reinforcement from Bruges and the surrounding district which came to their support, they at last obtained the victory. The Normans and all who were with them were utterly defeated, killed or drowned, not a single one escaping in the general slaughter. The news quickly spread through Flanders and Hainault and thence reached the two armies facing each other at Thun-l'Évêque. It brought joy to the Hainaulters, the Flemings and the men of Brabant, but dejection to the French.

After winning this victory, the English King spent the whole of the night, which was midsummer eve,[1] on board his ships at sea, amid such a banging and blowing of cymbals and trumpets, drums and cornets that God's own thunder would not have been heard above it. He was visited by emissaries from Flanders, and he asked those from Bruges for news of James van Artevelde. They replied that he had gone to the support of the Count of Hainault against the Duke of

1. Froissart is a day out. The battle was actually fought on midsummer day, 24 June.

Normandy with a force of over sixty thousand Flemings. The next day the King entered harbour and disembarked with all his men. He went on foot, accompanied by a throng of knights, to the Church of Our Lady at Ardenburg. After hearing mass there and dining, he mounted on horseback and arrived that same day at Ghent, where he was welcomed joyfully by the Queen. All his men with their baggage rejoined him there little by little.

Soon after Sluys, a one-year truce between England and France interrupts their confrontation in the Low Countries. Renewed fighting with the Scots ends in an English victory in 1342. Operations against the French are resumed in Brittany, a largely independent dukedom to which the succession is disputed. Edward supports Countess Jeanne de Montfort against Philip VI's candidate, Charles de Blois. In January 1343, two cardinals delegated by the Pope procure a three-year truce between Edward and the Duke of Normandy, commanding the French forces in Brittany. For a short time, there is peace between the chief contenders.

The Order of the Garter (1344)

A T that time King Edward of England conceived the idea of altering and rebuilding the great castle of Windsor, originally built by King Arthur, and where had first been established the noble Round Table, from which so many fine men and brave knights had gone forth and performed great deeds throughout the world. King Edward's intention was to found an order of knights, made up of himself and his sons and the bravest and noblest in England *and other countries too*.[1] There would be forty of them in all and they would be called the Knights of the Blue Garter and their feast was to be held every year at Windsor on St George's Day. To institute the feast, the King called together the earls, barons and knights of the whole country and told them of his intentions and of his great desire to see them carried out. They agreed with him whole-heartedly, because they thought it an honourable undertaking and one which would strengthen the bonds of friendship among them.

Forty knights were then chosen from among the most gallant of them all and these swore a solemn oath to the King always to observe the feast and the statutes, as these were agreed and drawn up. In the castle of Windsor, the King founded and had built the Chapel of St George and established canons to serve God in it, giving them a generous endowment. In order to make the feast known in all countries, the King sent his heralds to announce it in France, Scotland, Burgundy, Hainault, Flanders and Brabant, and also in the German Empire. All knights and squires who wished to come were given safe-conducts for fifteen days after the feast for their return home. There were to be jousts against forty home knights, challenging all comers, and forty squires as well. The feast was to be held on the following St George's Day in the year 1344, at Windsor Castle. The Queen of

1. Addition from the Rome MS.

England was to be there accompanied by three hundred ladies and young girls, all of noble or gentle birth, and all similarly dressed.[1]

To press on with the building-works at Windsor, which were decided upon and begun in the year 1343, workmen were brought in from all over England and paid punctually on Saturdays. They had a clerk to supervise them and pay their wages called William of Wykeham. Later, he became one of the great masters of England as bishop and chancellor and everything passed through his hands. He stood so high in the King's favour that, in his time, everything was done in England by his consent, and nothing was done without it.[2]

1. Froissart's account needs certain corrections. The original Knights of the Garter numbered twenty-six, not forty. It seems certain that the Order was formally instituted in 1348 or 1349, after Crécy and Calais, though it is very possible that the idea did originate in a tournament at Windsor in 1344. Froissart, though he writes elsewhere of the attachment of Edward III to the Countess of Salisbury, makes no attempt to connect the Order with the loss of that lady's garter at a ball. He therefore provides no help in explaining the motto, *Honi soit qui mal y pense*. The connexion between Windsor and Arthur's Round Table was of course a legend, apparently of recent growth in Froissart's day.

2. This last paragraph is an addition from the Rome MS.

The Campaign of Crécy (1346)

AFTER *a second tournament at Windsor (April 1345) Edward formally terminates the truce with Philip, alleging French violations. He sends one of his commanders, Thomas Dagworth, to Brittany, where the local struggle is still raging. At the request of the pro-English Gascon nobles, he sends a larger force to Bordeaux, under Henry of Derby, to repel French encroachments in Aquitaine. (The duchy had already been declared confiscate by Philip VI, after Edward's retraction of his homage.) Derby is at first highly successful, but in 1346 a powerful French army under the Duke of Normandy wipes out many of his gains and lays siege to the English-held castle of Aiguillon.*

Froissart's statement that Edward's campaign in Northern France which followed, and led to Crécy and the acquisition of Calais, was originally planned as a relief expedition to Gascony, is not discounted by responsible historians and has documentary support (Rymer, Foedera).

When the King of England heard how hard pressed his men were in the Castle of Aiguillon and learnt that his cousin, the Earl of Derby, who was at Bordeaux, was not strong enough to take the field and raise the siege, he decided to assemble a large army and lead it to Gascony. He gave orders for full preparations to be made, mobilized men from his own kingdom and engaged mercenaries in other countries where they could be found.

At that time Sir Godfrey of Harcourt, having been banished from France, arrived in England. He went straight to the King and Queen, who were then at Chertsey, a town on the Thames some fifteen miles from London. He was received with open arms and was immediately made a member of the King's household and council. A large estate was assigned to him in England to enable him to maintain himself and his followers on a lavish scale. Soon after this the King completed the first stage of his preparations. A large fleet was brought

68

together in Southampton harbour, and all kinds of men-at-arms and archers were assembled there.

At about midsummer 1346 the King took leave of the Queen, whom he left in the care of his cousin, the Earl of Kent. He appointed Lord Percy and Lord Neville to be guardians of his kingdom together with four prelates, the Archbishops of Canterbury and York and the Bishops of Lincoln and Durham. He left sufficient forces in England to defend it if need be, then rode down to Southampton to wait for a favourable wind. When it came, he boarded his ship, as did his son the Prince of Wales, Sir Godfrey of Harcourt, and the other lords, earls and barons, according to the order of embarkation. There must have been four thousand men-at-arms and ten thousand archers, without counting the Irish and Welsh who followed his army on foot. . . .

They set sail in accordance with the will of God, the wind and the sailors, and made a good start towards Gascony, where the King intended to go. But on the third day the wind changed and drove them back to the coasts of Cornwall, where they lay at anchor for six days. At this point the King held a new council at the suggestion of Sir Godfrey, whose advice was that it would be a better venture to make a landing in Normandy. 'Normandy,' said Sir Godfrey, 'is one of the richest countries in the world. I promise you, on my life, that once you reach it, it will be easy to land there. There will be no serious resistance, for the inhabitants have no experience of arms and the whole cream of the Norman knights are at the siege of Aiguillon with the Duke. You will find large towns and fortresses completely undefended, in which your men will win enough wealth to make them rich for twenty years to come. Your fleet will be able to follow you almost as far as Caen. If you see fit to take my advice, you and all of us will profit by it. We shall have gold, silver, food supplies and everything else in abundance.'

The King of England, who was then in his prime and desired nothing better than to meet the enemy and see action, readily agreed with Sir Godfrey, whom he called his cousin. He ordered his seamen to change course for Normandy and, taking the admiral's flag from the Earl of Warwick, made himself admiral and led the fleet for that voyage. With the wind now in their favour, they sailed to the port of La Hogue in the Cotentin Peninsula. The news that the English had arrived soon spread and the townships of Cotentin sent messengers at all speed to the King of France in Paris. King Philip already knew that the English King had been assembling a large army and that his fleet had been seen passing the coasts of Normandy and Brittany, but it was not known where he was making for. So as soon as he received the news of the landing in Normandy, he summoned his Commander-in-Chief, the Count of Guines, and the Count of Tancarville, who had both recently arrived from Gascony, and ordered them to go to Caen to be ready to defend the town and its approaches against the English. They promised to do their utmost and set out from Paris accompanied by a large force of men-at-arms, whose ranks were constantly swollen by new arrivals. Reaching Caen, they were greeted with joy by the citizens and the people from the surrounding country who had taken refuge there. They began to put the town in a state of defence (it was not walled at that period) and to see that the inhabitants were armed and equipped each according to his standing.

To return to the English fleet which had entered La Hogue: when it was drawn up and anchored on the shore, the King came off his ship. But as his foot touched the ground, he stumbled and fell so heavily that the blood gushed from his nose. The knights who were round him took this for a bad omen and begged him to go back on board for that day. 'Why?', retorted the King without hesitation. 'It's a very good sign for me. It shows that this land is longing to embrace me.' They were all greatly cheered by this answer. So the King encamped on the beach for that day and night and the whole of the next.

Meanwhile the horses were unloaded from the ships with all their gear and a council was held to decide how they should proceed. The King appointed Sir Godfrey of Harcourt and the Earl of Warwick to be Marshals of the army, with the Earl of Arundel as Commander-in-Chief. The Earl of Huntingdon was directed to remain with the fleet with a hundred men-at-arms and four hundred archers. At a second council they decided their order of march. The men were divided into three columns, one to take the right flank and follow the coast, another the left, while the third marched in the centre under the King and the Prince of Wales. Each night the flanking columns led by the two Marshals were to join up again with the King.

Following this plan, the English army began its advance. The fleet sailed along the coast, seizing every vessel, large or small, that they fell in with. Archers and foot-soldiers marched near them within sight of the sea, robbing, pillaging and carrying off everything they came across. They moved forward by land and sea until they reached Barfleur, a seaport and fortified town which they took immediately because the inhabitants surrendered in the hope of saving their lives, though this did not prevent the town from being emptied of its gold, silver and jewelry. They found so much of it there that the very servants in the army turned up their noses at fur-lined gowns. All the men in the town were taken and put on board the ships so that there should be no danger of their rallying afterwards and harassing them in the rear.

After capturing and plundering Barfleur, though without burning it, they spread out over the country, though they still kept near the coast. They did whatever they pleased, for no one resisted them. They came in time to a large wealthy town and port called Cherbourg. They sacked and burnt part of it, but found the citadel too strongly defended to be taken, so they went on towards Montbourg and Valogne. This last they sacked completely and then set fire to it. They did the same to a number of other towns in the region, taking so much valuable booty that it would have been an impossible task to count it.

Continuing from Valogne, the Earl of Warwick's column takes and sacks the fortified town of Carentan. The other two columns meet with similar success, amassing huge quantities of plunder in the form of household possessions and the livestock in which Normandy abounds.

So was the good, fat land of Normandy ravaged and burnt, plundered and pillaged by the English, until news of the havoc they were wreaking reached the King of France in Paris. When he heard of it, King Philip swore that they should not go home without being brought to battle and made to pay dearly for the misery and destruction they were inflicting on his subjects. He immediately caused a number of letters to be written. The first were to his friends in the Empire because they were the most distant from him: to the good King of Bohemia, who was very dear to him, and also to his son Charles of Bohemia, who at that time styled himself King of Germany, and by general consent was its king thanks to the influence and support of his father and of the King of France. Indeed, he had already assumed the arms of the Empire.

King Philip urgently requested them to join him with all their available forces in the campaign he was preparing against the English who were ravaging his country. They made no excuses, but assembled men from Germany, Bohemia and Luxemburg and came to France in strength to aid its king. The latter also wrote to the Duke of Lorraine, who brought more than four hundred lances to serve him. The Count of Salm, the Count of Saarbrück, the Count of Flanders and Count William of Namur came also, each with a very handsome company. King Philip sent another letter with a special summons to Sir John of Hainault[1] who had recently become his ally through the influence of his son-in-law, Count Louis of Blois, and of the Lord of Fagnolle. Sir John responded by bringing a large and splendidly equipped force of good knights from Hainault and elsewhere. His arrival so delighted the King that he attached him to his personal service and made him a member of his inner council. In this way the King of France summoned fighting men from every possible quarter and assembled one of the largest forces of great lords, dukes, counts, barons and knights that had been seen in France for a hundred years. But he had to bring them from such distant countries that it took a long time to collect them;

1. The same man who had assisted Queen Isabella and the young Edward III in 1326-7.

and meanwhile the King of England had devastated the whole region of Cotentin and Normandy.

The tale of plunder continues. The inhabitants, who have never experienced war, flee at the mere mention of the English, leaving their houses and barns filled with provisions for the taking. The army find an abundance of everything they need except wine, and there are reasonable stocks even of that. They capture Saint-Lô, where they acquire such quantities of cloth that 'they would have let it go cheap if they had had anyone to sell it to'.

When the King of England and his men had done as they pleased with the town of Saint-Lô, they marched on towards Caen, which was three times larger and full of wealth in the form of cloth and other goods, with rich citizens, noble ladies and very fine churches. In particular, there are two big and extremely wealthy abbeys, that of St Stephen and that of the Trinity, situated at either end of the town. One of them housed a hundred and twenty nuns, all fully endowed. Besides this, one of the strongest and finest castles in Normandy lies on one side of the town. Its captain at that time was a gallant Norman knight called Sir Robert de Wargnies, commanding a garrison of three hundred Genoese.

In the town itself were the Count of Eu and Guines, Constable of France, and the Count of Tancarville with a large number of good fighting men. The King of England advanced cautiously towards them, ordered his columns to join up, and encamped that night in open country five miles from the town. His fleet kept constantly near him and came to a port called Ouistreham, some six miles from Caen on the River Orne, which flows through Caen. The Constable of France and the other lords with him kept good watch over the town that night and were not over concerned about the English. The next morning they armed themselves, ordering their men and all the townspeople to do the same, and then held a council to decide their plan of action. The Constable and the Count of Tancarville wished to keep all their forces in the town to hold the gates, the bridge and the river, and to abandon the outskirts to the English because they were not fortified. It would be difficult enough to hold the main part of the town, since the river was its only line of defence.

The townspeople refused to agree and insisted on marching out to the fields to meet the English there, saying that they were numerous and strong enough to fight them. When the Constable heard their decision, he replied: 'So be it then, and God be with us. If you fight, I and my men will fight with you.' They marched out of the town in good enough order at the beginning. They seemed ready to risk their lives courageously and to put up a good defence.

On that day the English rose very early and made ready to advance. The King heard mass before sunrise, then mounted his horse, as did his son the Prince and Sir Godfrey of Harcourt, on whose advice the King largely relied. They moved forward in perfect order, with the Marshals' banner-bearers in the van, until they came close to the town of Caen and its defenders. These were waiting drawn up in the fields, apparently in excellent shape. But no sooner did the townsmen see the English advancing upon them in three solid, close-ordered divisions and catch sight of the banners and the innumerable pennons waving and fluttering in the wind and hear the shouting of the archers – all things of which they had had no previous experience – than they were so filled with dismay that nothing in the world could have stopped them taking to their heels. They turned and fled in confusion, in spite of everything the Constable could do. In a few moments their whole order of battle had broken up and they were rushing in terror to reach the safety of the town. Many of them stumbled and fell in the struggle to escape, while others piled on top of them in their panic.

The Constable and the Count of Tancarville with a few knights reached a gate at the entry to the bridge in safety. Since their men had broken, they could see that the battle was already lost. The English were now among them, killing as they liked without mercy. A few knights and squires and others who knew the way managed to reach the castle, where they were admitted by Sir Robert de Wargnies, who had plenty of room and provisions. There they were out of danger. Meanwhile the English, men-at-arms and archers, were continuing the slaughter of the fugitives, sparing none. Looking out from the gate-tower where they had taken refuge and seeing the truly horrible carnage which was taking place in the street, the Constable and the Count began to fear that they themselves might be drawn into it and fall into the hands of archers who did not know who they were. While they were watching the massacre in dismay, they caught sight of a gallant English knight with only one eye, called Sir Thomas Holland, and five or six other knights with him. They recognized him because they had campaigned together in Granada and Prussia and on other expeditions, in the way in which knights do meet each other. They were much relieved when they saw him and called out to him as he passed: 'Sir Thomas, come and speak to us.' On hearing his own name the knight stopped dead and asked: 'Who are you, sirs, who seem to know me?' They gave their names, saying: 'We are so-and-so. Come to us in this gate-tower and make us your prisoners.'

When he heard this Sir Thomas was delighted, not only because he could save their lives but also because their capture meant an excellent day's work and a fine haul of valuable prisoners, enough to bring in a hundred thousand gold *moutons*. So he brought the whole of his troop to the spot as quickly as possible and went up with sixteen of his men into the gate-tower, where he found the lords who had called to him and at least twenty-five knights with them, all looking very uneasy at the slaughter they could see in the town. They surrendered immediately and pledged themselves to be Sir Thomas's prisoners. Leaving sufficient of his men to guard them, the knight rode on through the streets. He was able that day to prevent many cruel and horrible acts which would otherwise have been committed, thus giving proof of his kind and noble heart. Several gallant English knights who were with him also prevented a number of evil deeds and rescued many a pretty townswoman and many a nun from rape.

Fortunately for the English, the river which flows through

Caen and which can float large ships was so low and sluggish that they could easily pass across it without troubling about the bridge.

In this way the King of England became master of Caen, though at a heavy price in men. For some of the inhabitants went up to the garrets overhanging the narrow streets and flung down stones and beams and masonry, killing and injuring several hundred of the English. The King was enraged when this was reported to him in the evening and gave orders for the whole population to be put to the sword on the next day and the town to be set on fire. Sir Godfrey of Harcourt forestalled this order by saying to him:

'Beloved sire, be a little less impetuous and content yourself with what you have done. You still have a long way to go before you reach Calais, as you intend. There are large numbers of people in this town who will defend themselves from house to house if they are attacked. To destroy the place might cost you dear and cripple your expedition. Remember that your enemy King Philip is certain to march against you in full strength and engage you, for good or ill, so there is still plenty of fighting before you, for which you will need all the forces you have and more. We can be masters of this town without further killing. Both men and women will be quite ready to give up everything they have to us.'

The King saw that Sir Godfrey was right and that things might well fall out as he said. So he changed his mind and replied: 'Sir Godfrey, you are our Marshal. Go and give whatever orders you see fit. For this once I leave everything in your hands.'

Sir Godfrey sent his banner through all the streets and had it proclaimed, in the King's name, that none should dare, on pain of the gallows, to start a fire, kill a man or rape a woman.

This proclamation reassured the townspeople and they allowed some of the English into their homes, without attempting to harm them. Some opened their chests and strong-boxes and gave up all they had, on condition that their lives were spared. But notwithstanding this and the orders of the King

76

and the Marshal, there were many ugly cases of murder and pillage, of arson and robbery, for in an army such as the King of England was leading it was impossible that there should not be plenty of bad characters and criminals without conscience.

For three days the English remained in possession of Caen, where they won an amazing quantity of wealth for themselves. They used the time to put their affairs in order and sent boats and barges laden with their gains – clothes, jewelry, gold and silver plate and many other valuable things – down the river to Ouistreham where their main fleet lay. They decided after long deliberation to send the fleet back to England with the booty and the prisoners. The Earl of Huntingdon remained in command of it, with two hundred men-at-arms and four hundred archers. The King of England bought the Count of Guines, Constable of France, and the Count of Tancarville from Sir Thomas Holland and his companions for twenty thousand nobles in cash.

So the King sent back his fleet full of conquered spoils and of good prisoners, including more than sixty knights and three hundred wealthy citizens, with a host of loving greetings to his wife, my lady Philippa, the gracious Queen of England.

The English ravage the country west of the Seine, but without attacking the fortified places, 'because the King wished to husband his men and artillery (i.e., siege-engines)'. They follow the left bank of the river as far as Poissy, some twenty miles from the capital.

They found all the bridges over the Seine destroyed, so went on until they came to Poissy. Here the bridge had also been broken down, but the piles and cross-beams were still in the river. The King halted there for five days until the bridge had been rebuilt strongly enough for his army to cross with ease and safety. His Marshals made forays nearly to Paris, burning Saint-Germain-en-Laye and La Montjoie, Saint-Cloud, Boulogne and Bourg-le-Reine. At this the people of Paris grew alarmed, for the city was not fortified at that time and they were afraid that the English would come right into it.

King Philip bestirred himself and had all the penthouses in

Paris removed to make it easier for his men to ride through the streets. Then he prepared to leave for Saint-Denis, where the King of Bohemia, Sir John of Hainault, the Duke of Lorraine, the Counts of Flanders and Blois and many barons and knights were waiting.

When the people of Paris saw that their King was leaving, they were more alarmed than ever. They came and knelt before him, saying: 'Beloved sire and noble king, what are you about to do? Will you abandon your good city of Paris in this way? The enemy are only five miles from us. When they hear that you have gone they will be here in an instant, and we shall have no one to defend us against them. Sire, we beg you to stay and help protect your loyal city.'

The King answered: 'My good people, you have nothing to fear. The English will come no nearer. I am going to Saint-Denis to be with my soldiers, for I mean to march against the English and fight them, whatever the outcome.'

In this way the King of France calmed the people of Paris, who were in great fear of being attacked and destroyed, so suffering the same fate as Caen. But the King of England lodged in the Abbey of Poissy-les-Dames and held his solemn state on the Feast of the Assumption, in the middle of August. He sat at table in a sleeveless scarlet gown trimmed with ermine.

The English leave Poissy on 16 August and move rapidly north. They skirt Beauvais, burning the suburbs, and take several smaller places before they reach Vimeu, the district west of Amiens and Abbeville. King Philip is now in close pursuit with a much superior army. On his orders the bridges over the Somme have either been destroyed or are so strongly defended that the English probe in vain to find a way across. They are in danger of being hemmed in against the river. At this point in the narrative, the French are at Amiens and the English have just decamped from the neighbouring town of Airaines to move to Oisemont, a few miles farther on. King Philip has sent a detachment under Sir Godemar du Fay to guard the last remaining crossing of the Somme, the ford of Blanchetaque, below Abbeville.

Having given these orders, King Philip, who was eager to

come up with the English and engage them, left Amiens with his whole force. At about noon he reached Airaines, which the King of England had quitted in the early morning. The French found that large quantities of provisions had been left behind. There was meat on the spits, there were loaves and pies in the ovens, barrels and kegs of wine, and many tables ready laid, for the English had left in great haste.

At Airaines King Philip's advisers said to him: 'Sire, you should halt here and wait for the rest of your army. It is certain now that the English cannot escape you.' So the King took up his quarters in the town and, as the various lords arrived, they were lodged there also.

To return to the King of England, who was in the town of Oisemont and well aware that the King of France was following him in full strength thirsting for battle. He would have given much to be across the River Somme with his men. When his two Marshals returned in the evening, after ranging the country as far as the gates of Abbeville and reaching Saint-Valery-sur-Somme, where there had been a sharp skirmish, he called together his council and, sending for some prisoners from Vimeu and Ponthieu, he said to them in a kindly voice:

'Do any of you know of a crossing – it must be below Abbeville – by which we and our army can pass safely? If anyone can guide us to it, we will set him free with twenty of his comrades.'

There was a certain groom called Gobin Agace who knew the ford of La Blanchetaque as well as any man, having been born and bred near it and having crossed over it several times that year. This man came forward and said:

'Yes indeed, sire. I promise you on my life that I can take you to a place where you can cross quite safely. There are some shallows wide enough for twelve men to walk over abreast, with the water no higher than their knees. When the tide is in, the river is too deep to ford. But when it goes out, which happens twice a day, it is low enough to be crossed on horseback or on foot. That is the only place where it can be done, except by the bridge at Abbeville, but that is a fortified town with a strong garrison. The ford I am telling you about, my lord, has a firm bottom of white gravel which will bear the weight of carts. That is why it is called Blanchetaque.'

When the King heard this, he was as pleased as if he had won a fortune, and he said: 'Well, friend, if what you tell me proves to be true, I will set you free with all your comrades and give you a hundred gold nobles.'

'On my life I swear it,' said Gobin Agace. 'But make your arrangements now to be on the bank before sunrise.'

'Certainly,' said the King. He gave orders for the whole army to be armed and ready to move on again at the sound of the trumpets.

He slept little that night, but rose at midnight and had the trumpeters sound the signal to strike camp. Soon everything was ready, the pack-horses loaded and the wagons filled. Leaving Oisement at first light, they made such good progress guided by the groom that by sunrise they were near to the ford. But the tide was in and they could not cross, so the King was obliged to wait for the rest of his men to catch up with him. When the tide had gone out it was mid-morning and by that time Sir Godemar du Fay, the knight whom King Philip had sent to guard the crossing, had appeared with a large force on the opposite bank.

King Philip had given him a thousand men-at-arms and five thousand foot-soldiers, including the Genoese, and he had been joined on the way by large numbers of local men, so that they were at least twelve thousand strong when they drew up along the bank to dispute the crossing.

This brought no change to the King of England's plans. He ordered his Marshals to strike at once into the water and his archers to shoot steadily at the French opposite. The two Marshals of England sent their banner-bearers forward, in the name of God and St George, and followed closely themselves. The bravest knights hurled their horses into the water, with the best mounted in the lead. There were many jousts in the river and many unhorsings on both sides, for Sir Godemar and his men defended the crossing bravely. A number of his knights, with others from Artois and Picardy, had decided not to wait on the bank but to ride into the ford and fight there in order to win greater distinction. So there was, as I have said, many a joust and many a skilled piece of fighting, for the knights sent to defend the shallows were picked men who stood in good order at the neck of the crossing and clashed fiercely with the English as these came up out of the water. The Genoese also did much damage with their cross-bows, but the English archers shot so well together that it was an amazing sight to see. And while they were harassing the French, the mounted men got through.

When the English were finally across, though not without considerable losses, they spread out over the fields, with the King, the Prince of Wales and all their nobles. After this, the French order was broken and those who could get away from the ford made off like defeated men. Some went towards Abbeville, others towards Saint-Riquier. There was great slaughter among them because those on foot had no means of escape. The pursuit went on for more than three miles and many from Abbeville, Montreuil, Rue and Saint-Riquier were killed or captured. On the other hand, some of the English were attacked before they could get over the river by squires from the French army who had come out looking for a fight. These belonged in particular to the Empire, to the King of Bohemia and to Sir John of Hainault. They captured some horses and equipment and killed or wounded a number in the English rear who were still trying to cross.

King Philip had left Airaines that morning and was riding rapidly forward when news was brought him of the English crossing and Sir Godemar's defeat. He was extremely angry, for he had been expecting to find the English on the bank of the Somme and fight them there. He halted in open country and asked his Marshals what was the best thing to do. They replied: 'Sire, you cannot cross the river yourself because the tide is in again now.' So the King turned back in fury and took up his quarters in Abbeville with all his people.

When the English had scattered the enemy and cleared the ground, they formed up in excellent order, assembled their supply-train and moved off in their habitual way. Knowing that the Somme was behind them they were full of confidence. The King of England thanked and praised God many times that day for bringing him safely over the water and making him overcome his enemies in battle. He then sent for the groom who had guided him to the ford, set him free with all his comrades, and gave him a hundred gold nobles and a good horse. I do not know what became of him afterwards.

As the King and his army rode slowly and joyfully along, they thought of quartering for the night in the nearby town of Noyelle. But when they learnt that it belonged to the Countess of Aumale, the sister of the late Robert of Artois, they spared the town and the lady's lands for his sake – an act of friendship for which she thanked them warmly. The King halted instead in open country near La Broye, while the Marshals made an incursion to Crotoy, on the coast, which they took and burnt to the ground. In the harbour they found a number of ships and barges laden with Poitou wines which belonged to merchants from Saintonge and La Rochelle. They quickly bought up the lot and the Marshals had some of the best of them sent to the King's army encamped a few miles away.

Early the next day the King struck camp and moved towards Crécy in Ponthieu. The Marshals led their forces on either side of him. One pushed forward as far as the gates of Abbeville, then turned away towards Saint-Riquier, burning and devastating the country. The other kept near the coast and reached the town of Rue. Then at noon on that Friday the three divisions joined up again and the whole army came to a halt not far from Crécy.

Knowing that the King of France was close behind him and eager for battle, King Edward said to his men:

'I will take up my position here and go no further until I have a sight of the enemy. I have good reason to wait for him, for I am on the land I have lawfully inherited from my royal mother, which was given to her as her marriage portion. I am ready to defend my claim to it against my adversary Philip of Valois.'

The King encamped in the open fields with his army and, since he was willing to risk the fortunes of battle with numbers which he knew were only an eighth of those of the King of France, he had to give urgent thought to his dispositions. He ordered his Marshals, the Earl of Warwick and Sir Godfrey of Harcourt, and with them that stout and gallant knight Sir Reginald Cobham, to consider the best place in which to draw up their forces. The three commanders rode round the fields and carefully studied the terrain to find the most advantageous position. Then they brought the King to it, with many others as well. Meanwhile, scouts had been sent out towards Abbeville, where they knew the King of France would cross the Somme, to discover if he was leaving that day to take the field. They reported that there was no sign of this.

So King Edward stood down his men for the day, with orders to assemble early next morning at the sound of the trumpets, in readiness to fight at once on the chosen positions. They all went to their quarters and busied themselves in checking and polishing their arms and armour.

The King of France spends the same day (Friday, 25 August) in Abbeville, also preparing for battle. His scouts have reconnoitred the position of the English and reported that they are evidently waiting for him. He moves some troops out of the town in readiness to march the next day. In the evening he gives a supper for the principal nobles, at which they pledge themselves to behave as brothers-in-arms. King Edward also gives a supper for his commanders and then retires to his oratory. Froissart continues:

He knelt before his altar, devoutly praying God to grant that, if he fought the next day, he should come through the business with honour. He rose fairly early in the morning and heard mass with his son the Prince of Wales. They took communion and most of their men also confessed and put themselves in a state of grace.

The King then gave orders for every man to go to the positions decided upon the day before. Close to a wood in the rear he had a large park set up, in which all the wagons and carts were put. All the horses were led into this park, leaving every man-at-arms and archer on foot. The park had only one entrance.

He caused his Constable and his Marshals to divide the army into three bodies. In the first was his son the young prince, and to fight beside him he chose the Earl of Warwick, the Earl of Oxford, Sir Godfrey of Harcourt, Sir Reginald Cobham, Sir Thomas Holland, Sir Richard Stafford, the Lord of Man, the Lord Delawar, Sir John Chandos, Sir Bartholomew Burghersh, Sir Robert Neville, Sir Thomas Clifford, the Lord Bourchier, the Lord Latimer and many other brave knights and squires, whom I cannot name in full. In the Prince's division there would have been about eight hundred men-at-arms, two thousand archers and a thousand light infantry including the Welsh. This body moved on to its positions in good order, each knight marching beneath his banner or pennon, or among his men.

In the second division were the Earls of Northampton and Arundel, the Lord Ros, the Lord Lucy, the Lord Willoughby, the Lord Basset, the Lord St Aubin, Sir Lewis Tufton, the Lord Multon, the Lord Alasselle and a number of others. This body consisted of about five hundred men-at-arms and twelve hundred archers.

The third division was the King's and was made up, as was fitting, of numerous good knights and squires, amounting to seven hundred men-at-arms and two thousand archers. When the three divisions had taken up their positions and each earl, knight and squire knew what he had to do, the King mounted a small riding-horse and, holding a white baton in his hand, rode slowly round the ranks escorted by his Marshals, encouraging his men and asking them to stand up for his honour and help defend his rights. He spoke to them in such a smiling, cheerful way that the most disheartened would have plucked up courage on hearing him. When he had gone round the whole army it was about midday. Returning to his own division, he gave orders for all the men to stand down and eat and drink at their ease. Having done this and packed up the pots, kegs and provisions in the carts again, they went back to their battle-positions. They sat down on the ground with

their helmets and bows in front of them, so as to be fresh
and rested when the enemy arrived.

That Saturday morning the King of France rose early and
heard mass in the Abbey of St Peter in Abbeville, where he
had his quarters. All the great lords and commanders who
were in Abbeville, the King of Bohemia, the Count of
Alençon, the Count of Blois, the Count of Flanders and others
followed his example. It should be said that not all had been
quartered in Abbeville, for there would not have been room
for them. Some had lodged in the surrounding villages and a
large number at Saint-Riquier, which is a fortified town. The
King moved out of Abbeville after sunrise with such a great
force of fighting men as has been rarely seen. Accompanied by
the King of Bohemia and Sir John of Hainault, he rode very
slowly to allow his men to catch up with him. When he had
advanced about six miles in the direction of the enemy, his
officers said to him:

'Sire, it would be advisable to put your divisions in order
and to let all the foot-soldiers go forward to avoid being
trampled down by the horsemen. And you should send some
of your knights ahead to reconnoitre the enemy's position.'

The King readily agreed and sent forward four gallant
knights, Le Moine de Bazeilles, the Lord of Noyers, the Lord
of Beaujeu and the Lord of Aubigny, who approached so
near to the English that they obtained a very good view of
their disposition. The English saw clearly what they were
doing, but they made no move and let them ride off unmolested.

The four returned towards the King of France and his
commanders, who had been walking their horses until they
came back and halted when they saw them. The knights
pushed through the crowd to reach the King, who called to
them: 'Well, my lords, what news?' They looked at each
other without answering, for none of them wished to be the
first to speak, as a matter of courtesy towards his companions.
At last the King turned to Le Moine de Bazeilles, who was
esteemed as one of the bravest and most chivalrous of knights

and one of the most experienced in war, and formally commanded him to give his opinion. This knight was a dependent
of the King of Bohemia, who always felt more secure when
he had him with him.

'Sire,' said Le Moine de Bazeilles, 'I will speak since it is
your wish, subject to correction by my companions. We rode
forward. We viewed the English lines. I have to report that
they are drawn up in three divisions, very prettily disposed,
and show no sign of intending to retreat. They are obviously
waiting for you. So my advice – always subject to a better
opinion – is that you should halt all your men now and en-
camp in the open for today. Before the rear can come up with
you and you can put your divisions in some order, it will be
getting late. Your men will be tired and in no sort of shape
and you will find that the enemy are fresh and rested and in
no doubt of the way they plan to fight. In the morning you
will be able to give more thought to your battle-order and
make a closer study of the enemy's position to see which is
the best line of attack. You can be sure that they will still be
there.'

The King fully approved this advice and ordered his Marshals to put it into execution. One of them rode forward and
the other back, shouting to the standard-bearers: 'Halt
banners on the King's orders, in the name of God and St
Denis!' At this command the leaders halted, but those behind continued to advance, saying that they would not stop
until they had caught up with the front ranks. And when the
leaders saw the others coming they went on also. So pride
and vanity took charge of events. Each wanted to outshine his
companions, regardless of the advice of the gallant Le Moine
and with the disastrous consequences of which you shall
shortly hear. Neither the King nor his Marshals could restrain
them any longer, for there were too many great lords among
them, all determined to show their power.

They rode on in this way, in no order or formation, until
they came within sight of the enemy. For what they did then
the leaders were much to blame. As soon as they saw the
English they reined back like one man, in such disorder that

those behind were taken by surprise and imagined they had already been engaged and were retreating. Yet they still had room to advance if they wished to. Some did, while others stopped where they were.

The countryside was also covered with countless volunteers from the district. They crowded the roads between Abbeville and Crécy, and when they came within ten miles of the enemy they drew their swords and shouted: 'Kill! Kill!' Yet they hadn't seen a soul.

There is no one, even among those present on that day, who has been able to understand and relate the whole truth of the matter. This was especially so on the French side, where such confusion reigned. What I know about it comes chiefly from the English, who had a good understanding of their own battle-plan, and also from some of Sir John of Hainault's men, who were never far from the King of France.

The English, who were drawn up in their three divisions and sitting quietly on the ground, got up with perfect discipline when they saw the French approaching and formed their ranks, with the archers in harrow-formation[1] and the men-at-arms behind. The Prince of Wales's division was in front. The second, commanded by the Earls of Northampton and Arundel, was on the wing, ready to support the Prince if the need arose.[2]

It must be stressed that the French lords – kings, dukes, counts and barons – did not reach the spot together, but arrived one after another, in no kind of order. When King

1. The most plausible interpretation of this phrase, *en manière de berse*, is that the archers formed hollow wedges pointed towards the enemy, at each end of a body of foot-soldiers and positioned slightly in advance of these. The formation would look like this:

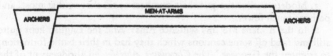

2. The King's division remained in reserve and, according to Froissart's account, took no part in the battle, as appears later.

Philip came near the place where the English were and saw them, his blood boiled, for he hated them. Nothing could now stop him from giving battle. He said to his Marshals: 'Send forward our Genoese and begin the battle, in the name of God and St Denis.'

He had with him about fifteen thousand[1] Genoese bowmen who would sooner have gone to the devil than fight at that moment, for they had just marched over eighteen miles, in armour and carrying their crossbows. They told their commanders that they were not in a state to fight much of a battle just then. These words came to the ears of the Count of Alençon, who grew very angry and said: 'What is the use of burdening ourselves with this rabble who give up just when they are needed!'

While this argument was going on and the Genoese were hanging back, a heavy storm of rain came on and there were loud claps of thunder, with lightning. Before the rain, huge flocks of crows had flown over both armies, making a deafening noise in the air. Some experienced knights said that this portended a great and murderous battle.

Then the sky began to clear and the sun shone out brightly. But the French had it straight in their eyes and the English at their backs. The Genoese, having been marshalled into proper order and made to advance, began to utter loud whoops to frighten the English. The English waited in silence and did not stir.[2] The Genoese hulloa'd a second time and advanced a little farther, but the English still made no move. Then they raised a third shout, very loud and clear, evelled their crossbows and began to shoot.

At this the English archers took one pace forward and poured out their arrows on the Genoese so thickly and evenly that they fell like snow. When they felt those arrows piercing

1. Modern authorities put their numbers at six thousand at most, and perhaps much fewer.

2. In the Amiens MS this sentence runs: 'And the English kept quite still and fired off some cannons which they had in their battle-formation, to frighten the Genoese.' The *Chroniques Abrégées*, an abridgement of the *Chronicles* of late date attributed to Froissart, also mentions the firing of 'two or three bombards'. See *Cannon* in Glossary.

their arms, their heads, their faces, the Genoese, who had never met such archers before, were thrown into confusion. Many cut their bowstrings and some threw down their cross-bows. They began to fall back.

Between them and the main body of the French there was a hedge of knights, splendidly mounted and armed, who had been watching their discomfiture and now cut off their retreat. For the King of France, seeing how miserably they had performed, called out in great anger: 'Quick now, kill all that rabble. They are only getting in our way!' Thereupon the mounted men began to strike out at them on all sides and many staggered and fell, never to rise again. The English continued to shoot into the thickest part of the crowd, wasting none of their arrows. They impaled or wounded horses and riders, who fell to the ground in great distress, unable to get up again without the help of several men.

So began the battle between La Broye and Crécy in Ponthieu at four o'clock on that Saturday afternoon.

The noble and gallant King of Bohemia, also known as John of Luxemburg because he was the son of the Emperor Henry of Luxemburg, was told by his people that the battle had begun. Although he was in full armour and equipped for combat, he could see nothing because he was blind. He asked his knights what the situation was and they described the rout of the Genoese and the confusion which followed King Philip's order to kill them. 'Ha,' replied the King of Bohemia. 'That is a signal for us.' He then asked for news of his son Charles, King of Germany, and was told: 'My lord, we have none. We believe he must be fighting on some other part of the field.' Then the King said a very brave thing to his knights: 'My lords, you are my men, my friends and my companions-in-arms. Today I have a special request to make of you. Take me far enough forward for me to strike a blow with my sword.'

Because they cherished his honour and their own prowess, his knights consented. Among them was Le Moine de Bazeilles, who rode beside him and would never willingly have left him, and there were several other good knights from the County of Luxemburg. In order to acquit themselves well and not lose the King in the press, they tied all their horses together by the bridles, set their king in front so that he might fulfil his wish, and rode towards the enemy.

It is true that too few great feats of arms were performed that day, considering the vast number of fine soldiers and excellent knights who were with the King of France. But the battle began late and the French had had a long and heavy day before they arrived. Yet they still went forward and preferred death to a dishonourable flight. There present were the Count of Alençon, the Count of Blois, the Count of Flanders, the Duke of Lorraine, the Count of Harcourt,[1] the Count of Saint-Pol, the Count of Namur, the Count of Auxerre, the Count of Aumale, the Count of Sancerre, the Count of Saarbrück and many other lords, barons and knights.

There also was Lord Charles of Bohemia, who bore the title and arms of King of Germany, and who brought his men in good order to the battlefield. But when he saw that things were going badly for his side, he turned and left. I do not know which way he went.

Not so the good King his father, for he came so close to the enemy that he was able to use his sword several times and fought most bravely, as did the knights with him. They advanced so far forward that they all remained on the field, not one escaping alive. They were found the next day lying round their leader, with their horses still fastened together.

The King of France was in great distress when he saw his army being destroyed piecemeal by such a handful of men as the English were. He asked the opinion of Sir John of Hainault, who was at his side. 'Well, sire,' Sir John answered, 'the only advice I can give you now is to withdraw to some place of safety, for I see no hope of recovery. Also, it will soon

---

1. Brother of the English commander, Sir Godfrey of Harcourt. Froissart later records that he was killed in the battle, as were nearly all the other nobles listed here.

be dark and you might just as easily fall in with your enemies and meet disaster as find yourself among friends.'

The King, shaking with anger and vexation, made no immediate reply, but rode on a little farther as though to reach his brother the Count of Alençon, whose banners he could see at the top of a small rise. The Count was launching a very well-ordered attack on the English, as was the Count of Flanders from another quarter. They moved their forces along the flank of the archers and reached the Prince of Wales's division, which they engaged fiercely for a long time. King Philip would gladly have joined them had it been possible, but there was such a throng of archers and men-at-arms in front of him that he could not get through. The farther he advanced, the smaller his numbers grew. . . .

The lateness of the hour harmed the French cause as much as anything, for in the dark many of the men-at-arms lost their leaders and wandered about the field in disorder only to fall in with the English, who quickly overwhelmed and killed them. They took no prisoners and asked no ransoms, acting as they had decided among themselves in the morning when they were aware of the huge numbers of the enemy.

Yet some French knights and squires, and with them Germans and Savoyards, succeeded in breaking through the Prince of Wales's archers and engaging the men-at-arms in hand-to-hand combat with swords. There was much brave and skilful fighting. On the English side, Sir Reginald Cobham and Sir John Chandos distinguished themselves, as well as others too numerous to be named, for all the flower of the English knighthood was there with the Prince. At that point the Earls of Northampton and Arundel, commanding the second division on the wing, sent support over to the Prince's division. It was high time, for otherwise it would have had its hands full. And because of the danger in which those responsible for the Prince found themselves, they sent a knight to King Edward, who had his position higher up on the mound of a windmill, to ask for help.

When he reached the King, the knight said: 'Sire, the Earls of Warwick and Oxford and Sir Reginald Cobham, who are with the Prince, are meeting a very fierce attack by the French. So they ask you to bring your division to their support, because if the attack grows any heavier, they fear it will be about as much as your son can deal with.' The King asked the knight, whose name was Sir Thomas of Norwich: 'Is my son dead or stunned, or so seriously wounded that he cannot go on fighting?' 'No, thank God,' replied the knight, 'but he is very hard pressed and needs your help badly.'

'Sir Thomas,' the King answered, 'go back to him and to those who have sent you and tell them not to send for me again today, as long as my son is alive. Give them my command to let the boy win his spurs, for if God has so ordained it, I wish the day to be his and the honour to go to him and to those in whose charge I have placed him.'

The knight went back to his commanders and gave them the King's message. It heartened them greatly and they privately regretted having sent him. They fought better than ever and must have performed great feats of arms, for they remained in possession of the ground with honour.

Late in the evening, as it was growing dark, King Philip left the field in despair, accompanied by five lords only. These were Sir John of Hainault, the first and nearest to him, and the Lords of Montmorency, Beaujeu, Aubigny, and Montsault. The King rode lamenting and mourning for his men until he came to the castle of La Broye. He found the gate shut and the drawbridge up, for it was now fully night and pitch-dark. He called for the captain of the castle, who came to the look-out turret and shouted down: 'Who comes knocking at this hour?' 'Open your gate, captain,' King Philip answered. 'It is the unfortunate King of France.'

The captain came out at once, recognizing the King's voice and having already heard of the defeat from fugitives who had passed the castle. The drawbridge was lowered and the King entered with his whole troop, but he was warned that it would be unwise to stay shut up inside there. So he and his men took a drink and left the castle again at about midnight, taking guides with them who knew the country. They rode so hard that by daybreak they reached Amiens, where the King stopped and lodged in an abbey, saying he would go no farther until he had news of the fate of all his army.

It must be said that fearful losses had been inflicted on the French and that the kingdom of France was greatly weakened by the death of so many of her brave nobility. If the English had mounted a pursuit, as they did at Poitiers, they would have accounted for many more, including the King himself. But this did not happen. On the Saturday they never once left their lines to pursue the enemy, but stayed on their positions to defend themselves against attack.

Froissart insists again on the part played by the English archers, and repeats that a decisive factor was the discomfiture of the Genoese crossbowmen at the beginning, with the confusion into which this threw the French horsemen. He says his last word on the actual battle:

However, among the English there were pillagers and irregulars, Welsh and Cornishmen armed with long knives, who went out after the French (their own men-at-arms and archers making way for them) and, when they found any in difficulty, whether they were counts, barons, knights or squires, they killed them without mercy. Because of this, many were slaughtered that evening, regardless of their rank. It was a great misfortune and the King of England was afterwards very angry that none had been taken for ransom, for the number of dead lords was very great.

When night had fully come and no more shouting or whooping or rallying-cries could be heard, the English concluded that the enemy were routed and the field was theirs. So they lit great numbers of lanterns and torches because it was very dark. King Edward, who had not put on his battle-helmet all that day, came down with his whole division to his son the Prince. He embraced him and said: 'Dear son, God grant that you may long go on in this way. You are indeed my son, for you have done your duty most loyally this day. You have proved yourself worthy to rule a land.' The Prince bowed very low and humbly did honour to his father, as was right.

It was natural that the English should be filled with joy when they realized that they had won the day. They hailed it as a glorious victory and were full of praise for their leaders and veteran captains. And several times that night they gave thanks to God for showing them such great mercies.

On the King's order there were no noisy celebrations, and the night passed quietly. When Sunday morning dawned there was a heavy mist, making it impossible to see farther than about fifty yards. So the King and his Marshals sent out a force of some five hundred men-at-arms and two thousand archers, who were to ride round and see if any of the French had reassembled. Levies of townsmen from Rouen and Beauvais had set out that morning from Abbeville and Saint-Riquier, knowing nothing of the previous day's defeat. To their misfortune they fell in with the English and went right up to them, thinking they were their own people. When the English recognized them, they charged down on them fiercely. There was a sharp engagement and the French were soon fleeing in disorder. More than seven thousand of them were killed in the open fields or under hedges and bushes. If the weather had been clear not a man would have escaped.

Not long after, the English ran into another force led by the Archbishop of Rouen and the Grand Prior of France, who also knew nothing of the defeat and had heard that the King of France would not fight until that Sunday. These also mistook the English for their own side and went towards them, and once again the English attacked lustily. There was another fierce engagement, for the two French lords had some good men-at-arms with them. But they could not hold out long and soon nearly all were killed, including the two leaders. No prisoners were taken for ransom.

So the English rode about that morning looking for adventures. They came across a good many French who had lost touch with their leaders the day before and had slept out in the open. These met with short shrift at their hands, being all put to the sword. I was told that the number of levies from the cities and towns who were killed on that Sunday morning was over four times greater than the number who died in the main battle on the Saturday.

The King of England was just coming away from mass when his horsemen and archers returned from their reconnaissance. They reported all they had seen and done and said that there was no sign that the French were re-forming. The King therefore decided to have the dead examined to find out what nobles had fallen. Two gallant knights, Sir Reginald Cobham and Sir Richard Stafford, were instructed to go out, taking with them three heralds to identify the dead by their arms and two clerks to write down their names. They were amazed at the number they found. They searched all the fields as thoroughly as they could, working on until late evening. Returning just as the King was about to go to supper, they gave him an exact report of what they had seen. Eleven princes lay dead on the field, eighty bannerets, twelve hundred ordinary knights and about thirty thousand other men. . . .[1]

The English remained there for that night and prepared to leave on the Monday morning. As an act of grace the King caused the bodies of all the chief nobles to be taken up and buried in consecrated ground in the nearby church at Maintenay. He accorded the people of the district a three days' truce to go over the battlefield and bury the other dead. He then made for Montreuil-sur-mer, while his Marshals went towards Hesdin and burnt Waben and Beaurain. But the castle at the last place was too strong for them to do any damage to it. They camped that Monday by the river which runs through Hesdin, on the Blangy side, and went on towards Boulogne the next day. On their way they burnt Saint-Josse and Neufchâtel, and then Étaples and Rue and the country round

1. Froissart's total of 1,291 for the dead nobility is reasonably close to the figure of '1,541 good men-at-arms' given by an English eye-witness, Michael de Northburgh, in a letter written a few days after the battle. Northburgh gives no figure for what he calls 'the commons and foot-soldiers', but Froissart's 'thirty thousand' for these other ranks is usually considered to be at least three times too high. In the Amiens MS he has: 'fifteen to sixteen thousand'.

Boulogne. They passed between the woods of Boulogne and the Forest of Hardelot until they came to the large town of Wissant. There the King, the Prince and the whole army took up their quarters and rested for one day. On the Thursday they left it and came before the fortified town of Calais.

The Siege of Calais (1346-7)

As soon as the King of England arrived before Calais, he began in earnest to make full preparations for a regular siege. Between the town, the river and the bridge of Nieuley he had houses built of heavy planks, thatched with straw and brushwood and set out in properly ordered streets, as though they were to be lived in for a dozen years. He was determined to stay there through winter and summer till Calais was his, without regard for the time and effort it might cost him. His new town had everything that an army could need and more, including a place to hold markets on Wednesdays and Saturdays. There were haberdashers and butchers' shops, stalls selling cloth and bread and all other necessities, so that almost anything could be bought there. All these things were brought over daily by sea from England and goods and foodstuffs were also supplied from Flanders. In addition, the English made frequent raids on the surrounding country, going as far as the gates of Saint-Omer and Boulogne, and bringing back much plunder to replenish their stocks of food. The King made no assaults on Calais, for he knew that the effort would be wasted. Desiring to spare his men and artillery, he said that he would starve the place out, however long it took, unless King Philip of France came to fight him again and raise the siege.

When Sir Jean de Vienne, the military commander of Calais, saw that the English were preparing for a long siege, he gave orders for all the poorer people, who had no stocks of provisions, to leave the town immediately. One Wednesday morning more than seventeen hundred of them, men, women and children, came out and tried to pass through the English army. When asked why they were leaving, they replied that they had nothing to live on. The King gave them permission to pass safely through and ordered that a hearty meal should be provided for them and that each should be given two pence.[1] This merciful act was highly praised, with good reason.

While Edward is besieging Calais, David II of Scotland invades England, but is defeated and taken prisoner at Neville's Cross. According to Froissart, Edward's queen, Philippa, accompanied the English army to the battlefield, returning to London after the victory with the prisoners.

The Queen of England, soundly advised by her men, had the King of Scotland, the Earl of Moray and the other Scottish lords put in the Tower under close guard and then turned to her other business. What she particularly desired was to go over to Calais to see her husband the King and her son the Prince of Wales. She hurried on with her preparations and, embarking at Dover, had such a favourable wind that, thanks to God, she was soon across. As can be imagined, she was welcomed with joy and she and all her ladies were soon lodged as honourably and comfortably as if they had been in London. They had landed on 29 October. On All Saints Day the King held a court in honour of the Queen and gave a dinner for all his lords and especially for the ladies. A large number had come over, both to accompany the Queen and to see their fathers, brothers and friends who were at the siege.

The siege went on for a long time and was the occasion for many fine exploits and feats of arms on land and sea, much too numerous for me to record. The King of France had posted so many good fighting men in the fortresses lying on the borders of Guines, Artois and Boulogne, and around Calais, and he kept so many Genoese, Normans and other sailors at sea, that when the English went out foraging or raiding they rarely had it their own way and often ran into fierce encounters. There were also frequent skirmishes near the gates and moats of the town which always took their toll in killed and wounded. Sometimes one side would come off best, sometimes the other, as is usual in this type of fighting. King Edward and his council now gave much thought to the construction of various machines to harass the besieged, but against these the defenders of Calais took counter-measures

1. *Estrelins.* See also note on p. 51.

and were so successful that they suffered no damage from them. Since they could not be reduced in these ways, the only course was to starve them out. Supplies could only reach them clandestinely, and if they did so it was thanks to two master mariners called Marant and Mestriel, both from Abbeville. These two would slip boldly into Calais with their ships, often at great risk to themselves. They were often pursued and nearly caught between Boulogne and Calais, but they always escaped. Many of the English were killed or drowned in attempting to stop them.

During the siege Edward finds time for diplomacy. The Flemish burghers to the east still support him and, during his march from Normandy to Crécy, their forces have been active south of Calais, no doubt with the idea of eventually linking up with the English army. But they have fallen back after failing to take Béthune. The Flemish ruling house, however, is still at loggerheads with the burghers and supports the French. The Count of Flanders has been killed at Crécy fighting beside King Philip. His fifteen-year-old son and successor also favours the French and is prepared to marry the daughter of the Duke of Brabant, now a French supporter. King Edward proposes an English marriage instead and offers his daughter Isabella. Knowing that this would seal an Anglo-Flemish alliance, the burghers get the young Count into their power and try to force him to change his mind.

For a long time the young Count was in the hands of the Flemings, who kept him a prisoner, though in comfortable conditions. But he grew sick of this, for it was not what he was used to, and in the end he changed his attitude – whether sincerely or not I do not know – and told his people that he would do as they advised, since he had more to gain from them than from any other nation. At this they were delighted and released him. Some of his pleasures were restored, such as freedom to go hawking for waterfowl, a sport of which he was very fond. But he was followed everywhere by guards who were entirely favourable to the King of England and had sworn on their lives not to let him escape. They watched him so closely that he was hardly able to go and piss. This went on for some time, until the Count agreed with his people that he would marry the King of England's daughter. The Flemings therefore invited the King and Queen, who were outside Calais, to come to the Abbey of Bergues and bring her with them. They would bring their young lord, and the marriage would be arranged.

As may be imagined, the King and Queen were very pleased by this news and said that the Flemings were excellent people. A day was agreed by both parties for the meeting at Bergues, to which the most prominent notables from the Flemish towns came in great state with the young Count. He bowed courteously to the King and Queen of England who had already arrived with a large suite. The King took him gently by the right hand, complimenting him as he did so. Then he asked him to forgive him for the death of his father and said that, as God was his witness, he had neither seen nor heard anything of the Count of Flanders during the whole of the battle of Crécy, or the day after. The young Count appeared to be fairly well satisfied with this apology.

They then discussed the marriage and drew up the various clauses of an agreement which all parties swore to observe. The Count was betrothed to the King of England's daughter, Princess Isabella, whom he promised to marry. The ceremony was postponed until a later date when they would have more leisure and the Flemings returned to Flanders with their lord and the English sovereigns to Calais. So things remained for a time. King Edward prepared to celebrate the wedding with great pomp and provided himself with costly jewels to be distributed on the day. The Queen did the same, for she was accounted the most gracious and bountiful lady of her time and she wished to be true to her reputation.

After the young Count had gone home he still went hawking and seemed to be very pleased at the prospect of the marriage. The Flemish were almost entirely reassured and no longer had him watched so closely. But they were far from understanding their young lord's mind, for in spite of his outward behaviour he was entirely French at heart, as he was soon to show.

One day when he had gone out hawking near the river –

it was in the very week when he was to marry the English princess – his falconer loosed a falcon at a heron and the Count did the same. As the two falcons flew after their prey, the Count rode in pursuit, shouting: 'O-ee! O-ee!' as though to lure them. When he had gone a little way and had open country before him, he clapped his spurs to his horse and galloped off, leaving his guards far behind. He reached the province of Artois, where he was safe. From there he went to France to King Philip, to whom he told his adventures and explained by what clever tricks he had escaped from his own people and the English. King Philip and the French said that he had done very well, but the English for their part said that he had betrayed them.

However, the King of England continued to be friendly to the Flemish. He knew that the Count had not been acting on their advice and that they were greatly displeased by what he had done. He therefore easily accepted the apologies which they made to him.

In the summer of 1347 King Philip gathers an army to relieve Calais, which is being steadily reduced by famine. His easiest way of approach would have been from the east, but the Flemings refuse to allow him to pass. He therefore follows much the same route as that which had led him to Crécy the year before and reaches the village of Sangatte, a few miles to the west of Calais:

When the King of England saw that King Philip had come with such a large army to raise the siege of a place which had already cost him so dear in money, lives and personal hardship – and this at a time when he had it in so tight a grip that it could not hold out much longer – it went entirely against his will to abandon his prize. He reflected that the French army had only two ways of approach to Calais – either along the dunes bordering the sea, or over country full of dikes and swamps which could only be crossed by the single bridge of Nieuley. He therefore had all his ships brought in near the dunes and loaded with bombards, crossbowmen, longbowmen, siege catapults and such things, for fear of which the French army dare not and could not pass that way. On the bridge he posted his cousin the Earl of Derby with a large force of men-at-arms and archers, so blocking the only road across the marshes.

Between the hill of Sangatte and the coast towards Calais there was a high tower guarded by thirty-two English archers which stood directly in the path of the French if they went over the dunes. It was strongly protected by big double ditches. The levies from the French towns saw this tower and the men of Tournay, who were a good fifteen hundred strong, advanced resolutely towards it. The archers who were inside shot at them, wounding a number. This only angered the men of Tournay and they went fiercely to the assault of the tower, forced their way across the ditches and reached the mound on which the tower stood with their picks and mattocks. Many more of the attackers were wounded in the struggle which followed, but they fought on until they had taken the tower. All those inside were killed and the tower demolished. This was hailed in the French army as a great achievement.

When his army was encamped on the hill of Sangatte, the French king sent forward the Lord of Beaujeu and the Lord of Saint-Venant, who were Marshals of France at that time, to reconnoitre the best line of approach to the enemy. They made a thorough inspection of the country, then came back and told the King that they could see no way of reaching the English without suffering further heavy losses. So things remained for the rest of that day and the following night.

After mass the next morning, King Philip sent four envoys, on the advice of his council, to the King of England. They were Sir Geoffroy de Charny, Sir Eustache de Ribemont, Sir Guy de Nesle and the Lord of Beaujeu. With the Earl of Derby's permission they crossed the bridge of Nieuley and as they went they looked closely at its strong defences and formed a high opinion of the dispositions of the Earl and his men who were guarding it. They rode on unmolested, on King Edward's orders, until they came to where the King himself was waiting, surrounded by a large number of his knights. They immediately dismounted and bowed before the

King, who received them fittingly. Sir Eustache de Ribemont, acting as their spokesman, then said:

'Sire, the King of France has sent us to inform you that he
has come to this place and halted on the hill of Sangatte with
the intention of fighting you, but he cannot see any way by
which to reach you. Yet he would dearly like to, in order to
raise the siege of his loyal town of Calais. He sent out his
marshals to try to discover some way of approaching you,
but the thing is impossible. He would therefore take it as a
favour if you would call your council together – and he would
do the same – and, according to the decision they came to,
agree on a spot where we could fight each other. Such is the
message and request which we have been charged to bring
you.'

After a brief consultation with his advisers, the King of
England replied: 'My lords, I fully understand the request
which you bring from my adversary, who is wrongly retain-
ing possession of my lawful heritage, to my great displeasure.
Kindly tell him from me that I have every right to be where
I am and where I have been for nearly a year, as he must
have known, and he could have come to me sooner if he had
wished to. But he has let me stay for so long that I have spent
my resources heavily and I believe I have now done enough
to be shortly master of the town and castle of Calais. So I am
not disposed to do very much to suit his plans and convenience, or let slip the thing I have so strongly desired and
bought so dearly. Tell him that if he and his men cannot get
through that way, they must go on looking until they find
another.'

*The envoys take this answer back to King Philip, who receives it
with anger and frustration. Two cardinals delegated by the Pope then
intervene in an attempt to arrange general peace terms, but after three
days negotiations break down on the question of the possession of Calais,
on which neither king will yield. The defenders of Calais, their provisions exhausted, look on helplessly at the comings-and-goings between
the two stationary armies. Finally, King Philip gives up. Early one
morning his army strikes camp and marches off.*

After the departure of King Philip and his army, the people

of Calais realized that the support on which they had been counting had failed them, and at the same time they were so weakened by hunger that the biggest and strongest among them could hardly stand. So they took counsel together and decided it would be better to throw themselves on the mercy of the King of England, if they could not obtain better terms, than to die one by one of starvation; for hunger might drive many of them frantic and cost them their souls with their bodies. They so entreated the Governor, Sir Jean de Vienne, to negotiate that at last he consented. He went on to the battlements and signalled to those outside that he wished to talk with them. When King Edward heard of this, he immediately sent out Sir Walter Manny and Lord Basset. They came to Sir Jean de Vienne and heard him say:

'My dear lords, you are very gallant knights with much experience of war, and you know that the King of France whom we serve sent us to this place to hold the town and castle for as long as our honour and his interests might require it. We have done everything in our power, but now our help has failed us and you are pressing us so hard that we have nothing left to eat. We must all die or go mad with hunger if the noble king whom you serve does not take pity on us. So I ask you, dear lords, to beg him humbly to have mercy on us and allow us to go away just as we are, taking for himself the town and citadel and all the things in them. He will find enough to satisfy him.'

To this Sir Walter Manny replied: 'Sir John, Sir John, we know something of the intentions of our lord the King, for he has told us of them. We must warn you that it is not his purpose to let you go free as you suggest. His intention rather is that you should place yourselves entirely in his hands, to be ransomed or put to death as he chooses. The people of Calais have caused him so much trouble and vexation, have cost him so much money and so many lives, that you cannot wonder that he should be enraged against them.'

Sir Jean de Vienne replied: 'It would be too hard for us to agree to such conditions. Inside here we are a little band of knights and squires who have served our master loyally to the best of our ability, as you would serve yours in the same case, and we have undergone many hardships and sufferings in so doing. But we would rather suffer more than any man has yet endured than consent that the humblest groom or servant in the town should be worse treated than the greatest among us. We beg you, in the kindness of your heart, to go back to the King of England and entreat him to spare us. That would be a chivalrous act on your part. And we hope that his noble heart will move him to have pity on us.'

'Indeed, yes,' said Sir Walter Manny, 'I will do that willingly, Sir John. And I sincerely hope he will listen to me, for it will go better with all of you if he does.'

The two English knights went off, leaving Sir Jean de Vienne standing on the battlements, for they were soon to return. King Edward was waiting for them at the entrance to his quarters, eager to have news of the state of Calais. With him were the Earl of Derby, the Earl of Northampton, the Earl of Arundel and several other English lords. His envoys bowed and went up to him and Sir Walter Manny began:

'Sire, we have seen the captain of Calais and have had a long conversation with him. It appears that he and his companions in arms as well as the citizens would be quite ready to surrender the town and castle and everything in them to you, on the sole condition that they were allowed to leave unharmed.'

'Sir Walter,' the King answered, 'you know something of our intentions concerning Calais. What was your reply?'

'Before God, sir,' said Sir Walter, 'I told them that you would agree to nothing, except that they should put themselves entirely in your hands, to live or die as you chose. When he heard this, Sir Jean de Vienne admitted that they were on the point of starvation but said that rather than surrender on those terms they would sell their lives as dearly as men ever did.'

'Sir Walter,' replied the King, 'there is not the slightest hope or prospect of my changing my mind.'

Sir Walter Manny went closer to the King and reasoned

with him, saying, to help the defenders of Calais: 'My lord,
you may well be mistaken, and you are setting a bad example
for us. Suppose one day you sent us to defend one of your
fortresses, we should go less cheerfully if you have these
people put to death, for then they would do the same to us if
they had the chance.' This argument did much to soften the
King's heart, especially when most of his barons supported it.
So he said: 'My lords, I do not want to be alone against you
all. Walter, go back to Calais and tell its commander that this
is the limit of my clemency: six of the principal citizens are
to come out, with their heads and their feet bare, halters
round their necks and the keys of the town and castle in their
hands. With these six I shall do as I please, and the rest I will
spare.'

'My lord,' said Sir Walter, 'I will do as you say.'

He went back to Calais to where Sir Jean de Vienne was
waiting and told him what the King had said, adding that that
was the most he could obtain. 'I am sure that is true,' said Sir
Jean. 'Now I must ask you to be so good as to wait here while
I report all this to the townspeople. It was they who sent me
here to talk with you and they, I think, who must give you
the answer.'

Sir Jean left the battlements and went to the market-place,
where he had the bells rung to summon the people together.
They all came, men and women, eager to hear the news, though
they were so weak with hunger that they could scarcely stand.
When they were assembled, Jean de Vienne quietly repeated
all that had been said, telling them that nothing more could
be hoped for and asking them to consult together and give
their answer quickly. When he had finished speaking they
began to cry out and weep so bitterly that their lamentations
would have moved the stoniest heart. For a time they were
unable to say anything in reply and Sir Jean himself was so
moved that he also was weeping.

At last the richest citizen of the town, by name Master
Eustache de Saint-Pierre, stood up and said:

'Sirs, it would be a cruel and miserable thing to allow such a population as this to die, so long as some remedy can be found. To prevent such a misfortune would surely be an act of great merit in Our Saviour's eyes and, for my part, I should have such strong hopes of receiving pardon for my sins if I died to save this people that I wish to be the first to come forward. I am willing to strip to my shirt, bare my head, put the rope round my neck, and deliver myself into the King of England's hands.'

When Master Eustache de Saint-Pierre had said this, his hearers were ready to worship him. Men and women flung themselves at his feet weeping bitterly. It was indeed a pitiful scene.

Then another greatly respected and wealthy citizen, who had two beautiful daughters, stood up and said that he would go with his friend Master Eustache de Saint-Pierre. His name was Master Jean d'Aire. A third, called Master Jacques de Wissant, who owned a rich family estate, offered to accompany them. Then his brother, Master Pierre de Wissant, and a fifth and a sixth, said they would go, too.

These six burghers stripped to their shirts and breeches there and then in the market-place, placed halters round their necks as had been stipulated and took the keys in their hands, each holding a bunch of them. Sir Jean de Vienne mounted a pony – for he could only walk with great difficulty – and led them to the gates. The men, women and children of Calais followed them weeping and wringing their hands. Sir Jean de Vienne had the gate opened and closed behind him, so that he stood with the six burghers between it and the outer barriers. He went to where Sir Walter Manny was waiting and said to him:

'Sir Walter, as the military commander of Calais and with the consent of the poor people of this town, I deliver up to you these six burghers. I swear that they have been and are to this day the most honourable and prominent citizens of Calais, by reason of their personal characters, their wealth and their ancestry, and that they carry with them all the keys of the town and citadel. And I beg you, noble sir, to intercede with the King of England not to have these good men put to death.'

'I do not know,' said Sir Walter, 'what the King will decide to do with them, but I promise you that I will do all I can.'

The barriers were then opened and Sir Walter Manny led off the six burghers, in the state I have described, straight towards the King's quarters, while Sir Jean de Vienne went back into the town.

At that time the King was in his chamber with a large company of earls, barons and knights. Hearing that the men of Calais were coming as he had ordered, he went out to the open space before his quarters, followed by his nobles and by great numbers of others who were curious to see them and learn what would happen to them. Even the Queen of England, who was far advanced in pregnancy, went out with her lord the King. When Sir Walter Manny arrived with the six burghers, he went up to the King and said: 'Sire, here is the deputation from Calais at your orders.'

The King kept quite silent and looked at them very fiercely, for he hated the people of Calais because of the losses they had inflicted on him at sea in the past. The six burghers knelt down before him and, clasping their hands in supplication, said: 'Most noble lord and king, here before you are we six citizens of Calais, long established and wealthy merchants of the town. We surrender to you the keys of the town and the castle, to do with them as you will. We put ourselves as you see us entirely in your hands, in order to save the remaining inhabitants of Calais, who have already undergone great privations. We pray you by your generous heart to have mercy on us also.'

None of the brave men present, lords, knights or men-at-arms, could refrain from shedding tears of pity when they heard this. It was indeed a moving sight to see men so humiliated and in such mortal danger.

But the King continued to glare at them savagely, his heart so bursting with anger that he could not speak. When at last he did, it was to order their heads to be struck off immediately.

All the nobles and knights who were there begged the King to have mercy, but he would not listen. Sir Walter Manny spoke up for them: 'Noble sire, curb your anger. You have a reputation for royal clemency. Do not perform an act which might tarnish it and allow you to be spoken of dishonourably. If you do not spare these men, the world will say that it was a cruel deed and that it was too harsh of you to put to death these honourable citizens who have voluntarily thrown themselves on your mercy to save the others.'

At this the King ground his teeth and said: 'That is enough, Sir Walter, my mind is made up. Let the executioner be sent for. The people of Calais have killed so many of my men that it is right that these should die in their turn.'

Then the noble Queen of England, pregnant as she was, humbly threw herself on her knees before the King and said, weeping: 'Ah, my dear lord, since I crossed the sea at great danger to myself, you know that I have never asked a single favour from you. But now I ask you in all humility, in the name of the Son of the Blessed Mary and by the love you bear me, to have mercy on these six men.'

The King remained silent for a time, looking at his gentle wife as she knelt in tears before him. His heart was softened, for he would not willingly have distressed her in the state she was in, and at last he said: 'My lady, I could wish you were anywhere else but here. Your appeal has so touched me that I cannot refuse it. So, although I do this against my will, here, take them. They are yours to do what you like with.'

The Queen thanked him from the bottom of her heart, then rose to her feet and told the six burghers to rise also. She had the halters taken from their necks and led them into her apartment. They were given new clothes and an ample dinner. Then each was presented with six nobles and they were escorted safely through the English army and went to live in various towns in Picardy.

After King Edward had handed over the six burghers to the Queen, he called Sir Walter Manny and his two Marshals and said to them: 'Sirs, take these keys of the town and castle of Calais and go and assume possession of them. Take the knights who are there and make them prisoners or else put them on parole; they are gentlemen and I will trust them on their word. All other soldiers, who have been serving there for pay, are to leave the place just as they are, and so is everyone else in the town, men, women and children, for I wish to repopulate Calais with pure-blooded English.' . . .

Now in my opinion it is very sad to reflect on the fate of those great burghers and their noble wives and their handsome children, who with their forefathers had been living for generations in Calais. There were many such on the day when it fell. It was harrowing for them to have to abandon their fine houses, their estates, their furniture and possessions; for they could take nothing away and they received no restitution or compensation from the King of France, for whose sake they had lost everything. I will say no more about them. They managed as well as they could, and the majority went to the town of Saint-Omer.[1] . . .

When King Edward returned to London, he gave serious thought to the repopulation of Calais, sending there thirty-six wealthy and responsible citizens with their families, and more than three hundred other men of lesser standing. Their numbers grew continually because the King granted them such great liberties and privileges that many became eager to settle there.

1. It appears that many of the French inhabitants were either not dispossessed, or were re-admitted after a few weeks. One who was confirmed in his possessions and given a post of special responsibility was the heroic Eustache de Saint-Pierre. It is also established that Philip VI made efforts to compensate those who were expelled, by conferring various offices and rights upon them.

Black Death, Flagellants and Jews [1] (1349)

IN the Year of Grace 1349, the penitents went about, coming first out of Germany. They were men who did public penance and scourged themselves with whips of hard knotted leather with little iron spikes. Some made themselves bleed very badly between the shoulders and some foolish women had cloths ready to catch the blood and smear it on their eyes, saying that it was miraculous blood. While they were doing penance, they sang very mournful songs about the nativity and passion of Our Lord.

The object of this penance was to entreat God to put a stop to the mortality, for in that time of death there was an epidemic of plague. People died suddenly and at least a third of all the people in the world died then. The penitents of whom I am speaking went in companies from town to town and from city to city and wore long felt hoods on their heads, each company with its own colour. Their rules forbade them to sleep more than one night in each town and the length of their goings-out was fixed by the thirty-three and a half years which Jesus Christ spent on earth, as the Holy Scriptures tell us; each of their companies went about for thirty-three and a half days, and then they returned to the towns or castles from which they had come. They spent very little money on their journeys, because the good people of the towns which they visited asked them to dinner and supper. They slept only on straw, unless illness forced them to do otherwise. When they entered a house in which they were to dine or sup, they kneeled down humbly on the threshold and said three paternosters and three *Ave Marias*, and did the same when they left. Many reconciliations were achieved through the penitents as they went about, for instance, over killings which had taken place and about which it had so far been impossible to reach an accord; but by means of the penitents peace was made.

1. From the Rome MS.

III

Their rules contained some quite reasonable and acceptable things which agreed with such natural human inclinations as to journey about and do penance, but they did not enter the Kingdom of France because Pope Innocent,[1] who was at Avignon at that time with his cardinals, considered the practice and opposed it very strongly, declaring in condemnation of the penitents that public penance inflicted by oneself was neither right nor lawful. They were excommunicated for doing it, and especially those clergy who went with them. A number of priests, canons and chaplains who supported them were deprived of their benefices. Any who wished for absolution had to go to Avignon to get it. So this movement was broken up and came to nothing when it was seen that the Pope and the King of France were against them, and they did not go beyond Hainault. If they had gone to Cambrai or Saint-Quentin, the gates would have been shut in their faces.

As soon as the penitents appeared and the news of them spread round, the sect of the Jews contemplated and feared their own destruction,[2] for they had a prophecy made over two hundred years earlier which said in cryptic language: 'Knights will come bearing links of iron who will be very cruel, but they will have no leaders and their power and their works will not extend beyond the Empire of Germany. But when they come, we shall all be destroyed.' Their prophecy came true, for in those days all the Jews were indeed destroyed, though more in one country than in another. The Pope, and the Kings of Castile, Aragon and Navarre, accepted great numbers of them and laid them under tribute beneath them.

1. Until 1352 it would be his predecessor, Clement VI.

2. First version: 'At that time the Jews were taken and burnt everywhere throughout the world, and their possessions seized by the rulers under whom they lived, except in Avignon and the domains of the Church beneath the protection of the Pope.'

After this, one manuscript (B6) has the addition: 'for the Church does not hold that they should be put to death, because they would be saved if they were willing to return to our faith.'

Sea Battle off Winchelsea (1350)

AT that time there was bitter feeling between the English and the Spanish on account of various acts of violence and plunder which the Spaniards had committed against English ships at sea. So it happened that in the year 1350, while the Spanish were in Flanders for trading purposes, they were told that the English were intending to waylay them on their voyage back home. They were not greatly disturbed by the news, but equipped their ships, lying at Sluys, with all kinds of weapons and powerful artillery, and engaged all the mercenaries, archers and crossbowmen who were willing to serve them for pay. They went on with their purchases of goods, just as they had planned, and meanwhile waited for each other, so as to sail in one fleet.

When King Edward, who had no love for them, heard of these warlike preparations, he said angrily: 'We have had long experience of Spanish ways. They have done us many wrongs and, far from making amends, they go on arming themselves against us. They must be intercepted on their way back.' His men readily agreed, sharing the same desire that the Spaniards should be fought. A special summons was sent out to all the gentry then in England and the King left London for Sussex, a county extending along the sea-coast between Southampton and Dover, opposite the districts of Ponthieu and Dieppe. He took up his quarters in an abbey overlooking the sea, to which the Queen herself accompanied him.

At that date there came to join the King, at the place which I have just mentioned, that gallant knight Robert of Namur, who had recently returned to England. The King received him gladly and he was fortunate enough to take part in the expedition. As soon as King Edward heard that the Spanish were preparing to pass through the Straits, he put to sea with a fine company of men-at-arms, knights and squires, and more great nobles than had ever accompanied him on any previous venture.

In that year the King had created his cousin, Henry Earl of Derby, Duke of Lancaster, and had made the Baron of Stafford an Earl. So these two were with him in the enterprise, as were his two sons the Prince of Wales and John, Earl of Richmond.[1] The latter was still too young to bear arms but the Prince, who was very fond of him, took him with him in his own ship. Also there were the Earls of Arundel, Northampton, Hereford, Suffolk and Warwick, Sir Reginald Cobham, Sir Walter Manny, Sir Thomas Holland, Sir Louis de Beauchamp, Sir James Audley, Sir Bartholomew Burghersh, the Lords Percy, Mowbray, Neville, Clifford, Ros, Berkeley and many others. The King was also accompanied by four hundred knights. All these were now at sea on board the ships, armed and equipped to engage the enemy who, as they knew, would be making the passage very shortly. They waited at anchor for three days between Dover and Calais.

After the Spaniards had completed their trading and had laden their ships with cloth, linens and all the goods which it seemed profitable to take back to their country, they embarked at Sluys in the knowledge that the English were waiting for them. Together with the great quantity of projectile-throwers with which they had provided themselves, they had heavy iron bars specially made to hurl at ships and sink them, as well as piles of stones for the same purpose. When they saw that the wind was with them, they raised anchor. There were forty big ships all sailing together, so powerful and splendid that they made a beautiful sight. At the top of the masts were wooden castles loaded with stones of different sizes and manned by irregular soldiers to throw them. On the masts also were streamers bearing their various colours and emblems which waved and fluttered in the wind. If the English were thirsting for a fight, they appeared to be even more so, and this proved to be the case, as you will hear. In men, these Spanish were at least ten to one, thanks to the mercenaries they had hired in Flanders. They considered themselves

1. The Black Prince and John of Gaunt.

quite strong enough to engage the King of England and all his might at sea. In this frame of mind they sailed on towards Calais, with the wind full astern.

King Edward had already drawn up his fleet and decided how he wished to fight the battle, and he had appointed Sir Robert of Namur master of a ship called the *Salle du Roi*, on board of which was all his household equipment. He stood in the bows of his own ship, wearing a black velvet jerkin and a black beaverskin cap which greatly suited him. On that day, I was told by some who were with him, he was in a gayer mood than he had ever been seen before. He told his minstrels to strike up a dance tune which Sir John Chandos, who was there beside him, had recently brought back from Germany. And out of sheer high spirits he made Sir John sing with the minstrels, to his own vast amusement. At the same time he kept glancing up at the mast, on which he had posted a look-out to espy the coming of the Spaniards. While the King was enjoying this gaiety and his knights were cheerful at seeing him so cheerful, the look-out shouted: 'Ship ahoy! And she looks like a Spaniard.' The minstrels stopped playing, and the man was asked if he saw more than one. In a moment he answered: 'Yes, there are two, now three, now four.' And then, seeing the huge fleet, he shouted: 'There are so many, God help me, I can't count them!' The King and his men realized that it must be the Spanish. The trumpets were sounded and the ships drew close together so as to be in battle order and more safely positioned. They were sure now that they would have their fight, since the Spaniards were coming in such strength. It was already late, somewhere about four o'clock. The King therefore had wine served to himself and all his knights. Then he and the others put on their battle-helmets.

The Spanish were coming so fast that, had they wished, they could have sailed clean through without engaging. They were in big ships, well trimmed, with the wind astern, and need never have tangled with the English unless they wanted to. But such was their pride and confidence that they scorned to slip by without fighting. Instead, they prepared to give battle in earnest with their full strength.

When King Edward saw how things were shaping, he called to the helmsman of his ship: 'Steer at that ship straight ahead of us. I want to have a joust at it.'

The seaman would never have dared to disobey the King's orders, so he put his helm towards the Spaniard which was bearing down on them rapidly with the wind. The King's ship was stoutly built and timbered, otherwise it would have been split in two, for it and the Spanish ship, which was tall and heavy, collided with a crash like thunder and, as they rebounded, the castle of the King's ship caught the castle of the Spaniard with such force that the mast on which it was fixed broke and it was flung into the sea. The men in it were killed or drowned. The King's ship was so shattered by the collision that its seams cracked and water began to pour in. His knights did not tell the King of this yet, but set to work to bale out the water. Then the King, looking at the ship with which he had jousted and which was lying before them, said: 'Grapple my ship to that one. I want to have it.' 'Let that one go,' his knights answered. 'You'll get a better one.' So that ship went on and another big one came up. The knights flung out hooks and chains and fastened their own ship to it. A fierce battle began between them, the English archers shooting and the Spanish defending themselves lustily, and soon the fighting had spread to a dozen different places. Wherever the English found themselves at close quarters, they threw out their grapnels and performed prodigies of valour. The advantage was by no means with them for, the Spanish ships being bigger and higher than theirs, they were able to shoot down at them and hurl the great iron bars which did considerable damage.

The knights in the King of England's ship, seeing that it was making so much water that it was in danger of foundering, made desperate efforts to capture the ship to which they were grappled. They fought so well that in the end the Spaniard was taken, and all the men on board it thrown into the sea. Only then was the King told of the danger they were in of sinking and urged to move into the ship they had just captured. This he did, with his knights and all the others, leaving

116

their own ship abandoned. They then prepared to continue the attack on the enemy vessels, which were making a stout fight of it and whose archers were wreaking particular havoc with the bolts from their powerful crossbows.

This hotly contested sea-battle began late. The English therefore redoubled their efforts to finish the business and defeat their enemies before nightfall. Yet the Spanish, who are used to the sea and had better ships, did their utmost and never flinched. The young Prince of Wales and his company were engaged in another quarter. They were grappled and held fast by a big Spanish ship which inflicted great damage on them. Their ship was holed in several places, through which the water came pouring in. However fast they baled, they could not stop her from settling lower and lower. This filled the Prince's men with great anxiety and made them fight all the harder to take the Spanish ship. But it put up such a stout defence that they could not manage it. While they were in this perilous situation, the Duke of Lancaster came sailing alongside them. He saw that they were getting the worst of it and that their ship was in a dangerous state, for water was being thrown out on every side. So he went round to the other side of the Spaniard, shouting: 'Derby to the rescue!' whereupon the Spanish were boarded and engaged so fiercely that they did not hold out for long. Their ship was taken and they were all thrown overboard with no quarter for any. The Prince of Wales and his men went on board, and hardly had they done so than their own ship sank. Then they realized fully the great danger they had been in.

The English knights and barons were fighting in other places, following the plan of battle which had been made. They had need of all their strength and skill, for they were up against no weak enemy. For example, late in the evening, the ship carrying the King's household, commanded by Sir Robert of Namur, was grappled by a big Spanish ship and hotly engaged by it. In order to master the English ship at their leisure and capture both it and everyone in it, the Spaniards decided to carry it off with them. They hoisted their sails and moved forward with the wind, in spite of everything that Sir Robert and his seamen could do. The Spaniard being the heavier and taller ship, its advantage was too great to be resisted.

So linked together, they passed near the King's ship, and the English shouted: 'Rescue the *Salle du Roi!*' But in the growing dark they were not heard, or if they were, they were not aided. It looked as though the Spaniards would carry them away as they pleased, when one of Sir Robert's men called Hanekin performed a notable feat of daring. With his drawn sword in his hand, he braced himself and sprang on board the enemy ship, forced his way to the mast, and cut the sail cable so that the sail sagged and no longer drew. Then he skilfully severed the four main ropes which stayed the mast and the sail, so that this collapsed and the ship came to a stop.

Seeing this, Sir Robert of Namur and his men leapt eagerly on board the Spaniard, with their swords drawn. They attacked its crew so heartily that they killed them all and threw them overboard, and captured the ship.

I cannot describe all the brave deeds that were done there, but can only say that the battle was fierce and bitter as long as it lasted, and that the Spanish gave King Edward plenty of trouble. But finally the day was with the English. The Spanish lost fourteen ships, while the rest sailed on and escaped. When they had all passed and the English had no one left to fight, they sounded the retreat on their trumpets and set their course towards England, reaching land at Rye and Winchelsea a little after nightfall.

At that same hour the King and his sons, the Prince and the Earl of Richmond, with the Duke of Lancaster and some of the barons who were there, disembarked, obtained horses in the town, and rode to the abbey where the Queen was staying only two miles away. She was overjoyed to see her lord and her children, for during that day she had suffered great anxiety. The whole battle had been watched from high ground on that part of the English coast, the weather being very fine and clear. The Queen had been told – for she insisted on knowing – that the Spanish numbered more than forty large ships. Hence her relief when she saw her husband and sons again.

The night was passed in great rejoicings by the lords and ladies and in conversations on arms and love. The next day the greater part of the barons and knights who had been at the battle rejoined the King. He thanked them for their brave conduct and loyal service. Then they took their leave of him and returned each to his own home.

The Siege of Breteuil and the Poitiers
Campaign (1356)

IN *the year of the sea-battle off Winchelsea, Philip VI of France died and was succeeded by John II, 'the Good'. Though there was a temporary lull in the war with England, the new King's internal difficulties were soon increased by the intrigues of his cousin, Charles ' the Bad', King of Navarre, who had rival claims to the French throne. Early in 1356 Charles of Navarre was seized and put in prison, but his family and the vassals of his fiefs in Normandy continued to give trouble, in alliance with the English. The Duke of Lancaster led a small expedition to Normandy in support of them, but avoided battle when John the Good marched against him and retired on Cherbourg. The French King used his forces to capture Evreux, a stronghold of the Navarrese, then laid siege to Breteuil, another dependency of Charles the Bad.*

The French who were besieging Breteuil lost no time in devising various means of attack to wear down the garrison. In reply, those inside strove constantly to find ways of hitting back at them. The besiegers set up great engines to hurl missiles by night and day on to the roofs of the towers, which did much damage. The King of France also set numbers of carpenters to work at building a large 'belfry' or wooden tower with three storeys which could be moved about on wheels. Each storey could hold a good two hundred men, with enough room to use their weapons. This tower was provided with loopholes and padded with leather as a protection against heavy bolts. Some called it a cat-house and others an assault-machine. While it was being constructed and made ready, the peasants of the district were ordered to bring up great quantities of wood and unload them in the moats, then to spread straw and earth on top so that the tower could be wheeled against the walls to assault the defenders. It was a full month before the moat was filled at the place where the attack was to be made. When everything was complete, a large force of knights and squires who wanted to win distinction got into the tower which was then wheeled up to the walls.

The garrison had seen the tower being built and had formed a fairly clear idea of the French plan of attack. They had accordingly equipped themselves with cannons casting fire and big, heavy bolts of great destructive power. They made ready to assault the tower and defend themselves with great spirit. First, before using their cannons, they engaged in open combat with the men in the tower, fighting them hand-to-hand. Many fine feats-of-arms were performed. When they had had enough of this, they began to fire their cannons and to fling fire on top of the tower and inside it, and with it heavy volleys of their big bolts, by which many of the besiegers were killed and wounded and the others so harassed that they did not know which way to turn. The fire, which was Greek fire, set the roof of the tower alight, forcing the men in it to abandon it hurriedly, to save themselves from being burnt to death. When the fighting men of Breteuil saw this, they raised a great cheer and began to shout: 'St George! Loyalty and Navarre! Loyalty!' And then they shouted: 'Well, you French, you didn't get us as easily as you thought you would!'

What was left of the tower remained in the moat, and no attempt was made to man it again. But the French worked on at filling the rest of the moat, using fifteen hundred men to do nothing else every day.

Meanwhile the Black Prince, now aged twenty-five, had sailed from England to Bordeaux in the autumn of the previous year and had struck down towards the south-east with a combined force of English and Gascons. His object was to terrorize the districts which were inclining towards the French and perhaps bring to battle King John's lieutenant in Languedoc, Count Jean d'Armagnac. The expedition was a complete success in the way of punitive devastation and loot, but there was no battle of armies. After penetrating as far as Carcassonne and Narbonne the Prince returned to Bordeaux in December 1355, and prepared for another strike northwards when the winter was over.

While the King of France was besieging Breteuil, the Prince

of Wales left Bordeaux, where he had been all this time completing his preparations for a campaign. He intended to make a foray far into French territory, and perhaps reach Normandy and the frontiers of Brittany to aid the Navarrese, for he was well aware that his father King Edward was in close alliance with the princes of Navarre and the Harcourt family. He set out on this occasion with two thousand men-at-arms and six thousand archers, including irregulars. With him in particular were all the barons and knights who had accompanied him on the expedition to Carcassonne and Languedoc, and whom there is no need to name again here.

The Prince and his men moved forward in good military order. They crossed the Garonne at Bergerac and then, entering Rouergue, crossed the Dordogne.[1] In Rouergue they began to make war seriously, exacting ransom-money from towns and castles, or else burning them, taking prisoners and capturing supplies in quantity. The country was well stocked, but they left it broken and devastated behind them. Then they entered Auvergne, where they crossed and re-crossed the River Allier several times and found none to oppose them. From Limousin they chose a route to bring them to the rich and prosperous region of Berry and the River Loire. They found more than enough provisions for themselves, so burnt or otherwise destroyed what was left over.

News of the Black Prince's movements is brought to Breteuil to King John, who becomes impatient to end the siege. Terms of surrender are agreed upon.

The defenders of Breteuil negotiated a surrender to the King of France, for the siege-engines, which were in action continuously, were inflicting great damage on them and they saw no sign of relief from any quarter. They knew that, if they were taken by assault, they would all be slaughtered without mercy. The King of France, for his part, was anxious to campaign against the English who were devastating his country, and was, moreover, thoroughly weary of being immobilized before that fortress to which he had brought sixty thousand

1. *Sic* Froissart. But Bergerac is on the Dordogne. To enter Rouergue from there they presumably crossed the River Lot.

men whom he was maintaining at great expense. He therefore agreed to spare their lives and let them go with whatever possessions they could carry with them, but nothing more. The knights and squires of Breteuil withdrew to Cherbourg, as far as which the King gave them a safe-conduct. The King took possession of the castle and had it put into thorough repair. He then struck camp and returned towards Paris, but dismissed none of his men-at-arms, since he expected to use them elsewhere.

Leaving Paris, the King of France assembles a new and larger army at Chartres, at the same time reinforcing the garrisons of various fortresses to block off the English from the north. Meanwhile, the English reach Bourges, which they take, together with the nearby town of Vierzon, and there decide to turn west through Touraine and Poitou. Their plan is to make a destructive sweep through those provinces and thence regain Bordeaux. They are now being shadowed by a French force of three hundred lances. These skirmish with a detachment of the English, who get the better of them and pursue the survivors as far as Romorantin, where they take refuge in the castle. The town itself is occupied without resistance.

News reached the Prince that his men had been in action. He asked with whom and was told of the result of the engagement, and how his men had driven the enemy into the castle of Romorantin. 'We will ride that way,' said the Prince. 'I would like to have a closer look at them.' The whole army set out in that direction and reached the town of Romorantin. This was now full of their own men, who were busy studying the best way to attack the castle. The Prince rode up to it in full armour, mounted on a black charger, with Sir John Chandos at his side. They too began to examine the castle and weigh it up, and they concluded that it could well be taken. The Prince called Sir John Chandos and said: 'John, go up to the barriers and speak to the knights inside there. Ask them if they would be ready to surrender quietly, without undergoing an assault.'

Leaving the Prince, Sir John rode up to the barriers and made signs that he had something to discuss. The guards inquired his name and asked who had sent him. He told them who he was and said that he had come from the Prince. They took all this information to their commanders. Lord Boucicaut and the Hermit of Chaumont came down to the barriers, where Sir John saluted them and said:

'Sirs, I have been sent to you by the Prince, who is willing to make you what I think is a very generous offer. He says that, if you will become his prisoners and surrender this fortress which is not defensible, he will spare your lives and give you the most honourable treatment.' 'Sir John,' replied Lord Boucicaut, 'very many thanks to the Prince for his generous offer, but we do not feel disposed to accept it. God forbid that he should capture us so easily.' 'What, Lord Boucicaut,' said Sir John, 'do you think yourselves such splendid knights that you can hold this fortress against the Prince and his army, with no prospect of relief from any quarter?' 'Chandos, Chandos,' replied Boucicaut, 'I don't consider myself a splendid knight, but we should be crazy to accept the kind of terms you are offering, and crazier still to give ourselves up when there is as yet no need for it. Please tell my lord the Prince to do whatever he thinks best, and we will await him here in all confidence.'

Sir John Chandos left them and returned to the Prince, to whom he related the whole of this conversation. When the Prince learnt of Lord Boucicaut's reply, he thought none the less of him for it and gave orders for his men to take up quarters for the rest of that day and the night. He proposed to attack the fortress on the following day and see if he could take it by assault.

Early the next morning, all his fighting men armed themselves, including the archers. They assembled under their banners and began a fierce assault on the castle. The archers stood along the banks of the moat, shooting so steadily that the defenders hardly dared to show themselves on the battlements. Others launched out on doors and hurdles with picks and mattocks, or bows and arrows, in their hands. Reaching the foot of the wall, they hacked and hammered away at it.

Up above were the Lord of Craon, Lord Boucicaut and the Hermit of Chaumont, heading a lusty defence. They hurled down stones and flints and pots of quicklime, which inflicted terrible wounds on those they fell upon. Among those killed on the English side was a fine Gascon squire called Raymond de Zedulach, belonging to the Captal de Buch's troop, whose death was greatly regretted. The assault went on the whole day, with hardly any respite, until finally the attackers withdrew to their quarters, where the whole tended the wounded, and so they passed the night.

The assault is renewed the next day even more fiercely, but without success. The Black Prince grows impatient at his losses and expresses his determination to capture the castle and its defenders unconditionally.

So they attacked more heavily on every side to gain their objective, and because the Prince had spoken so strongly. Some of the wiser men-at-arms reflected that they were striving in vain and letting their men be killed and wounded to no purpose, since they would never take the castle just by shooting arrows and hurling stones. They therefore ordered cannons to be brought forward to shoot bolts and Greek fire into the courtyard. If the fire caught there, it might well spread to the roofs of the castle towers, which were thatched with straw at that time. Unless this tactic succeeded, they could not see any way of taking the castle and the knights who were defending it.

Accordingly, fire materials were brought up and shot from bombards and cannons into the courtyard, where they caught and spread so rapidly that everything began to burn. The fire reached the thatched roof of a big tower in which were the three knights who had fought so gallantly on that and the previous day. When they saw the fire above their heads and realized that they must either surrender or perish where they stood, their confidence deserted them. They came down hurriedly and surrendered to the Prince unconditionally. Had they not done so, he would have refused them, because of the strong and angry words which he had spoken. So the Prince had these knights as his prisoners and made them ride on with him, together with several other gentlemen who had been in the castle of Romorantin. The castle itself was left burnt, ruined and empty. The Prince's men plundered and carried off everything they found there and in the town.

The Prince moves in a south-westerly direction through Touraine, still devastating the country. King John leaves Chartres and advances south through Blois, Amboise and Loches to La Haye-en-Touraine, collecting more men on the way. Independently, the Cardinal de Périgord, who had been dispatched by the Pope on a so far fruitless peace mission to the King of France, travels to Poitiers in the hope of averting a clash between the two armies.

News reached the King of France that the Prince of Wales was forcing the pace to get back to the district from which he had started. The King, who desired above all things to bring him to battle, began to fear that he would escape him. He therefore left La Haye-en-Touraine, followed by all his army, and rode on to Chauvigny, which was reached on the evening of Thursday, 15 September 1356. A large number of his nobles lodged in the town of Chauvigny itself, and others outside in a big meadow bordering the river. The next day, after his morning drink, the King crossed the bridge of Chauvigny expecting to find the English before him, but they were not there. In all, sixty thousand horsemen crossed the river at that point during the day in pursuit of the English, while many others crossed it at Châtellerault. As soon as they were over, they took the road to Poitiers.

For their part, the Prince and his men knew nothing of the enemy's movements and had no means of knowing. They had of course heard that they had taken the field, but they had no idea of their exact whereabouts, beyond supposing that they were not far off, because their own foragers were unable to find supplies; as a result of this the army was very short of food. Many regretted the wanton destruction they had wrought in Berry, Anjou and Touraine and their neglect to stock up more fully with provisions.

On the Saturday, a scouting detachment of the English clash with a contingent of French who have lagged behind the main army. Prisoners are taken, from whom the Prince discovers where the enemy is.

When the Prince and his commanders learnt that the King

126

of France was in front of them with his army, having crossed the bridge at Chauvigny on the Friday, so making it impossible for them to leave the district without fighting, they closed up and came to a halt in the open fields. Orders were given by the Prince that without special authority no one was to ride out ahead of the Marshals' banners, on pain of death. This order was strictly observed and the English rode on for the whole of that day until they were within four miles of Poitiers. Then four knights, the Captal de Buch, Sir Aymon de Pommiers, Lord Bartholomew Burghersh and Sir Eustace d'Aubrecicourt, were detailed to lead a reconnoitring force of two hundred men in armour, all mounted on excellent horses. These rode forward until they obtained a view of the King's main division, and saw all the country around covered with men-at-arms. They could not resist charging into the rear of the French. They felled some to the ground and took promises of ransom from others, until the main army began to bestir itself to attack them. News of this was brought to the King of France, just as he was about to enter the city of Poitiers.

When he knew the truth – that his enemies, whom he was so eager to meet, were behind him and not ahead – he was highly pleased. He reined round and ordered his whole army to turn about well outside the town and take up quarters in the open country. It was late at night before they were all settled. The Prince's scouts went back to him and described a part of the French forces, saying that there were an inordinate lot of them.

The Prince was in no way disturbed by this, but said: 'May God be with us! Now we must consider how to fight them to the best advantage.' That night the English encamped in a strong position, among hedges, vines and bushes. They set a strong guard to keep careful watch, as did the French on their side.

The next morning the French prepare for battle, organizing their army in three main divisions, each, according to Froissart, numbering sixteen thousand men. Four knights are sent out to reconnoitre the English force. They return to the King and make their report.

'Sire,' said Sir Eustace de Ribemont, acting as spokesman

for the others, as they had asked him, 'we have seen and observed the English. We would estimate their numbers at two
thousand men-at-arms, four thousand archers, and fifteen
hundred light-armed men.' 'And how are they disposed?'
asked the King. 'Sire,' replied Sir Eustace, 'they are in a very
strong position and, although we are convinced that they have
only one division, it is extremely skilfully placed. They have
chosen a length of road strongly protected by hedges and
bushes, and they have lined the hedge on both sides with their
archers, so that one cannot enter that road or ride along it
without passing between them. Yet one must go that way
before one can fight them. There is only one way in and out of
that hedge, through which perhaps four men-at-arms could
ride abreast, the same as along the road.[1] At the end of the
hedge, among vines and thorn-bushes between which it would
be impossible to march or ride, are their men-at-arms, all on
foot, and they have placed their archers in harrow-formation[2]
in front of them. It is a very skilful piece of work in our
opinion, for if one wants to engage them by force of arms, the
only way in is between those archers, whom it will not be easy
to overcome.'

'Well, Sir Eustace,' said the King, 'how would you advise
proceeding?'

'Sire,' replied the knight, 'with everyone on foot, except for
three hundred of the most vigorous and experienced knights
in your army, mounted on first-rate horses, to break through
those archers and scatter them. And then your formations of
men-at-arms would follow quickly on foot and engage their
men-at-arms hand-to-hand. That is the best plan I can think of,
but if anyone knows of a better, let him say so.'

The King thoroughly approved of this suggestion and said
he would act on it.

1. All authorities on the battle assume that the 'hedge' ran frontally to
the two armies, while the 'road' passed through a gap in it and led to the
main English body positioned, dismounted, in the rear. From Froissart's
account alone, however, it would be equally possible that the hedge was
a double one, lining each side of the road at right angles to the French
line of advance.

2. See p. 87 above.

On his orders, accordingly, the two Marshals set out and, riding from division to division, they made a choice of three hundred knights and squires, the toughest and best fighters of the whole army, all fully equipped and mounted on superb horses. Immediately afterwards the battalion of the Germans was formed. Led by the Counts of Saarbrück, Nidau and Nassau, this was to remain on horseback to support the Marshals.

King John of France was there, with nineteen others bearing similar arms.[1] He had placed his eldest son (the Duke of Normandy) in the charge of the Lord of Saint-Venant, Sir Jean de Landas and Sir Thibaut de Voudenay and his three younger sons, Louis, Jean and Philippe, in the care of other good knights and squires. The King's sovereign banner was carried by Sir Geoffroy de Charny, as the wisest and bravest knight of them all. Sir Regnault de Cervoles, known as the Archpriest, wore the arms of the young Count of Alençon.

When the King's forces were mustered and armed, with each commander among his men under his own banner, and each fully aware of the part he had to play, orders were given for everyone to dismount, except those who had been chosen by the Marshals to break through the archers. All who had lances were to cut them down to a length of five feet, in order to make handier weapons of them, and they were also told to take off their spurs. These orders were obeyed to the letter, for everyone accepted them as right and proper.

Just as they were about to advance, to all appearances eager to engage the enemy, the Cardinal de Périgord came riding up, spurring and lashing his horse towards the King. He had left Poitiers in the early morning, and he now bowed humbly before the King and begged him with uplifted hands, in the name of Almighty God, to hold off for a moment until he had had a word with him. King John, who was accessible to any reasonable request, consented and said: 'Willingly. What do you wish to say?'

'My very dear lord,' said the Cardinal, 'you have with you

1. A practice sometimes adopted to confuse the enemy.

here the whole cream of your kingdom's nobility, pitted against what in comparison is a mere handful of the English. If you could overcome them without a fight by accepting their surrender, it would redound more to your honour and advantage than if you risked this large and splendid army in battle. I therefore beg you humbly, in the name of God, to let me ride over to the Prince and persuade him of the great peril he is in.'

To this also the King consented, saying: 'Sir, we agree, but do not be too long about it.'

Upon this, the Cardinal went hurriedly over to the Prince of Wales, whom he found standing among his men in the thickest part of a vineyard, awaiting the French attack with every sign of confidence. Having dismounted and bowed to him, the Cardinal said: 'I am sure, my son, that if you had seen the King of France's army and formed a correct idea of its size, you would allow me to try to arrange terms between you, if it is at all possible.' The Prince, who was still a young man, answered: 'Sir, subject to the honour of myself and my men, I would be ready to listen to any reasonable proposal.' 'My son,' said the Cardinal, 'that was well said. I will bring you to an agreement if I can. It would be a thousand pities if all these fine men here, on both sides, were to meet in battle. Too much misery could come of it.'

Without saying more, the Cardinal returned to the King of France and began to work out grounds for agreement and put forward suggestions, saying to the King, in order to make him more amenable: 'Sire, you need be in no great hurry to fight them. You can have them all without striking a blow, for they cannot retreat or escape you. So I beg you to forbear for this one day and grant them a truce until sunrise tomorrow.'

On hearing this, the King became thoughtful and at first refused the Cardinal's repeated requests for a truce, for some of his council were against it – in particular Sir Eustace de Ribemont and Sir Jean de Landas, who were very close to him. But the Cardinal, sparing no efforts in a good cause, begged and exhorted him so fervently that at last he gave in and agreed to a truce until the next morning. This decision was quickly carried by the Cardinal to the Prince and his men, who found it not unwelcome because they were continually improving their dispositions and their battle-plan.

The King caused a tent of vermilion silk, very elegantly and richly made, to be pitched in the fields on the same spot where he had granted the truce, then dismissed all his men to their quarters except for the battalion of the Constable and the Marshals. He also kept with him his sons and the most important members of his family on whom he depended for advice.

During the whole of that Sunday the Cardinal rode to and fro from one to the other, and would gladly have brought them to an agreement had it been possible, but he found the King and his council so unyielding that they refused to negotiate unless four-fifths of all the English became their prisoners and the Prince and his men surrendered unconditionally, which they would never have done. There were many discussions and offers, and various proposals were made. I was told some time ago by followers of the Cardinal, who were present on that occasion and certainly thought they knew something about it, that the Prince offered to restore to the King of France everything he had taken on that campaign, towns and castles, to hand over all his prisoners, and to swear not to take up arms against France for the next seven years. But the King and his council would not hear of it. They insisted on this as their final condition: that the Prince and a hundred of his own knights should become the King's prisoners, in return for letting the others go; but this was a stipulation which the Prince and his council would never have accepted.

During the truce, knights from both sides ride about examining the other army. Among the English who do this is Sir John Chandos.

Just as Sir John Chandos had ridden round observing part of the French dispositions, so one of the French Marshals, Sir Jean de Clermont, had gone out reconnoitring the English. In doing this, it so happened that their paths crossed and that some strong words and very ugly insults were exchanged. I

will tell you why. These knights, who were young and in love
– for that must certainly have been the explanation – were
both wearing on their left arms the same emblem of a lady
in blue embroidered in a sunbeam. They always wore this on
their outer garment, whether they were in armour or not. Sir
Jean de Clermont was by no means pleased to see his emblem
on Sir John Chandos and he pulled up dead in front of him
and said: 'I have been wanting to meet you, Chandos. Since
when have you taken to wearing my emblem?' 'And you
mine?' said Sir John. 'It is just as much mine as yours.' 'I
deny that,' said Sir Jean de Clermont, 'and if there were not a
truce between us, I would show you here and now that you
have no right to wear it.' 'Ha,' replied Sir John, 'tomorrow
morning you will find me more than ready to prove by force
of arms that it belongs to me as much as to you.'

With these words, they each turned away, but Sir Jean de
Clermont shouted, as a further provocation: 'That's just the
sort of boast you English make. You can never think of anything new yourselves, but when you see something good you
just take it!'

Nothing more was said or done for the moment. Each went
back to his own army and the matter was left at that.

Having achieved nothing by his attempts at mediation between the two sides, the Cardinal de Périgord returned to
Poitiers late on the Sunday evening. The French also withdrew to their quarters and made themselves comfortable over
a good meal. They had plentiful supplies of provisions,
whereas the English were extremely short. It was this which
troubled them most, for they were hemmed in so closely that
they could not send out foragers, nor could they move from
there without exposing themselves to the French. It is fair to
say that they had much less fear of a battle than of being
pinned down where they were and starved out like a be-
leaguered garrison.

During the whole of that Sunday they applied themselves to
the business in hand and made the best use they could of the
time. The archers strengthened their position by digging

trenches and setting up obstructions round them. On the Monday morning the Prince and his men were quickly ready for battle again, as also were the French. At about sunrise the Cardinal reappeared and made another attempt to reconcile the two sides, but in vain. The French told him angrily to go back to Poitiers, or wherever else he liked, and to bring no more peace proposals, or it might be the worse for him. The Cardinal, who had been inspired in all his efforts by the best intentions, nevertheless did not want to endanger himself. He took his leave of the King of France and, going over to the Prince of Wales, said to him: 'My son, do your best. You will have to fight. I cannot see that the King of France has the slightest desire to reach an agreement with you.'

This last remark only irritated the Prince and strengthened his resolution. He replied: 'That is just what we mean to do, and may God defend the right!'

The Cardinal then rode off towards Poitiers, but among his followers were some warlike squires and men-at-arms who favoured the King rather than the Prince. When they saw that there would be a battle, they stole away from their master and joined the French army, choosing as their leader the Castellan of Amposta, an experienced soldier who was attached at that time to the Cardinal's household. The Cardinal knew nothing of this until he was back in Poitiers. If he had known, he would never have allowed it, since he had tried to be an impartial mediator between both sides.

The battle-order of the English was exactly as the four French knights had reported it on the Sunday morning, except that since then they had detailed some of their best knights to remain on horseback to counter the battalion of the French Marshals, and in addition had placed on their right wing, on a gently sloping hill, three hundred mounted men-at-arms and the same number of mounted archers. These were to ride right round the hill under cover and to make a flank attack on the Duke of Normandy's division which was drawn up on foot beneath it. These were the only changes they had made. The Prince waited among the vines with his main body, all of them fully armed and with their horses near at hand, ready to be mounted at once if necessary. On the most exposed side, by which alone they could be approached, they were protected by the baggage-wagons and the equipment.

Froissart gives a list of the principal knights, English, Gascons and others, who were with the Prince, and adds that whereas the English strength, all told, was only eight thousand the French had at least fifty thousand men, including three thousand knights.

Having exhorted his men to fight bravely, the Prince gives permission to two of his knights, James Audley and Eustace d' Aubrecicourt (a Hainaulter), to ride out and make the first attack on the enemy.

I related earlier, when describing the battle-order of the French, that the Germans who were on the flank of the Marshals all remained mounted. Sir Eustace d'Aubrecicourt lowered his lance and gripped his shield and spurred his horse out between the armies. A German knight called Sir Louis de Recombes, whose arms were argent, five roses gules, while Sir Eustace's were ermine, two humets gules, came out from the Count of Nassau's detachment to which he belonged, and lowered his lance to meet him. They hit each other at full speed and were both unhorsed, but the German was wounded in the shoulder and could not get up as quickly as Sir Eustace. When the latter was on his feet, he grasped his lance and rushed at his fallen opponent, full of determination to press home the attack. But he had no chance of doing so, for five German men-at-arms leapt upon him and bore him to the ground. He was so overpowered, lacking support from his own men, that he was captured and taken to the Count of Nassau's people, who paid little attention to him just then. I do not know whether or not he made a formal surrender, but they tied him on a baggage-cart with their spare gear.

Very soon after Sir Eustace d'Aubrecicourt's capture, the fighting became general. The Marshals' battalion had already advanced for action, headed by the men who were to break through the ranks of the archers. All on horseback they entered the road which had the thick hedge on either side. No sooner were they engaged in it than the archers began to shoot murderously from both flanks, knocking down horses and piercing everything before them with their long barbed arrows. The injured and terrified horses refused to go on. They swerved or turned back, or else fell beneath their riders, who could neither use their weapons nor get up again, so that the battalion of the Marshals never got near the Prince's division. A few of the best mounted knights and squires did force their horses past and broke through the hedge, but these also failed to reach the Prince.

One of the French Marshals, Arnoul d'Audrehem, clashes with the English captain, Sir James Audley. He is wounded and taken prisoner.

Meanwhile, the other Marshal of France, Sir Jean de Clermont, fought most gallantly beneath his banner for as long as he could hold out, but at last he was felled never to rise again, or to be spared for ransom. There he died in the service of his King; and some attributed this to the angry words he had exchanged the day before with Sir John Chandos. Rarely have skilled fighting-men suffered such losses in so short a time as were inflicted on the battalion of the Marshals, for they became jammed against each other and could make no headway. Seeing the carnage and unable to advance themselves, those behind turned back and ran up against the Duke of Normandy's division, whose ranks were close and numerous in front. But the rear ranks soon began to melt away when they learnt that the Marshals had been defeated. Most of them took to their horses and rode off, for the English detachment which had ridden round the hill with their mounted archers in front of them charged in and took them on the flank. If the truth must be told, the English archers were a huge asset to their side and a terror to the French; their shooting was so heavy and accurate that the French did not know where to turn to avoid their arrows. So the English kept advancing and slowly gaining ground.

When the Prince's men-at-arms saw that the Marshals' battalion was routed and that the Duke of Normandy's division was wavering and beginning to break up, their strength flooded back to them and their spirits rose. They made for their horses which they had kept near them and scrambled on to them. Having quickly mounted, they all came together and began to shout: 'St George! Guyenne!' the more to confuse the enemy. It was then that Sir John Chandos made this great and memorable remark to the Prince: 'Ride forward, sir, victory is yours! Today you will hold God in your hand. Let us make for your adversary, the King of France, that's where the real business lies. I know he is too brave to run away, so he can be ours, with the help of God and St George, but only if we tackle him. You said just now that you would show how well you can fight.' These words fired the Prince and he answered: 'Come on, John, come on. You won't see me hanging back. It's forward now.' Then he called to his banner-bearer: 'Advance, banner, in the name of God and St George!'

The banner-bearer did as the Prince commanded and soon they were in the thick of the fighting. Many men were unhorsed, with little chance of getting up again unless they were helped by others. As the Prince with his banner-bearer was riding into the enemy followed by his men, he glanced right towards a small bush and saw under it the dead body of Sir Robert de Duras with his banner beside him – it was a French banner with a red saltire – and a dozen of his followers lying around. The Prince called to two of his squires and three archers and said to them: 'Put the body of that knight on a shield and carry it to Poitiers. Take it from me to the Cardinal de Périgord and say that I have sent it him with my compliments.' The men made haste to carry out the Prince's orders.

Now some would say that he had acted in mockery, but I will tell you what moved him to do this. He had already learnt that some of the Cardinal's people had stayed on the battlefield to fight on the other side, which was quite improper according to all the rules of war. Those who belong to the Church and attempt in good faith to mediate between two sides should not take up arms in favour of either, for obvious reasons. It was because these had done so that the Prince was indignant with the Cardinal and sent him his nephew's body, as just related. He also wanted to behead the Castellan of Amposta, who was taken prisoner, and would certainly have done so in his anger, if Sir John Chandos had not stopped him by saying: 'Sir, be patient and wait till you know more about this. Perhaps the Cardinal will give such good excuses for his people that you will be satisfied.' So the Prince went on, leaving orders for the Castellan to be kept under close guard.

After the Marshals' battalion had been irrevocably defeated and the Duke of Normandy's division had begun to break up, and many in it who ought by right to have stayed fighting had taken to their horses to escape, the English, now all mounted, made straight for the battalion of the Duke of Athens, Constable of France. There followed a great mêlée, in which many were unhorsed. French knights and squires fighting in groups raised their cry of 'Montjoie Saint-Denis!' while the English shouted: 'St George! Guyenne!' Prodigies of valour were performed, for down to the humblest they were worthy men-at-arms. Next, the Prince and his men clashed with the German battalion led by the Counts of Saarbrück, Nassau and Nidau. These did not last long, but were soon beaten and put to flight.

No one could face the heavy, rapid fire of the English archers, who in that encounter killed and wounded many who found no chance of offering ransoms or pleading for mercy. But the three Counts just mentioned were taken prisoner in a fairly regular manner, while many of their knights and squires were killed or captured. In this engagement Sir Eustace d'Aubrecicourt was rescued by men who knew that he had been captured by the Germans and went looking for him, Sir Jean de Ghistelles in particular. He was found and put on a horse and went on to do great deeds that day, taking and ransoming some important prisoners who later brought him in considerable sums which contributed greatly to his advancement.

When, as I have said, the Duke of Normandy's division saw the Prince's forces approaching after the defeat of the

Marshals and the Germans, most of them were demoralized and thought only of flight. Among them were the King's own sons, the Duke of Normandy, the Count of Poitiers and the Count of Touraine, who were very young and inexperienced at that time and easily influenced by their advisers. Only Sir Guichard d'Angle and Sir Jean de Saintré, who were attached to the Count of Poitiers, refused to flee and charged into the thick of the battle. But the three princes made off, as they had been advised, and with them more than eight hundred lances, complete and unblooded, who took no part in the fighting. They went off in the direction of Chauvigny.

You read earlier in this chronicle about the Battle of Crécy, and heard how unfavourable fortune was there to the French. At Poitiers similarly it was unfavourable, fickle and treacherous, for the French were at least seven to one in trained fighting-men. But it must be said that the Battle of Poitiers was fought much better than Crécy. Both armies had greater opportunities to observe and weigh up the enemy, for the Battle of Crécy began without proper preparation in the late afternoon, while Poitiers began in the early morning, and in good enough order, if only luck had been with the French. There were incomparably more fine feats of arms than at Crécy, though not so many great lords were killed. And all who fell at Poitiers or were taken prisoner did their duty so loyally to their king that their heirs are still honoured for it and the gallant men who fought there are held in perpetual esteem. Nor should it be said that the King of France ever showed dismay at anything he saw or heard reported. He remained on the field from beginning to end, like the brave knight and stout fighter he was. He had shown his determination never to retreat when he commanded his men to fight on foot and, having made them dismount, he did the same and stood in the forefront of them with a battle-axe in his hands, ordering forward his banners in the name of God and St Denis, with Sir Geoffroy de Charny bearing the principal one. So, in good order, the King's main division came face-to-face with the English.

The fighting was fierce and bloody; many hard blows were dealt with axes, swords and other weapons of war. King John and his youngest son Philip closed with the battalion of the English Marshals, the Earls of Warwick and Suffolk. There were also Gascons among them: the Captal de Buch, the Lord of Pommiers, Sir Aimery de Tastes, the Lord of Mussidan, the Lord of Longueren, the Souldich de Latrau.

The King fully realized that his men were in danger. He saw their ranks wavering and breaking and the banners and pennons falling or moving back under the weight of the enemy's assault. Yet he still hoped to recover everything by force of arms.

Froissart names a number of French knights who remained fighting beside the King, and adds:

Also in the King's division was Earl Douglas of Scotland, who fought bravely enough for a time. But when he saw that total defeat was imminent, he left and did his utmost to escape. He would never have allowed himself to fall into the hands of the English but would have preferred death in battle, knowing for certain that they would never have agreed to ransom him.

Finally the King's division collapses altogether and the situation becomes chaotic.

As their ranks broke and crumbled, there were taken prisoner quite near the King the Count of Tancarville and Lord Jacques de Bourbon, at that time Count of Ponthieu, and Lord Jean d'Artois, Count of Eu. A little farther off, Lord Charles d'Artois surrendered to the Captal with many other knights. The pursuit of the routed French went on as far as the walls of Poitiers, where there was a fearful slaughter of men and horses, for the inhabitants of Poitiers shut the gates and refused to let anyone in. Consequently a horrible scene of killing and maiming took place in the road and before the main gate. The French surrendered at the mere sight of an Englishman and some of these, archers and others, had four, five or six prisoners each. Never before had there been so disastrous a rout.

The Lord of Pons, a great baron from Poitou, was killed

there with many other knights and squires. The Viscount of Rochechouart, the Lord of Poyane and the Lord of Parthenay were captured, and the Lord of Montendre in Poitou. Sir Jean de Saintré was taken prisoner, so battered that he never recovered his health; yet he was held to be the best and most valiant knight in France. Sir Guichard d'Angle, who had fought very courageously that day, was left for dead among the other dead.[1]

Meanwhile Sir Geoffroy de Charny had been fighting gallantly near the King. The whole of the hunt was upon him, because he was carrying the King's master-banner. He also had his own banner in the field, gules, three inescutcheons argent.[2] The English and Gascons came in such numbers from all sides that they shattered the King's division. The French were so overwhelmed by their enemies that in places there were five men-at-arms attacking a single knight. Sir Geoffroy de Charny was killed, with the banner of France in his hands. Sir Baudouin d'Annequin was captured by Lord Bartholomew Burghersh, and the Count of Dammartin by Sir Reginald Cobham. Round the King of France himself there was a great jostling and turmoil, with everyone struggling to take him prisoner. Those who were near enough to recognize him cried: 'Surrender, surrender, or you're a dead man!' There was a knight there from Saint-Omer called Sir Denis de Morbecque who had been with the English for five years because he had been banished from France in his youth after killing a man in a family feud. He had become a paid retainer of the King of England. Fortunately for this knight he found himself near to King John during the scuffle to capture him. He forced his way through the press, for he was a big, strong man, and said in good French, by which he attracted the King's attention better than the others: 'Sire, give yourself up!' Seeing himself in this desperate plight and feeling that resistance was useless, the King looked at him

1. He survived and later changed sides, to become one of the Black Prince's commanders, tutor to Richard II, and ultimately Earl of Huntingdon.

2. i.e. three small silver shields on a red ground.

and said: 'To whom shall I surrender? To whom? Where is my cousin, the Prince of Wales? If I could see him, then I would speak.' 'Sire,' replied Sir Denis, 'he is not here. But surrender to me and I will take you to him.' 'Who are you?' the King asked. 'Sire, I am Denis de Morbecque, a knight from Artois. But I serve the King of England because I have been exiled from France and have forfeited all my possessions.' Then, as I was informed, the King answered, or probably answered: 'I surrender to you', and gave him his right-hand glove. The knight took it with delight. But there was still a great commotion round the King, with each man clamouring: 'I took him! I took him!' and neither the King nor his young son Philip could move a step forward.

We will now leave the King for a moment and return to the Prince of Wales and the battle.

The Prince, who had been like a raging lion under his battle-helmet and had revelled in the fighting and the rout of the enemy, was hot and exhausted towards the end of the day. So Sir John Chandos, who had never left his side, said to him: 'Sire, it would be a good thing to halt here and raise your banner on this bush to rally your men who are getting very scattered. The day, thank God, is yours. I can see no French banners or pennons or any body capable of reforming. You should sit and cool off a little, for you look very over-heated.'

The Prince acted on this suggestion and had his banner raised on a tall bush. He ordered the trumpets to be sounded and took off his battle-helmet. His personal attendants and the knights of his chamber hurried to him. They put up a small crimson tent into which he went and where drink was brought to him and the lords with him. Their numbers grew constantly as they returned from the pursuit. They all stopped there or thereabouts, busying themselves with their prisoners.

As soon as the two Marshals, the Earls of Warwick and Suffolk, had come back, the Prince asked them if they had any news of the King of France. They said no, nothing definite. They thought he must have been either killed or captured, since he had certainly not left the battle-field. The Prince then turned anxiously to the Earl of Warwick and Sir Reginald Cobham and said: 'Please go out again and ride about until you have found out the true position.' The two commanders mounted their horses and rode them up a hillock from which they had a view all round. They saw a great mob of men-at-arms on foot moving very slowly towards them. In the midst. of it was the King of France in grave danger, for English and Gascons had got hold of him, having snatched him away from Sir Denis de Morbecque, who was no longer near. The strongest were shouting: 'I took him, he's mine!' The King, who understood their eagerness to get possession of him, attempted to end this dangerous situation by saying: 'Sirs, sirs, take me in a gentlemanly way, and my son with me, to my cousin the Prince, and stop this brawling over my capture. I am a king, and great enough to make each one of you rich.' These words satisfied them for a moment, but soon the brawling broke out again and they came to blows at every step they took.

Seeing this crowd in the distance, the two commanders decided to go towards it. They spurred up to it and said: 'What's happening? What's going on here?' Someone answered: 'It's the King of France, and a dozen knights and squires squabbling to get him.' Wasting no more words, the two knights pushed their horses through the crowd and ordered every man there to stand back and stay back, if he valued his life. No one dared to disobey this order, so they drew well away from the King and the two barons, who sprang to the ground and bowed humbly before him. He was indeed glad to see them, for they had delivered him from great danger.

Warwick and Cobham escort King John to the Prince's tent, where he is received with every mark of courtesy.

So that battle was fought as you have heard, in the fields of Maupertuis, six miles from the city of Poitiers, on the nineteenth day of September, 1356. It began in the early morning and was finished by mid-afternoon, although many of the English did not return from the pursuit until late evening. That was why the Prince hoisted his banner on the bush – to recall and rally his men. There died that day, it was said, the finest flower of French chivalry, whereby the realm of France was sorely weakened and fell into great misery and affliction, as you will hear later. With the King and his youngest son Philip, seventeen counts were taken prisoner, besides the barons, knights and squires; while between five and seven hundred men-at-arms were killed, and six thousand men in all.[1]

By the time the English were all back round the Prince they found that their prisoners were twice as numerous as themselves, so they conferred together and decided to ransom most of them on the spot. The captured knights and squires found the English and Gascons very accommodating and many of them bought their liberty there and then, or were freed simply on their promise to surrender themselves at Bordeaux by Christmas or to deliver the payment there.

The English took up their quarters for the night on the edge of the battle-field. Some disarmed, but not all, and they disarmed their prisoners. They made them as comfortable as they could, each attending to his own, for the prisoners captured in the battle were theirs personally, to be freed and ransomed as they chose.

Thus all who took part in that glorious battle under the Prince became rich in honour and possessions, not only because of the ransoms but also thanks to the gold and silver which they captured. They found plate and gold and silver belts and precious jewels in chests crammed full of them, as well as excellent cloaks, so that they took no notice of armour, arms or equipment. The French had come to the battle splendidly provided, like men who felt certain in advance of victory.

That evening the Prince of Wales gave a supper for the King of France and most of the captured counts and barons. The Prince seated King John and his son Philip, with Lord Jacques de Bourbon, Lord Jean d'Artois, the Count of

1. The exact numbers vary in different manuscripts, but all approximate to these figures.

Tancarville, the Count of Étampes, the Count of Dammartin, the Lord of Joinville and the Lord of Parthenay, at a high table, lavishly provided, and the rest of the nobles at other tables. He himself served in all humility both at the King's table and at the others, steadfastly refusing to sit down with the King in spite of all his entreaties. He insisted that he was not yet worthy to sit at the table of so mighty a prince and so brave a soldier as he had proved himself to be on that day. He constantly kneeled before him, saying: 'Beloved sire, do not make such a poor meal, even though God has not been willing to heed your prayers today. My royal father will certainly show you every mark of honour and friendship in his power, and will come to such a reasonable understanding with you that you and he will always remain firm friends. In my opinion, you have good cause to be cheerful, although the battle did not go in your favour, for today you have won the highest renown of a warrior, excelling the best of your knights. I do not say this to flatter you, for everyone on our side, having seen how each man fought, unanimously agrees with this and awards you the palm and the crown, if you will consent to wear them.'

At these words all those present murmured their approval, French and English remarking to each other that the Prince had spoken nobly and to the point. Their esteem for him increased and it was generally agreed that in him they would have a most chivalrous lord and master if he was granted life to go on in the same auspicious way.

Next morning, after the nobles had heard mass and had drunk and eaten a little and the servants had packed up everything and assembled the wagon-train, they moved on towards Poitiers. Into Poitiers on the previous night had come Sir Mathieu de Roye, with a good hundred lances, having missed the battle. But he had met the Duke of Normandy out in the country near Chauvigny when the latter was retreating towards French territory, as previously described. The Duke had told him to go to Poitiers with his whole force and to be the governor and captain of the city until further orders. Sir

Mathieu had set a strong guard on the gates and ramparts that night and in the morning had ordered all the men in the town to arm themselves in its defence. But the English passed by without attacking. They were so encumbered with booty and valuable prisoners that they had no time or inclination to attack fortresses on their way home. They considered that it would be a sufficient achievement to return safely to Bordeaux with the King of France and the spoils. Unable to go fast because of the laden pack-animals and the long wagon-train, they advanced by short marches, never covering more than twelve to fifteen miles a day and halting in the early afternoon. They kept together in one close-ordered body, except for the detachment of the Marshals who rode ahead with five hundred armoured men to reconnoitre the country and open up the route. But they met with no obstacles the whole way and had no encounters. The country was so stunned by the disaster of Poitiers, the death or surrender of the French nobles and the capture of their King that no one lifted a finger to oppose them. All fighting men kept very quiet indeed and stayed inside their fortresses.

THE THREE ESTATES; THE FREE COMPANIES

I F the English and their allies were jubilant at the capture of King John, the kingdom of France was deeply disturbed by it. There was cause enough, for it brought loss and suffering to people of all conditions, and the wiser heads predicted that greater evils were to come. Their sovereign was a prisoner and all the best of their knights were also in prison or dead, and the three princes who had escaped, Charles, Louis and John, were very young in age and experience, so there was little chance of recovery through them.

In addition, those knights and squires who had returned from the battle were so blamed and detested by the commons that they were reluctant to go into the big towns. There was much intriguing and mutual recrimination, until some of the wiser ones realized that things could not be allowed to go on in this way, but that something must be done about it. There was a force of English and Navarrese in the Cotentin, under Sir Godfrey of Harcourt, which was ranging over the whole region and laying it waste.

So all the prelates of the Church, bishops and abbots, all the nobility, lords and knights, the Provost of the merchants of Paris [1] and the burgesses, and the councillors of the French towns, met together in Paris to consider how the realm should be governed until their King should be set free. They also wanted to find out what had happened to the vast sums which had been raised in the past through tithes, levies on capital, forced loans, coinings of new money and all the other extortionate measures by which the population had been tormented and oppressed while the soldiers remained underpaid and the country inadequately protected. But of these matters no one was able to give an account.

1. Étienne Marcel.

It was therefore agreed that the prelates should elect twelve good men from among them, with powers, as representatives of the clergy, to devise suitable means of dealing with the situation described. The barons and knights also elected twelve of the wisest and shrewdest of their number to attend to the same matters, and the burgesses twelve in the same way. It was then decided by common consent that these thirty-six persons should meet frequently in Paris to discuss the affairs of the realm and put them in order. Questions of all kinds were to be referred to these Three Estates. Their acts and ordinances were to be binding on all the other prelates, nobles and common people of the cities and towns. Nevertheless, even at the beginning, several of those elected were viewed unfavourably by the Duke of Normandy[1] and his council.

As a first measure, the Three Estates stopped the coining of the money then being minted and took possession of the dies. Secondly, they required the Duke to arrest his father's Chancellor, with Sir Robert de Lorris, Sir Simon de Bucy, Jean Poillevilain [Master of the Mint] and the other financial officers and former counsellors of the King, in order that they should render a true account of all the funds which had been levied and collected on their advice. When these high officials heard of this, they completely disappeared and were wise to do so. They left the kingdom of France as quickly as they could and went to live in other countries until the situation should have changed.

Next, they appointed on their own authority officials with the duty of raising and collecting all the levies, taxes, tithes, loans and other duties payable to the crown and they had new coinage of fine gold minted, called *moutons*.[2] They would also have liked to have the King of Navarre[3] released from the

1. King John's eldest son, later Charles V. He assumed the powers of Regent within a fortnight of the defeat of Poitiers.

2. So called because one side represented the 'Lamb of God'. The coin had been current in earlier reigns.

3. Charles 'the Bad', King of Navarre, had been seized and imprisoned by King John a few months before Poitiers.

castle of Arleux in the Cambrésis, where he was held prisoner, for many of them felt that, provided he was willing to be loyal and cooperative, the kingdom would be strengthened by such a measure, since after the defeat of Poitiers there were very few great lords who could act as leaders. They therefore requested the Duke of Normandy to set him free, saying that he appeared to have been greatly wronged and they did not know why he was held in prison. The Duke very prudently replied that he dared not release him nor advocate doing so, since it was his father the King who had put him there for reasons which he did not know. The King of Navarre was consequently not released just then.

At that time a knight called Sir Regnault de Cervoles, commonly known as the Archpriest, took command of a large company of men-at-arms assembled from many countries. These found that their pay had ceased with the capture of King John and could see no way of making a living in France. They therefore went towards Provence, where they took a number of fortified towns and castles by assault and plundered the whole country as far as Avignon under the sole leadership of Sir Regnault. Pope Innocent VI and his cardinals who were at Avignon at that date were in such fear of them that they hardly knew where to turn and they kept their household servants armed day and night. After the Archpriest and his men had pillaged the whole region, the Pope and his College opened negotiations with him. He entered Avignon with most of his followers by friendly agreement, was received with as much respect as if he had been the King of France's son, and dined several times at the palace with the Pope and the cardinals. All his sins were remitted him and when he left he was given forty thousand crowns to distribute among his companions. The company left the district but still remained under the command of the Archpriest.

At that time also there arose another company of men-at-arms and irregulars from various countries, who subdued and plundered the whole region between the Seine and the Loire. As a result, no one dared to travel between Paris and Vendôme, or Paris and Orléans, or Paris and Montargis, and no one dared to remain there. All the inhabitants of the country districts fled to Paris or Orléans. This company had a Welsh captain called Ruffin,[1] who had himself made a knight and became so powerful and rich that his wealth was uncountable. These companions often carried their raids almost to Paris, or at other times towards Orléans or Chartres. No place was safe from being attacked and pillaged unless it was very strongly defended. . . . They ranged the country in troops of twenty, thirty or forty and they met no one capable of putting up a resistance to them. Elsewhere, along the coast of Normandy, there was a larger company of English and Navarrese pillagers and marauders commanded by Sir Robert Knollys, who conquered towns and castles in the same way and also found no one to oppose them. This Sir Robert Knollys had been following this practice for a long time and had acquired at least a hundred thousand crowns. He had a large number of mercenaries at his command and paid them so well that they followed him eagerly.

These activities of what were known as the Free Companies, who attacked all travellers carrying valuables, began under the administration of the Three Estates. The nobles and the prelates began to grow tired of the institution of the Estates and left the Provost of the Merchants and some of the burgesses of Paris to go their own way, finding that these were interfering more than they liked with the conduct of affairs.

It happened one day, when the Duke of Normandy was at the palace with a large company of nobles, knights and prelates, that the Provost of the Merchants also assembled a great crowd of the common people of Paris who supported him, all wearing similar caps by which they could recognize each other. He went to the palace surrounded by his men and entered the Duke's room, where he asked him very sharply to shoulder responsibility for the affairs of the realm and give some thought to them, so that the kingdom – which would eventually be his – should be properly protected from the

1. Also known as 'Griffon', so perhaps 'Griffith' or 'Gruffydd'.

depredations of the Free Companies. The Duke replied that he would be quite ready to do so if he had the means at his disposal, but that it should be done by whoever collected the revenue and taxes belonging to the realm.

I do not know exactly how it happened, but such an angry argument arose that there, in the presence of the Duke of Normandy, three of the chief members of his council were killed, so close to him that his robe was splashed with blood and he himself was in great danger. But he was given one of the people's caps to put on his head and was forced to pardon the murder of his three knights, two of them soldiers and the third a legal officer. The first were Sir Robert de Clermont, a nobleman of high standing, and the Lord of Conflans. The lawyer was Master Regnault d'Acy, the Advocate General.

On the initiative of the Provost, the King of Navarre is released from prison and brought to Paris. (Although Froissart places this after the killings just described, it occurred in fact some three months before them.)

When the King of Navarre had been in Paris for a short time, he called together a variety of people, prelates, knights, clerks of the University of Paris and any others who wished to attend, and delivered a speech to them. Speaking at first in Latin, with the Duke of Normandy present, he complained very temperately and reasonably of the wrongs and violence which had been done to him without good cause. He said that no one should feel any fear of him, since he was ready to live and die defending the kingdom of France – as indeed he was bound to, for he was descended in the direct line on both his father's and his mother's side. And he let it be understood clearly enough that, if he ever wished to lay claim to the French crown, he could show that he had a better right to it than the King of England. His speech and his arguments were listened to with approval, and in such ways he gradually acquired great popularity among the Parisians, until they came to prefer him to the Regent, the Duke of Normandy. The same thing happened in a number of other French cities and towns.

THE JACQUERIE (1358)

Not long after the King of Navarre had been set free, there were very strange and terrible happenings in several parts of the kingdom of France. They occurred in the region of Beauvais, in Brie and on the Marne, in Valois, in Laonnais, in the fief of Coucy and round Soissons. They began when some of the men from the country towns came together in the Beauvais region. They had no leaders and at first they numbered scarcely a hundred. One of them got up and said that the nobility of France, knights and squires, were disgracing and betraying the realm, and that it would be a good thing if they were all destroyed. At this they all shouted: 'He's right! He's right! Shame on any man who saves the gentry from being wiped out!'

They banded together and went off, without further deliberation and unarmed except for pikes and knives, to the house of a knight who lived near by. They broke in and killed the knight, with his lady and his children, big and small, and set fire to the house. Next they went to another castle and did much worse; for, having seized the knight and bound him securely to a post, several of them violated his wife and daughter before his eyes. Then they killed the wife, who was pregnant, and the daughter and all the other children, and finally put the knight to death with great cruelty and burned and razed the castle.

They did similar things in a number of castles and big houses, and their ranks swelled until there were a good six thousand of them. Wherever they went their numbers grew, for all the men of the same sort joined them. The knights and squires fled before them with their families. They took their wives and daughters many miles away to put them in safety, leaving their houses open with their possessions inside. And those evil men, who had come together without leaders or arms, pillaged and burned everything and violated and killed all the ladies and girls without mercy, like mad dogs. Their barbarous acts were worse than anything that ever took place between Christians and Saracens. Never did men commit such vile deeds. They were such that no living creature ought to see, or even imagine or think of, and the men who committed the most were admired and had the highest places among them. I could never bring myself to write down the horrible and shameful things which they did to the ladies. But, among other brutal excesses, they killed a knight, put him on a spit, and turned him at the fire and roasted him before the lady and her children. After about a dozen of them had violated the lady, they tried to force her and the children to eat the knight's flesh before putting them cruelly to death.

They had chosen a king from among them who came, it was said, from Clermont in Beauvaisis; and they elected the worst of the bad. This king was called Jack Goodman. Those evil men burned more than sixty big houses and castles in the Beauvais region round Corbie and Amiens and Montdidier. If God had not set things right by His grace, the mischief would have spread until every community had been destroyed and Holy Church afterwards and all wealthy people throughout the land, for men of the same kind committed similar acts in Brie and in Pertois. All the ladies of the region, with their daughters, and the knights and squires, were forced to flee one after another to Meaux in Brie as best they could, in no more than their tunics. This happened to the Duchess of Normandy and the Duchess of Orléans and to a number of other great ladies, like the humbler ones, as their only alternative to being violated and then murdered.

Other wicked men behaved in just the same way between Paris and Noyon, and between Paris and Soissons and Ham in Vermandois, and throughout the district of Coucy. That was where the worst violators and evil-doers were. In that region they pillaged and destroyed more than a hundred castles and houses belonging to knights and squires, killing and robbing wherever they went. But God by His grace provided a remedy – for which He is devoutly to be thanked – in the manner of which you shall now hear.

When the gentry of the Beauvaisis and of the other districts where those wicked men assembled and committed their barbarous deeds saw their houses destroyed and their friends killed, they sent to their friends in Flanders, Hainault, Brabant and Hesbaye to ask for help. Soon they arrived in considerable numbers from all sides. The foreign noblemen joined forces with those of the country who guided and led them, and they began to kill those evil men and to cut them to pieces without mercy. Sometimes they hanged them on the trees under which they found them. Similarly the King of Navarre put an end to more than three thousand of them in one day, not far from Clermont in Beauvaisis. But by then they had increased so fast that, all taken together, they easily amounted to a hundred thousand men. When they were asked why they did these things, they replied that they did not know; it was because they saw others doing them and they copied them. They thought that by such means they could destroy all the nobles and gentry in the world, so that there would be no more of them. . . .

At the time when these evil men were plaguing the country, the Count of Foix and his cousin the Captal de Buch came back from Prussia. On the road, when they were about to enter France, they heard of the dreadful calamities which had overtaken the nobility, and were filled with horror. They rode on so fast that they reached Châlons in Champagne in a single day. Here there were no troubles from the villeins, for they were kept out from there. They learnt in that city that the Duchess of Normandy and the Duchess of Orléans and at least three hundred other ladies and their daughters, as well as the Duke of Orléans, were waiting at Meaux in a state of great anxiety because of the *Jacquerie*. The two gallant knights decided to visit the ladies and take them whatever support they could, although the Captal de Buch was English. But at that time there was a truce between the Kingdoms of France and of England, so that the Captal was free to go wherever he wished. Also he wanted to give proof of his knightly qualities, in company with the Count of Foix. Their force was made up of about forty lances and no more, for they were on their way back from a journey abroad, as I said.

They rode on until they came to Meaux in Brie. There they

went to pay their respects to the Duchess of Normandy and the ladies, who were overjoyed to see them arrive, for they were in constant danger from the Jacks and villeins of Brie, and no less from the inhabitants of the town, as it soon became plain. When those evil people heard that there were a large number of ladies and children of noble birth in the town, they came together and advanced on Meaux, and were joined by others from the County of Valois. In addition, those of Paris, hearing of this assembly, set out one day in flocks and herds and added their numbers to the others. There were fully nine thousand of them altogether, all filled with the most evil intentions. They were constantly reinforced by men from other places who joined them along the various roads which converged on Meaux. When they reached that town, the wicked people inside did not prevent them from entering, but opened the gates and let them in. Such multitudes passed through that all the streets were filled with them as far as the market-place.

Now let me tell you of the great mercy which God showed to the ladies, for they would certainly have been violated and massacred, great ladies though they were, but for the knights who were in the town, and especially the Count of Foix and the Captal de Buch. It was these two who made the plan by which the villeins were put to flight and destroyed.

When these noble ladies, who were lodged in the market-place – which is quite strong, provided it is properly defended, for the River Marne runs round it – saw such vast crowds thronging towards them, they were distracted with fear. But the Count of Foix and the Captal de Buch and their men, who were ready armed, formed up in the market-place and then moved to the gates of the market and flung them open. There they faced the villeins, small and dark and very poorly armed, confronting them with the banners of the Count of Foix and the Duke of Orléans and the pennon of the Captal de Buch, and holding lances and swords in their hands, fully prepared to defend themselves and to protect the market-place.

When those evil men saw them drawn up in this warlike order – although their numbers were comparatively small –

they became less resolute than before. The foremost began to fall back and the noblemen to come after them, striking at them with their lances and swords and beating them down. Those who felt the blows, or feared to feel them, turned back in such panic that they fell over each other. Then men-at-arms of every kind burst out of the gates and ran into the square to attack those evil men. They mowed them down in heaps and slaughtered them like cattle; and they drove all the rest out of the town, for none of the villeins attempted to take up any sort of fighting order. They went on killing until they were stiff and weary and they flung many into the River Marne.

In all, they exterminated more than seven thousand Jacks on that day. Not one would have escaped if they had not grown tired of pursuing them. When the noblemen returned, they set fire to the mutinous town of Meaux and burnt it to ashes, together with all the villeins of the town whom they could pen up inside.

After that rout at Meaux, there were no more assemblies of the Jacks, for the young Lord de Coucy, whose name was Sir Enguerrand, placed himself at the head of a large company of knights and squires who wiped them out wherever they found them, without pity or mercy.

THE LAST DAYS OF ÉTIENNE MARCEL (1358)

Meanwhile the burghers of Paris under Étienne Marcel have acquired control of the city and completed its fortifications. They are virtually besieged by the Regent, who has withdrawn to the outskirts from which he harries the capital with a strong force of mercenaries. The King of Navarre also leaves the capital and installs himself at Saint-Denis with his own army of mercenaries. These are ostensibly maintained for the protection of the Parisians, who are providing their pay. But, while pretending to support the burghers, the King enters into a secret pact with the Regent.

The Provost of the Merchants and his faction, knowing that they had incurred the resentment and hatred of their sovereign lord the Duke of Normandy, began to feel uneasy. They often

visited the King of Navarre at Saint-Denis, pointing out to
him gently but plainly that he was the cause of the danger
in which they found themselves; for they had freed him from
prison and brought him to Paris and would gladly have made
him their lord and king had they been able to, and had indeed
connived at the killing of the three councillors in the palace
because they were opposed to him. They entreated him not
to fail them or to place too much trust in the Duke of Normandy and his council. The King of Navarre, realizing that
the Provost and his supporters were growing anxious and
remembering their friendly behaviour towards him in the past,
reassured them as well as he could by saying: 'My dear sirs
and friends, you will never suffer any harm from me. Now,
while you are in control of Paris with no one daring to thwart
you, I would advise you to make provision for the future by
building up a fund of gold and silver in some place where you
can lay hands on it in case of need. If you send it here to Saint-
Denis and entrust it to me, I will keep it for you and use it
secretly to maintain a force of men-at-arms with whom you
can fight your enemies if necessary.' The Provost of the
Merchants agreed to this. Twice a week from then on he
sent two pack-horses laden with florins to Saint-Denis to the
King of Navarre, who received them with jubilation.

Now it happened that inside Paris itself there had remained
a large number of English and Navarrese mercenaries who
had been retained by the Provost and the commons to help
defend them against the Duke of Normandy. As long as the
fighting lasted these men had behaved loyally and well.
When peace was made between them and the Duke, some of
them left, but not all. Those who left went to the King of
Navarre, who took them on his strength, but more than three
hundred stayed on in Paris, enjoying themselves and spending
their money freely, as soldiers do in such towns. A disturbance arose between them and the Parisians, in which more
than sixty of the soldiers were killed, either in the streets or in
their lodgings. The Provost of the Merchants was highly
incensed by this and blamed the Parisians bitterly. But nevertheless, to appease the people, he took some hundred and fifty

of the soldiers and imprisoned them in the Louvre, telling the citizens, who were clamouring to kill them, that he would punish them according to their crimes. This quietened the Parisians and after nightfall the Provost, who wished to propitiate those English mercenaries, released them from prison and sent them on their way. They all joined the King of Navarre at Saint-Denis. . . .

When they were all assembled at Saint-Denis, they decided to avenge their comrades and the treatment inflicted on themselves. They sent a declaration of war to the Parisians and began to rove about outside the city killing and hacking to pieces any of the inhabitants who were bold enough to venture out. These were in such fear of the English that soon no one dared to go outside the gates. For this the Provost was held responsible and, afterwards, openly accused.

When the people of Paris found themselves harried like this by the English soldiers, they were frantic with rage and demanded that the Provost should arm some of their community and send them out to fight. He agreed and said he would go with them, so one day they set out, over two thousand strong. Hearing that the English were somewhere near Saint-Cloud, they decided to divide into two bodies and take two separate roads, so as to make sure that the enemy should not escape them. They were to meet again at a certain spot not far from Saint-Cloud. So the two forces parted company, the Provost taking the smaller one, and spent most of the day circling around Montmartre[1] and finding no trace of what they were looking for.

About mid-afternoon the Provost, having accomplished nothing and growing tired of wandering about the country, returned to Paris by the Porte Saint-Denis. The other body knew nothing of this and stayed out longer; if they had known, they would have gone back also. In the evening they

1. The apparent illogicality of looking for the enemy in the wrong direction – Montmartre was north of Paris, Saint-Cloud west – seems explained by the fact, not recorded by Froissart, that the King of Navarre helped to lead the expedition and had no desire to clash with the English mercenaries.

did make for home, marching without order, like men who had no expectation of meeting the enemy. They moved along in groups, looking thoroughly sick and tired of the whole business. Some carried their helmets in their hands or let them hang from their necks, some, through weariness and apathy, trailed their swords along the ground or wore them slung from their shoulders. Slouching along in this way, they took the road leading into Paris through the Porte Saint-Honoré. Suddenly at a turning of the road they were attacked by the English soldiers, who were at least four hundred strong and all of one sort and one mind. They dashed in shouting among the French, striking out at them lustily. Over two hundred were accounted for at the first onslaught.

Taken completely by surprise, the French were too shaken to attempt an organized resistance. They took to flight and let themselves be cut to pieces like cattle. Those who could fled back into Paris, but over seven hundred were killed in the pursuit which continued as far as the barriers of the city. The Provost was fiercely blamed for this occurrence, many saying that he had betrayed them.

The next morning, the relatives and friends of those who had been killed went out with carts and wagons to fetch their bodies and give them burial. But on the way they were ambushed by the English and over a hundred more of them were killed or wounded. The people of Paris fell into such distress and confusion that they no longer knew whom to trust. They began to murmur and be suspicious of everyone. The King of Navarre was growing cool towards them, both because of the pact with his brother-in-law the Duke of Normandy and because of the way they had attacked the English mercenaries who had remained in Paris. He was quite willing for them to be punished and so pay more dearly for that evil deed. The Duke of Normandy for his part would not intervene as long as the Parisians were still ruled by the Provost of the Merchants. He sent them a public notification in writing that he would not make peace with them unless twelve of the citizens, to be chosen by himself, were surrendered to him at discretion. It is easy to understand why the Provost and others who knew that they were inculpated were filled with alarm. They saw clearly enough, on considering the situation, that things could not continue as they were for long, for the people of Paris were beginning to cool in their enthusiasm for them and their party. They spoke of them contemptuously, and this was known to them.

Finally they concluded that if the choice lay between remaining alive and prosperous and being destroyed, it would be better for them to kill than to be killed. On that conclusion they based their whole plan of action and entered into secret negotiations with the English soldiers who were harrying Paris. A pact was made between the two parties, according to which the Provost and his supporters were to seize possession of the Porte Saint-Honoré and the Porte Saint-Antoine and to open those two gates at midnight to a combined force of English and Navarrese, who would come ready armed to ravage and destroy Paris. These plunderers were to spare neither man nor woman, of high or low degree, but to put everyone to the sword, except for some who would be recognized by marks on their doors and windows.[1]

On the very night when this was to happen, an inspiration from God awoke some of the citizens who had an understanding with the Duke of Normandy and whose leaders were Sir Pepin des Essarts and Sir Jean de Charny. These by divine inspiration – for so it must be supposed – learnt that Paris was to be plundered and destroyed. They immediately armed themselves and all their friends and caused the news to be whispered about secretly, so as to gain more supporters.

Pepin des Essarts and others, well armed and numerous, raised the banner of France to the cry of: 'Up with the King and the Duke!' and were followed by the people. They went

1. In Froissart's account the villain of the piece is Étienne Marcel, and too little is made of the dubious part played by the King of Navarre in these events. In spite of his secret understanding with the Regent, he seems to have been anxious to gain possession of Paris for himself and was at least rumoured to have intended pressing on with his claim to the French throne, to the exclusion both of the Regent and of the captive King John.

to the Porte Saint-Antoine, where they found the Provost of the Merchants with the keys of the gate in his hands. There they met Jean Maillart, who had had a quarrel earlier that day with the Provost and with Josseran de Mâcon[1] and had come over to the Duke of Normandy's party. Bitter accusations were hurled at the Provost and he was attacked and forced back. The people were in a tumult, clamouring and hooting. They shouted: 'Death to the Provost and his friends! They have betrayed us! Kill them!'

In the midst of the commotion the Provost, who was standing on the steps of the Saint-Antoine blockhouse, would gladly have escaped had he been able to, but was so close-pressed that he could not. Sir Jean de Charny hit him on the head with an axe and stretched him on the ground. There he was struck by Master Pierre de Fouace and others, who did not leave off until he was dead, together with six others of his faction, including Philippe Guiffart, Jean de Lille, Jean Poiret, Simon Le Paonnier and Gilles Marcel. Several other traitors were caught and put in prison. A search was made through the streets and the city was put in a state of defence and strong guards posted over it for the remainder of the night.

As soon as the Provost and his supporters had been killed or caught, which took place on the evening of Tuesday, 31 July 1358, messengers were sent in haste with the news to the Duke of Normandy, who was at Meaux. He was naturally delighted and prepared to come to Paris. But before his arrival, the King of Navarre's Treasurer, Josseran de Mâcon, and Charles Toussac, an alderman of Paris, were executed as traitors on the Place de Grève. The bodies of the Provost and the others killed with him were dragged to the courtyard of St Catherine's Church in the Val des Écoliers. Gashed and naked as they were, they were laid in front of the cross in the courtyard and left there for a long

1. The King of Navarre's Treasurer. According to another source, the *Grandes Chroniques de France*, Étienne Marcel had ordered the keys of one of the gates to be handed over to him, but Jean Maillart, the captain of the guard, had refused.

time, so that any who wished to see them could do so. Afterwards they were thrown into the Seine.

BRIGANDRY, WARFARE AND PREDICTIONS

Acclaimed by his supporters, the Duke of Normandy re-enters Paris and takes up residence in the Louvre. For a time Charles of Navarre continues his campaign of brigandage round Paris, but finally makes peace with the Regent. His brother Philip, however, continues to pillage the country, in connivance with the English. Elsewhere also English, or so-called English, bands maintain a reign of terror, virtually paralysing trade and agriculture.

The kingdom of France was plundered and pillaged in every direction, so that it became impossible to ride anywhere without being attacked. Sir Eustace d'Aubrecicourt maintained himself in Champagne, of which he was the virtual master. Whenever he liked he could assemble at a day's notice seven hundred to a thousand fighting men. He or his men made raids almost daily, sometimes towards Troyes, sometimes towards Provins, or as far as Château-Thierry or Châlons. The whole of the low country was at their mercy, on both sides of the Seine and the Marne. This Sir Eustace performed many fine feats of arms and no one could stand up to him, for he was young and deeply in love and full of enterprise. He won great wealth for himself through ransoms, through the sale of towns and castles, and also through the redemption of estates and houses and the safe-conducts which he provided. No one was able to travel, either merchants or others, or venture out from the cities and towns without his authority. He had a thousand soldiers in his pay and held ten or twelve fortresses.

Sir Eustace at that time was very sincerely in love with a young lady of high breeding, and she with him. There is no harm in giving her name, since she later became his lawful wife. She was Madame Isabel de Juliers, daughter of the Count of Juliers by one of the daughters of the Count of Hainault. The Queen of England was her aunt, and as a girl she had been married in England to the Earl of Kent, but he died young. This lady was still young and she had fallen in love with Sir Eustace for his great exploits as a knight, of which accounts were brought to her every day. While he was in Champagne, she sent him several hackneys and chargers, with love-letters and other tokens of great affection, by which the knight was inspired to still greater feats of bravery and accomplished such deeds that everyone talked of him.

Sir Eustace d' Aubrecicourt is defeated and captured in a skirmish, to be ransomed later. As a result, the English evacuate a number of castles, but still hold others.

Sir Peter Audley remained none the less at Beaufort and Jean de Ségur at Nogent and Albrecht at Gyé-sur-Seine. At that time there departed this life in rather strange circumstances, in the castle of La Hérelle which he held, ten miles from Amiens, Sir Jean de Picquigny, strangled, it was said, by his chamberlain. One of his most trusted knights, called Sir Lus de Bethisi, also died in the same way. May God have mercy on their souls and forgive them their misdeeds.

A very strange thing happened at about the same time to an English squire belonging to the troop of Sir Peter Audley and Albrecht. They had gone raiding one day to a village called Ronay and began plundering it just as the priest was chanting high mass. This squire entered the church and went up to the altar and, seizing the chalice in which the priest was about to consecrate the blood of Our Lord, he spilt the wine on the ground. When the priest protested, he gave him a back-hand blow with his gauntlet, so hard that the blood spurted on to the altar. After this, they all left the village and, while they were riding across the country, with the robber who had committed the outrage carrying the chalice, the plate and the communion cloth against his breast, this thing suddenly happened which I will relate; it was a true example of God's anger and vengeance and a warning to all other pillagers. His horse and he on it began whirling madly about in the fields and raising such an outcry that none dared to go near them; until at last they fell in a heap with their necks broken and were immediately turned to dust and ashes. All this was witnessed by the comrades who were present and who were so terrified that they swore before God and Our Lady that they would never again violate a church, or rob one. I do not know whether they kept their promise.

In the autumn of 1359 Edward III led an expedition from Calais through north-eastern France with the object of bringing the Regent to heel and enforcing a peace treaty which would consolidate the gains of Poitiers. He besieged Rheims unsuccessfully before finally reaching Chartres.

While Rheims was being besieged, the English nobles were dispersed about the neighbouring country, where they could live more easily and could guard the roads to stop supplies from entering the city. That fine soldier and great English baron, Lord Bartholomew Burghersh, had his quarters with his whole contingent of men-at-arms and archers in the town of Cormicy, where there was an excellent castle belonging to the Archbishop of Rheims. The Archbishop had entrusted its defence to a knight from Champagne called Sir Henry de Vaulx, who had a number of good soldiers with him. The castle seemed safe from all assaults, having a great square tower with thick walls and strong battlements.

When Lord Burghersh, having invested the castle and considered its strong construction, had seen that he could not take it by assault, he summoned a band of miners whom he had in his service and ordered them to do their work of mining the fortress, adding that they would be well paid for it. 'Right,' they said. They started their mine and by digging continually night and day they made such progress that they came right under the great tower. All the time they were mining they were putting in props, but the men in the castle did not know they were working. When the tower was directly over the mine, so that it could be brought down at any moment, the miners went to Lord Burghersh and said: 'Sir, we've pushed on so far with the job that the big tower can be dropped whenever you give the word.' 'That's good,' said the knight, 'but do nothing more until you have my orders.' 'Right,' they said.

Lord Burghersh mounted his horse and, taking one of his companions, Jean de Ghistelles, with him, he rode up to the

castle and signalled that he wished to speak with the men inside. Sir Henry came on to the battlements and asked him what
he wanted. 'What I want,' said Lord Burghersh, 'is for you to
surrender. If not, you will all be dead men before long.'
'What?' said the French knight, beginning to laugh. 'We are
all safe and sound in here and well supplied with everything
we need, and you ask us to surrender like that! No sir, never.'
'Come, Sir Henry,' said the English knight, 'if you knew what
a mess you were in, you would surrender at once without
arguing.' 'And what mess are we in, sir?' asked the French
commander. 'Just come outside and I'll show you,' said Lord
Burghersh, 'on condition that if you want to go back into
your tower I'll let you. You have my promise of that.'

Sir Henry took the English knight at his word and accepted
the offer. He came out of his fortress with only three companions and joined Lord Burghersh and Sir Jean de Ghistelles outside. They took him at once to their mine and let him
see that the great tower was only supported by wooden props.
When the French knight realized the danger they were in, he
said to Lord Burghersh: 'Certainly, sir, you were quite right
and it was a really gentlemanly act to do what you did. We put
ourselves at your disposal with everything we have with us.'

Lord Burghersh accepted them as his prisoners and brought
all their men out of the tower together with their possessions.
Then he had fire set to the mine. When the props burnt
through, the huge square tower split down the middle and
collapsed. 'Look at that,' said Lord Burghersh to Sir Henry de
Vaulx and the rest of the garrison. 'Didn't I tell you?' 'Yes,
sir,' they replied. 'We will remain prisoners at your discretion
and we are grateful for your courteous dealing. If the Jack
Goodmans who were once uppermost in this district had got
the better of us as you did just now, they would never have
treated us in this generous way.'

That was how the garrison of Cormicy was captured and
the castle demolished.

You may like to know that on this campaign the great English lords and men of substance took with them tents of various sizes, mills for grinding corn, ovens for baking, forges for shoeing the horses and all other necessities. To carry all this, they had fully eight thousand wagons, each drawn by four good, strong rounseys which they had brought over from England. They also carried on the wagons a number of skiffs and other small boats so skilfully made from leather that they were a sight worth seeing. Each could take three men over the biggest lake or pond to fish whatever part of it they liked. This was a great standby for them at all seasons, including Lent, at least for the lords and the royal household, but the common soldiers had to manage with what they found. In addition, the King had for his personal use thirty mounted falconers and their loads of birds and sixty couples of big hounds and as many coursing-dogs, with which he went either hunting or wild-fowling every day. Many of the nobles and wealthy men also had their hounds and hawks like the King. Their army was always divided into three bodies, each moving independently with its own vanguard and rearguard and halting for the night three miles behind the preceding one. The Prince commanded one division, the Duke of Lancaster another, and the King the third and largest. They kept this formation the whole way from Calais until they reached the city of Chartres.

In those days there was a Franciscan friar at Avignon, a very learned and intelligent man, called Brother Jean de la Rochetaillade. He was kept imprisoned by Pope Innocent VI in the castle of Bagnols because of the extraordinary misfortunes which he predicted, firstly for the prelates and princes of the Church, on account of the excessive luxury and pomp in which they lived; and also for the Kingdom of France and the great lords of Christendom, because of the way in which they oppressed the common people. This Friar John claimed to prove his utterances by the Apocalypse and the ancient books of the holy prophets, whose sense was made clear to him, he said, by the grace of the Holy Spirit. Many of his predictions were hard to believe, yet some came true within the period in which he placed them. He did not speak as a prophet, but knew about them through the old Scriptures and by the grace of the Holy Spirit – as one says – who had granted him understanding to make clear all those ancient prophecies and writings, so as to announce to all Christians the year and the date when the troubles were to come. He composed several books, well written and based on sound theological knowledge, one of which appeared in the year 1356. In it he described so many strange events for the years 1356 to 1360 that they seemed incredible, although several of them in fact occurred. And when he was asked about the war between the French and English he replied that what had been seen so far was nothing beside what was to come, and that there would be no peace nor end before the realm of France had been wasted and destroyed in every district and region. That came true, for France was indeed ravaged, wasted and destroyed, and in particular during the time which the friar predicted, in '56, '57, '58, and '59, in all its regions, so savagely that none of the princes or nobles dared to show his face before those people of low degree, drawn from many different countries, coming one after another, with no highly placed leaders at all. And the realm was defenceless before them, as you have already heard.

King John's Return to England and his Death (1363-4)

PEACE *terms were at last agreed in 1360 at Brétigny. The English were confirmed in possession of Aquitaine, Calais and Ponthieu (the district round the mouth of the Somme). King John II, a prisoner in London since Poitiers, was released on the promise of a huge ransom, but important hostages were retained to guarantee payment. One of these, his son Louis, Duke of Anjou, broke his parole not long afterwards. It was partly, at least, with the very honourable intention of repairing this act of bad faith, that King John returned voluntarily to England in 1363.*

I was informed at the time – and it was perfectly correct – that King John became set on going to England to visit his brother King Edward and his sister the Queen, and with this intention called together part of his council. No one could dissuade him from his purpose, though he was strongly advised against it, several of the French prelates and barons telling him that it would be a most hazardous step to place himself in the King of England's power. His answer was that he had found the King his brother, the Queen and their sons so full of good faith, honour and courtesy, that he feared nothing from them and was sure they would behave in the same way to him in all circumstances, and also that he wished to apologize for his son the Duke of Anjou, who had gone back to France. No one dared to go against this argument, since the question was already settled in his mind. Immediately after he appointed his son the Duke of Normandy to be regent and governor of France until his return. . . .

[After visiting Amiens and Hesdin] he travelled on to Boulogne and lodged in the abbey of that town, waiting for a favourable wind. With him were Lord Jean d'Artois, Count of Eu, the Count of Dammartin, the Grand Prior of France, Lord Boucicaut, Marshal of France, Sir Pierre de Villiers, Sir Jean Danville, Sir Nicolas Braque and several others, who

167

were all to accompany him across the sea. When their ships were loaded and the sailors saw that the wind was right, the King was informed. He went aboard his vessel at about midnight, while his men embarked in the others. They remained anchored off Boulogne until daylight, waiting for the tide to turn. When they raised anchor, they had all the wind they needed and steered for England, reaching Dover towards evening; the date was 4 January, two days before Twelfth Night.

News of their arrival was brought to the King and Queen of England who were at Eltham, a very fine royal manor about seven miles from London. Some of the household knights, Lord Bartholomew Burghersh, Sir Alan Buxhull and Sir Richard Pembridge, were immediately sent down to Dover, where the King of France had remained since his arrival. They greeted him with all possible respect, telling him that King Edward was delighted that he had come. The next morning King John mounted his horse and rode with all his followers to Canterbury, which they reached at dinner-time. Entering the Cathedral of St Thomas, the King paid humble devotion to the body of the Saint and offered it a rich jewel of great value. After spending two days at Canterbury, he rode on towards London and, travelling in short stages, came to Eltham where the King and Queen of England were waiting to receive him with a great company of knights and ladies. He arrived on a Sunday in the afternoon, and between then and supper there was time for much dancing and merriment. The young Lord de Coucy[1] in particular took great pains to dance and sing well when his turn came. He was much applauded by both French and English, for whenever he did a thing he did it well.

It would be impossible for me to record all the honours with which the King and Queen of England received King John, but finally he left Eltham and entered London. There he was welcomed by people of all conditions, who came out in companies to meet him, greeting him with the greatest respect.

1. Enguerrand de Coucy, who later married Edward III's daughter Isabella. He was in England as a hostage.

Amid a great playing of musical instruments he was escorted
to the Palace of the Savoy, which had been got ready for him,
and where he was lodged with the members of his family and
the French hostages. Chief among them were his brother the
Duke of Orléans, his son the Duke of Berry, his cousin the
Duke of Bourbon, the Count of Alençon, Guy de Blois, the
Count of Saint-Pol, and many others.

King John spent the rest of the winter there cheerfully
and sociably. He was visited frequently by the King of
England and his sons, the Dukes of Clarence and Lancaster
and Lord Edmund. They held several big entertainments and
parties together, dinners, suppers and so forth, either at the
Savoy or at the Palace of Westminster situated near by, to
which the King of France went privately whenever he liked
by boat along the Thames.

*Froissart records briefly that King John fell ill and died at the
Palace of the Savoy (April 1364). His eldest son, the Duke of
Normandy, succeeded him as Charles V of France.*

The Battle of Montiel and Death of
Peter the Cruel (1369)

DURING *the peace between England and France many men from the Free Companies were drawn off to fight in Spain, serving under regular commanders, such as Du Guesclin and the Black Prince. The crown of Castile was disputed between Peter the Cruel and his bastard brother, Henry of Trastamara. With French support, Henry supplanted Peter for a short time in 1366–7, but Peter recovered the throne with the Black Prince's help. He behaved with such ruthlessness and treachery that the Black Prince withdrew his aid, and Henry then struck back at him, again supported by the French, and defeated him at Montiel.*

This battle of Spaniards against Spaniards and between the two kings and their allies, fought not far from the castle of Montiel, was a grim and murderous affair. There were many good knights on King Henry's side, Bertrand du Guesclin, Geoffroy Ricon, Arnaut Limosin, Yvain de Lakonnet, Jean de Berguettes, Gauvain de Bailleul, Le Bègue de Villaines, Alain de Saint-Pol, Éliot de Tallay and the Bretons who were there; from the kingdom of Aragon the Viscount of Rocaberti and the Viscount of Roda and several others whom I cannot all name. They performed many fine feats of arms and indeed they had to, for among the forces against them were some very strange people, such as Saracens and Portuguese. The Jews who were there soon turned their backs and took no part in the fighting, but the men from Granada and Morocco fought well. They were armed with bows and assegais which they knew how to use and their shooting and throwing were skilful in the extreme. In the thick of the battle was the king Don Pedro, a stout fighter indeed, wielding an axe with which he dealt such lusty blows that none dared to come near him. The banner of his brother King Henry was brought up opposite his, closely surrounded and supported by good fighters, shouting their war-cries and thrusting fiercely with their lances. King Peter's men began to waver and lose heart. Don Fernando de Castro, whose duty was to advise and watch over the King, soon saw, with his quick eye, that their ranks were about to break in defeat; they had never recovered from the shock of being taken by surprise. He therefore said to King Peter: 'Sire, leave the field and make for the Castle of Montiel which we left this morning. If you retreat there, you will be safe. But if the enemy capture you, you will be killed without mercy.'

King Peter took this advice and withdrew as quickly as possible to Montiel. He reached it so opportunely that he found the gates open, and the commander let him in accompanied by a dozen men only.

Meanwhile, the others went on fighting scattered over the country, and some did all that could be expected of them. The Saracens who were there and did not know the country [and the possible hiding-places] preferred to brave death rather than be hunted down in a long pursuit, so some of them sold their lives very dearly. News was brought to King Henry and Sir Bertrand du Guesclin that King Peter had retreated to Montiel and shut himself inside there, pursued by Le Bègue de Villaines and his troop. The castle could only be entered and left by one narrow road, across which Le Bègue de Villaines was now installed, and on which he had planted his pennon.

The castle of Montiel was strong enough to have held out for a long time if it had been supplied with provisions. But when King Peter entered it, there were supplies for only four days,[1] to the great alarm of the King and his men, for they were watched so closely by night and day that not even a bird could have left the castle without being seen. King Peter, who was inside there in a state of anguish at seeing himself encircled by his foes, who he knew would not grant him peace on any terms, became greatly apprehensive. So, having considered the danger in which he lay and his lack of

1. Froissart has previously related that Peter lodged in the castle the night before the battle and 'was given what entertainment he could' by the governor. No doubt this had already reduced the stocks of provisions.

provisions, he agreed to leave the castle by night with guides
to lead him safely round the besieging army, trusting in God's
help to bring him through. He accordingly stole out secretly
towards midnight with twelve followers, including Don
Fernando de Castro. The sky was overcast and it was very
dark.

At that hour Le Bègue de Villaines was keeping watch with
over three hundred men. When King Peter and his party
came out of the castle and were descending the steep path
which led down from it, moving so quietly that one would
hardly know they were there, Le Bègue de Villaines, who was
continually on the alert for fear that he should bungle the
business and lose everything, thought he heard the sound of
hooves on the paving-stones and said to the men with him:
'Keep very quiet. Don't raise the alarm, but I hear people
moving. We must find out who is abroad at this hour. It may
be people taking supplies to the castle, for their stocks must be
nearly exhausted.'

He moved forward with his dagger in his hand and his
comrades beside him and, coming upon a man near the King,
said: 'Who goes there? Speak, or you're a dead man!' This
man was English, so he said nothing but broke away and
dashed on. Le Bègue let him go and stopped another, who was
King Peter. Although it was very dark, he thought he recognized him because of the likeness to his bastard brother Henry,
whom he strongly resembled. Holding the dagger to his
breast, he said: 'And you? Who are you? Give your name
and surrender, or you're a dead man!' While speaking he
had seized the horse's bridle, so that this man should
not escape like the first, although that one was captured by
others.

Seeing a large force of armed men in front of him and
knowing that he could not escape, King Peter said to Le
Bègue, whom he recognized: 'Bègue, I am King Peter of
Castile, a man much slandered by evil tongues. I surrender
to you and place myself, with all my men here – there are
only twelve of us – in your keeping at your discretion. I
ask you, in the name of chivalry, to take us all to safety. I will

pay you whatever ransom you care to ask since, thank God, I still have plenty to draw on. But keep me out of the hands of my bastard brother Henry.'

Le Bègue's answer, so I was informed and assured later, was that the King and his party could confidently come with him, and that his brother would never hear anything of the matter through him. On that understanding they went off. The King was taken to Le Bègue de Villaines' quarters, and more exactly to the room of Sir Yvain de Lakonnet.[1]

He had not been there an hour when King Henry and the Viscount of Rocaberti, with a small company of their men, arrived at the same quarters and entered the room where King Peter was. As he came in he said: 'Where's that Jewish son of a whore who calls himself King of Castile?' Then King Peter stepped forward, that bold and bloody man, and said: 'You're the son of a whore. I'm the son of good King Alfonso.' With these words he seized his brother in his arms and, pulling him towards him in a wrestler's grip, he mastered him and forced him down under him on to an *ambarda*,[2] in other words, a bed with a silk mattress. He got his hand to his dagger and would certainly have killed him if the Viscount of Rocaberti had not caught hold of his foot and twisted him over so that King Peter was underneath and King Henry was on top. The latter drew a long Castilian knife which he carried slung from his shoulder and drove it upwards into his brother's body. His men came running in and helped to finish him off. They also killed at his side an English knight called Sir Ralph Helme, who was formerly known as the Green Squire, and a squire called Jacques Rollans because they attempted to resist. But no harm was done to Don Fernando de Castro and the others. They remained the prisoners of Le Bègue de Villaines and Sir Yvain de Lakonnet.

1. Froissart's careful account is in contradiction with that of Spanish historians, who attribute King Peter's betrayal to Du Guesclin, saying that he was taken to the quarters of the French commander-in-chief.

2. Froissart: *ambarde*. There is no Spanish word with the required sense resembling this. Either there is a scribal error or possibly Froissart, who very rarely quotes foreign words, overreached himself here in an attempt to supply local colour.

So ended King Peter of Castile, who once had reigned in great prosperity. Those who had killed him left him lying on the ground for three days, which in my opinion was an inhuman thing to do. And the Spaniards came and mocked at him.

The Sack of Limoges (1370)

IN 1369 the peace between England and France was broken. Du
Guesclin, who had remained in Spain for a time with King Henry, was
sent for by Charles V of France to take part in a campaign against
the Black Prince in Aquitaine. The French commanders ravage the
country and capture fortresses, while other fortresses go over to them
without resistance. They besiege Limoges, which has some English
garrison, but is really commanded by the Bishop of Limoges, a
trusted lieutenant of the Black Prince.

Sir Bertrand's arrival at the siege greatly heartened the
French and made a deep impression both inside the city and
outside. He immediately went to work on the negotiations
which had already begun between the Bishop of Limoges and
the Duke of Berry and concluded them so skilfully that the
Bishop and the defenders of Limoges went over to the French
side. The Dukes of Berry and Bourbon, Lord Guy de Blois
and the chief French nobles entered Limoges amid general
rejoicing and received the homage and pledges of loyalty of
its inhabitants. After three days spent in resting and refreshing
themselves, they decided to break off campaigning for that
season, as the Duke of Anjou had already done, and go back
home to guard their towns and fortresses against Sir Robert
Knollys, who was leading an army through France. They
considered they had done enough by taking a city such as
Limoges. The French lords therefore dispersed, while Sir
Bertrand remained in the Limousin region with two hundred
lances, basing himself on the castles of the Lord of Melval
who had turned French.

Before the Duke of Berry left Limoges, he had instructed
Sir Jean de Villemur, Sir Hugues de la Roche and Roger de
Beaufort to remain in the city with a hundred men-at-arms at
the Bishop's request. Then he withdrew to Berry and the
Duke of Bourbon to the Bourbonnais and the other nobles
from the distant marches returned to their domains.

When news reached the Prince of Wales that Limoges had gone over to the French and that the Bishop of the place, who was the godfather of one of his children and in whom he had always placed the greatest trust, had been concerned in all the negotiations and had been a party to the surrender, he was furiously angry and lost much of his esteem for churchmen, in whom he had previously had great faith. He swore on the soul of his father – an oath which he never broke – that he would attend to no other business until he had won the city back and had made the traitors pay dearly for their disloyalty. When assembled, his army numbered twelve hundred lances, knights and squires, a thousand archers and three thousand foot-soldiers. With the Prince when he left Cognac were his two brothers, the Duke of Lancaster and the Earl of Cambridge, and the Earl of Pembroke, whom they also called their brother.[1] With him also were the Poitevin knights Sir Guichard d'Angle, Sir Louis d'Harcourt and others; the Lord of Montferrant, the Lord of Chaumont and many others, Gascons; Sir Thomas Percy, Sir William Beauchamp, Sir Michael de la Pole and others, English; the Hainaulter Sir Eustace d'Aubrecicourt; and from the Companies, Sir Perducat d'Albret, Naudon de Bageran, Lamit, the Bastard of Lesparre, the Bastard of Breteuil, Espiote, Bernadet de Wist and numerous others.

All these warlike men set out in full array and took the field, and the whole country began to tremble before them. By that time the Prince was no longer able to ride a horse, but was taken on a litter with a splendid escort. They moved forward until they reached Limoges and immediately established themselves round it. The Prince swore that he would not leave until he had it at his mercy. The Bishop and the chief citizens knew that they had acted very wrongly and had incurred the Prince's wrath, and they regretted it bitterly. But there was nothing they could do, for they were not masters in their city. Sir Jean de Villemur, Sir Hugues de la Roche and Roger de Beaufort, its captains, did their best to reassure

1. Their brother-in-law John Hastings, Earl of Pembroke, married Margaret, youngest daughter of Edward III.

them, when they saw how frightened they were, by saying:
'Sirs, take courage. We are strong and numerous enough to
resist the Prince's army. He cannot take us by assault or do
us much harm. We are too well provided with artillery.'

It was quite true that when the Prince and his marshals had
thoroughly examined the massive fortifications of Limoges
and had learnt the number of the knights and squires in the
garrison, they recognized that they would never be able to
take it by assault. So they put a different tactic into operation.

The Prince habitually took with him on his expeditions a
large body of those rough labourers called miners. These
were immediately set to work and began driving rapidly forward with their mine.

For about a month, certainly not longer, the Prince of Wales
remained before Limoges. During that time he allowed no
assaults or skirmishes, but pushed on steadily with the mining.
The knights inside and the townspeople, who knew what was
going on, started a countermine in the hope of killing the
English miners, but it was a failure. When the Prince's miners
who, as they dug, were continually shoring up their tunnel,
had completed their work, they said to the Prince: 'My lord,
whenever you like now we can bring a big piece of wall down
into the moat, so that you can get into the city quite easily and
safely.'

The Prince was very pleased to hear this. 'Excellent,' he
said. 'At six o'clock tomorrow morning show me what you
can do.'

When they knew it was the right time for it, the miners
started a fire in their mine. In the morning, just as the Prince
had specified, a great section of the wall collapsed, filling the
moat at the place where it fell. For the English, who were
armed and ready waiting, it was a welcome sight. Those on
foot could enter as they liked, and did so. They rushed to the
gate, cut through the bars holding it and knocked it down.
They did the same with the barriers outside, meeting with no
resistance. It was all done so quickly that the people in the
town were taken unawares. Then the Prince, the Duke of

Lancaster, the Earl of Cambridge, Sir Guichard d'Angle, with all the others and their men burst into the city, followed by pillagers on foot, all in a mood to wreak havoc and do murder, killing indiscriminately, for those were their orders. There were pitiful scenes. Men, women and children flung themselves on their knees before the Prince, crying: 'Have mercy on us, gentle sir!' But he was so inflamed with anger that he would not listen. Neither man nor woman was heeded, but all who could be found were put to the sword, including many who were in no way to blame. I do not understand how they could have failed to take pity on people who were too unimportant to have committed treason. Yet they paid for it, and paid more dearly than the leaders who had committed it.

There is no man so hard-hearted that, if he had been in Limoges on that day, and had remembered God, he would not have wept bitterly at the fearful slaughter which took place. More than three thousand persons, men, women and children, were dragged out to have their throats cut. May God receive their souls, for they were true martyrs.

When they first broke into the town a contingent of the English made for the Bishop's palace. He was discovered and seized, and brought without ceremony before the Prince, who looked at him very grimly. The kindest word he could find to say was that, by God and St George, he would have his head cut off. Then he had him removed from his presence.

As for the knights who commanded in Limoges, Sir Jean de Villemur, Sir Hugues de la Roche, and Roger de Beaufort, son of the Count of Beaufort, when they saw the disaster which had overtaken them, they said: 'There's no hope for us, but we'll sell our lives dearly, as knights ought to do.' Sir Jean de Villemur said to Roger de Beaufort: 'Roger, you must be made a knight.' Roger replied: 'Sir, I am not yet worthy of knighthood, but all my thanks for thinking of it.' Nothing more was said, indeed there was no time for much conversation. They took up position in a square with their backs against an old wall, and there Sir Jean and Sir Hugues unfurled their banners and put themselves in a posture of defence. They had about eighty men altogether. Soon the Duke of Lancaster and the Earl of Cambridge with their company came upon them and, dismounting when they saw them, attacked them lustily. Their men did not last long against the English, but were soon scattered and either killed or captured.

There was a long hand-to-hand combat between the Duke of Lancaster and Sir Jean de Villemur, who was a fine knight, strong and of superb physique; also between the Earl of Cambridge and Sir Hugues de la Roche, and between the Earl of Pembroke and Roger de Beaufort. Those three against three gave a masterly display of skilful fighting. The others let them fight it out; it would have gone ill with any who tried to interfere. Presently the Prince came that way in his wheeled litter and watched them with keen interest, until he grew calmer and his anger ebbed away at the sight of them. At length the three Frenchmen stopped fighting with one accord and said, giving up their swords: 'Sirs, we are yours, you have beaten us. Treat us according to the law of arms.' 'By God, Sir Jean,' said the Duke of Lancaster, 'we would never dream of doing anything else. We accept you as our prisoners.' That, as I was informed later, was how the three Frenchmen were captured.

But there was no respite elsewhere. The city of Limoges was pillaged and sacked without mercy, then burnt and utterly destroyed. The English left, taking their prisoners with them, and returned to Cognac, where the Princess was, and where the Prince dismissed all his fighting men. He did nothing more that season, for he felt very unwell and was growing worse daily, to the great concern of his brothers and his men.

Now, as to what happened to the Bishop of Limoges, who was in grave danger of losing his head – the Duke of Lancaster requested him of the Prince, who agreed to give him up and handed him over to his brother to do as he liked with. The Bishop had friends on the road they were travelling, and these informed Pope Urban, who had recently arrived in

Avignon from Rome. This was a fortunate chance for the Bishop, who otherwise would have lost his life. The Pope requested the Duke to hand him over to him in such persuasive and amicable terms that the Duke felt unable to refuse. He complied and sent the Bishop to him, for which the Pope was duly grateful.

The Turn of the Tide

DU GUESCLIN APPOINTED CONSTABLE (1370)

WHEN the King of France heard of the retaking and destruction of Limoges, he was greatly angered and his heart ached for the sufferings of its inhabitants. It was therefore decided by the council of the nobles and prelates, strongly supported by the common feeling of the whole kingdom, that it was a necessity for the French to have a supreme commander, with the title of Constable, for Sir Moreau de Fiennes wished to resign that office. What was needed was an enterprising soldier who was himself a brave fighter and popular with all the knights and squires. After full consideration, Sir Bertrand du Guesclin was unanimously chosen, provided he was willing to accept, as the worthiest and most suitable man for the post, as well as the most gallant and successful leader fighting at that time in the service of France.

Du Guesclin is sent for and at first refuses the honour, on the grounds that he is too poor and humble a knight to command the great nobles of France, and particularly the dukes and princes of the royal family. The King overrides this objection.

The King answered and said: 'Sir Bertrand, you cannot excuse yourself on those grounds. I have neither brother nor cousin nor nephew, nor count, nor baron in my kingdom who would refuse to obey you. If any did, it would anger me so much that he would soon hear about it. So take the post with an easy mind. I beg you to.'

Sir Bertrand saw that none of the excuses he could make or think of would have any weight, so finally he gave in to the King's demands, though very much against his will. He was invested amid great rejoicing with the office of Constable of France and, in order to strengthen his authority, the King placed him next to him at his table and showed him all possible favours. With the office, he made him several handsome gifts of domains and rents for himself and his heirs in perpetuity. The Duke of Anjou took an active part in securing his promotion.

LA ROCHELLE GOES OVER TO THE FRENCH (1372)

The tide of war begins to turn. Towns and castles are going over to the French in territories recognized as English by the Treaty of Brétigny. A powerful factor in this change of heart are the military successes of Du Guesclin, who in 1372 conducts a campaign in Poitou. When the city of Poitiers is threatened, the English commander of the neighbouring port of La Rochelle, Sir John Devereux, takes about half his own garrison to reinforce it. Other events supervene. The citizens of Poitiers themselves open their gates to Du Guesclin, while La Rochelle is blockaded by a fleet provided by the King of Castile, Henry of Trastamara.

The people of La Rochelle were in secret negotiation with Owen of Wales,[1] who had been blockading them by sea, and with the Constable of France who was at Poitiers. But they dared do nothing openly because their castle was still held by the English, and without the castle they would not contemplate going over to the French. When John Devereux, as I have recorded earlier, went to carry support to the people of Poitiers, he left in charge a squire called Philippot Mansel, a happy-go-lucky sort of fellow, with about sixty soldiers under him.

The mayor of La Rochelle at that time was a very sharp-witted man, shrewd in all his undertakings, and a good Frenchman at heart, as he was to show. When he saw that the moment had come, he put his scheme into operation, having already consulted some of the citizens who were of the same mind. This mayor, whose name was Jean Caudourier, knew that Philippot, though a good fighting soldier, was neither cautious nor very astute and had not an ounce of guile in him.

1. An independent military leader who had offered his services to the King of France and claimed descent from the native Welsh rulers dispossessed by Edward I in the previous century. Froissart says that he held joint command of the blockading fleet with the Spanish admiral.

So one day he invited him to dinner with some of the burgesses. Suspecting nothing, Philippot accepted the invitation and went. Before they sat down, Jean Caudourier, who had already laid his plans and told his companions about them, said to Philippot: 'Yesterday I received a message from our very dear lord the King of England which I am sure will interest you.' 'What was it?' asked Philippot. 'I will show you,' said the mayor, 'and I will have it read out to you, as of course it should be.'

He went to a chest and took out an opened letter which had been sealed some time before with the great seal of Edward III and had no connexion with the present matter. But the mayor made it appear to have and said to Philippot: 'Here it is.' He showed him the seal, which quite convinced him because he recognized it. But he could not read, which made him easy to trick. Jean Caudourier then called a secretary, whom he had already rehearsed in what he had to do, and said: 'Read this letter to us.' The secretary took the letter and pretended to read a message which he himself made up, to the effect that the King of England ordered the mayor to hold a parade of all the fighting men in the city of La Rochelle and to report their numbers to him by the bearer of the present letter. The same was to be done for the men in the castle, because he expected to visit the place himself before long.

When all this had been said, as though it was being read out from the letter, the mayor said to Philippot: 'Captain, you have heard the orders which our lord the King sends me. I accordingly command you in his name to parade your men tomorrow on the square in front of the castle, and immediately after your parade I will hold mine in the same place, where you can see it. We will then each write back to our very dear sovereign lord, giving him an exact account of our numbers. And another thing: if your fellow-soldiers need money, I have a strong feeling that, after the parade, I shall lend you some to bring their pay up to date. That will meet what the King tells me in another, private, letter, in which he instructs me to pay them out of my own funds.'

Philippot, who completely believed everything he had

heard, said: 'By God, yes, mayor! Since I have to hold a parade I will be glad to do it tomorrow, and the fellows will be glad to turn out, if it means they're going to be paid. Money is what they need.'

The matter was taken as settled. They went in to dinner and had a thoroughly enjoyable time. After dinner, Philippot returned to the castle and told his men what had happened, adding: 'Cheer up, lads. Immediately after tomorrow's parade you are going to be paid. The King has sent orders about it to the mayor of this town, and I've seen the letters.'. The soldiers, who really did need money, for they were owed three months' pay or more, answered: 'That's wonderful news!' They began to polish their helmets, scour their armour, and shine up their swords or whatever weapons they had.

That evening Jean Caudourier made his secret preparations and informed most of the townspeople whom he knew to be on his side, giving them instructions as to how they should act the next day. Quite near to the castle and in the square where the parade was to be held, there were some old, uninhabited houses. In these the mayor had decided to post four hundred men in hiding, chosen from among the most martial in the town. When the soldiers had come out from the castle, these were to appear behind them and bar their way back, so trapping them. That was the best way he could see of getting the better of them. This plan was followed and the townsmen who were to take part in the ambush were chosen. They went secretly to their posts at dead of night, armed to the teeth and primed on what they had to do.

Soon after sunrise next morning the mayor and the councillors, accompanied only by some of their officials, set off completely unarmed, as a cover to lure out the garrison more easily, and arrived in the square for the parade. They were all mounted on big, strong horses, so as to get away quickly when the trouble began. At the sight of them, the captain of the castle hurried his men on, shouting: 'Come on, down to the square! They're waiting for us.'

The garrison poured out of the castle unsuspectingly, eager to parade and looking forward to their money, leaving only the menials inside. They left the gate wide open because they expected to go back through it before long and they got ready to be reviewed by the mayor and council. While they were all standing there in a bunch, the mayor kept up the deception by going from one to another and saying: 'You haven't got all your equipment with you to draw full pay. You must put that right,' and they answered: 'Yes, *sir*.' With such jokes and quips he held their attention until the ambushers came out, armed to the last buckle, placed themselves between the garrison and the castle, and seized the gate.

At that point the mayor and councillors galloped off, leaving their men to deal with the soldiers, who were very quickly mastered and taken prisoner, for they saw that resistance was useless. They were disarmed one by one in the square and imprisoned in various places in the town, in towers and gatehouses, with never more than two of them together. Soon afterwards, the mayor came back to the square fully armed, followed by over a thousand men. He made for the castle, which surrendered to him immediately, since there were none but humble people, maids and menservants, inside. These were only too glad to be allowed to surrender and be left in peace. In that way the castle of La Rochelle was retaken.

The people of La Rochelle retain control of their town and refuse to open the gates to the French without certain guarantees.

Now as to the conditions on which the people of La Rochelle stood firm and insisted: to begin with, they sent twelve of the most prominent citizens to the King in Paris, after delivery of a safe-conduct from him for the journey in both directions. The King, who desired to have them as his friends and subjects, received them well and was ready to listen to their demands, which were these:

Their first requirement, before they swore fealty to the King, was that the castle at La Rochelle should be demolished. Next, they demanded that the King of France and his heirs in perpetuity should hold La Rochelle as a crown domain, which should never be alienated in consequence of any peace-treaty, agreement, marriage or pact whatsoever with the

King of England or any other lord. Thirdly, they requested
the King to have minted in their town coinage of exactly the
same value and alloy as that minted in Paris. Fourthly, they
demanded that no King of France, his heirs or successors,
should have power to impose upon them or their tenant-
farmers any income or property-tax, levy, salt-tax, duty,
hearth-tax or anything similar, without their free consent.
Fifthly, they desired and requested of the King that he would
have them absolved of the promises and oaths which they had
sworn to the King of England, to break which would be
gravely prejudicial to their souls and would weigh heavily on
their consciences; wherefore they desired the King, at his
own expense, to obtain for them from their Holy Father the
Pope absolution and dispensation for all their infringements.

*The King does not easily agree to these conditions, but after some
stiff bargaining he accepts them all. Du Guesclin is sent to La
Rochelle and receives the homage of the townspeople as the King's
representative.*

JOHN OF GAUNT'S FRUITLESS EXPEDITION (1373)

*The war continues to run in favour of the French. More castles near
La Rochelle and in other parts of Poitou change sides voluntarily or
are taken by Du Guesclin. A relief expedition led by Edward III in
person is prevented from landing by contrary winds and returns to
England. The struggle is carried successfully to Brittany, whose Duke,
King Edward's ally and son-in-law, flees to England. Probably in
order to create a diversion in his favour, an English army crosses to
Calais in the late summer of 1373.*

This army was to be commanded by the King's son, Lancaster, and the Duke of Brittany. They were to arrive in the
harbour of Calais and then pass through Picardy. Their intention was, unless the weather proved unfavourable, to make
their way between the Seine and the Loire, find supplies for
themselves in Normandy and Brittany, carry support to the
fortresses which remained English – Bécherel, Saint-Sauveur,
Brest and Derval – and fight the French wherever they found
them, if they were willing to come to battle. . . .

So they were at Calais with three thousand men-at-arms and six thousand archers, and at least two thousand other men. Among this force were three hundred lances made up of native Scotsmen who served the King of England for pay.[1] The Constable of the whole army was Edward, Lord Despenser, one of the great barons of England, a spirited, courteous and gallant knight and a fine leader of men, who had been appointed to the post by the King himself. The Marshals were the Earls of Warwick and Suffolk.

Striking out into Picardy, the English find the fortified places forewarned and closed against them. They meet French contingents in occasional skirmishes, but achieve nothing decisive. Meanwhile, Charles V has begun to recall his chief commanders from Brittany to face the invasion.

The Dukes of Lancaster and Brittany with their men reached Vaux near Laon, where they halted for three days and obtained plentiful supplies. They found the country round there rich and stocked with food, for it was harvest-time. They held the farms and big villages to ransom on the threat of burning them, and were brought wine and sacks of flour, bullocks and sheep. The English plainly showed that they desired nothing more than to engage the French in battle, but the King of France, being doubtful of the result, would not permit his men to fight. Instead, he had the English closely followed and harried by five to six hundred lances who kept them in such a state of uncertainty that they never dared to disperse. In the city and on the hill of Laon were three hundred Breton and French lances who could see the English beneath them at Vaux, yet they never came down to attack them at evening, night or dawn. The English struck camp and went in the direction of Soissons, always keeping to the rivers and the most fertile country. As they went they were continually flanked by a good four hundred lances led by the Lord of Clisson, the Lord of Laval, the Viscount of Rohan and others. Sometimes they rode so near to each other that they could very easily have fought had they wanted to, and sometimes they talked to one another. For example, Sir Henry Percy, one

1. There was a four-year truce between the two kingdoms.

of the most gallant of the English knights, was once riding across country with his troop and Sir Guillaume des Bordes and Sir Jean de Bueil were riding with theirs, and each was keeping exactly to its own trail. Sir Henry Percy, who was on a white charger, said to Sir Aimery of Namur, the son of the Count, who was nearest to him on the left: 'It's a fine day for hawking. Why don't you fly for a kill, since you've got wings?' 'Yes, Sir Percy,' said Sir Aimery, moving a little out of line and making his horse curvet, 'that's a true word, it's good hawking for us. If it depended on me we would fly out after you.' 'I know you would, Aimery. Just persuade your friends to peel off. There's good game to be had.' In this bantering mood Sir Henry Percy rode for some time alongside the French, talking to that spirited young soldier, Aimery the Bastard of Namur. The two sides could have clashed often enough had they wished to, but they rode straight forward with perfect discipline.

The whole way from Arras to Épernay only two partial engagements take place, both to the disadvantage of the English.

After the two engagements at Ribemont and Ouchy, the Duke of Lancaster and his men had not a single encounter worth recording while they were on French territory. They passed through many narrow and dangerous places, keeping well together and moving cautiously, but the French King's council gave him this advice: 'Let them go on. They cannot rob you of your heritage by fires and smoke. They will grow tired and crumble away to nothing. Sometimes a great storm-cloud appears over the country, but later it passes on and disperses of itself. So will it be with these English soldiers.'

This seemingly passive attitude is criticized by some who feel that the nobility are failing in their duty by not bringing the English to open battle. A conference of military leaders is held in Paris to reconsider their strategy.

When the principal members of the royal council were assembled, they went to a private room where the King opened the discussion on the situation just described and asked each to give his opinion upon it, with his reasons in favour of fighting or not fighting. The Constable was asked to speak first because of his experience of big set battles against the English. He made lengthy excuses and was unwilling to reply until the great nobles present, the Duke of Anjou, the Duke of Berry, the Duke of Burgundy and the Count of Alençon, had given their opinion. However, he was pressed so hard by all of them that finally he was obliged to speak. He said to the King:

'Sire, these who talk of fighting the English do not consider the risk they may be running. I do not say they should not be fought, but I want it to be done from a position of advantage, as *they* know how to do so well and have done so often – at Poitiers, at Crécy, in Gascony, in Brittany, in Burgundy, in France, in Picardy, in Normandy. All those victories of theirs have done great harm to your kingdom and its nobility and have filled them with such pride that they despise all other nations because of the huge ransoms they have had from them, which have made them grow rich and arrogant. My fellow-soldier here, the Lord of Clisson, can speak with more knowledge of them than I can,[1] since he was brought up among them in his youth. He has a better acquaintance with their ways and character than any of us. So I will ask him, if it is your pleasure, my lord, to speak in support of what I have been saying.'

The King looked at the Lord of Clisson and, in order to satisfy Sir Bertrand, asked him in the most courteous way if he would kindly give his opinion. The Lord of Clisson did not hesitate to accept, and spoke strongly in support of the Constable, saying that his advice was excellent, for reasons which he presently gave:

'As God hears me, my lords, the English are so filled with their own greatness and have won so many big victories that they have come to believe they cannot lose. In battle they are the most confident nation in the world. The more blood they

1. Olivier de Clisson came of a great Breton family which served both the French and English crowns at different times. After his father's execution for treason in Paris (1343) the young Olivier, aged seven or eight, was taken by his mother to England and brought up at the court of Edward III, who treated him generously. He fought on the English side for a considerable time, going over openly to the French only in January 1370.

see flowing, whether it is their enemy's or their own, the fiercer and more determined they grow. And they say that their luck will always hold, as long as their King is alive. So in my humble opinion it would be inadvisable to fight them unless they can be taken at a disadvantage, in the way one should take one's enemy. I notice that the affairs of France are now prospering and that what the English took from us by skilful strategy, they have now lost. Therefore, my dear lord, if you approved of the advice which the Constable gave you, go on approving it.'

'Yes indeed,' said the King. 'I have no intention of marching out and hazarding my knights and my kingdom for a bit of farming land. From now on I again entrust you, together with the Constable, with the whole responsibility for my realm, because I think your opinion is the right one. And you, my brother of Anjou, what would you say?'

'Simply this,' said the Duke of Anjou, 'that anyone who gave you different advice would be betraying our interests. We shall still be waging war against the English, just as before. But when they expect to find us in one part of the country, we shall be in another, and we shall take from them when it best suits us the few pieces of territory they still hold. I hope to do so well, with the help of our two friends here, that before long it will be possible to say that, within the borders of Aquitaine and Upper Gascony, they haven't got much left.'

This satisfied the King completely and the decision was taken not to fight the English, except in the way that had been proposed. After the conference, the Constable and Sir Olivier de Clisson left Paris with some five hundred lances and made for Troyes. The English were heading that way, having crossed and recrossed the Marne without difficulty. Wherever they found the bridges destroyed, over that or any other river, they made use of the carpenters and other workmen they had with them, who quickly built a new bridge, provided they could find the wood. They had brought skilled men of all trades from England with them.

The army of the two Dukes lay before the towns of Vertus and Épernay. They forced the whole country round there to supply them with provisions. They found much plunder and booty near that fine river, the Marne, of which they were lords and masters, since none came out against them. Then they moved up-river towards Châlons in Champagne, but they did not go very near it and branched off (south) towards Troyes. There the Dukes of Burgundy and Bourbon had already arrived with the Constable and the Lord of Clisson. Their forces now numbered at least twelve hundred lances. They garrisoned the town and waited for the English, who were devastating the surrounding country.

The English appear outside Troyes, but there is no fighting, except for minor skirmishes. Two papal legates have reached the armies in the hope of arranging a cessation of hostilities, but neither side is interested. Eventually the English move on.

So the Dukes of Lancaster and Brittany campaigned across the kingdom of France at the head of their men, never finding anyone to meet them in a real battle, though they asked nothing better. Many times they sent their heralds to the commanders who were pursuing them, demanding battle and proposing various arrangements. But the French refused to listen; none of the challenges and proposals that the English sent to them came to anything. They shadowed them at one hour on the right and the next on the left, as the courses of the rivers demanded, and they were quartered nearly every night in strong towns or castles, where every comfort was to be had. But the English camped in the open country, living on very short commons and exposed to the cold when winter came, for they passed through some very poverty-stricken districts in Limousin, Rouergue and the Agenois. The greatest and grandest among them sometimes went for six days without tasting bread. Indeed, that often happened from the moment they entered Auvergne, for towards the end of their ride they were being followed by as many as three thousand lances and they dared not go out foraging unless all of them went together. In this plight nevertheless they crossed all the rivers between the Seine and Bordeaux, the Loire, the Allier, the Dordogne, the Garonne and several other big streams which run down from the mountains of Auvergne. But as to their wagon-train, it is not hard to guess what became of that. Less than a third of it reached Bordeaux, either because the horses succumbed or because it could not get over the mountain passes. And many knights and squires died on the way of the cold or the sicknesses which they caught in the winter, for it was after Christmas when they entered the city of Bordeaux. Other knights contracted illnesses of which they died later, in particular the Constable of the army, Edward Lord Despenser,[1] who was deeply mourned by all his friends. He was a noble heart and a gallant knight, open-handed and chivalrous. May God have mercy on his soul.

1. Edward Le Despenser, grandson of the younger Despenser executed in 1326, died in 1375. He had been a patron of Froissart's during the latter's stay in England in the thirteen-sixties.

IN 1376 King Edward of England celebrated his jubilee, having ruled for fifty years. The same year had seen the death of his eldest son Edward, Prince of Wales and of Aquitaine, the flower of the world's knighthood at that time and the most successful soldier of his age. This most gallant man and chivalrous prince died at the palace of Westminster outside the city of London on Trinity Sunday, the eighth of June, 1376. He was deeply mourned for his noble qualities and on his deathbed he made a full repentance and professed his firm faith and humblest submission to God. In order to show him the utmost honour and respect, as he so richly deserved on account of his exploits in war, his body was embalmed and placed in a lead coffin, in which it was sealed, except for the face, and was thus kept until Michaelmas, when all the prelates, barons and knights of England came to his funeral at Westminster.

As soon as the King of France was informed of the death of his cousin the Prince of Wales, he had his obsequies performed with great solemnity in the Sainte Chapelle in Paris. They were attended by his brothers and by many of the principal French barons and knights. And the King of France maintained that the Prince had ruled his domains nobly and worthily.

When All Saints Day came, King Edward sent his envoys to the peace talks at Bruges,[1] as previously arranged. They were Sir John Montagu, Lord Cobham, the Bishop of Hereford and the Dean of St Paul's in London. The King of France sent the Count of Saarbrück, the Lord of Châtillon and Sir Philibert de l'Espinasse. The two papal legates were again there as negotiators. These envoys and negotiators remained at Bruges for a long time, but they accomplished little. Nothing came to a head, for the English made demands and the French also.

1. Initiated inconclusively the previous year.

Towards Lent, however, a secret draft treaty was agreed between them. The English envoys were to take their copy to England and the French to France, each submitting it to their King. They, or other emissaries of the two kings, were to meet again at Montreuil-sur-mer, and on that condition the truces were extended to the first of May. The two delegations returned to their respective countries and made a report on the state in which they had left things. The French then sent to Montreuil-sur-mer the Lord de Coucy, the Lord de La Rivière, Sir Nicolas Braque and Nicolas Le Mercier, and the English Sir Guichard d'Angle, Sir Richard Stury and Geoffrey Chaucer. These nobles and envoys had long discussions about a marriage between the young Richard, son of the Prince of Wales, and Princess Marie, the daughter of the King of France. Then the English returned to England and the French to France and the truces were extended for another month.

I forgot to mention that on Christmas Day of that year (1376) the King of England held a great and solemn feast in his palace of Westminster, which all the prelates, earls, barons and knights of England were commanded to attend. And there Richard, the Prince's son, was raised up and carried before the King, who invested him, in the presence of the lords just mentioned, with the succession to the throne of England, to hold it after his death; and he seated him beside him. He required an oath from all prelates, barons, knights, officers of the cities and the towns, of the ports and frontier-posts of England, that they would recognize him as their king. After this, the noble King Edward fell into a sickness of which he died within a year, as I shall record later. But first let us return to the ineffectual negotiations and peace talks.

This time an English delegation is sent to Calais and a French delegation to Montreuil. No doubt because of growing suspicions of each other they never meet face to face. Their only contact is through the papal legates who journey to and fro between them.

Their negotiations still bore on the marriage mentioned above, the French offering, with the daughter of their king, twelve cities in France, that is to say, in the Duchy of Aquitaine; but they wanted to see Calais demolished.[1] So the negotiations were broken off and matters were left in suspense. There was no further extension of the truce. The French returned to France and the war was renewed.

During the whole time since the fruitless peace negotiations had begun at Bruges, the King of France had been keeping a powerful fleet at sea, which he intended to use against England. King Henry of Spain had supplied him with galleys and big ships and had lent him one of his principal admirals, Don Fernán Sánchez de Tomar,[2] the French admiral being Sir Jean de Vienne. With him were a number of experienced knights and squires from Burgundy, Champagne and Picardy. These sailors were now cruising about, waiting only for word that the war had been renewed. The fact was well known in England, since the commanders of the English islands, Jersey, Guernsey and Wight, had reported it to the King's council. The King himself was now very ill and unable to attend to the affairs of the realm, which were referred to his son, the Duke of Lancaster. He was, indeed, so weak that the doctors had given up hope of his recovery. So Sir John Arundel was sent to Southampton with two hundred men-at-arms and three hundred archers to guard the harbour, town and coast against the French.

On 21 June 1377, the gallant and noble King Edward III departed this life, to the deep distress of the whole realm of England, for he had been a good king for them. His like had

1. Describing the first round of negotiations in 1375, Froissart had written: 'The King of England made impossible demands, to which the French would never have consented: restoration of all the territories which the King of France or his dependents had taken from him, payment of all money which was still due when the above-mentioned peace was broken, and the Captal de Buch released from prison. For his part the King of France wanted to have the town and castle of Calais razed to the ground, as a first condition of any agreement and, as to the money, quite the opposite: he wanted the entire sum which his father King John and he himself had paid to be returned to him. These were things which the King of England would never have agreed to: the return of the money and the destruction of Calais.'

2. Froissart: Dan Ferrans Sanses de Touwars.

not been seen since the days of King Arthur, who once had also been King of England, which in his time was called Great Britain. So King Edward was embalmed and placed with great pomp and reverence on a bier borne by twenty-four knights dressed in black, his three sons and the Duke of Brittany and the Earl of March walking behind him, and carried thus at a slow march through the city of London, the face uncovered. To witness and hear the grief of the people, their sobs and screams and lamentations on that day, would have rended anyone's heart.

So the body of the noble king was taken through London to Westminster and buried beside his wife, Philippa of Hainault, Queen of England, as they had appointed in their lifetime. . . .

After the funeral, it was seen that England could not remain for long without a king and that it was in the interests of the whole country to crown as early as possible the successor whom the late king had invested in his lifetime. The prelates, earls, barons, knights and commons of England therefore arranged a date in the near future on which to crown the heir, the young Richard, son of the Prince of Wales; and they reached this decision unanimously.

In the same week in which the King died, the envoys who had been at Calais, the Earl of Salisbury and Sir Guichard d'Angle, returned to England. Great was their grief when they learnt of the King's death, but they had to submit to God's will. All the frontiers of England were then closed, and no one left the country at any point whatever. This was to give time to put the affairs of the realm in order before the death of its great king was known.

Now I will turn to the French forces at sea. On the eve of St Peter's and St Paul's day, 29 June, the French landed in Sussex near the borders of Kent, in a fairly large town of fishermen and sailors called Rye. They pillaged and plundered it and burnt it completely. Then they returned to their ships and went down the Channel to the coast of Hampshire, but they did not land there just then.

When news of this reached London, where the whole

country was assembling to crown the young King Richard, it caused great consternation. The nobles and the population with them said: 'We must make haste to crown our king and then go against these French before they do us more damage.' So the young Richard was crowned in the Palace of Westminster on the eighth of July, 1377, in his eleventh year. On the same day he created nine knights and five earls. As I do not know the names of the knights, I will pass them over, but I can name the earls. First, his uncle Thomas was made Earl of Buckingham; Sir Henry Percy became Earl of Northumberland; the King's brother, Sir Thomas Holland, became Earl of Kent; his tutor, Sir Guichard d'Angle, Earl of Huntingdon and Sir John Mowbray, Earl of Nottingham. Immediately after this ceremony and the coronation, it was decided who should go to Dover to guard the port and who should be sent elsewhere. The two brothers, the Earls of Cambridge and Buckingham, were chosen for Dover with four hundred men-at-arms and six hundred archers, and the Earl of Salisbury and his brother Sir John Montagu were sent to another good seaport called Pesk[1] with two hundred men-at-arms and three hundred archers.

The French land on the Isle of Wight, disembark their horses, and go marauding over the island. They re-embark and make for 'Hamptonne' (Southampton or Portsmouth), where they are fought off by Sir John Arundel, who is guarding the Hampshire coast. They then sail east and, after failing to land at 'Pesk', defended by Montagu and Salisbury, they land at 'a good big village on the sea with a fine priory, which is called Lyaus'. This would be Lewes, a riverport on the Sussex Ouse (though the landing was in fact at Rottingdean). The defenders of Lewes are defeated and the town and some of the surrounding villages burnt. From the English prisoners taken back to France is learnt the first news of the death of Edward III.[2]

1. Probably Pevensey.
2. The chronology of this summarized passage in Froissart, like some of the topography, is confused. The landing near Lewes occurred soon after the sack of Rye, as part of the same operation, and it is quite credible that prisoners taken then gave the first news of the King's death. The landing on the Isle of Wight came later: on 21 August according to Walsingham's *Historia Anglicana*.

When the King of France learnt of the death of his adversary the King of England and the accession of King Richard, he was no less preoccupied than before. But he showed no signs of it and prepared to commemorate the death of his cousin of England, whom, as long as peace had lasted, he had called brother. His obsequies were celebrated in the Sainte Chapelle of Paris with as much pomp and ceremony as if King Edward had indeed been his cousin german. By this the King of France proved himself to be a most honourable man, for he could well have dispensed with it if he had wished to.

BOOK TWO

(1376–85)

Papal Affairs and the Great Schism (1376–9)

IN 1309 the seat of the Papacy had been moved, partly owing to French influence, from Rome to Avignon. Here, in the County of Provence, it was just outside the King of France's domains and safe from the interference of the Holy Roman Emperors in the unsettled state of Italy at that time. For nearly seventy years the Popes used Avignon as their sole official seat, until the developments described by Froissart took place.

When Pope Gregory XI, who at that time occupied the Holy See of Rome in the city of Avignon, saw that he could not bring about a peace between the Kings of France and England – to his great displeasure, for he and his cardinals had worked hard to that end – he formed the devout intention of revisiting Rome and the Holy See that St Peter and St Paul had established there. Also he had promised God as a young man that, if in later life he ever rose to so high an office as the pontificate, he would do his utmost to have his seat in the place where St Peter had had it, and nowhere else. This pope was of delicate constitution and particularly afraid of the effects of over-work, for he was often ill. At Avignon he was so taken up by the affairs of France and so harried by the King and his brothers, that he hardly had a moment to attend to his health, so he thought that he would get away from them to have more peace. He ordered preparations to be made for his journey on a scale befitting the great dignitary he was and he told his brother cardinals that he intended to go to Rome. They were dismayed by his decision, for they feared the Romans and would have dissuaded him had they been able to, but they could not.

When the King of France heard of it, he was greatly disturbed, because at Avignon the Pope was much nearer his reach than elsewhere. He wrote to his brother the Duke of Anjou, who was at Toulouse, asking him to go immediately to Avignon and persuade the Pope to countermand his

journey. The Duke went there and was received with delight
by the cardinals and lodged in the Pope's palace so that he
should have greater opportunities to talk with him. I need
hardly say that he did his utmost to present the arguments
against the plan, but the Pope refused to listen to him, and
the whole time the Duke was in Avignon the preparations for
the journey went on. However, four cardinals were designated
to remain in Avignon to attend to cismontane affairs. They
were given full powers by the Pope to do all that could be
done by them, with the reservation of certain papal matters
which he cannot delegate to anyone.

When the Duke of Anjou saw that he would not succeed by
eloquence or argument, he took leave of the Pope, saying as
he did so:

'Holy Father, you are going to a country and among people
where they have little love for you, and leaving the source of
the faith and the kingdom in which the Church has more influence and excellence than anywhere else in the world. This
act of yours may well bring great disaster upon the Church,
for if you die out there – which, by what your doctors tell
me, is very probable – the Romans, who are strange and
treacherous people, will become lords and masters of all the
cardinals and will force a pope of their own choosing to be
elected.'

In spite of these and other arguments, the Pope set out on
his journey and reached Marseille where the galleys of Genoa
were ready waiting for him, while the Duke of Anjou went
back to Toulouse.

Pope Gregory embarked at Marseille with a large and
handsome retinue and had a smooth voyage as far as Genoa,
where he landed. The galleys were reprovisioned and they
then sailed on without incident to put in near Rome. Rejoicing
at his arrival, the leading citizens came out on draped horses
and led him in triumph into Rome. He took up his residence
in the papal palace and paid visits to a church within the city
called Santa Maria Maggiore, for which he had a great pre-
dilection and which he had endowed with fine works of art.
It was there that he died not very long after his arrival, on

28 March 1378. His obsequies were held in the noble style befitting a pope. He was buried in that church and there his body lies.

Immediately after his death, the cardinals met in conclave in the Palace of St Peter. As soon as they had gone in to hold their customary election of a pope who would work for the good of the Church, the Roman people assembled in violent crowds and made for the Vatican quarter. There were many thousands of them, all in a mood to cause trouble if things did not go according to their wishes. They said this kind of thing: 'Listen, our lord cardinals, hurry up and elect a pope, you are taking too long about it. And see that he's a Roman, we want no other kind. If he was from anywhere else, the Roman people and the Council would not recognize him as pope and you will all be in danger of your lives.'

The cardinals, who were at the mercy of the Romans, felt very uneasy when they heard these threats. They did what they could to appease the crowds, but feeling mounted so high that those nearest to the conclave-hall, hoping to intimidate the cardinals and make them obey their will, broke into it. In fear of their lives, the cardinals fled in disorder, but the Romans did not stop at that. They rounded them up, willing or not, and told them to elect a pope. Seeing themselves entirely in the power of the Romans and in great danger, the cardinals made haste to satisfy them. Nevertheless, they did it by means of a proper election, choosing a very saintly man who was a native of Rome and had been made a cardinal by Urban V. He was known as the Cardinal of St Peter.

This choice pleased the Romans greatly and the worthy man was given all the rights belonging to the pontificate, but he lived for only three days. This was why: the Romans were so delighted to have this pope that they took the good man, who was at least a hundred years old, set him on a white mule and paraded him round and round in the city, celebrating their triumph and exulting over the cardinals, until he became exhausted by the jolting and the terror he was in and on the third day took to his bed and died. He was buried in the Basilica of St Peter, and there he lies.[1]

The cardinals were distressed by the death of this pope, for they knew that it meant that further trouble was in store. Before he had died, they had planned to keep up a façade in Rome for two or three years and then transfer the See elsewhere, to Naples or Genoa, away from the reach of the Romans. But now everything had to be started afresh. They met again in conclave in worse conditions than before, for the Romans all gathered in St Peter's Square and showed only too plainly that they would break in and massacre everyone if things did not go as they wished. They shouted to the cardinals inside: 'Make quite sure, our lord cardinals, you give us a Roman pope, and one that lasts this time. If not, we'll come and make your heads redder than your hats.'

These threats terrified the cardinals, who preferred to die as confessors rather than martyrs. They therefore made haste to elect another pope. The man they chose was not one of their brother cardinals, but the Archbishop of Bari, a great cleric who had done much good work for the Church.

After his election, the Cardinal of Geneva put his head out of one of the windows of the conclave-hall and called to the crowds: 'Calm yourselves now, you have a Roman pope, Bartholomew of the Eagles, Archbishop of Bari.' The people shouted back all together: 'He's all right for us!'

The Archbishop was not in Rome on that day. I believe he was in Naples. He was quickly sent for, came to Rome delighted at the news, and presented himself to the cardinals. They gave him a great reception, he was taken and raised up among them and invested with all the rights of the Papacy, taking the name of Urban VI. The Romans were extremely pleased by this name, because of good Pope Urban V, who had held them in great affection.

His creation was announced in all the churches of Christen-

1. Though it seems a pity to spoil a good story partially, the Cardinal of St Peter was never elected pope. He was merely presented as such to the mob, in an endeavour to placate them. Also, he died some five months later.

dom; also to the emperors, kings, dukes and counts. The cardinals wrote to their friends that they now had a properly elected pope – words which some of them later regretted having used so emphatically. The new pope revoked all dispensations granted previously. Clergy of all ranks accordingly left their homes for Rome to obtain new ones.

THE GREAT SCHISM

[Not long after Urban VI had been made pope] a number of the cardinals decided to come together at a favourable opportunity and elect another, because this pope was doing no good to them or the Church, being too arbitrary and capricious. When he discovered that he was great and powerful and saw various Christian kings writing to him to declare their allegiance, he grew presumptuous and began to act violently and wilfully, removing certain of their rights from the cardinals, contrary to the customary practice. They were greatly offended and, discussing it among themselves, they concluded that he would never act in their interests and was unworthy to hold sway. Several then proposed to elect a different pope who would be both wise and powerful and rule the Church well.

The cardinals put a great deal of work into this plan, particularly the one who was later made pope. They were a whole summer debating it inconclusively, for those who favoured a new election dared not act openly for fear of the Romans. During the vacation of the court a number of the cardinals left Rome to forget their cares in various places of their choice. Urban went to Tivoli, and remained there for some time. During this vacation, which could not be extended for too long because a large number of clergy from different parts of the world were in Rome waiting for dispensations, of which many had been promised and approved, those cardinals who were in agreement met together to institute a pope. Their choice fell on Robert of Geneva, who had first been bishop of Thérouanne, then bishop of Cambrai, and was now known as the Cardinal of Geneva. After this election, at which the majority of the cardinals were present, he took the name of Clement.

At that time a very gallant knight from Brittany, called Silvester Bude, was in the neighbourhood of Rome, with two thousand Bretons under his command. They had all fought very bravely in previous years against the Florentines, whom Pope Gregory had excommunicated and made war upon because of their rebellion. Silvester Bude had done so well that they had surrendered unconditionally. Pope Clement, and the cardinals who supported him, now sent secretly for him and his men. They came into the Vatican quarter and established themselves in the Castle of Sant'Angelo outside Rome, to coerce the Romans from there. Urban did not dare to leave Tivoli, neither did the cardinals who supported him. There were not many of these, for fear of the Bretons. These were in considerable strength and were all violent men, who overthrew everything they came up against.

When the Romans found themselves in this situation, they sent for other German and Lombard mercenaries, who skirmished every day with the Bretons. Meanwhile, Clement granted indulgences and had his papal name published throughout Christendom. When the King of France was informed of it, he was greatly surprised at first. He called together his brothers, the chief barons, the prelates and the rector, masters and doctors of the University of Paris to consider which of the two popes he should recognize. It took some time to decide the matter, for many of the clergy were at variance, but finally all the French prelates favoured Clement, as did the King's brothers and the greater part of the University of Paris. King Charles of France was strongly advised by all the great clerics of his realm to give his allegiance to Clement as the rightful pope. He published a special edict throughout his kingdom, by which everyone was to honour Clement and obey him as God's viceroy on earth. The King of Spain took the same course, as did the Count of Savoy, the Lord of Milan and the Queen of Naples. The fact that the King of France supported Clement greatly helped his cause, for the realm of France is the main bastion of Christianity, of religious excellence and faith, because of the noble churches and the great prelatures which it has.

Charles of Bohemia, King of Germany and Holy Roman Emperor, was still alive then, living in Prague, where the news of these surprising events was brought to him. Although all in the German Empire, except the Archbishop of Trier, believed wholeheartedly in Urban and would not even hear of his rival, the Emperor hid his preferences as long as he lived[1] and gave replies, when asked about it, which satisfied the prelates and barons of his empire. Nevertheless the churches of the Empire followed Urban, as did the whole realm of England; but the kingdom of Scotland followed Clement. Count Louis of Flanders did much to injure Clement in the regions of Brabant, Hainault, Flanders and Liège, for he was a convinced Urbanist who said that that pope had been wronged. The Count had great influence in the territories near his own, so that their churches and secular lords followed his lead: except in Hainault, where the churches and the lords in alliance with them remained neutral, recognizing neither pope. For this reason the then Bishop of Cambrai, called John, lost all his temporal revenues.

It was then that Pope Clement despatched the Cardinal of Poitiers, a shrewd, worthy and learned cleric, to inform and exhort the people of France, Hainault, Flanders and Brabant. He had taken part in the first election and was able to explain how they had been forced to choose the Archbishop of Bari as pope. The King of France and his brothers and the prelates received him favourably and listened readily to his arguments. They felt they were very sound and placed great reliance on them. When he had stayed in France for as long as he wanted, he went on to Hainault and was well received by Duke Albert. So he was in Brabant by the Duke and Duchess, but he achieved nothing more there. He thought at first of going to Liège, but was so strongly advised not to that he changed his mind and went back to Tournay. He intended going to Flanders to see the Count, but dropped that plan also on

1. He died at the end of November 1378, about a month after Clement VII's enthronement.

receiving word that he was not wanted there, since the Count supported Urban and always would do, and in that conviction would live and die. He therefore left Tournay and went to Valenciennes and from there to Cambrai. Here he remained for some time, still hoping for better news.

In this way the Christian kingdoms were at variance over the two popes and the churches were also divided. The greater number were for Urban, but the richest in terms of revenue gave their full allegiance to Clement. Accordingly, with the consent of his cardinals, he sent to Avignon to have the town and the palace got ready; his intention was to move there as soon as possible. Meanwhile, he went to the city of Fondi and continued the grant of dispensations. He was followed there by clerics of all ranks who desired to have them. In the villages round Rome were large numbers of soldiers engaged in harrying the city and the quarter of St Peter's. They tormented the inhabitants night and day with skirmishes and attacks. Others in the Castle of Sant'Angelo, outside Rome, also gave the citizens much trouble. But the Romans brought German soldiers to their support and these were so numerous, when added to the men the citizens could muster, that one day they took the quarter of St Peter's by force. All the Bretons who could get away withdrew into the Castle of Sant'Angelo, but, once there, they were attacked so fiercely that they surrendered the castle in return for their lives. They came out and retired on Fondi and the lowlands round it, while the Romans destroyed the castle and burned the whole of St Peter's quarter. When Sir Silvester Bude, who was out in the country, heard what had happened, he was enraged and considered how he could get his revenge on the Romans. His spies told him that all the notables of the city were to meet in council in the Capitol. Upon this, he formed a column, made up of the men-at-arms he had with him, and, riding secretly towards Rome along hidden ways, came into the city by evening through the Naples Gate. Once the Bretons were inside, they made for the Capitol, reaching it at the very moment when the councillors had come out of the council-chamber and were standing about in the square. Those Bretons lowered their lances and spurred their horses and crashed in among them, knocking down and killing a vast number, including all the chief notables of the town. Seven knights banneret and a full two hundred other prominent men died there in the square, without counting the many who were injured.

Having achieved their aim, the Bretons withdrew. It was now late and they were not pursued, partly because of the darkness, partly because there was such confusion in Rome that no one knew what to do, apart from attending to their dead and wounded friends. They spent the night in great anxiety, burying the dead and nursing the wounded. In the morning, as an act of vengeance, they decided on a very barbarous act. They hunted down the poor clerics who were staying in Rome and had had nothing to do with the attack on the Capitol, and killed or wounded over three hundred of them. In particular, Breton clergy who fell into their hands were dealt with mercilessly. So great calamities occurred round Rome because of the quarrel of the popes, and people who were not to blame for it paid the penalty every day.

Queen Joanna of Naples visits Pope Clement at Fondi and offers him the gift of all her domains in fact or in right. She wishes him to assign them to some powerful prince, preferably French, who will defend them against her enemy, Charles of Sicily. Among these domains is the County of Provence.

Shortly after this, Pope Clement reflected that it was not to his advantage to stay too long in the neighbourhood of Rome, and that Urban and the Romans were working hard to make friends with the Neapolitans and Charles of Sicily. He feared that the sea and land routes for his intended return to Avignon might soon be blocked; but the main consideration which decided him to return was the desire to bestow on the Duke of Anjou, in the same way as he himself had received them, the rights which the Queen of Naples had made over to him. He prudently made his preparations in secret and embarked with all his cardinals and their familiars in galleys and ships sent from Aragon and Marseille, with the Count of Rocaberti, a gallant Aragonese, on board them. They reached Marseille safely after a smooth voyage, to the great joy of that whole region. From there the Pope travelled to Avignon, announcing his arrival to the King of France and his brothers, who were very glad to hear of it. The Duke of Anjou, then at Toulouse, came to visit him and was given all the titles which the Queen of Naples had assigned to the Pope. The Duke, who was always interested in great estates and honours, accepted them with gratitude for himself and his heirs and told the Pope that as soon as he was able he would go to those countries outside France in sufficient strength to withstand all the enemies of the Queen of Naples. After staying about a fortnight with the Pope he returned to his wife the Duchess at Toulouse and Pope Clement remained in Avignon. But he left his men-at-arms, Sir Silvester Bude, Sir Bernard de la Salle and Florimont to combat and harass the Romans.

The Peasants' Revolt in England (1381)

WHILE these negotiations and discussions were going on,[1] there occurred in England great disasters and uprisings of the common people, on account of which the country was almost ruined beyond recovery. Never was any land or realm in such great danger as England at that time. It was because of the abundance and prosperity in which the common people then lived that this rebellion broke out, just as in earlier days the Jack Goodmans rose in France and committed many excesses, by which the noble land of France suffered grave injury.

These terrible troubles originated in England from a strange circumstance and a trivial cause. That it may serve as a lesson to all good men and true, I will describe that circumstance and its effects as I was informed of them at the time.

It is the custom in England, as in several other countries, for the nobles to have strong powers over their men and to hold them in serfdom: that is, that by right and custom they have to till the lands of the gentry, reap the corn and bring it to the big house, put it in the barn, thresh and winnow it; mow the hay and carry it to the house, cut logs and bring them up, and all such forced tasks; all this the men must do by way of serfage to the masters. In England there is a much greater number than elsewhere of such men who are obliged to serve the prelates and the nobles. And in the counties of Kent, Essex, Sussex and Bedford in particular, there are more than in the whole of the rest of England.

These bad people in the counties just mentioned began to rebel because, they said, they were held too much in subjection, and when the world began there had been no serfs and could not be, unless they had rebelled against their lord, as Lucifer did against God; but they were not of that stature, being neither angels nor spirits, but men formed in the image

1. Between John of Gaunt, Duke of Lancaster, and the Scots, with a view to renewing the truce between England and Scotland.

of their masters, and they were treated as animals. This was a
thing they could no longer endure, wishing rather to be all
one and the same;[1] and, if they worked for their masters, they
wanted to have wages for it. In these machinations they had
been greatly encouraged originally by a crack-brained priest
of Kent called John Ball, who had been imprisoned several
times for his reckless words by the Archbishop of Canterbury. This John Ball had the habit on Sundays after mass,
when everyone was coming out of church, of going to the
cloisters or the graveyard, assembling the people round him
and preaching thus:

'Good people, things cannot go right in England and never
will, until goods are held in common and there are no more
villeins and gentlefolk, but we are all one and the same.[2] In
what way are those whom we call lords greater masters than
ourselves? How have they deserved it? Why do they hold us
in bondage? If we all spring from a single father and mother,
Adam and Eve, how can they claim or prove that they are
lords more than us, except by making us produce and grow
the wealth which they spend? They are clad in velvet and
camlet lined with squirrel and ermine, while we go dressed in
coarse cloth. They have the wines, the spices and the good
bread: we have the rye, the husks and the straw, and we drink
water. They have shelter and ease in their fine manors, and
we have hardship and toil, the wind and the rain in the fields.
And from us must come, from our labour, the things which
keep them in luxury. We are called serfs and beaten if we are
slow in our service to them, yet we have no sovereign lord
we can complain to, none to hear us and do us justice. Let us
go to the King – he is young – and show him how we are
oppressed, and tell him that we want things to be changed, or
else we will change them ourselves. If we go in good earnest
and all together, very many people who are called serfs and
are held in subjection will follow us to get their freedom. And

1. Since Froissart uses no word exactly corresponding to 'equal', it has
been avoided in translation. His phrase is: '... *mais vouloient être tout un*'.
See also next footnote.
2. Or 'unified' Froissart: '*tout-unis*'.

when the King sees and hears us, he will remedy the evil, either willingly or otherwise.'

These were the kind of things which John Ball usually preached in the villages on Sundays when the congregations came out from mass, and many of the common people agreed with him. Some, who were up to no good, said: 'He's right!' and out in the fields, or walking together from one village to another, or in their homes, they whispered and repeated among themselves: 'That's what John Ball says, and he's right.'

The Archbishop of Canterbury, being informed of all this, had John Ball arrested and put in prison, where he kept him for two or three months as a punishment. It would have been better if he had condemned him to life imprisonment on the first occasion, or had him put to death, than to do what he did; but he had great scruples about putting him to death and set him free; and when John Ball was out of prison, he went on with his intrigues as before. The things he was doing and saying came to the ears of the common people of London, who were envious of the nobles and the rich. These began saying that the country was badly governed and was being robbed of its wealth by those who called themselves noblemen. So these wicked men in London started to become disaffected and to rebel and they sent word to the people in the counties mentioned to come boldly to London with all their followers, when they would find the city open and the common people on their side. They could then so work on the King that there would be no more serfs in England.

These promises incited the people of Kent, Essex, Sussex, Bedford and the neighbouring districts and they set off and went towards London. They were a full sixty thousand and their chief captain was one Wat Tyler. With him as his companions were Jack Straw and John Ball. These three were the leaders and Wat Tyler was the greatest of them. He was a tiler of roofs, and a wicked and nasty fellow he was.

It was on the Monday before Corpus Christi day, in the year 1381, that those people left their homes to go to London to see the King and be freed from serfdom. They reached Canterbury, and with them was John Ball, who was expecting to find the Archbishop, but he was in London with the King. Wat Tyler and Jack Straw were also at Canterbury. When they entered the place, they were cheered by everyone, for the whole town was on their side. They consulted together and decided that, while they were on the way to London, they would send men across the Thames to Essex and Sussex and to the counties of *Stanfort* and Bedford[1] to tell all the people to come towards London from the other side, so that they would surround the city, and the King would be unable to bar their way. Their intention was to join forces on Corpus Christi or the day after. Those who were at Canterbury went into the Cathedral of St Thomas and did much damage there. They sacked the Archbishop's chambers and while they were plundering and carrying the things outside they said: 'This Chancellor of England got this furniture on the cheap. Soon he will have to render us an account of the revenue of England and the huge sums he has levied since the King's coronation.'[2]

After sacking the Abbey of St Thomas and the Abbey of St Vincent on the Monday, they left the next morning for Rochester, with all the common people of Canterbury with them. They drew in all the people from the villages they went near, and they passed by like a tornado, levelling and gutting the houses of lawyers and judges of the King's and Archbishop's courts, and showing them no mercy. When they reached Rochester, they were greeted with enthusiasm, for the people of that town were of their party. They went to the castle and took prisoner its captain, Sir John Newton, who was also the governor of the town. They told him: 'You must come with us to be our leader and captain and do whatever

1. Froissart's geography has often been the despair of his exegetists. In this and certain other passages he places Sussex north of the Thames. Read, probably, Suffolk. By *Stanfort* he usually means Stafford, which is undeniably north of the Thames. But if he meant Hertford here, it would fit the geographical and historical facts quite well.

2. The Archbishop of Canterbury, Simon Sudbury, was also Chancellor at that date.

we ask of you.' The knight tried to refuse, giving several reasons, but it was no good. They told him: 'Sir John, if you will not do as we wish, you are a dead man.' The knight saw all those men in furious mood getting ready to kill him. He feared death and obeyed them, joining their march against his will.

The men from the other districts of England, Essex, Sussex, Kent, *Stanfort*, Bedford, and from the bishopric of Norwich as far as *Gernemue*[1] and (King's) Lynn, behaved in just the same way. They got the knights and nobles into their power – such as the Lord of Morlais,[2] a great baron, Sir Stephen Hales and Sir Stephen de Cosington – and compelled them to go with them. Just consider what devilry was abroad. If their plans had succeeded, they would have destroyed all the nobility of England; and afterwards, in other nations, all the common people would have rebelled; they had been inspired and influenced by the people of Ghent and Flanders who rebelled against their lord. And in that very year the Parisians did the same, making themselves long iron hammers to the number of over twenty thousand. But first to continue with the English rebels from the counties I have named.

When that multitude which had halted in Rochester had achieved their purpose there, they crossed the river (Medway) and came to Dartford, still relentlessly pursuing their course of destroying the houses of lawyers and judges whenever they passed near them. They cut off the heads of a number of men and went on to within about twelve miles of London, where they halted on a hill known as Blackheath. And as they went they said they stood for the King and the noble commons of England.

When the inhabitants of London heard that they were quartered so near to them, they shut the gates of London Bridge and posted guards over it. This was done on the orders of the Lord Mayor, Sir William Walworth, and a number of wealthy citizens who were not of the rebel party, though

1. *Sic* Froissart. This may be (Great) Yarmouth. For *Stanfort*, see note 1, page 214.
2. Probably Sir William Morley.

more than thirty thousand of the small people in London were. The men who were at Blackheath now decided to send their knight to the King in the Tower to ask him to come and talk with them, and to say that all they were doing was in his interest: since for many years past the realm of England had been misgoverned, both as regarding its prestige and the welfare of the common people, and all this thanks to his uncles and his clergy, and principally the Archbishop of Canterbury, his Chancellor, from whom they demanded an account. The knight did not dare to refuse them but went to Thames-side opposite the Tower and had himself rowed across the water.

Sir John Newton delivers his message, begging the King to give him an answer to take back, because his children are being held as hostages for his return. Richard promises to speak to the rebels in person on the next day.

On the morning of Corpus Christi day, King Richard heard mass in the Tower of London with all his nobles and afterwards entered his barge, accompanied by the Earls of Salisbury, Warwick, Oxford and others. They were rowed downstream in order to cross the Thames near Rotherhithe, one of the King's manors, where about ten thousand of the Goodmen, having come down from the hill, were waiting to see the King and talk to him. When these saw the royal barge coming, they all began to shout and raised such a din that it sounded as though all the devils in hell had been let loose. They had brought with them their knight, John Newton, and if the King had not come and they found that he had tricked them, they would have set on him and hacked him to pieces; that was what they had promised him. When the King and his nobles saw the frenzied crowds on the bank, the boldest of them were frightened and his barons advised the King not to land. They began to turn the barge away and upstream again. The King called: 'Sirs, what have you to say to me? Tell me. I came here to talk to you.' Those who could hear him shouted with one voice: 'Come on land, you! It'll be easier that way to tell you what we want.' The Earl of Salisbury, speaking for the King, replied: 'Sirs, you are not in a fit condition for the King to talk to you now.' Nothing was added to this and the King went back, as advised, to the Tower of London from where he had started.

When those people saw that they would obtain nothing more, they were aflame with fury. They went back to the hill where the main body was and reported what had been said to them and that the King had gone back to the Tower. The whole mass of them began shouting together: 'To London! Straight to London!' They started off and swept down towards the city, ransacking and destroying the houses of abbots, lawyers and court officials, and came to the immediate outskirts, which are fine and extensive. They levelled several fine buildings and, in particular, the King's prisons, which are called Marshalseas, setting free all the prisoners inside. They committed many outrages in the suburbs and, when they reached the bridge, they began to threaten the Londoners because they had closed its gates. They said they would set fire to all the suburbs and then take London by storm, burning and destroying it. The common people of London, many of whom were on their side, assembled together and said: 'Why not let these good people come into the town? They are our own people and they are doing all this to help us.' So the gates had to be opened and all those famished men entered the town and rushed into the houses which had stocks of provisions. Nothing was refused them and everyone made haste to welcome them in and set out food and drink to appease them. After that, their leaders John Ball, Jack Straw and Wat Tyler, with more than thirty thousand men, went straight through London to the Palace of the Savoy, a very fine building on the Thames as you go towards the King's Palace of Westminster, and belonging to the Duke of Lancaster. They quickly got inside and killed the guards, and then sent it up in flames. Having committed this outrage, they went on to the palace of the Hospitallers of Rhodes, known as St John of Clerkenwell, and burnt it down, house, church, hospital and everything. Besides this, they went from street to street, killing all the Flemings they found in churches, chapels and houses. None was spared. They broke into many

houses belonging to Lombards[1] and robbed them openly,
no one daring to resist them. In the town they killed a wealthy
man called Richard Lyon, whose servant Wat Tyler had
once been during the wars in France. On one occasion Richard
Lyon had beaten his servant and Wat Tyler remembered it.
He led his men to him, had his head cut off in front of him,
and then had it stuck on a lance and carried through the
streets. So those wicked men went raging about in wild
frenzy, committing many excesses on that Thursday throughout London.

Towards evening, they all collected together for the night
in a square called St Katharine's, just outside the Tower of
London. They said they would not budge from there until
they had the King in their power and had got him to grant all
their demands. They also said that they wanted to have an
account from the Chancellor of all the sums of money which
had been raised in the kingdom during the past five years, and
that unless he could give a good and satisfactory account of
them, it would be the worse for him. With those intentions,
after a day spent in doing much harm to the foreigners in
London, they settled for the night beneath the walls of the
Tower.

You can well imagine what a frightening situation it was
for the King and those with him, with those evil men all
shouting and yelling outside like devils. In the evening the
King, with his brothers and the barons round him, had agreed
to a plan proposed to them by the Mayor of London, Sir
William Walworth, and other prominent citizens. It was, that
they should come at midnight, fully armed, down four different streets, and fall on those evil men, the whole sixty thousand of them, while they were asleep. They would all be drunk
and could be killed like flies, since not one in twenty of them
was armed. And it may be said that the loyal and wealthy
people in London were quite in a position to do this. They had
secretly assembled their friends in their houses, and their

---

1. Lombards and Flemings: two types of foreigner personifying the
banker and the merchant.

servants all carried weapons. Thus, Sir Robert Knollys was there in his house guarding his treasure with over six score fighting men all in readiness, who would have sallied out at once if the word had been given. It was the same with Sir Perducat d'Albret, who was in London at that time. They could have mustered between seven and eight thousand men, all fully armed. But none of this was done, for fear of the rest of the common people in London. The wiser heads, such as the Earl of Salisbury, told the King: 'Sire, if you can appease them by fair words, that would be the better course. Promise them everything they are asking. If we begin something that we are unable to finish, there will be no stopping things before we and our heirs are destroyed and all England is laid in ruins.'

This advice was followed and the Mayor was given new orders to remain inactive and do nothing at all which might cause trouble. He obeyed, as was his duty. Now, together with the Mayor, the City of London has twelve aldermen. Nine were with him and the King, as their actions showed, and three were on the side of those evil men, as it became apparent later. They paid very dearly for it.

On the Friday morning, the crowds in St Katharine's Square beneath the Tower began to stir and raise a great outcry, saying that if the King would not come and speak to them, they would take the Tower by force and kill everyone inside. For fear of these boasts and threats, the King decided to do as they asked and sent word that they were all to go out of London to a fine open space which is called Mile End, situated in the middle of a pleasant meadow, where the people go for recreation in summer. There the King would grant them all they were demanding or might demand. The Mayor of London announced this to them and he had it cried, in the King's name, that whoever wanted to talk to the King should go to the place just mentioned, in the certainty that the King would be there. Then those people, the commons of the villages, began to move off in that direction, but all did not leave, nor were they all of the same sort. There were many whose only object was to destroy the nobles and seize their wealth and to loot and ransack London. That was the main reason why they had begun all this. They quickly showed their hand, for no sooner had the gate of the Tower been opened and the King had come out with the Earls of Salisbury, Warwick and Oxford, Sir Robert of Namur, the Lord of Vertaing, the Lord of Gommegnies and several others, than Wat Tyler, Jack Straw and John Ball entered the castle by force with some four hundred men, and went from room to room until they found the Archbishop Simon of Canterbury. That wise and worthy man, Chancellor of England, who had just celebrated divine service and said mass before the King, was seized by those scoundrels and instantly beheaded. So were the Grand Prior of the Hospital of St John,[1] and a Franciscan friar who was a physician attached to the Duke of Lancaster, which was the reason why he was killed, to his master's subsequent anger, and a serjeant-at-arms of the King, called John Legge. Their four heads were placed on long lances and carried before the crowd through the streets. When they had sported with them long enough, they set them up on London Bridge, as though they had been traitors to the King and the realm. Those scoundrels also entered the room of the Princess of Wales and tore her bed to pieces, so terrifying her that she fainted. Her menservants and maids carried her down in their arms to the river-gate and put her in a small boat which took her along the river to the Tower Royal, where she was placed in a house known as the Queen's Wardrobe. She remained there for a day and night, like a half-dead woman, until she was comforted by her son the King, as I will describe later.

As the King was going towards Mile End outside London, his two brothers, the Earl of Kent and Sir John Holland, left him for fear of death, and with them also went the Lord of Gommegnies. They dare not show themselves to the populace at Mile End. When the King arrived there, accompanied by the other nobles named above, he saw over sixty thousand men from different districts and villages in the English

1. Sir Robert Hales, Treasurer of England.

counties. He rode right in among them and said very amiably: 'Good people, I am your lord and king. What are you asking for? What do you want to say to me?' Those who were near enough to hear him replied: 'We want you to make us free for ever and ever, we and our heirs and our lands, so that we shall never again be called serfs or bondmen.' The King answered: 'That I grant you. Now go back home in your village-companies as you came here, but leave two or three men behind to represent each village. I will have letters written at once and sealed with my Great Seal for them to take back with them, granting you all that you ask freely, faithfully and absolutely. And in order to reassure you still more, I will order my banners to be sent to you in each baili-wick, castlewick and borough. You will find no hitch in any of this, for I will never go back on my word.'

These words did much to calm those humble people, that is, the raw, simple, good folk who had flocked there without really knowing what they wanted, and they shouted: 'Hurrah! That's all we ask for!' So these people were placated and be-gan to go back to London. The King said another thing which pleased them greatly: 'Between you, good men of Kent, you shall have one of my banners, and you of Essex one, and you of Sussex another, and those of Bedford yet another, and those of Cambridge one, those of *Gernemue* one, those of Stafford one, and those of Lynn one. I pardon you everything you have done until now, provided that you follow my banners and go back to your own places in the way I told you.' All of them answered: 'Yes!'

These people went back to London, while the King ordered over thirty clerks to write letters of authority on that same Friday, to be sealed and delivered to them. Those who had the letters left to go back to their counties, but the main source of trouble remained behind – Wat Tyler, Jack Straw and John Ball. They said that, although some people were satisfied, they would not leave like that, and more than thirty thousand supported them. So they stayed in London and did not press very hard to have the King's letters of authority, but were chiefly intent on spreading such unrest through the

town that the rich and noble would be killed and their houses
looted. This was just what the citizens of London had feared
and was the reason why they had privately assembled their
friends and servants inside their houses, each according to his
resources.

When the small people who felt satisfied had received their
letters and had started back for their own towns, King
Richard went to the Queen's Wardrobe, where his mother the
Princess had taken refuge in a state of terror. He comforted
her, as he well knew how to do, and stayed with her for the
whole of that night.

I would like to tell you also of an incident caused by those
evil men outside the city of Norwich, while they were being
led by a captain they had, called Geoffrey Litster.[1]

On that same day of Corpus Christi, when those other
wicked people entered London, burned the Palace of the
Savoy and the church and house of the Hospitallers of St
John, broke open the King's prison of Newgate and set free
all the prisoners, and committed all the other excesses I have
recorded, the men of the following districts: *Stanfort*, Lynn,
Cambridge, Bedford and *Gernemue* had risen and come together. They moved towards London to join their comrades,
for that was part of their plan, and they had as their leader
that very bad character, Litster. As they went, they made
everyone come with them, so that not a single able-bodied
man remained behind. They halted outside Norwich, for a
reason which you shall hear.

The captain of that town was a knight called Sir Robert
Salle. He was not of gentle birth, but in appearance, reputation and fact he was a brave and experienced fighting-man.
King Edward had knighted him for his sterling worth and
physically he was the best-built and strongest man in all
England. Litster and his followers thought that they would
take this knight with them and make him their commander, in
order that they should become both more feared and more

1. Froissart has: *Guillaume* (William) *Listier, qui était de Stanfort*
(? Suffolk), but there is little doubt that Geoffrey Litster is meant.

popular. They sent a message asking him to come out and speak with them, or else they would storm the city and burn it. The knight considered that it would be better to comply than risk such a disaster, so he took his horse and rode alone out of the town to where they were waiting. They greeted him with all respect and asked him to get off his horse to talk with them. He did so, which was an act of folly. As soon as he was on the ground, they surrounded him and began pleading with him frankly but gently: 'Robert, you are a knight and you have a great reputation round here as a brave and worthy man. Of course you are one, but we know very well that you are not a gentleman, but the son of a common mason, of the same sort as us. Come with us and you shall be our master and we will make you so great a lord that the fourth part of England will be under your rule.'

When the knight heard this, he was astonished and greatly offended, for he would never have struck such a bargain. Glaring at them fiercely, he said: 'Away from me, you wicked people, false and evil traitors that you are, do you think I would abandon my natural lord for dung like you, and dishonour myself utterly? I would rather see you all hanged, as you will be, for that's the only end you deserve.'

With these words he tried to get back on his horse, but his foot slipped in the stirrup and the horse took fright. They began to yell at him and shout: 'Put him to death!' Hearing this, he let go of his horse, drew a long Bordeaux sword which he carried, and began cutting and thrusting all around him, a lovely sight to see. Few dared to come near him, and of those who did he cut off a foot or a head or an arm or a leg with every stroke he made. Even the boldest of them grew afraid of him. On that spot Sir Robert gave a marvellous display of swordsmanship. But those wicked men were more than sixty thousand strong and they hurled and flung and shot their missiles at him until his armour was pierced through. To tell the truth, even if he had been a man of iron or steel, he could still not have got out alive, but first he killed a dozen of them stone dead, apart from those he wounded. Finally, he was brought down and they cut off his arms and legs and carved up his body piece by piece. So died Sir Robert Salle; it was a pitiful end, and later, when the news was known, all knights and squires in England were deeply angered by it.

On the Saturday morning the King left the Queen's Wardrobe in the Tower Royal and went to Westminster to hear mass in the abbey, together with all his nobles. In a small chapel in the abbey there is an image of Our Lady which has great virtues and performs miracles and in which the Kings of England have always placed great faith. The King said his prayers before the statue, dedicating himself to it, then got on horseback with all the barons who were round him. It was somewhere about nine in the morning. He started with his followers along the road which leads into London, but when he had gone a little way, he branched off to the left to pass outside it. The truth was that no one knew where he intended to go when he took this road leading round London.

On the morning of the same day all the bad men, led by Wat Tyler, Jack Straw and John Ball, had assembled together and gone to hold a confabulation at Smithfield, where the horse-market is held on Fridays. There were over twenty thousand of them, all of one kind. Many more were still in the town breakfasting in the taverns and drinking Languedoc wine and Malmsey in the Lombards' houses, free of all charge. Anyone able to provide them with food and drink was only too happy to do so. The crowds assembled at Smithfield had with them the royal banners given them on the previous day and the scoundrels were contemplating running amok through London and looting and plundering. The leaders said: 'We have achieved nothing yet. The rights the King has granted us won't bring us in much. Now let's all decide together: let's sack this rich and mighty town of London before the men of Essex, Sussex, Cambridge, Bedford and the other far-off counties of Arundel, Warwick, Reading, Berkshire, Oxford, Guildford, Coventry, Lynn, Stafford, *Gernemue*, Lincoln, York and Durham come – for they all will come. We know that Bakier[1] and Litster will

1. *Sic* Froissart. Perhaps Baker.

bring them. But if we are masters of London and of the gold and silver and riches we find in it – for they are there all right – we shall have the first pick and we shall never regret it. But if we just leave them, the men who are coming, we tell you, will get them instead.'

They were all agreeing to this plan when suddenly the King appeared, accompanied by perhaps sixty horsemen. He had not been thinking about them, but had been intending to go on and leave London behind. When he reached the Abbey of St Bartholomew which stands there, he stopped and looked at the great crowd and said that he would not go on without hearing what they wanted. If they were discontented, he would placate them. The nobles who were with him stopped when he did, as they must. When Wat Tyler saw this, he said to his men: 'Here's the King, I'm going to talk to him. Don't budge from here unless I give you the signal, but if I make this sign (he showed them one), move forward and kill the lot. Except the King, don't touch the King. He's young, we will make him do as we want, we can take him with us anywhere in England and we shall be the lords of the realm. No doubt of that.' There was a tailor there called John Tickle, who had delivered sixty doublets for some of those scoundrels to wear, and Tyler was wearing one himself. Tickle said to him: 'Hi, sir, who's going to pay for my doublets? I want at least thirty marks.' 'Be easy now,' said Tyler. 'You'll be paid in full by tomorrow. Trust me, I'm a good enough guarantee.'

With that, he stuck his spurs into a horse he had mounted, left his companions and went straight up to the King, going so near that his horse's tail was brushing the head of the King's horse. The first words he said to the King were: 'Well, King, you see all those men over there?' 'Yes,' said the King. 'Why do you ask?' 'Because they are all under my command. They've sworn their sacred oath to do anything I tell them.' 'Good,' said the King, 'I see nothing wrong in that.' 'So,' said Tyler, who only wanted a quarrel, 'do you think, King, that these men here, and as many again in London, all under my command, are going to leave you without getting their letters? No, we're going to take them with us.'

'It's all in hand,' said the King. 'They have to be drawn up separately and given out one after another. Simply go back to your men, my friend, and get them to withdraw from London quietly, and remember what your interests are. It is our intention that each of you, by villages and boroughs, should have your letter as agreed.'

On hearing this, Wat Tyler looked across at one of the King's squires, who was behind the King and bore his sword. He was a man whom Tyler hated, because they had had words in the past and the squire had abused him. 'Well,' said Tyler, 'so you are here? Give me your dagger.' 'Never,' said the squire. 'Why should I?' The King looked at his servant and said: 'Give it him.' Very unwillingly the squire did so. When Tyler had it, he began toying with it and then turned again to the squire and said: 'Give me that sword.' 'Never,' said the squire, 'it's the King's sword. It's not for such as you, you're only a boor. If you and I were alone in this place, you would never have asked me that – not for a heap of gold as high as that church of St Paul's over there.' 'By God,' said Tyler, 'I'll have your head, if I never touch food again.'

Just then the Lord Mayor of London arrived on horseback with a dozen others, all fully armed beneath their robes, and broke through the crowd. He saw how Tyler was behaving and said to him in the sort of language he understood: 'Fellow, how dare you say such things in the King's presence? You're getting above yourself.' The King lost his temper and said to the Mayor: 'Lay hands on him, Mayor.' Meanwhile Tyler was answering: 'I can say and do what I like. What's it to do with you?' 'So, you stinking boor,' said the Mayor, who had once been a King's Advocate, 'you talk like that in the presence of the King, my natural lord? I'll be hanged if you don't pay for it.'

With that he drew a great sword he was wearing and struck. He gave Tyler such a blow on the head that he laid him flat under his horse's feet. No sooner was he down than he was entirely surrounded, so as to hide him from the crowds who were there, who called themselves his men. One of the King's squires called John Standish dismounted and thrust his sword into Tyler's belly so that he died.

Those crowds of evil men soon realized that their leader was dead. They began to mutter: 'They've killed our captain. Come on, we'll slay the lot!' They drew themselves up in the square in a kind of battle-order, each holding before him the bow which he carried. Then the King did an extraordinarily rash thing, but it ended well. As soon as Tyler was dispatched, he left his men, saying: 'Stay here, no one is to follow me,' and went alone towards those half-crazed people, to whom he said: 'Sirs, what more do you want? You have no other captain but me. I am your king, behave peaceably.' On hearing this, the majority of them were ashamed and began to break up. They were the peace-loving ones. But the bad ones did not disband; instead they formed up for battle and showed that they meant business. The King rode back to his men and asked what should be done next. He was advised to go on towards the country, since it was no use trying to run away. The Mayor said: 'That is the best thing for us to do, for I imagine that we shall soon receive reinforcements from London, from the loyal men on our side who are waiting armed in their houses with their friends.'

While all this was going on, a rumour spread through London that the King was being killed. Because of it, loyal men of all conditions left their houses armed and equipped and made for Smithfield and the fields nearby, where the King now was. Soon they were some seven or eight thousand strong. Among the first to arrive were Sir Robert Knollys and Sir Perducat d'Albret, accompanied by a strong force of men, and nine of the London aldermen with over six hundred men-at-arms, and also an influential London citizen called Nicholas Brembre, who received an allowance from the King, and now came with a powerful company of men-at-arms. As they arrived they all dismounted and drew up in battle formation near the King, on one side. Opposite were all those evil men, drawn up also, showing every sign of wanting a fight, and they had the King's banners with them. There and then the King created three new knights. One was William Walworth, Mayor of London, the second John Standish and the third Nicholas Brembre. The leaders conferred together, saying: 'What shall we do? There are our enemies who would gladly have killed us if they thought they had the advantage.' Sir Robert Knollys argued frankly that they should go and fight them and kill them all, but the King refused to agree, saying that he would not have that done. 'But,' said the King, 'I want to have my banners back. We will see how they behave when we ask for them. In any case, by peaceful means or not, I want them back.' 'You're right,' said the Earl of Salisbury. So the three new knights were sent over to get them. They made signs to the villeins not to shoot, since they had something to discuss. When they were near enough for their voices to be heard, they said: 'Now listen, the King commands you to give back his banners, and we hope that he will have mercy on you.' The banners were handed over at once and taken back to the King. Any of the villeins who had obtained royal letters were also ordered in the King's name to give them up, on pain of death. Some did so, but not all. The King had them taken and torn up in front of them. It may be said that as soon as the royal banners had been removed, those bad men became just a mob. Most of them threw down their bows and they broke formation and started back for London. Sir Robert Knollys was more than angry that they had not been attacked and all killed. But the King would not hear of it, saying that he would take full vengeance later, as he did.

So those crazy men departed and split up, some going one way, some another. The King, with the nobles and their companies, went back in good order into London, to be received with joy. The first thing the King did was to visit his lady mother the Princess, who was still in the Tower Royal. When she saw her son, she was overjoyed and said: 'Ah, my son, how anxious I have been today on your account!' 'Yes, my lady,' the King answered, 'I know you have. But now take comfort and praise God, for it is a time to praise him. Today I have recovered my inheritance, the realm of England which I had lost.'

The King remained with his mother for the whole day and

the lords and nobles went back peaceably to their houses. A royal proclamation was drawn up and cried from street to street, ordering all persons who were not natives of London or had lived there for less than a year to leave at once. If they were still found there at sunrise on the Sunday, they would be counted as traitors to the King and would lose their heads. When this order became known, none dared to disobey it. Everyone left in haste on that same Saturday and started back for their own districts. John Ball and Jack Straw were found hiding in an old ruined building, where they had hoped to escape the search. But they did not; their own people gave them away. The King and the nobles were delighted by their capture, for then their heads were cut off, and Tyler's too, although he was dead already, and posted up on London Bridge in place of those of the worthy men whom they had beheaded on the Thursday. News of this quickly spread around London. All the people from the distant counties who had flocked there at the summons of those wicked men set off hurriedly for their own places, and never dared to come back again.

When these troubles were over and *Thomas Baquier*[1] had been executed at St Albans, Litster at *Stafort*,[2] and Tyler, John Ball and Jack Straw and several others in London, the King decided to make a tour of his kingdom, going round all the bailiwicks, boroughs, castlewicks and boundaries of England to punish the evil-doers and take back the letters which he had been forced to grant to various places, and to restore the kingdom to proper order.

He therefore secretly summoned a number of men-at-arms to come together on a certain day. They amounted to at least five hundred lances and an equal number of archers. When they were ready, the King set out from London, accompanied only by his household, and took the road to Kent, where the

1. *Sic* Froissart. Baker (?).
2. *Sic* Froissart. Possibly Suffolk was intended here, since Litster's activities were in East Anglia. More accurately, it seems established that Litster was captured and executed at North Walsham, fifteen miles from Norwich.

first rising of those evil men had occurred. The men-at-arms followed him on the flanks and did not ride with him. He entered the county and came to Ospringe. The mayor and all the men in the town were called together, and when they were assembled the King caused one of his counsellors to expound to them how it was that they had been disloyal to him and had come very near to bringing all England to ruin and disaster. He then said that, since the King knew that this thing had been the work of a few, not of all, and it was better that the few should suffer than the many, he demanded that they should point out the guilty to him, on pain of incurring his anger for ever after and being branded as traitors to their king. When the people heard this demand and the innocent saw that they could purge themselves of the crime by naming the guilty, they looked at one another and said: 'Sire, there is the man who was the first to cause trouble in this town.' The man was immediately seized and hanged, and altogether seven were hanged at Ospringe. The letters which had been granted them were called for. They were brought and handed to the legal officers, who tore them up and scattered them in the presence of the whole population, and then said: 'We command all you who are here assembled, in the King's name and on pain of death, to return peaceably each to his own home, and nevermore to rise in revolt against the King and his ministers. That offence, by the punishment which has been inflicted, is now remitted you.' They all answered with one voice: 'God save the King and his noble counsellors!'

After Ospringe, the King proceeded in the same way at Canterbury and Sandwich, at *Gernemue*, Orwell and elsewhere, in all parts of England where his people had rebelled. Over fifteen hundred were put to death by beheading and hanging.

Affairs of Flanders (1381–2)

AT the time when these events were taking place in England, the struggle in Flanders continued as before, the Count[1] against the people of Ghent, and they against the Count. You know how Philip van Artevelde had risen to power in Ghent, being elected captain-general on the initiative of Pierre du Bois, who advised him, when he took office, to be stern and ruthless, so as to make himself feared. Philip adopted this policy, for he had not been governing long when he caused twelve men to be beheaded. According to some, it was because they had played a leading part in his father's[2] death, and he was taking vengeance. He began to rule with great energy and made himself feared, but also loved, by many people, especially by the soldiers belonging to the Free Companies. To line the pockets of these and keep in their good books, he refused nothing. Everything was abandoned to them.

I may be asked how the people of Ghent were able to sustain a war. The answer is this, according to what I heard from them later. They were so united that, when it was necessary, they all dipped into their purses, the rich taxing themselves according to their means and sparing the poor, and this solidarity gave them lasting strength. Also Ghent, all things considered, is among the strongest towns in the world, because neither Brabant, Hainault, Holland nor Zealand desire to make war on it. But if those four countries should ever be hostile to it, with Flanders, it would be encircled, helpless and doomed to starvation. However, those countries never did combine against it, for which reason it could make war more effectively and hold out longer.

1. Louis de Male, whose father had been killed at Crécy and who had avoided marrying Edward III's daughter during the siege of Calais.
2. James van Artevelde, Captain-general of Ghent, murdered there in 1345.

In the early days of Philip van Artevelde's rule, the Master of the Weavers was accused of treason. He was arrested and imprisoned and his house was searched to discover if the charge against him was true. Newly prepared saltpetre[1] was found there, which he had failed to produce for use during the whole year they had been under siege. The Master was beheaded and drawn through the town by the shoulders as a traitor, to give an example to the others.

The Count of Flanders lays siege a second time to his defiant subjects in Ghent, but is still unsuccessful and withdraws to Bruges. He tries to bring them to heel by cutting off the supplies which would normally reach them from other places. Although the blockade is not complete, food becomes very scarce in Ghent. On the Duchess of Brabant's initiative a reconciliation is attempted, but negotiations break down because of the intolerably hard conditions insisted on by the Count. On his return from the abortive talks to the now desperate situation in Ghent, Philip van Artevelde addresses the townspeople:

'Good people of Ghent, the only course I can see before us is to make a definite decision quickly. You know how short of food we are and that there are thirty thousand mouths in this town which have not eaten bread for the past fortnight. We must do one of three things. The first is to shut ourselves up in this town, blocking up all the gates, make our sincere confessions and go into the churches and chapels, there to die shriven and repentant, like martyrs on whom none will take pity. In that event, God will have mercy on our souls and, wherever the news is known, it will be said that we died like brave and faithful people. Secondly, we can all of us go, men, women and children, with halters round our necks, barefoot and bare-headed, and throw ourselves on the mercy of the Count of Flanders. His heart is surely not so hard that, seeing us in that state, he will not grow kinder and take pity on his humble people. If it will appease his anger, I will be the first to offer him my head. I am ready to die for the sake of the people of Ghent. Or thirdly, we will pick five or six thousand of the fittest and best-armed men in this town and will go after him at Bruges and fight him. If we are killed in that

---

1. Used in making gunpowder.

venture, it will be an honourable death. God will have pity on us and men also. They will say that we have fought for our cause bravely and loyally to the end. If God is good to us in the battle, as in times of old, as our reverend fathers tell us, he strengthened the hand of Judith who killed Holophernes, leader and master of Nebuchadnezzar's knights – whereby the Assyrians were defeated – we shall be the most highly honoured of any people since the Romans. Now consider which of these three things you wish to do. It must be one or the other.'

The third course is chosen. The men are to leave on the next day.

On that understanding, all the townspeople who had been at this meeting in the place of the Friday markets, dispersed and went home to prepare for what they had to do. They kept their town shut so tight on that Wednesday that not a soul came in or out until the Thursday morning, when those who were to leave were ready. There were about five thousand of them and no more. They loaded about two hundred wagons with cannon and artillery and seven only with provisions, five with baked bread and two with wine. All of this was contained in two casks, leaving none in the town. That shows how near they were to the end of their resources. When they left there were moving scenes between those who were going and those who stayed behind. The latter said: 'Dear friends, you see what you are leaving behind you. You have nothing to hope for if you return without victory. You know there is nothing more here. And if the news comes that you are dead or defeated, we shall immediately set fire to the town and destroy ourselves like desperate men.'

Those who were going replied, to comfort them: 'All you have said is right and true. Pray to God for us. We have hopes that He will help us, and you also before we meet again.'

So the five thousand left Ghent with their meagre supplies and camped for that Thursday night about five miles from the town. They did not touch their provisions, but managed with what they could get from the country. They marched for the whole of Friday and again used none of their own food. Their foragers found something in the country which did

them for that day. By evening they were a few miles from
Bruges, so they halted and chose a place to await their enemy.
There was a big pond ahead of them and they used this to
protect them on one side and placed their baggage-carts on the
other. There they spent the night.

The Saturday dawned fine and clear. It was St Helena's day,
the third of May. That is the very day of the festival and procession at Bruges, and for that reason there were more people
in the town than at any other time in the year. The word
quickly spread in Bruges: 'Do you know what? The Ghent
men have come for our procession!' There was a great stir
in the town, with people going from street to street and saying: 'What are we waiting for? Why don't we go and fight
them?' When the Count of Flanders heard of it in his palace,
he was astonished and said: 'The crazy, impudent people!
May the devil take them now! Not one shall escape of the
whole lot of them. This is going to be the end of this war.'

He then went to mass, and soon knights from Flanders,
Hainault and Artois who were in his service came flocking in
to inquire what he wanted to do. He showed his pleasure at
seeing them and said: 'We're going to fight those wicked
men. Yet they are brave,' he added. 'They would rather die
by the sword than from hunger.'

On that Saturday morning, Philip van Artevelde gave orders
for everyone to turn devoutly towards God and for mass to
be sung in several different places, for they had some friars
among them. Each man was to confess and say his prayers
sincerely, putting himself in a right frame of mind to receive
God's grace and compassion. All this was done. Mass was
celebrated in seven different parts of the army, and with each
mass there was a sermon, which lasted for over an hour and a
half. They were told by the clergy, Franciscan friars and
others, that they were like the people of Israel, who were long
held in subjection by Pharaoh; until, by God's grace, they
were delivered and led towards the Promised Land by Moses
and Aaron, and Pharaoh and the Egyptians were slain and
destroyed. 'In like manner,' said these friars in their sermons,

'you are held in servitude by your lord, the Count of Flanders, and by your neighbours of Bruges, before whose town you have halted. Do not doubt that they will attack you. They are determined men, who count your strength for little. But pay no heed to that. God, who is all-seeing and all-powerful, will uphold you. And give no thought to what you have left behind you, for you know, if you are defeated, that there is no second chance. Sell your lives dearly and courageously and die, if you must, with honour. Do not be dismayed if a great multitude comes out from Bruges against you, for victory goes not to the greatest number, but there where God bestows it, according to His grace. There are many examples, such as that of the Maccabeans and the Romans, of a humble people of good will, trusting in the grace of Our Lord, striking down a mighty people who boasted in their numbers. In this struggle, your cause is just and right for many reasons. Take heart and courage from that.'

With such arguments and many others the preaching friars exhorted the men of Ghent on that Saturday morning, so comforting them greatly. Three-quarters of the army took communion and all behaved most devoutly and showed themselves to be filled with the fear of God.

They are next exhorted by Philip van Artevelde, who repeats that they have been forced into this situation and must fight to the death since they have nothing more to lose.

At the end of his address he said: 'Sirs, you see in front of you the whole of your provisions. Please share them out fairly between you, as between brothers, with no disputes. When they are finished, you will have to conquer more if you want to eat.'

Upon this, they formed up very quietly. The wagons were unloaded and the sacks of bread distributed by companies and the two casks of wine up-ended. They breakfasted reasonably well on the bread and wine, each having enough to satisfy him for the time. Afterwards, they felt strong and in good heart, more robust and active than they had been before. When the breakfast, which they made their dinner, was over, they formed up for battle, all squatting down behind their ribalds.[1] These are high wheelbarrows, banded with iron, with long iron spikes sticking out from the front, which they are accustomed to wheel along with them. On this occasion they grouped them in front of their ranks and hedged themselves in with them.

The Count comes out of Bruges with his mounted men-at-arms, preceded by a much larger body of townspeople on foot. But it is now near evening and he is advised to put off fighting until the morrow.

The Count agreed and would have liked to follow this course. But the men of Bruges in their pride were so eager to fight that they would not wait. They thought that they would soon have defeated them and be going back to their town. In spite of the orders of the men-at-arms, of whom the Count had a large number, more than eight hundred lances, the Bruges townsmen went forward and began to fire cannons. Then the Ghent men came together and closed their ranks and fired off over three hundred cannons at once. They wheeled round the pond, so that the men of Bruges had the sun in their eyes, to their great disadvantage, and charged at them, shouting 'Ghent!'

No sooner did the men of Bruges hear these battle-cries and the sound of the cannons, and see the enemy coming straight at them in a determined way, than they broke like cowards, puffed up with nothing but false courage. They allowed the Ghent men to drive into them without resistance, threw down their pikes and turned to run.

The men of Ghent in their close, solid ranks, soon saw that the enemy were beaten and began striking them down in front of them, killing and going straight ahead, never once breaking formation but marching on at a steady pace. They kept up their cry of 'Ghent! Ghent!' and said to each other: 'Forward! Forward! Follow up closely. They're beaten and running. We'll get into Bruges with them. God has shown us great mercies on this day.' . . .

When the Count of Flanders and the men-at-arms saw the poor showing of the townspeople and the way they had de-

1. The 'ribald' was an early form of anti-personnel gun, firing through several small tubes or barrels. Froissart's description helps to define it.

feated themselves, with no apparent hope of recovery, they also were seized by panic and began to break up and flee in different directions. No doubt if they had seen any sign of resistance or of a rally among the men of Bruges, they might well have gone into action and harassed the Ghent men. They might even have turned the day. But it was not so, and they fled pell-mell towards Bruges. The son did not wait for his father, or the father for his son. Many indeed decided not to go towards Bruges, because the crush was so great in the fields and on the road that it was horrible to see it and to hear the cries and groans of the wounded, with the Ghent men on the heels of the Bruges men shouting 'Ghent! Ghent!' and slaughtering and striding on without stopping.

The Count escapes into Bruges ahead of the rout and goes to his palace. He gives orders for the gate to be guarded and for the remaining men in the town to assemble in the market-place.

While the Count was in his palace and was sending the clerks of the guild-masters from street to street to tell every man to go to the market-place to defend the town, the men of Ghent, treading on their enemies' heels, came rapidly on and followed them straight inside. The first place they went to, without turning to left or right, was the market, and there they halted and drew up. One of the Count's knights, Sir Robert Le Marescal, had been sent, while the Count was still issuing his orders, to see how they were doing at the gate. He found it split off its hinges and the Ghent men in possession of it. He found some Bruges men nearby, who said to him: 'Robert, Robert, go back and get away if you can. The men of Ghent are masters of the town.' He went back as quickly as he could to the Count, who was just leaving his palace for the market-place, riding his horse and preceded by a large number of torches. The knight made his report, but the Count, bent on winning everything back, nevertheless made for the market. As he was about to enter it among a mass of torches, shouting his battle-cry of: 'Flanders! The Lion! The Count!' the men at his horse's head and in front of him looked and saw that the whole place was filled with Ghent men. 'In God's name, sir,' they said, 'turn back. If you go on you will be killed, or captured at the best. Your enemies are all drawn up in the market-place waiting for you.' It was true. The men of Ghent were saying already as they saw the stream of torches coming out from the side-street: 'Here's our lord and master, here's the Count, he's coming right into our arms.' Philip van Artevelde had had the word passed along the ranks: 'If the Count attacks us, be sure that no one harms him. We will take him back to Ghent alive and well, and be able to make the peace that suits us best.' . . .

[Other men of the Count's insisted]: 'If you enter the market-place you will be killed. You are in great danger any way. There are plenty of other men from Ghent going from street to street searching for their enemies, and there are Bruges men with them taking them into the houses to find the ones they want to get. It won't be easy for you to escape. All the gates are held by the Ghent men, and you can't go back to your palace. A big troop of Ghent men is on the way to it.'

It was a hard blow to the Count to hear this. He began to grow frightened and to realize the danger he was in. He had all the torches put out and said to the men with him: 'I see there is no hope of winning back the town. I dismiss you all. Find your own ways to safety if you can.' His orders were carried out. The torches were extinguished and thrown into the gutters and the men dispersed quickly. The Count went up a side-street, had himself disarmed by one of his servants and his weapons and armour thrown away, and put on his servant's robe. He told him to go his own way and escape if he could, and if he fell into the enemy's hands, to keep his mouth shut about his master. The servant answered: 'Sir, they can kill me first.' So the Count remained alone.

For some time at this late hour – it was about midnight or a little after – the Count of Flanders wandered desperately through streets and alleys, until he felt forced to go into some house or other. If not, he would be caught by the mercenaries from Ghent, and other men from Bruges, who were hunting for him all over the town. So he entered a poor woman's house. It was no lordly manor, with halls and chambers and courtyards, but a poor grimy hovel, blackened by the smoke of the peat fire. The house consisted simply of one miserable room on the street, with an old sheet of smoke-stained cloth in it to shield the fire, and overhead a cramped little loft which was reached by a ladder with seven rungs. In the loft was a wretched bed in which the poor woman's children were sleeping.

Distraught and trembling, the Count went in and said to the woman, who was terrified at his appearance: 'Woman, save me. I am your lord the Count of Flanders. But now I must hide, my enemies are after me. If you help me, I shall reward you well.'

The poor woman recognized him, for she had often been to his door for alms. She had seen him coming and going when he went about his princely pleasures. She made up her mind quickly, which was a good thing for the Count, because if she had hesitated for a moment he would have been caught talking to her by the fire. 'Sir,' she said, 'go up to the loft and get under the bed where my children are sleeping.' He did as she told him, while she stayed looking after the fire and seeing to another small child which lay in a cradle.

When the Count entered the loft he slipped as quietly as he could between the blanket and the mattress and huddled there, making himself as small as possible. Then the mercenaries of Ghent arrived at the house, some of them saying that they had seen a man going in. They found the poor woman nursing her baby by the fire. 'Woman,' they asked her, 'where is the man we just saw coming in and shutting the door behind him?' 'Bless your hearts,' she replied, 'I've seen no man come in here tonight. I went out myself a few minutes ago to throw out some water, and then shut the door again. Where could I hide him? You can see all I've got here. There's my bed and my children are upstairs in another.'

One of them took a candle and went up the ladder. He poked his head into the loft and saw nothing but the little bed with the children in it. He looked round carefully and said to his comrades: 'Come on, we're wasting our time here. The woman's telling the truth. There's no one here but her and the kids.'

With this they left the house and continued their search elsewhere. No one else came with evil intentions.

The Count of Flanders had heard the whole conversation as he lay huddled in the little bed. The state of fear he was in can be imagined. What thoughts must he have had who in the morning could say, 'I am one of the great princes of Christendom', and that same night was reduced to such littleness? Well could he say that the chances of this world are precarious.

Francis Ackerman was one of the great captains of mercenaries and had been sent by Philip van Artevelde and Pierre du Bois to make the street-to-street search through Bruges. They also held the market-place, and held it all that night until the next morning, when they saw that they were in entire control of the town. These mercenaries were strictly forbidden to harm the traders and good people from other places who were in Bruges at the time, since they had nothing to do with this war. The order was quite well observed and Francis and his men did no harm or damage to any strangers. But vengeance was decreed by the Ghent men upon the four guilds of Bruges, the tailors, the glaziers, the butchers and the fishermen. All who could be found were to be killed, with no exceptions, because they had supported the Count outside Oudenarde and elsewhere. They went through the houses searching for those good people and killed them mercilessly wherever they found them. More than twelve hundred of them died that night and there were a number of other murders, robberies and crimes which never came to light. Many houses were plundered and women raped and killed and chests broken open, on such a scale that the poorest men of Ghent became rich.

At seven o'clock on the Sunday morning the joyful news reached Ghent of how their men had defeated the Count and the Bruges men and were lords and masters of the city by right of conquest. The effect of the news on the population of

Ghent, which had been in such desperate straits, can be imagined. There were processions and thanksgivings in the churches and praises to God who had shown them his mercy and lent them his aid to win the victory. More and more good news reached them as the day wore on, making them so wild with joy that they hardly knew what they were doing. . . .

Inquiries were made in Bruges as to what had become of the Count. Some said that he had left the town on the Saturday. Others said he was still in Bruges, hidden somewhere where he might yet be found. The leaders of the Ghent men took little notice. They were so elated by the victory and their ascendancy over their enemies that they thought nothing of any count, baron or knight in Flanders, but considered themselves so great that they would soon be the masters of everything. Philip van Artevelde and Pierre du Bois remembered how, when they had left Ghent, it was completely empty of wine and foodstuffs. They sent some of their men to Damme and Sluys to take possession of those towns and the supplies inside them, so as to re-provision the town of Ghent.

I was told at the time, and I believe it was true, that the Count of Flanders got out of Bruges on the Sunday night. How, I do not know, nor whether someone let him through the gates; I think they probably did. In any case, he came out alone and on foot, clad in a cheap and simple robe. Finding himself in the country, his spirits revived and he felt he was over the worst danger. He walked on at random until he came to a large bush and stopped under it to consider which way to go. He did not know the country or the roads and had never been along them on foot. While he was squatting there he heard a man speaking. It was one of his knights who had married an illegitimate daughter of his and whose name was Sir Robert Le Marescal. He recognized his voice and called to him as he went past: 'Is that you, Robin?' 'Yes, sir,' said the knight, recognizing his voice also. 'You've given me a lot of trouble looking for you round Bruges. How did you get away?' 'Come, come, Robin,' said the Count, 'this is no time to relate our adventures. Try and get me a horse, I'm tired of walking. And take the Lille road, if you know which it is.' 'Yes, sir, I do know,' his knight replied.

They walked all that night until sunrise next morning before they could find a horse. The first which the Count had was a mare belonging to some worthy man in a village. The Count got on its back, with no saddle or saddle-cloth, and rode it like that till the Monday evening, when he came across country to the castle of Lille. The majority of the knights who had escaped from the battle of Bruges were also making their way there, some on horseback and some on foot. Not all, however, took that road. Some went by sea to Holland and Zealand and stayed there to await developments.

Ghent prospers for a short time, ruled by Philip van Artevelde in almost princely state. Many Flemish towns desert the Count and join him, except for Oudenarde, which he besieges through the summer. The Count invokes the aid of the young King of France, acting through the Duke of Burgundy, his own son-in-law. Van Artevelde for his part looks to England and sends a mission to London which offers the English an unopposed entry through the Flemish ports and at the same time demands repayment of a loan of 200,000 francs made to Edward III nearly forty years previously. The royal council is highly amused and keeps the mission waiting. By the time their answer is sent, offering an alliance, it is too late.

The French support the Count in strength. An army assembled at Arras finds a way across the River Lys, intended as the Flemish line of defence, and moves on Ypres. Ypres goes over to them, together with a number of other towns. Leaving the siege of Oudenarde, Van Artevelde marches confidently to meet them. The two armies confront each other near Roosebeke, today Westrozebeke, a village some two miles north of Passchendaele. The Golden Mount (Goudberg) which lay between the French and the Flemings is the same high ground which marked the limit of the British-Canadian advance in the offensive of 1917.

Battle of Roosebeke (1382)

WHEN the Flemings had settled down for the night – while keeping good watch, for they knew that the enemy were within three miles of them – I was told that Philip van Artevelde had his girl with him: she was a young lady from Ghent who had accompanied him on the campaign. While Philip was asleep on a camp-bed near the coal fire in his tent, this woman went out at about midnight to look at the sky and the weather and find out the time, because she was unable to sleep. She looked towards Roosebeke and saw smoke and sparks in several parts of the sky, coming from the camp fires which the French had lit under hedges and bushes. She then thought she heard a great commotion between their army and the French army, with shouts of 'Montjoie!' and other cries. It seemed to come from the Golden Mount between them and Roosebeke. Thoroughly frightened, she went back into the tent and roused Philip, saying: 'Get up quickly and arm yourself. I can hear a great noise on the Golden Mount. I think the French are coming to attack you.' Philip got up at once and put a cloak on. Picking up an axe, he went out of the tent to see if there was anything in what she said.

He heard the same thing that she had heard. There seemed to be some great disturbance going on. Going back to the tent, he ordered his trumpet to be blown to give the alert. The whole army recognized its sound, got up and began to arm. The men who were keeping watch ahead of them sent some of their comrades to Philip to ask what they had missed, since everyone was arming. Word went back to them that they were held greatly to blame for having heard all this commotion in the enemy's direction and not having given the alarm. 'Ha,' they said, 'go back and tell Philip that we did hear some noise on the Golden Mount and we sent men to find out what it was. They reported that it was nothing, they found and saw nothing. Since there were no signs of movement we decided not to rouse the army, for fear of getting into trouble.'

When Philip was told this, he was reassured. But in his own mind he wondered what it could have been. Some say that it was the devils of hell revelling and whirling round on the spot where the battle was to be fought, in anticipation of the huge prey they would get from it.

After this alert the Flemings could not settle down again, fearing constantly that they might be taken by surprise. So they armed themselves at a leisurely pace, lit big fires by their tents and ate a good breakfast, for they had plenty of food and wine. About an hour before daybreak Philip said: 'It would be a good thing to move into the open and draw up our men. Then, if the French attack when it grows light, we shall be waiting for them and ready to fight our own battle.'

All agreed to this and they left their encampment and marched to a stretch of heathland next to a wood. In front of them they had a fairly wide ditch which had been newly dug. Behind them was a thick patch of brambles, gorse and other brushwood. In this strong position they drew up without haste, forming one large division, deep and solid. According to the reports made by their Constables they numbered about fifty thousand, all picked men chosen for their strength, their fighting skill and daring, and their readiness to hazard their lives. There were about sixty English archers who had deserted from the garrison at Calais to make more money with Philip. In their encampment they left all the baggage they had, trunks, beds and other things – everything except their arms – and their carts, horses and pack-animals, women and servants. But Philip van Artevelde had his page beside him mounted on a magnificent horse, good enough for a lord and worth five hundred florins. He brought it with him, not because he intended to run away and leave his men, but through pride and so that he could mount it if there were a pursuit of the French. Then he could command his troops and shout: 'Kill! Kill them all!'

He had in his army about nine thousand men from Ghent whom he kept beside him, having greater confidence in them than in the others. These were in the van with their banners, together with the men from the castlewicks of Alost and Grammont. Behind them were those from the castlewick of Courtrai, and then the men of Bruges, of Damme and of Sluys. Most of those from the district round Bruges were armed with hammers and picks, and wore iron helmets and coats and gauntlets of whaleskin. Each carried a shaft having an iron spike with a ferrule. The men from each town or castlewick had similar uniforms so as to recognize each other: one company wore coats with horizontal blue and yellow bands, another red coats with black bands, another had white chevrons on blue coats, another coats with wavy stripes of green and blue, another chequered black-and-white bands, another black and red quarterings, another blue coats with one red quartering, another had the top half red and the bottom white. Each company had the banners of their guilds and long knives stuck in their belts, and in this order they stood motionless waiting for day to break.

The French army is also ready for battle. With it are the young King Charles VI, his uncles, his Constable, Olivier de Clisson, the Lord de Coucy, the Count of Flanders and a glittering array of French and allied knights. In the early morning mist three knights go out on the usual reconnoitre of the enemy. They find the Flemish army on the move.

When the thick mist lifted on that Thursday morning, the Flemings, who had gone to their strong position before daylight and had stayed there till about eight o'clock without seeing any sign of the French, felt that they were in such huge numbers that they became over-confident. The captains began talking to each other and saying: 'What are we doing here, standing on our feet and getting chilled? Why not go boldly forward, since we feel like it, and seek out the enemy and fight him? It's no good waiting in this place. The French will never come to challenge us here. Let's go at least as far as the Golden Mount and get the advantage of the high ground.'

So many expressed the same opinion that they all agreed to move forward and go up the Golden Mount, which was between them and the French. To avoid the ditch in front of them, they went round behind the wood and had a clear march across the fields.

While they were doing this, the three French knights arrived at such an opportune moment that they could see their whole force and reconnoitre it at leisure. They rode over the fields skirting the battalions which closed up together, well within bow-shot of them, and when they had passed them on the left and gone beyond them, they came back on the right. In this way they had a thorough view of the army in breadth and depth. The Flemings saw quite well that they were there, but paid no attention and never broke their ranks. Also, the knights were so well mounted and so experienced in this exercise that they thought nothing of it. . . .

When the Flemings were ready to go up on the Golden Mount, they halted and re-formed in one close-ordered body and Philip said to them: 'Sirs, when the battle begins, remember how our enemies were shattered at the battle of Bruges by ourselves keeping steady and close together, so that our ranks could not be broken. Do that today. Let each hold his pike straight in front of him, and put your arms round each other, so that no one can get between you. Keep marching slowly and steadily forward without turning to left or right. And, just before the clash comes, let our bombards and cannons fire and our crossbowmen shoot. That will scare the enemy!'

Having given these instructions and seen that the men were drawn up in proper order, Philip van Artevelde posted himself on one of the flanks, surrounded by the men in whom he had the greatest trust. To his page who was riding his horse he said: 'Go and wait for me near that bush out of range. When you see that the French are beaten and running, bring up my horse and shout my battle-cry. The men will make way for you. Come right up to me, for I want to lead the pursuit.' The page obeyed. Philip also placed next to him the English archers who had come to serve him for pay.

You can see how well this Philip had made his dispositions. That is my opinion, and is the opinion also of many experienced soldiers. He made only one mistake, which was this: he left the strong position to which he had gone in the morning, where the enemy would never have come to fight him because they could not have reached him without suffering over-heavy losses.

The three French scouts return to the King and make an optimistic report. The French prepare to go into action.

A number of banners were taken out and unfurled. It was decided that, when the moment came to join battle, the King's division with the oriflamme should be in the forefront, while the vanguard should go right round on one flank and the rearguard on the other. They would attack the Flemings simultaneously with their lances, hemming them in and pressing upon those serried ranks, to their own great advantage. . . .

Soon afterwards the oriflamme was unfurled, carried by Sir Pierre de Villiers. Some people say that, according to the old records, it has never been unfurled against Christians except on that occasion. There was much debate about whether to use it or not on this campaign. However, after several considerations had been weighed, it was finally decided to unfurl it because the Flemish were of the opposite persuasion to Pope Clement and proclaimed themselves Urbanists. For this, the French said that they were unbelievers and outside the faith.

This oriflamme is a revered and famous banner. It was sent down mysteriously from heaven and is a kind of gonfalon. It brings great comfort to those who see it. Its virtues were proved then, for all morning the mist had been so thick that the men could hardly see each other, but as soon as the knight bearing it had unfurled it and held it up, the mist dispersed and the sky became as pure and clear as it had been the whole year. When they saw the sun shining out on this beautiful day, and had a clear view all round them and of the distance, the French nobles had good reason to feel heartened. Then it was a splendid sight to see those banners, those helms, that fine armour, those glittering lance-blades at the ready, those pennons and those coats-of-arms. And they kept absolutely still, none uttering a word, the front ranks watching the great army of the Flemings tramping towards them like a single man. They marched slowly in serried ranks, their pikes raised straight in the air, and the shafts were like a forest, so enormous was their number.

I was told by the Lord of Schoonvorst, who said he saw it himself, as did many others, that after the oriflamme had been raised and the mist had lifted, a white dove flew round several times above the King's division. When it was tired of flying and battle was about to be joined, it went and perched on one of the King's banners. This was taken as an excellent omen.

As the Flemings approached, they began to fire big bolts feathered[1] with bronze from their bombards and cannons; so the battle began. The King of France's division met the first shock, a weighty one. Those Flemings, proud and in great heart, came down at them fierce and hard from the high ground, butting their pikes at them with all the force of their chests and shoulders, as though they were wild boars; and they were knit so tightly together that their ranks could not be broken.

The first to be killed on the French side were the Lord of Wavrin, banneret, Morelet de Halewin and Jacques de Heere. The King's division was pushed back, but the vanguard and rearguard on the wings rode round and enveloped the Flemish, so that they became very hard-pressed. The men-at-arms began thrusting at their flanks with their stout, long-bladed lances of hard Bordeaux steel which penetrated their coats of mail to the flesh. Those who were attacked shrank back to escape the thrusts, for it would have been beyond human endurance for them to stand their ground and be impaled. They were rammed so closely together that they could not move their arms or use their pikes to defend themselves. Many lost strength and breath, falling on top of each other, so that they collapsed and died without striking a blow. Philip van Artevelde was surrounded, pierced with lances and borne down, with a number of the men of Ghent who were with him and loved him. When his page saw that his side was losing, he used the good horse on which he was mounted and rode off,

1. With projections like the feathers of an arrow.

leaving his master, since he could not help him. He went back towards Courtrai to return to Ghent.

So this battle took shape, and when the Flemings were hemmed in and squeezed on both flanks they stopped advancing because they could not use their weapons. The King's division, which had wavered a little at the beginning, recovered heart. Men-at-arms set about beating down Flemings lustily. Some had sharp axes with which they split helmets and knocked out brains, others lead maces with which they dealt such blows that they felled them to the ground. Hardly were they down than the pillagers came slipping in between the men-at-arms, carrying long knives with which they finished them off. They had no more mercy on them than if they had been dogs. So loud was the banging of swords, axes, maces and iron hammers on those Flemish helmets that nothing else could be heard above the din. I was told that if all the armourers of Paris and Brussels had been brought together, plying their trade, they would not have made a greater noise than those warriors hammering on the helms before them.

Knights and squires did not spare themselves, but went to work with a will, vying with one another. Some advanced too far into the press and were surrounded and crushed . . . for which reason there were a certain number of French dead. But they were not very many, because they came to each others' help whenever possible. There was a great pile of Flemish dead, long and high, but never before in so great a battle in which so many were killed had so little blood been seen flowing. This was because by far the greatest number were crushed or smothered to death, and these men did not bleed.

So on the Golden Mount were the Flemings defeated, and the pride of Flanders humbled and Philip van Artevelde slain; and with him nine thousand men from the town of Ghent and its dependencies. There died that day, the heralds reported, more than twenty-six thousand men on the field without counting the pursuit. The battle lasted only an hour-and-a-half from the time it was joined till the time it was won. After that victory, which was greatly to the honour and advantage of all Christendom and of all the gentry and nobility – for if the villeins had achieved their purpose, unexampled ravages and atrocities would have been committed by the commons in rebellion everywhere against the nobly born – the citizens of Paris with their long hammers became more cautious. How did they like the news of the defeat of the Flemings and the death of their leader? They were not cheered by it. Neither were the Goodmen in a number of other towns. . . .

When the King of France had retired from the battle-field to a tent of crimson silk very elegantly and richly designed, and had taken off his armour, his uncles and many French barons went there to congratulate him. Then he remembered Philip van Artevelde and he said to those around him: 'I would like to see that Philip, dead or alive.' His men replied that they would do their utmost to find him. It was announced throughout the army that whoever found Philip van Artevelde would be given ten francs. Grooms and servants began searching among the dead, who had already been stripped from head to foot. They were so filled with thirst for gain that in the end Philip was found and recognized by a man who had long been his servant and knew him well. His body was carried and dragged to the King's tent. The King looked at him for a time, and the lords also. He was turned over to see if he had died of wounds, but there were no wounds such as could have caused his death. He had been crushed in the press and had fallen into a ditch, with a great mass of Ghent men on top of him. When they had looked at him for a time they took him away and hanged him from a tree. Such was the final end of Philip van Artevelde.

On the next day, Friday, the King decamped from Roosebeke because of the stench of the dead and was advised to make for Courtrai, to rest and refresh himself there. On the day of the battle the Hare of Flanders[1] and various Flemish knights and squires who knew the country, some two hundred lances in all, had ridden over to Courtrai, entering the

1. Name given to the bastard son of the Count.

town without opposition. Women both rich and poor and numerous men took refuge in cellars and churches to escape death; it was pitiful to see them. So the first to enter the town had a fine haul of plunder, and after them little by little came French, Bretons and others, finding lodgings for themselves as they arrived. The King entered Courtrai on the first of December. A great massacre was at once begun, down below the town, of the Flemings who had retreated there, none being spared. The French hated the Flemings and those of Courtrai in particular, because of a battle which had been fought there in the past, in which Count Robert of Artois had been killed, with all the flower of French chivalry. Now their successors wanted to avenge them.

It came to the King's knowledge that in the Church of Notre-Dame at Courtrai was a chapel in which five hundred gilded spurs were hung. These spurs had belonged to the French knights killed in the battle mentioned, in the year 1302. Every year the citizens held a great festival round them, in celebration of their triumph. The King said that they should pay for it, as indeed they did, and that when he left the town should go up in fire and flames. So they would remember in time to come that the King of France had been there.

Charles VI Marries Isabella of Bavaria (1385)

I HAVE already related how the Duke of Burgundy and Duke Albert of Bavaria, Lord of Hainault, Holland, Zealand, and lease-lord of Friesland, had met at Cambrai for the marriage of their children,[1] to which wedding the young King of France also came, and a magnificent occasion it was. Now, according to my information, it was during that week when the King of France was there, with his uncles of Burgundy and Bourbon and Duke Albert and the ladies, the Duchesses of Burgundy and of Brabant and the Countess of Hainault, that on the initiative of Madame de Brabant secret discussions were held about a marriage between the young King of France and my lady Isabella, the daughter of Duke Stephen of Bavaria. It was recalled that on his death-bed King Charles V of France of happy memory had desired that, if a suitable match could be found, his son Charles should be married to some German lady. In this way the Germans and the French would be drawn into closer alliance, for he saw how the King of England's position had been strengthened by his marriage to the sister of the King of Germany.[2]

The Duchess of Brabant, who had a talent for this kind of thing, pointed out to the King's uncles and his council when at Cambrai that the young lady was the daughter of a great nobleman in Germany, the most powerful of the Bavarians, and that strong alliances with the Germans would result. Duke Stephen could influence the decisions of the highest lords in the Empire, for he was as great or greater than the King of Germany. It was this consideration which did most to persuade the King of France and his council to go on with the matter, but it was handled very discreetly and very few people

1. The double marriage of Margaret of Hainault to John of Burgundy, and William of Hainault to Margaret of Burgundy (Easter, 1385). Froissart's description of their wedding is omitted in this selection.
2. Richard II had married Anne of Bohemia in 1382.

knew about it until it was concluded. You may want to know the reason for this, and I will tell you.

It is the custom in France for any lady, however great her family may be, whom it is intended to marry to the King, to be seen and examined by ladies in a completely naked state, to decide whether she is fit and properly formed to bear children. Besides this, the lady lived in a country as far distant as Bavaria and it was not known, once she had been brought to France, whether she would be to the liking of the King. If not, the whole thing would be broken off. For these reasons everything was done in secret, and towards Whitsun the lady was taken to Brabant where the Duchess received her warmly and instructed her in French ways. With her was her uncle, Duke Frederick of Bavaria, who in fact had been the first person to suggest the marriage, in this way.

The very first time Duke Frederick had come to France to take part in the siege of Bourbourg,[1] he had been made much of by the King's uncles and the rest of the royal family, because he had come to help the King from the distant country of Bavaria, which is over six hundred miles away. He was felt to have rendered a very great service and was consequently always lodged near the King for friendship's sake and spent much time in the company of the King's uncles. When he had set out from Bavaria, he certainly supposed that the Kings of France and England would be meeting in battle either in Flanders or in France, since that was the common belief at the time throughout Germany, and for that reason King Charles and his uncles felt all the more grateful to him. So it happened, when they were all on that campaign around Bergues and Bourbourg, that the royal dukes, chatting together as great lords do, asked him whether he hadn't a marriageable daughter, because the King of France needed a wife, and they would rather have a Bavarian marriage than any other, since in former days there had always been Bavarians on the King's council. Duke Frederick had replied that he hadn't one, but that his elder brother, Duke Stephen, had a

1. In 1383, in the continuation of the Flanders campaign after Roosebeke.

very pretty one. 'What age?' asked the King's uncles. 'Between thirteen and fourteen.' 'That's just what we want,' they said. 'When you are back in Bavaria, talk it over with your brother and bring your niece on a pilgrimage to St John's of Amiens. The King will be there. If he sees her, perhaps he will desire her. He likes to see beautiful women around him and soon grows fond of them. If she finds the way to his heart, she will be Queen of France.'

That was how the first steps were taken, but nothing more was said or done and at that time the King himself had no idea that there had been talk of his marriage. When Duke Frederick returned to Bavaria, he reported all this to his brother Duke Stephen, who thought it over for a long time and then said: 'My dear brother, I quite believe that things are as you told me and my daughter would be happy indeed if she could rise so high as to be Queen of France. But it's a long way from here, and also there is that examination to be passed before she could become the wife of a king. I should feel exceedingly offended if, having sent my daughter to France, she was then brought back to me. I would prefer to marry her in my own time somewhere nearer home.'

Duke Frederick had to be satisfied with his brother's reply, and he wrote letters to that effect to the King's uncles, his own uncle Duke Albert, and Madame de Brabant, to whom he had mentioned the matter on his way home. He thought that the whole thing would now be forgotten. Besides, another match seemed to be in the air and it looked as though the King would soon be betrothed to the Duke of Lorraine's daughter, who was a very pretty young lady of about his own age, and of high and noble lineage, belonging to the Blois family. There was also talk of the Duke of Lancaster's daughter, who later became Queen of Portugal, but in her case no arrangement could be made on account of the war; so that project had to be dropped.

It was then that the Duchess of Brabant revived the idea of the Bavarian marriage on the occasion of the Burgundy–Hainault wedding at Cambrai, maintaining that, on account of the German connexions which it would bring, it was the most advantageous and honourable match that she could see for the King. 'True, dear lady,' replied his uncles. 'But the whole thing seems to be dead now.' 'Now you just keep quiet,' said the Duchess, 'and leave it to me. I will bring it up again and I promise that you will hear more about it this summer.' The Duchess made good her promise, for she worked so hard that Duke Stephen agreed to allow Duke Frederick to take his daughter off with him, and they gave out on their way that they were going on a pilgrimage to St John's of Amiens. Everyone believed this, because the Germans are much given to going on pilgrimages and it is an established custom with them.

When Duke Frederick and his niece, my lady Isabella of Bavaria, had stayed for three days with the Duchess of Brabant at Brussels, they took leave of her and went on. This was all part of the Duchess's plan and, as they were leaving, she promised that she would be at Amiens as soon as they, if not sooner, for she also meant to go there on pilgrimage. On that understanding, she set about making her arrangements.

Meanwhile Duke Frederick and his niece entered Hainault and went straight to Le Quesnoy, where they found the Duke and Duchess and William of Hainault, who styled himself Count of Ostrevant, and his wife, the daughter of the Duke of Burgundy, who all gave them a very friendly welcome; for Duke Albert was Duke Frederick's uncle, so the young lady was his niece too. 'And how did you manage to bring her away?' asked Duke Albert and his wife, who knew that Duke Stephen had been strongly opposed to it, for the reasons already given. 'Well,' said Duke Frederick, 'it was not at all easy. But I lectured and badgered my brother so much that he let me take her. But just as we were leaving, after he had kissed his daughter, he called me aside and said: "Frederick, brother Frederick, you are taking away my daughter with absolutely no certainty of the outcome, since if the King of France does not want her, she will be disgraced for the rest of her life. So think carefully what you are doing, for if you bring her back here you will have no worse enemy than me." Just consider, my dear uncle, and you, my dear aunt, what a predicament I have put myself into for my niece's advancement.'

'Have no fear, my dear nephew,' the Duchess replied. 'God will look after her, she will be Queen of France. Then your brother's threats will turn to gratitude.'

Duke Frederick and his niece remained at Le Quesnoy with their uncle and the Duchess and their children for a full three weeks. The Duchess, who was very experienced in such things, instructed the young Bavarian lady daily in manners and behaviour, although she was graceful and sensible by nature and had received a good upbringing, though she knew no French. The Duchess of Hainault could not leave her with the clothes and outfit she had come with, for they were too simple by French standards. She had her dressed, bejewelled and equipped as lavishly as if she had been her own daughter. When everything was perfect and it was time to set off, she and the Duchess and the Duchess's daughter-in-law left Le Quesnoy in great pomp along the Cambrai road. With Duke Albert, Duke Frederick, William of Hainault and their retinue, they made good progress until they came to Amiens.

To that place the Duchess of Brabant had come by another road. The King of France and his council and the Duke and Duchess of Burgundy were also there. The Lord de La Rivière and Sir Guy de La Trémoille, with barons, knights and squires, came out from Amiens to meet the Duchess of Hainault and escort her to her mansion. Once all these lords and ladies were lodged within the city, they began to exchange visits among themselves and to entertain lavishly. But very few people, except the three dukes and duchesses and their children and the Lord de La Rivière and Sir Guy de La Trémoille and the Lord de Coucy – whom the Duke of Berry had sent word to at Avignon a little previously, which brought him back with all speed – knew why they were assembled here. But the King could hardly sleep for eagerness to see his prospective bride, and he kept asking the Lord de La Rivière: 'When am I going to see her?' The ladies had some good laughs when they heard about this.

On the Friday, when the young lady had been dressed and

adorned as befitted her, the three duchesses led her before the King. As she came up to him, she sank in a low curtsey at his feet. The King went towards her and, taking her by the hand, raised her up and looked at her long and hard. With that look love and delight entered his heart. He saw that she was young and beautiful and was filled with a great desire to see her and have her. Then said the Constable of France to the Lord de Coucy and the Lord de La Rivière: 'This lady is going to stay with us. The King cannot take his eyes off her.'

Thereupon all those lords and ladies burst into conversation, while the young Isabella stood quite silent, moving not a feature of her face. Also at that date she knew no French.

After a little while, the ladies took their leave of the King and withdrew, taking their girl with them. She went back with Madame de Hainault and her daughter of Ostrevant. The King's intentions were still not known, but they soon became so, for when he also withdrew the Duke of Burgundy charged the Lord de La Rivière to ask him what he thought of the young lady and whether he liked her enough to marry her. The Duke did this because the King talked more freely to the Lord de La Rivière than to anyone else. So when they were in private he asked him: 'Sire, what do you think of the young lady? Is she to stay with us? Will she be Queen of France?' 'Upon my honour,' said the King, 'yes! We want no other. And tell my uncle of Burgundy, in God's name, to make haste about it.'

Leaving the King, the Lord de La Rivière went to another room where the Duke of Burgundy was waiting and reported this answer. 'So be it!' said the Duke. 'It is our wish, too.' He called immediately for his horse and went with a large escort to take the news to the Hainault household. It was greeted with delight and cries of 'Wonderful!' The lords and ladies met on that same Friday to decide where the marriage should take place. They agreed to leave Amiens and go to Arras for the wedding ceremony and festivities. Such was the decision of the King's uncles and his council, and on that understanding they broke off and went to bed.

On the Saturday morning the chamberlains and valets set

off for Arras to take over houses and prepare apartments. The lords and ladies expected to leave after dinner and spend the night at Ancre or Bapaume or Beauquesne. But this plan was altered, because when the King came away from mass and saw the servants packing up and getting ready to go, he said to the Lord de La Rivière: 'Gerald, where are we going to?' 'Sire, your uncle of Burgundy has arranged for you to go to Arras, to be married and hold the festivities there.' 'But why?' said the King. 'Is anything wrong with Amiens? This seems as good a place to be married in as Arras.' While he was speaking the Duke of Burgundy came in. 'Uncle,' said the King, 'it is our wish to be married in this fine cathedral of Amiens. We do not want any further delays.' 'Just as you say, my lord,' said the Duke. 'I must go and see my cousin of Hainault, then. She was last informed that she should leave here for Arras.'

Accompanied by several great lords, the Duke visited the Duchess and found her in her room with the bride who was to become his niece beside her. He bowed to them with fitting courtesy and then said to the Duchess, laughing: 'Madam and fair cousin, the King has countermanded our journey to Arras. He is obsessed by the prospect of this marriage. He admitted that he could not sleep last night for thinking of his bride-to-be. So the plan now is for you to stay here quietly today and tomorrow, and then on Monday we will find a cure for these two poor young invalids.' The Duchess burst out laughing and said: 'God's will be done!'

When Monday came Duchess Margaret of Hainault dressed and adorned the young lady who was to be Queen of France with all the pomp appropriate to a royal bride. The Duchess of Brabant joined them, accompanied by numerous ladies and maids-of-honour, and then the Duchess of Burgundy also arrived. The three duchesses led off the young Isabella of Bavaria in covered carriages of indescribable magnificence, wearing on her head the crown, worth a king's ransom, which the King had sent to her on the Sunday. Outside the cathedral church of Amiens they were met by Duke Albert, Duke

Frederick, William of Hainault and many barons and knights, coming in great state. Soon the King and the Duke of Burgundy arrived. So the young lady was led in by those lords and ladies with all possible honour, and married with due ceremony to the King by the bishop of the diocese.

After high mass and the solemn rites of marriage had been celebrated, they went on to the bishop's palace where the King was staying. A wedding-feast had been prepared there for the ladies, and a separate one for the King and the great nobles. They were served at table by none but counts and barons. So the day passed by in great feasting and merriment, and in the evening the ladies put the bride to bed, for that duty belonged to them. Then the King, who so much desired to find her in his bed, came too. They spent that night together in great delight, as you can well believe.

BOOK THREE

(1386–8)

At the Court of the Count of Foix (1388)

IN *the autumn of 1388 Froissart, wishing to obtain first-hand material for his Third Book, which he was writing under the patronage of Count Guy de Blois, undertook a journey to Orthez in Béarn. This was the seat of Gaston-Phoebus of Foix, an energetic, resourceful and not uncultivated prince who ruled a territory north of the Pyrenees made up of Béarn, the County of Foix and other domains. Bordering French territory in Languedoc, English territory in Gascony, and the Kingdom of Navarre in Spain, it was an ideal centre in which to gather information on happenings in the south, and particularly in Spain and Portugal, in which Froissart was then interested. The chronicler's journey on horseback took him westwards from Carcassonne into the Count's domains, where he joined a knight of the Count's, Sir Espan de Lyon, who was returning from a mission to Avignon. The two rode on together, Sir Espan talking informatively of events connected with the towns and castles they saw on their way. After several days in each other's company, they reach Orthez.*

[Leaving Morlaas] the next day, we reached Bougarber for dinner, then mounted our horses again, stopped for a drink at Arthez, and came into Orthez just at sunset. The knight went to his own house and I to the Hostelry of the Moon, kept by a squire of the Count's called Ernauton du Pin, who made me very welcome because I was French. Sir Espan de Lyon, in whose company I had travelled, presently went up to the castle to discuss his affairs with the Count. He found him in his gallery, having just had supper, for it had been the Count of Foix's custom since boyhood to have a sleep in the afternoon and to sup at midnight. The knight told him of my arrival. He immediately sent down to the hostelry to fetch me, for he was – and is now, if he is still alive – particularly interested in meeting strangers and in hearing their news. When he saw me, he welcomed me warmly and made me a member of his household, where I stayed for over twelve weeks, with my horses fed and well looked after in every way.

To show on what terms he was with me during that time, I should say that I had brought with me a book which I had composed at the request of my lord Wenceslas of Bohemia, Duke of Luxemburg and Brabant. Contained in this book, entitled *Meliador*, are all the songs, ballades, rondeaux and virelays which the noble Duke wrote in his time. These things, thanks to the skill with which I had inserted and arranged them in the book, pleased the Count greatly, and every night after supper I used to read some of them to him. While I was reading no one presumed to speak a word, for he insisted that I should be heard distinctly, and not least by himself. When I reached some point which he wanted to discuss, he was always eager to talk it over with me, speaking, not in his own Gascon, but in excellent French.

At the time when I was with him, Count Gaston of Foix was about fifty-nine. I can say that, though I have seen many knights, kings, princes and others in my life, I have never seen one who was so finely built, with better-proportioned limbs and body or so handsome a face, cheerful and smiling, with eyes which sparkled amiably when he was pleased to look at anyone. He was so accomplished in every way that it would be impossible to praise him too highly. He loved everything which it was right to love and hated whatever deserved hatred. He was a shrewd nobleman, bold in action and sound in judgement. He never kept unbelievers about him. He ruled his estates grandly. He said numerous prayers daily, reciting the Psalter at night, the Hours of Our Lady, of the Holy Spirit and of the Cross, with the Vigils for the Dead. Every day he had five francs given away in small coins for the love of God, and these alms were distributed at his door to all kinds of people. He was generous and open-handed. He knew exactly from whom it was proper to take and to whom to give. He loved dogs more than all other animals and was very fond of hunting, both in summer and winter. He took great pleasure in arms and love.

He always disliked excessive extravagance and required an account of his wealth once every month. He chose twelve prominent men from his country to receive his rents and administer his retainers. For each period of two months, two of them worked in his receiving-office and at the end of that time they were changed and two others took their place. The most outstanding of them, in whom he trusted most, was made his comptroller. To him all the others were responsible and rendered their accounts and receipts. The comptroller brought his accounts to his master on rolls or books, and left them for the Count to look over. He had a number of chests in his private room and from time to time, but not every day, he had money taken from them to give to some lord, knight or squire who had come to visit him, for no man ever left him without receiving a present. He was always increasing his wealth, as a precaution against the hazards of fortune which he feared. He was approachable and agreeable to everyone, speaking to them kindly and amiably. He had four secretaries to write and copy letters, and the four of them had to be ready waiting for him when he came out from his private apartment. He did not call them John or Walter or William, but when he had read his letters and wanted to dictate or give them some order, he addressed them without distinction as *You Shocking Servant*.

The Count of Foix lived in the way that I am describing to you. When he came out of his room at midnight to sup in his hall, twelve lighted torches were carried before him by twelve serving-men, and these twelve torches were held up in front of his table, giving a bright light in the hall, which was full of knights and squires and always contained plenty of tables laid for supper for any who wanted it. No one spoke to him at his own table unless he first asked him to. He usually ate much poultry – but only the wings and the legs – and drank little. He took great pleasure in minstrelsy, of which he had an excellent knowledge. He liked his clerks to sing songs, rondeaux and virelays to him. He would remain at table for about two hours, and he also enjoyed having travelling entertainers to perform between the courses. After he had watched them, he sent them round the tables of the knights and squires.

In short, I observed all this and reflected that, before I came to Orthez, I had been in many courts of kings, dukes, princes, counts and great ladies, but I had never been to one which pleased me more or in which there was more enthusiasm for deeds of arms. One saw knights and squires coming and going in the hall and the rooms and the courtyard, and one heard them talking of arms and love. Every subject of honour was discussed. Reports from every country and kingdom were to be heard, for, because of the reputation of the master of the house, they were brought there in great abundance. At Orthez I was informed of most of the feats of arms which had taken place in Spain, Portugal, Aragon, Navarre, England, Scotland and within the borders of Languedoc, for while staying there I met knights and squires from all those nations who had come to visit the Count. And so I gathered information either from them or from the Count himself, who was always willing to talk to me of such matters.

When I saw the rich and lavish scale on which the Count lived, I became extremely curious to discover what had happened to his son Gaston, or by what misadventure he had died, for Sir Espan de Lyon had been unwilling to tell me. I continued to inquire until an old and distinguished squire gave me the story. He told it me in these words:

'It is true that the Count of Foix and Madame de Foix, his wife, are estranged from each other, and have been for a very long time. The quarrel between them was caused by the lady's brother, the King of Navarre, after the King had gone surety for the Lord of Albret, whom the Count of Foix was holding to ransom for fifty thousand francs. The Count, who knew the King of Navarre to be cunning and deceitful, would not allow him credit for that sum, whereupon the Countess grew highly indignant with her husband and said to him:

' "My lord, you do little honour to my noble brother by refusing him credit for fifty thousand francs. Even if you never have any more men from Armagnac or from Albret in your power, as you have had them in the past, his word ought to satisfy you. And you know that you still have to provide fifty thousand francs for my marriage-settlement and to deliver the money into the hands of my brother, so you cannot lose in any case."

'"Lady," he said, "you are quite right. But if I thought that the King of Navarre might wriggle out of this payment, the Lord of Albret should never leave Orthez until I was paid to the last farthing. But since you ask me, I will do this, not for your sake, but for my son's."

'Upon this undertaking and the promise of the King of Navarre, who made himself responsible for the debt to the Count of Foix, the Lord of Albret was allowed to go free. He joined the French and was married in France to the sister of the Duke of Bourbon. He paid the fifty thousand francs at his convenience to the King of Navarre, according to his obligation, but the King did not send the money to the Count of Foix. Then the Count said to his wife:

'"Lady, you must go to Navarre and see your brother the King and tell him that I am most displeased at his failure to send on my money which he has received."

'The lady replied that she was willing to go and she left the Count with her retinue and went to her brother at Pamplona, where she was made welcome. She delivered her husband's message fairly and exactly. When the King had heard her, he said:

'"My dear sister, the money is yours since the Count of Foix owes it to you as your marriage-settlement, but it shall never leave the Kingdom of Navarre as long as I am in control of it."

'"Ah, my lord, that is a certain way of stirring up hatred between my husband and us. If you persist in what you have just said, I shall never dare to return to Foix, for my husband would say that I had deceived him and would kill me."

'"It is not for me," said the King, who was determined not to part with the money, "to say what you should do, whether you should stay here or go back. But I am the master of this money. I am holding it on your behalf, but it shall never leave Navarre."

'The Countess of Foix could obtain nothing more from him, so she stayed in Navarre, not daring to go back. The

Count, seeing the trickery of the King of Navarre, blamed his wife for it and began to hate her. Yet it was not her fault that she failed to go back as soon as she had delivered her message. It was more than she could risk, for she knew how harsh her husband could be when a thing displeased him.

'Things remained thus. Meanwhile Gaston, the son of my lord the Count, grew up and became a very handsome young man and was married to the daughter of the Count of Armagnac. This young lady was the sister of the present Count and of Sir Bernard of Armagnac. Thanks to this marriage there would have been a settled peace between Armagnac and Foix. The young nobleman must have been about fifteen or sixteen. A very good-looking squire he was, and very like his father in all physical respects. He was seized by a strong desire to go to Navarre to see his mother and his uncle. It was a most unhappy thing both for him and for the country.

'When he reached Navarre he was made welcome. He stayed for a time with his mother, then said good-bye to her, since by no word or entreaty could he persuade her to return to Foix with him. The lady had asked him whether his father had charged him to bring her back. He replied that when he left Foix there had been no mention of it, and for that reason she did not dare to risk going, but stayed where she was. The young man then went off to Pamplona to take leave of his uncle, the King. The King received him warmly and kept him there for ten days or more, giving handsome presents to him and his followers. The last present which he gave him was the young man's death. I will tell you how and why.

'When the time came for the young man to leave, the King took him privately to his room and gave him a very fine little purse filled with a certain powder – of such a kind that, if any living creature ate or touched it, he would immediately and infallibly die.

'"Gaston, my dear nephew," said the King, "you must do as I shall explain to you. You know that the Count of Foix has wrongly conceived a great hatred for your mother, my sister. This distresses me greatly, as it must you. However, to restore things to their proper state and put your father on good terms again with your mother, when a suitable moment comes you will take a little of this powder and will put it on your father's food, taking great care that no one sees you. As soon as he has tasted it, he will have one desire and one only: to have his wife, your mother, back with him, and they will love each other ever after so perfectly that they will never want to be separated again. That is a thing which you must desire with all your heart. But be very careful not to reveal what I am telling you to anyone who might repeat it to your father, for then you would ruin everything."

'The young man, who believed all that his uncle told him, replied: "Yes, certainly." Thereupon he left Pamplona and went back to Orthez. His father was pleased to see him, as was natural. He asked him about Navarre and wanted to know what jewels or other presents had been given to him. He showed them all, except the little purse containing the powder, which he was careful to hide.

'Now it was a frequent custom in the castle of Foix for Gaston and Yvain, his bastard brother, to sleep together in the same room. They were very fond of each other, as young brothers are, and they used the same clothes, for both were of about the same age and size. It happened one day that, playing and jumping about on their beds as boys do, they exchanged tunics and that Gaston's tunic, in which was the purse with the powder, fell on his brother's bed. Yvain, who was very sharp, felt the powder in the purse and said to Gaston: "What is this thing you are always wearing on your chest?"

'Gaston was not at all pleased to be asked this and he said: "Give me back my tunic, Yvain. It's nothing to do with you."

'Yvain threw his tunic back to him. Gaston put it on, and on that day he was much more thoughtful than he had been before. Three days later it so happened – as though God was working to protect the Count of Foix – that Gaston lost his temper with Yvain over a game of tennis and slapped his face. The young man was offended and angry and went in tears to his father's room, where he found him just after he had heard mass. When the Count saw him in tears, he asked him: "Yvain, what is the matter with you?"

'"By God, sir," said Yvain, "Gaston has thrashed me, but he deserves to be thrashed as much as I do, and more."

'"Why is that?" asked the Count, immediately growing suspicious, for he was quick to imagine harm.

'"Well, sir, ever since he came back from Navarre he has been wearing a little purse stuffed full of powder on his chest. I don't know what it is or what he means to do with it, except that he has told me once or twice that his mother will pretty soon be on better terms with you than she ever was."

'"Ha!" said the Count. "That's enough. And take care not to breathe a word of what you have told me to anyone else."

'"Certainly not, sir," said the young man.

'The Count of Foix reflected deeply and made no move until dinner-time, when he washed and sat down at table in his hall as on other days. Gaston was accustomed to serve him with all his dishes and to taste his food. As soon as he had placed the first dish before the Count and had done what he had to do, the Count looked at his son and saw the strings of the purse against his tunic. His blood boiled and he said:

'"Gaston, come nearer. I have something to say in your ear."

'The young man came up to the table. The Count gripped him by the chest and undid his tunic, then took a knife and cut the strings of the purse and held it in his hand. Then he said to his son:

'"What is in this purse?"

'The young man was taken completely aback and answered not a word. He grew pale with fear and bewilderment and began to tremble violently, for he felt that he had done wrong. The Count of Foix opened the purse and sprinkled some of the powder on a slice of bread, then whistled up a greyhound which he had near him and gave it the bread to eat. No sooner had the dog taken one bite than it rolled on its back and died. When the Count saw this happening he was furious – and no wonder. He got up from the table and took his knife and was about to stab his son. He would certainly have killed him, but knights and squires sprang up in front of him, saying:

'"For God's sake, my lord, do not act hastily. Find out more about the matter before you harm your son."

'The first words that the Count spoke were in his native Gascon:

'"*Zo, Gaston, traitour*, for your sake and to increase the inheritance which was to come to you, I have had war and hatred with the King of France, with the King of England, with the King of Spain, with the King of Navarre and the King of Aragon, and I have held out and struck back at them, and now you want to murder me. There is some evil thing in your nature. Now you shall die by this knife."

'He moved away from the table with the knife in his hand, intending to kill him on the spot. But knights and squires flung themselves weeping on their knees before him, and cried:

'"Ah, my lord, in God's name, do not kill Gaston. You have no other heir. Put him under guard and inquire into the matter. Perhaps he did not know what he was carrying and is quite innocent of this crime."

'"Quickly then," said the Count. "Put him in the tower, and let those who guard him be accountable for him."

'The young lord was put in the tower of the castle. The Count seized a number of those who served his son, but he did not get them all, for several escaped. One of them is today Bishop of Lescar, near Pau, outside the domain, who was under suspicion, as were several others still alive. But as many as fifteen were put to death very horribly, and the reason he gave was that they must have known his son's secrets and they ought to have warned him about the purse in Gaston's tunic. They had not done so and therefore several squires died horribly, which was a pitiable thing. In all Gascony there were none so fine, so handsome or so well turned-out as they, for the Count of Foix has always been served by a brilliant retinue.

'This matter affected the Count of Foix very deeply and he showed it. One day he summoned to Orthez all the nobles and prelates of Foix and Béarn, with all the notables of those two domains. When they were assembled, he explained why he had sent for them and told them that he had surprised his son in so black a crime that he intended to put him to death. They answered him as one man, saying: "My lord, with all respect, we do not want Gaston to die. He is your heir, and you have no other."

'When the Count heard his people begging for his son's life, he became a little more moderate. He thought that he would punish him with a few months' imprisonment and then send him away on a journey for two or three years until he had forgotten his anger and the young man, having grown older, had become wiser and more discreet. So he dismissed his people. But those of the County of Foix would not leave Orthez until the Count had promised them that Gaston should not die, for they loved the young man greatly. He gave them his word, but said that he would keep him in prison for a certain time. On receiving this promise they all went away and Gaston remained a prisoner at Orthez.

'News of these happenings spread far and wide and came to the Pope at Avignon. He immediately dispatched the Cardinal of Amiens to Béarn, with the mission of settling the affair by placating the Count of Foix and having his son released. But the Cardinal went about his business so slowly that he had got no farther than Béziers when news reached him that he was not needed in Béarn, since the Count's son, Gaston, was dead. As I have told you this much, I will also tell you how he died.

'The Count had him kept in a room in the tower at Orthez where there was little light, and there he remained for ten days. He ate and drank little, although enough food and drink were brought to him every day. But when he got his meals, he pushed them on one side and would not look at them. It was surprising that he was able to live so long, for several reasons. The Count kept him shut up with no guard in the room to keep him company, or to comfort and advise him, and the young man had only the clothes he stood up in when he was first thrown in there. So he grew melancholy and fretted excessively, for he had not been brought up to that. He cursed the hour when he was born if he was to end in that way.

'On the day of his death, the people who served his meals took the food in and said: "Gaston, here is some food for you." Gaston took no notice of it and said: "Put it over there." The man who was carrying it looked round the room and saw all the food he had brought on the previous days. He fastened the door again and went to the Count of Foix and said: "For the love of God, my lord, be careful about your son. He is starving in his prison. I do not think he has eaten since he was put in there, for I have seen all the dishes which have been taken to him standing on one side untouched."

'On hearing this, the Count grew very angry and left his room without a word to go to the tower. As ill luck would have it, he was holding a little knife with which he pared his nails. He had the prison door opened and went up to his son, holding the knife by the blade near the point – so near it, indeed, that the part which stuck out beyond his fingers was no longer than the thickness of a Tours shilling. By an evil chance, when he thrust that tiny point against his son's throat, saying: "Ha, traitor, why don't you eat?" he wounded him in some vein.

'The Count came away immediately, without saying or doing anything more, and went back to his room. The young man's blood had run cold with fear at the sight of his father, and in addition he was weak with fasting when he saw or felt the point of the knife pricking his throat. Lightly though it did so, it was in a vein. He turned his face away and died there and then.

'The Count had hardly got back to his room when a message came from the man who served the food:

'"My lord, Gaston is dead."

'"Dead?" said the Count.

'"As God is my witness, sir, he is."

'The Count would not believe that it was true. He sent a knight who was with him to find out. The knight went to the tower and came back to say that he really was dead. Then the

Count of Foix was distressed beyond measure. He grieved deeply for his son and said:

'"Ah, Gaston, what a miserable business this is! It was an evil day for you and for me when you went to see your mother in Navarre. Never again shall I know complete happiness."

'He sent for his barber and had his head shaved to the skin. He humbled himself and put on black, and ordered all his household to do the same. The young man's body was carried with weeping and lamentations to the Minorite Friars at Orthez, and there it was buried.

'That is the true account of the death of Gaston of Foix. It was his father who actually killed him, but his real assassin was the King of Navarre.'

The Haunting of Sir Peter

WHEN I heard the squire of Béarn's account of the death of young Gaston, I felt deeply sorry for the sake of the gallant Count, his father, whom I had found to be a lord with such admirable qualities, so noble, so open-handed and so chivalrous; and also for the sake of the country, which remained very unsettled for lack of an heir. Presently I took leave of the squire, after thanking him for his kindness in telling me the story. I often saw him again in the Foix household and we had many conversations together. One day I asked him whether Sir Peter of Béarn, the Count's bastard brother, who struck me as a knight of great character, was a wealthy man and married. He answered:

'Yes, he is married, but neither his wife nor his children live with him.'

'Why not?' I asked.

'I will tell you,' said the squire. 'Sir Peter of Béarn has a habit when he is asleep at night of getting up and arming himself. Unless great care is taken to prevent him, he draws his sword and fights, he does not know with whom. His chamberlains and servants, who sleep in his room and look after him, get up when they see or hear him, and wake him up. They tell him what he is doing and he says that he knows nothing about it and that they are lying. There was a time when they left no sword or other weapons in his room. But when he got up and could not find them, he raised such a raring and a roaring that it sounded as if all the devils of hell were in there with him. So they found it better to leave his weapons with him, for then he soon grows tired of arming and disarming and goes back quietly to bed.'

'And does he possess great estates through his wife?' I asked.

'By God he does,' said the squire. 'But the lady, who

brought him the inheritance, gets most of the income. Sir Peter of Béarn gets only a quarter.'

'And where does the lady live?'

'She lives in Castile with the present King, her cousin. Her father was the Count of Biscay. He was the first cousin of that King Peter who ruled so harshly, and who put him to death and also tried to get this lady into his power, and he seized all her land. As long as he was alive, the lady had nothing. On her father's death, people had come to this lady, who has the title of Countess of Biscay, and had said to her:

'"Escape, my lady, for if King Peter gets you, he will have you killed or put in prison. He is very angry with you because you seem to have been saying that he had the Queen his wife murdered in her bed (she who was the sister of the Duke of Bourbon and of the Queen of France). More faith is put in your word than in anyone else's, for you were a lady of her bedchamber."

'Filled with fear, the Countess Florence of Biscay left her home with a small retinue – for it is natural for any man or woman to flee from death – and travelled through the Basque country. After great difficulties she arrived here and told her whole story to my lord. The Count, who is gentle and kindly to all ladies, took pity on her. He let her stay and lodged her with the Lady of Corresse, an important baroness of this country, and he provided her with all that she required. His brother, Sir Peter, was a young knight at that time, without the warlike experience which he now has; he stood high in the Count's favour. He and the lady were married, and very soon after the marriage she recovered her estate. He has a son and a daughter by her, but they are in Castile with the lady, for they are still young and the mother does not choose to leave them with the father because she has strong claims of her own to the greater part of the property.'

'Holy Mary,' I said to the squire when I heard this, 'and what can be the cause of this delusion of Sir Peter of Béarn's of which you spoke, which makes him afraid to sleep alone in a room and, when he is asleep, to get up all by himself and lay about him like that? It really is an extraordinary thing.'

'Well now,' said the squire, 'he has often been asked, but he does not know the reason. The first time that anything was noticed was the night after he had been out in the woods of Biscay hunting an exceptionally big bear. This bear killed four of his hounds and wounded several others, so that the rest were afraid to go near. Sir Peter drew a Bordeaux sword which he was carrying and went up angrily – because of his hounds which he saw lying dead – to attack the bear. He fought it for a long time at great risk to himself and only got the better of it after much difficulty. But in the end he killed it and went back to his castle of Languidendon in Biscay, taking the bear with him. Everyone was impressed by the size of the beast and by the knight's bravery in attacking and overcoming it.

'When his wife, the Countess of Biscay, saw it, she showed signs of great distress and fainted. She was carried to her room and remained there very depressed for the rest of that day and the whole of the next. She would not say what was the matter with her, but on the third day she said to her husband:

'"My lord, I shall never be cured until I have made a pilgrimage to St James of Compostella. Give me permission to go and to take my son Peter and my daughter Adrienne with me. I ask you this as a special favour."

'Sir Peter agreed readily. The lady set off with a large escort, taking all her valuables which she had carried in front of her, gold, silver and jewels (since she knew very well she would not return) but no one paid much attention to this. She made her pilgrimage and then took the opportunity of visiting her cousin the King of Castile and the Queen. They gave her a friendly welcome. She is still there and she refuses to return or to send her children back.

'I told you that on the very night after Sir Peter had hunted and killed the bear, that delusion came to him while he was asleep in his bed. And people say that the lady knew what would happen as soon as she saw the bear, because her father had once hunted the same beast and had heard a voice saying (though there was no person in sight):

'"You hunt me although I mean you no harm. You will come to an evil end."

'When she saw the bear, the lady remembered how her father had related this, and she recalled how King Peter had had him beheaded without cause. That was the reason why she fainted and why she will never love her husband, but firmly maintains that he will suffer some terrible injury before he dies and that what has happened to him so far is nothing beside what is to come.

'Now I have told you about Sir Peter of Béarn, as you asked me,' said the squire, 'and the tale is quite true, for that is how it was and that was what happened. What do you think of it?'

The strange story had made me very thoughtful and I replied:

'I can quite believe it, and it may well be so. We read in books that in the old days gods and goddesses changed men into beasts and birds at will, and so did women. So it may be that that bear had been a knight hunting in the forests of Biscay. Perhaps he angered some god or goddess in his time and was changed into the shape of a bear and was working out his punishment, just as Actaeon was changed into a stag.'

'Actaeon?' said the squire. 'Good Master Froissart, tell me that tale, will you?'

'With pleasure,' I said. 'We learn from the old books that Actaeon was a skilful, gallant and handsome knight who loved hounds above all other pleasures. It happened one day that he was hunting in the woods of Thessaly and started an extraordinarily fine stag which he hunted all day, losing sight of all his men and of his hounds too. He was absorbed in pursuing the stag and he followed its tracks until he came to a wood or a kind of meadow fringed with tall trees, in the middle of which was a delightful little pool. In this pool Diana, the goddess of chastity, was bathing to cool herself, with her maidens round her. The knight came charging down on them before he even knew they were there; he had gone too far to retreat. Startled and embarrassed by his appearance, the maidens immediately gathered round their mistress to conceal her, for she was ashamed to be found naked. But she rose up above them all, looked at the knight, and said:

'"Actaeon, whoever sent you here was no friend of yours. I will not have you boast, when you are away from this place, that you have seen me or my maidens naked. For this offence you must be punished. My will is that you should take on the likeness and form of the stag which you have been hunting today."

'Actaeon was immediately changed into a stag, whose nature is to love hounds. A similar thing may have happened to the bear you told me about, and possibly the lady knows more about it, or knew more than she said at the time. If so, she ought not to be blamed.'

The squire replied: 'That may be so.'

With that, we ended our talk.

Reminiscences of the Bascot de Mauléon, Freebooter

FROISSART remains at Orthez for Christmas, which the Count celebrates with full religious observances and other festivities. Besides his own vassals numerous knights and squires from neighbouring territories come to Orthez to take part in the celebrations and to pay their court.

Among those who came to the Count's court I met a Gascon squire called the Bascot de Mauléon, a man of about fifty-five with the appearance of a bold and experienced soldier. He arrived with plenty of followers and baggage at the hostelry where I was staying at Orthez – at the sign of the Moon, kept by Ernauton du Pin. He had as many pack-horses with him as any great baron, and he and his people took their meals off silver plate. When I heard his name and saw how warmly he was welcomed by the Count and everyone else, I asked Sir Espan de Lyon: 'Isn't that the squire who gave up the Castle of Tuzaguet[1] when the Duke of Anjou was besieging Mauvezin?'

'Yes,' he said. 'He's a good soldier in these days and a great captain.'

On hearing this I made friends with him, since he was in the same hostelry, through a Gascon cousin of his with whom I was on very good terms, who was the captain of Carlat in Auvergne and was called Ernauton and also the Bourc de Caupenne. In the way one does start talking of arms and warfare, sitting at the fire one night after supper and waiting for midnight to come when the Count had his supper, this cousin set him talking about his past life and the battles he had fought in his time for better or worse, which he remembered very clearly.

1. Froissart has previously related how the Bascot surrendered the castle, a centre of brigandage, to the French forces in return for a safe-conduct to another castle. The Bascot refers to it later in recounting his life. See p. 289 below.

The Bascot asked me: 'Sir John, haven't you got what I'm going to tell you in your chronicle?'

'I don't know whether I have or not,' I said. 'Give me your account of it, for I am very interested to hear you talk of deeds of arms. I can't remember everything in it, and also there are things of which I may not have been informed.'

'True,' said the squire. Whereupon he took up his tale and said this:

'The first time I fought in battle was under the Captal de Buch at Poitiers, and by good luck I took three prisoners on that day, a knight and two squires, who brought me in three thousand francs between them. The next year I was in Prussia with the Count of Foix and his cousin the Captal, whose troop I still belonged to. On our way back through Meaux in Brie we came upon the Duchess of Normandy, the Duchess of Orléans and many other ladies, gentlefolk, whom the Jacks had surrounded in the market-place, and would have raped if God had not sent us there.[1] It was well within their power, for there were over ten thousand of them and the ladies were defenceless. We delivered them from that danger and killed more than six thousand of the Jacks. They never rebelled again.

'At that time there was a truce between the Kings of France and England, but the King of Navarre was making war on his own account against the Regent of France. The Count of Foix went back to his domains, but my master the Captal remained with the King of Navarre and drew his pay from him. We went, with others who were helping us, into the kingdom of France and especially into Picardy, where we started a fierce campaign and took many towns and castles in the bishoprics of Beauvais and Amiens. We became masters of the farmlands and the rivers and we and our friends won a great deal of wealth.

'When the truce between France and England came to an end, the King of Navarre stopped his war because peace was made between the Regent and him. Then the King of England crossed the sea with a great army and laid siege to Rheims.

1. See above, pp. 153-5.

He sent for my master the Captal, who was then at Clermont in Beauvaisis campaigning in support of him. We went to join the King and his sons.'

The squire stopped and said to me: 'But I expect you have all that, and how the King of England went on and reached Chartres, and how peace was made between the two kings?'

'True,' I said, 'I've got it all, and you're describing things exactly as they happened.'

The Bascot de Mauléon went on:

'When this peace was concluded, one of its conditions was that all fighting-men and companions-in-arms must clear out of the forts and castles they held. So large numbers of poor companions trained in war came out and collected together. Some of the leaders held a conference about where they should go and they said that, though the kings had made peace, they had to live somehow. They went to Burgundy and they had captains of all nationalities, English, Gascons, Spaniards, Navarrese, Germans, Scots and men from every country, and I was there as a captain. There were more than twelve thousand of us in Burgundy and along the Loire, counting everyone.

'And I tell you that in that assembly there were three or four thousand really fine soldiers, as trained and skilled in war as any man could be, wonderful men at planning a battle and seizing the advantage, at scaling and assaulting towns and castles, as expert and experienced as you could ask for – and didn't we show it at the battle of Brignais, when we thrashed the Constable of France and the Count of Forez with a good two thousand lances of knights and squires.

'That battle was a godsend to the companions, for they were very hard up. They all grew rich on good prisoners and the towns and fortresses they took in the archbishopric of Lyons and down the Rhône. The crowning touch to the campaign was the capture of Pont-Saint-Esprit, for then they made war on the Pope and the Cardinals and really made them squeal. They could not get rid of them, and never would have done until everything had been destroyed if they had not thought of a way out. They sent to Lombardy to invite the Marquis of Montferrat, who was at war with the Lord of Milan. When he reached Avignon the Pope and cardinals made an agreement with him and he talked to the English, Gascon and German captains. On payment of sixty thousand francs by the Pope and the cardinals, several captains of companies, such as Sir John Hawkwood, a fine English knight, Sir Robert Briquet, Carsuelle, Naudon of Bageran, the Bourc of Breteuil, the Bourc Camus, the Bourc of Lesparre, Bataillé, and several others gave up Pont-Saint-Esprit and went off to Lombardy, taking three-fifths of all the men with them. But we stayed behind, Sir Seguin de Badefol, Sir Jean Jouel, Sir Jacques Planchin, Lamit, Sir John Aimery, the Bourc of Périgord, Espiote, Louis Roubaut, Limosin, Jacques Tiriel, myself and several others. We had Anse, Saint-Clément, L'Arbresle, La Terrasse, Brignais, Mont-Saint-Denis, L'Hôpital-sous-Rochefort and more than sixty forts in the Mâconnais, in Forez, Velay, Lower Burgundy and on the Loire, and we held the whole country to ransom. They couldn't get rid of us, either by paying us good money or otherwise.

'We took La Charité in a night attack and held it for a year and a half and everything was ours along the Loire as far as Le Puy-en-Velay, for Sir Seguin de Badefol had left Anse and was holding Brioude in Auvergne, where he made a hundred thousand francs in gains from the country round, and down the Loire as far as Orléans, and also all along the River Allier. Even the Archpriest,[1] who commanded in Nevers and was a loyal Frenchman at the time, could do nothing about it, except through knowing the companions – on account of which we did do something for him when he asked us to. The Archpriest did a very good thing in Nivernais when he fortified the city of Nevers. Otherwise it would have been taken and plundered many times, because we held about twenty-seven towns and castles in the district round it and there was not a knight or squire or man of means who dared to venture out unless he had bought one of our safe-conducts. We were

1. Regnault de Cervoles, previously a captain of freebooters himself.

carrying on that particular war with the knowledge of the
King of Navarre, and in his name.

'Then came the battle of Cocherel,[1] at which the Captal was
in command for the King of Navarre. A good many knights
and squires from our district went to join him to get some
better fighting. Sir Jacques Planchin and Sir Jean Jouel took
two hundred lances to serve him. At that time I held a castle
called Le Bec d'Allier, fairly near to La Charité as you go towards the Bourbonnais. I had forty lances under my command and I was making very good gains just then in the
Moulins district and round Saint-Pourçain and Saint-Pierre-
le-Moûtier. But when I heard that my master the Captal was
assembling a big force in the Cotentin, I badly wanted to see
him again and left my fortress with twelve lances, joining Sir
Jean Jouel's and Sir Jacques Planchin's company. We reached
the Captal safely without any encounters on the way. I expect
you have all the facts about the battle in your chronicle.'

'Yes,' I said. 'The Captal was taken prisoner and Sir Jean
Jouel and Sir Jacques Planchin were killed.'

'That's right,' said the Bascot de Mauléon. 'I was taken
prisoner there, but I was very lucky. I was captured by a
cousin of mine, who was also the cousin of my cousin the
Bourc de Caupenne, who's sitting here now. He was a fellow
called Bernard de Terride. He was killed later in Portugal, in
the Juberot affair.[2] Bernard, who was then serving under Sir
Aymon de Pommiers, ransomed me on the field for a thousand francs and gave me a safe-conduct back to my castle at
Le Bec d'Allier. As soon as I got there, I called one of my men,
counted out the thousand francs and gave them him. He took
the money to Paris, and brought me back the discharge and
the receipt.

'In that same year Sir John Aimery, an English knight
and the greatest captain we had, was out marauding, and was

1. Between a French army commanded by Du Guesclin and the King of
Navarre's forces led, as Froissart says, by the Captal de Buch (May 1364).
2. The Battle of Aljubarrota, in which the Portuguese defeated the
Spanish (1385).

following the bank of the Loire to reach La Charité. He fell into an ambush laid by the Lords of Rougement and Voudenay and the Archpriest's men. They were too strong for him and beat him, and he was ransomed for thirty thousand francs, which he paid in cash. He was furious at his capture and the loss, and swore he would not return to his castle until he had got his own back. He assembled a large number of companions, and went to La Charité-sur-Loire, where he asked the captains, Lamit, Carsuelle, the Bourc of Périgord and myself, who was there on pleasure, if we were willing to go on a raid with him. We asked him where to. "This is it," he said. "We'll cross the Loire at Port Saint-Thibaut and go and capture and plunder the town and castle of Sancerre. I've sworn an oath not to go back to any fortress of mine until I've had a sight of the Sancerre boys.[1] If we could get the garrison and the boys inside, Jean, Louis and Robert, we should recover our losses and be sitting on top of the whole country. We could do it quite easily, because they are not expecting us, and then we're doing ourselves no good by sitting here."

' "That's true," we said.

'We all agreed to his plan and began our preparations at once.

'Now it happened,' the Bascot de Mauléon went on, 'that the garrison of Sancerre got to know of our scheme. At that time they had a captain, a fine soldier called Guichard Aubergeon who was a native of Lower Burgundy and who made a splendid job of guarding the town and castle of Sancerre, with the young lords inside it, who were all knights by then. This Guichard had a brother who was a monk in the Abbey of Saint-Thibaut, quite near Sancerre. The monk was sent by his brother to La Charité-sur-Loire to deliver some protection-money owed by some neighbouring towns. No one took much notice of him and somehow he found out the whole of our plan, with all the names of the captains of the forts round La Charité and the strength of their contingents, and also the

1. The Count of Sancerre and his two brothers, no doubt good for valuable ransoms.

time when we were going to cross the river at Port Saint-
Thibaut and the way we intended to do it. Thereupon he went
back and told his brother.

'The Sancerre boys, the Count and his brothers, began
their preparations against us as quickly as they could and sent
word to the knights and squires of Berry and the Bourbonnais
and the captains of the garrisons around, until they had at
least four hundred lances of first-class men. They set up a
well-laid ambush of two hundred lances in a wood outside
Sancerre.

'We left La Charité at sunset and rode in order at a brisk
pace as far as Pouilly. We had had a lot of boats brought together in the port down below to take ourselves and our
horses across. So we crossed the Loire as planned and by
about midnight we were all on the other side with our horses.
Because it would soon be light, we left a hundred lances to
guard the horses and the boats, while the rest of us went on
and marched right past the ambush, which let us go without
moving a finger.

'When we were about three-quarters of a mile past it, they
came out and fell upon our men on the river-bank. They got
in among them and thrashed them thoroughly, killing or capturing them all and taking the horses and boats as well. Then
they got on our horses and spurred them forward and reached
the town as soon as we did. They shouted: "Our Lady!
Sancerre!" because the Count was there with his men and it
was his brothers who had laid the ambush. We were properly
hemmed in and hardly knew which way to face. There was a
great set-to with lances, because, as soon as the mounted men
reached us, they got off the horses and attacked us fiercely.
What hampered us most was that we could not spread out,
because we were going along a road with tall hedges and
vines on both sides of it. Some of their men who knew the
country and this road well had climbed up the vine slopes
with their servants and were throwing stones at us from
above, which bruised us and threw us into disorder. We could
not retreat, yet it was very difficult to advance towards the
town because it lies on a steep hill.

'So they gave us a thorough mauling and our commander-in-chief, Sir John Aimery, was run right through the body by Guichard Aubergeon. Guichard made him his prisoner and did all he could to save him. He took him to a hostelry in the town and had him laid on a bed, and said to the host: "Take good care of this prisoner and make sure his wound is properly seen to. If he stays alive, he's big enough to pay me twenty thousand francs."

'After this, Guichard left his prisoner and returned to the battle, where he went on fighting beside the others. There also, in the company of the Sancerre boys, were Sir Guichard Dauphin, the Lord of Talus, the Lord of Mornay, Sir Gérard and Sir Guillaume de Bourbon, the Lord of Couzan, the Lord of La Pierre, the Lord of La Palice, the Lord of Nançay, Sir Louis de La Croise, the Lord of La Frète and others who had joined them for the love of arms and to help defend the region.

'I can tell you it was a hard and nasty battle, and we held out for as long as we could, so that there were a lot of killed and wounded on both sides. By the look of them they preferred to get us alive rather than dead. Finally, we were all captured, Carsuelle, Lamit, Naudon of Périgord, Espiote, the Bourc of Lesparre, Angerot de Lamongis, Philippe de Roie, Pierre de Curton, Lepesat de Pamiers, the Bourc of Ornesan and all our captains from round about. We were taken to the castle of Sancerre and greeted with shouts of joy. Never in the kingdom of France have the Free Companions had such a setback as we suffered then. Still, Guichard Aubergeon lost his prisoner, for the man who was looking after him, through sheer viciousness and carelessness, let him bleed so much that he died. That was the end of Sir John Aimery.

'As a result of the defeat at Sancerre, La Charité-sur-Loire and all the garrisons round it surrendered to the French, upon which all of us were set free and given safe-conducts out of France to go wherever we pleased. Very fortunately for us an expedition was mounted in that same year by Sir Bertrand du Guesclin, the Lord of Beaujeu, Sir Arnoul d'Audrehem

and the Count of La Marche to go to Spain in support of
King Henry against his brother, Don Pedro. But before that,
I was in Brittany at the battle of Auray under Sir Hugh Calveley. I recovered some of my losses, for we won that battle
and I had some good prisoners who earned me two thousand
francs. So I went to Spain under Sir Hugh Calveley with a
command of ten lances and we drove King Peter out. Later
on, when there was an alliance between King Peter and the
Prince of Wales and he wished to put him back on the throne
of Castile – which he did – I was there, again in Sir Hugh
Calveley's company, and I returned to Aquitaine with him.

'Then war was started again between the King of France
and the Prince. We were kept very busy because they fought
us really hard and many English and Gascon captains were
killed, though I stayed alive, thank God. First, Sir Robert
Briquet was killed in Orléanais at a place called Olivet between Blois and the domains of the Duke of Orléans. He and
his whole company were wiped out by a squire from Hainault, a tough fighting-man and a fine captain, called Alart de
Donstienne, who bore the arms of Barbançon because he came
of noble family. He was governor of Blois at the time and in
command of the whole district for my lords Louis, Jean and
Guy de Blois. Well, he happened to meet Sir Robert Briquet
and Sir Robert Cheney at Olivet. He thrashed them thoroughly
and they were both killed, with all their men. Not a single
prisoner was taken.

'Some time after that, at the battle of Niort in Saintonge,
Carsuelle was beaten and killed by Sir Bertrand du Guesclin,
and at least seven hundred English all died in that affair.
Then at Sainte-Sévère the English captains Richard Giles and
Richard Holme were also killed. I know of very few, except
myself, who were not killed somewhere in battle. But I have
always held the frontier and fought for the King of England,
for my family estate lies in the Bordeaux district. Sometimes I
have been so thoroughly down that I hadn't even a horse to
ride, and at other times fairly rich, as luck came and went.
Once Raymonnet de l'Épée and I were companions-in-arms
and we held three castles near Toulouse on the frontier of

Bigorre, the castle of Mauvezin, the castle of Tuzaguet and the castle of Lutilhous. They yielded us great gains for a time. Then the Duke of Anjou came and turned us out by force. Raymonnet de l'Épée was captured and went over to the French, but I remained a loyal Englishman, and shall be as long as I live.

'Now, after I had lost the castle of Tuzaguet and been taken to Castelculier and the Duke of Anjou had withdrawn to France,[1] I decided that I must do something to bring me in some money, if I was not to go on living in poverty. So I sent some men to prospect the town and castle of Thurie, near Albi, which castle has since brought me in, through plunder, protection-money and various strokes of luck which I've had, one hundred thousand francs. Let me tell you how I got it.

'Outside the place there is an excellent spring, to which the women from the town used to come every morning with their pitchers and buckets to draw water and carry it back on their heads. I determined to have the place and took fifty companions from the garrison of Castelculier, and we rode a whole day through woods and heathland. At about midnight I placed the men in ambush near the town and went on myself with five others dressed as women, with pitchers in our hands. We reached a meadow outside the town and hid ourselves in a haystack, for it was about midsummer and they had just cut the hay. When it was time for the gate to be opened and the women began coming out to the spring, all of us took our pitchers, filled them and started towards the town, covering our faces with kerchiefs. No one would have recognized us. The women we met on the way said: "Holy Virgin, how early you've got up!" We disguised our voices and answered in their patois: "Yes, haven't we?" and so went past them and reached the gate. We found no one there to guard it except a cobbler who was setting up his lasts and rivets. One of us blew a horn to bring up the others who were waiting in ambush. The cobbler was paying no attention to us, but when he heard

1. See above, p. 280.

the horn he asked us: "Hi, girls, who was that blowing a
horn?" One of us answered: "It's a priest going out for a
ride. I don't know if it's the vicar or the town chaplain."
"Oh yes," he said, "it's Master Francis, the parish priest. He's
very fond of going out in the morning after hares."

'Immediately after this the rest of us arrived and we entered
the town, where we found not a man ready to put hand to
sword in its defence.

'That was how I captured the town and castle of Thurie,
which has brought me in greater profits and income yearly –
and any day when it happened to be a good moment – than
the castle and all the dependencies of this place would fetch
if they were sold at their best price. But now I don't know
what I ought to do with it. I am negotiating with the Count of
Armagnac and the Dauphin of Auvergne who have been given
special powers by the King of France to buy towns and fortresses from companions who hold them in Auvergne,
Rouergue, Quercy, Limosin, Périgord, the Albigeois and the
Agenais, and from any who are fighting or have fought in the
King of England's name. Several have already given up their
castles and gone. But I don't know whether I shall give mine
up or not.'

At this point the Bourc de Caupenne broke in and said:
'You are right there, cousin. It's the same with my castle of
Carlat in Auvergne. That's why I've come to Orthez to find
out more about it at the Count's court. Lord Louis de Sancerre, Marshal of France, should be here soon. He's stuck at
Tarbes at the moment, or so I hear from people who've seen
him there.'

Thereupon they called for wine. It was brought, and we
drank, and then the Bascot de Mauléon said to me: 'Well, Sir
John, what do you say? Have I given you a good account of
my life? I have had quite a lot more adventures than I told
you of, but I can't and won't talk about them all.'

'Indeed, sir,' I said, 'it was well worth hearing.'

I set him talking again and asked him about Louis Roubaut,
a great fighting squire and captain of men whom I had once

seen in Avignon looking very prosperous. What had happened to him?

'I will tell you,' said the Bascot. 'A long time ago, after Sir Seguin de Badefol had held Brioude in Velay, thirty miles from Le Puy, and had harassed the country round and won enough from it, he went back to Gascony and gave Brioude and Anse on the Saône to Louis Roubaut and a companion of his called Limosin. At the time I am speaking of, the country was so bruised and battered and so full of companions in every place that hardly anyone dared to go out-of-doors. Now, from Brioude to Anse the distance is over seventy-five miles, all over mountainous country. But when Louis Roubaut wished to go from one to the other, he thought nothing of it, because they held several castles in the County of Forez and elsewhere in which they could break the journey. The gentry of Auvergne, Forez and Velay were so worn down by the war, or else were prisoners or paying ransoms, that they were afraid to take up arms against them. There were no great lords in France to lead forces into the country districts, for the King was young and had to attend to too many different parts of his kingdom. There were Companies everywhere and troops roving about or settling on the country and no one could get rid of them. The great lords were hostages in England[1] and meanwhile their people and their country were being pillaged and ruined and they could do nothing about it because their men had no stomach for fighting or even for defending themselves.

'Well, Louis Roubaut and Limosin, who were brothers-in-arms, became bitter enemies, for this reason: Louis Roubaut had a very beautiful woman at Brioude as his mistress, and he loved her passionately. During his journeys from Brioude to Anse, he used to entrust her to his great friend Limosin, in whom he had complete faith. Limosin looked after the good lady so well that he got all he wanted from her, until Louis Roubaut found out everything about it. The discovery

1. This was soon after the death of King John (1364), when many French nobles were still kept in England as hostages for the ransoms exacted after Poitiers.

filled him with such hatred for his friend that, so as to shame
him more, he told his servants to seize him and had him
stripped to his breeches and flogged through the town.
The trumpet was sounded ahead of him and at each cross-
roads his misdeed was announced; then he was declared
banished from the town as a traitor and thrown out just as
he was, with a cheap tunic to cover his back. That was
what Louis Roubaut did to Limosin, and Limosin took it
deeply to heart and said he would get his revenge when he
could.

'In Limosin's prosperous days, when he used to go marauding between Brioude and Anse and also plundering the district of Velay, he had always kept well clear of the lands of the
Lord of La Voulte, a baron living near the Rhône, because he
had served him as a boy. He thought he would go back into
his service and would ask his pardon and beg him to make his
peace for him in France, promising to be a good and loyal
Frenchman for ever after. He arrived at La Voulte – he knew the
way well enough – and went to an inn, for he was travelling
on foot. When he knew that it was the right time, he went up
to the lord's castle. They would not let him in, but he told
some sort of story and pleaded so hard that the porter allowed
him to stand in the gateway, forbidding him to come in any
farther without orders. He obeyed readily.

'In the evening the Lord of La Voulte took a stroll in the
courtyard and came to the gate. Limosin immediately flung
himself on his knees before him and said: "My lord, don't you
recognize me?" "Devil take it," said the lord of the castle,
"I don't." But after he had had a good look at him, he said:
"You're very like Limosin who used to be my servant." "Yes,
my lord," said the other, "I am Limosin, and your servant
too."

'Then he begged his forgiveness for all that had happened
in the past and told his whole story, describing how Louis
Roubaut had ill-treated him. At the end of it, the Lord of La
Voulte said: "Limosin, if things are as you say and you wish
to be a good and loyal Frenchman, I will make your peace
with everyone." "My lord, I promise you," he answered, "I

will do more good to the kingdom of France than I ever did it harm." "Well, we'll see," said the Lord of La Voulte.

'The lord kept him in the castle without allowing him to go out until he had made his peace with everyone round. When he could ride again as an honourable man, the Lord of La Voulte gave him a horse and armour and took him to the Seneschal of Velay at Le Puy, and introduced him. He was questioned closely about the state of things in Brioude and also about Louis Roubaut, and which roads he took when he was travelling about. He revealed everything and said: "When Louis rides out, he doesn't take more than thirty or forty lances with him. As for the roads, I know them all by heart, for I've covered them many times, with and without him. If you will mount an expedition of men-at-arms, I'll stake my head that you'll have him within a fortnight."

'The nobles took him at his word. Spies were set to work. Louis Roubaut was followed and it was found that he had gone from Brioude to Anse. When Limosin was sure of this, he said to the Lord of La Voulte: "Sir, give your orders, it's time now. Louis Roubaut is at Anse and will soon be going back. I will take you to the pass which he must go through."

An ambush is laid and Louis Roubaut is captured

'When Limosin saw that Louis Roubaut was caught, he showed himself to him and said reproachfully: "Louis, Louis, this is where friendship ends. Remember the shame and disgrace that you brought on me at Brioude because of your mistress. I would not have thought that for a woman, if she was willing and I was willing, you would have made me take what I did take. If you had done the same thing to me, I should never have minded, for two companions-in-arms, such as we were then, could surely, at a pinch, have overlooked a woman."

'On hearing this the lords began to laugh, but Louis did not find it funny.

'After Louis Roubaut's capture the garrison of Brioude surrendered to the Seneschal of Auvergne, for they were demoralized by the loss of their captain, and their best men with him.

The garrisons of Anse and the other fortresses they held in
Velay and Forez did the same and they were happy to be permitted to escape with their lives. Louis Roubaut was taken
to Annonay and imprisoned there. A written report of his
capture was sent to the King of France, who was delighted by
the news. Quite soon after he was sentenced. I believe, by
what I heard, that he was beheaded at Villeneuve near Avignon. So that was the end of Louis Roubaut. May God have
mercy on his soul!

'Well, my dear sir,' said the Bascot de Mauléon, 'I've done
a lot of talking to while away the time. But it's all true.'

'I'm sure it is,' I told him, 'and many, many thanks. I have
enjoyed hearing you talk as much as the others and your
words will not be wasted. If God permits me to return to my
native country, I shall include the events you have related in
my chronicles, together with all the other things I have seen
or found out on my journey. They will naturally have a place
in the important work of history which the most noble Count
of Blois has commissioned me to write, so that, with other
events I have described in the same work and, God willing,
shall describe in the future, they will always be remembered.'

On hearing this, the Bourc de Caupenne began speaking
and would readily, as I could see, have related the life-story
and adventures of himself and his brother, the Bourc Anglais,
and the fighting they had seen in Auvergne and elsewhere.
But he had no time to tell his tale, because the signal was
sounded at the castle to summon all those down in the town
who were expected to be present at the Count's supper. The
two squires had torches lit and we set out together from the
hostelry on our way up to the castle, as did all the other
knights and squires who were lodged in the town.

The Tale of the Familiar

THREE *years before Froissart's visit to Foix, the Portuguese had inflicted a crushing defeat on the Castilians at Aljubarrota. A strong contingent from Béarn had gone to fight for King Juan of Castile against their Count's advice, and the majority of them perished. The battle was fought on a Saturday (14 August 1385).*

I must tell you a very strange story which was told to me in the Count's castle by the same man who informed me about the battle of Aljubarrota and all that had happened in that campaign. Since I heard this squire's tale, which I will relate to you in a moment, I have thought about it a hundred times and shall remember it as long as I live.

'It is absolutely true,' the squire said to me, 'that on the day after the battle was fought the Count of Foix knew about it, though how he could have done was a complete mystery. On the Sunday, the Monday and the Tuesday after it, he stayed in the castle living so plainly and gloomily that no one could get a word out of him. He would not even leave his room during those three days, or see any of the knights and squires who were closest to him unless he sent for them specially. And to some he did send for he spoke not a word during the whole time. On the Tuesday evening he called in his brother, Sir Arnaut Guillaume, and said to him very quietly: "Our men have had a rough time. What I said would happen when they left has happened." Sir Arnaut Guillaume is a very shrewd man who understands his brother's ways and temperament, and he said nothing. The Count, who had nursed his depression long enough and wished to unburden himself, began speaking again, louder this time, and said: "By God, Arnaut, things are as I told you. We shall soon have the news of it, for it is a hundred years since the land of Béarn lost so many in a single day as have died this time in Portugal." Several knights and squires who were standing round heard the Count's words and remembered them, and within ten days they were confirmed by those who returned from the battle and related, first to the Count, and afterwards to everyone else who wanted to hear, exactly what had happened at Aljubarrota. The Count's grief was renewed and families were plunged into mourning for the brothers, fathers, sons and friends they had lost.'

'Holy Virgin!' I said. 'But how could the Count have known or guessed it from one day to the next? I should like to know that.' 'Anyway,' said the squire, 'he did know. It was obvious.' 'Does he have second sight?' I said, 'or does he have messengers who ride at night on the winds? He must possess some magic powers.' The squire laughed and said: 'He must know of these things by some kind of necromancy. We don't really know how he does it, except by his imaginings.' 'Come, my dear sir,' I said, 'tell me more about these "imaginings" you are thinking of, and you will earn my gratitude. If it is something which ought to be kept quiet, I will do so. As long as I am in this country, I will not say a word about it.' 'No, please don't,' said the squire. 'I wouldn't like anyone to know that I told you. But some people do talk about it privately when they are among friends.'

With that, he took me aside into an angle of the wall of the castle chapel and began his tale.

'Something like twenty years ago there was an influential baron in this country called Raymond, Lord of Corresse. Corresse, you understand, is a town with a castle about twenty miles from this town of Orthez. At the time of which I am speaking the Lord of Corresse had a case before the Pope's court in Avignon over the tithes of the church in his town. He was in dispute with a cleric from Catalonia, who was very learned in canon law and claimed to have a strong right to the Corresse tithes, which were worth at least a hundred florins a year. He clearly proved his case and Pope Urban V in consistory gave a definitive judgement in his favour and rejected the knight's plea. The cleric armed himself with documents showing this final decision of the Pope's, travelled to Béarn and produced them, and on the strength of the papal bull took possession of the tithe-rights. The Lord of Corresse was indignant with the cleric and all his works. He went to find him and said: "Master Peter (or Master Martin, or whatever his name was), do you think I am going to give up my inheritance because of your papers? I doubt if you will be so bold as to make off with things that are mine, for if you do you will be risking your life. Now go and look somewhere else for a benefice. You are not going to get anything from my estate, and once for all I'm telling you to keep off."

'The cleric was scared of the knight, who was a violent man, and he dared not insist. He gave up and decided to go back, either to Avignon or to his own country, but just before he left he went to the Lord of Corresse and said to him: "Sir, by force and not by right you are depriving me of the rights of my church, and in all conscience you are acting very wrongly. I am not as strong as you are in this country, but I would like you to know that as soon as I can I shall send you a champion who will frighten you more than I do." The baron made light of these threats and said: "Go with God, go along, do your worst. You might as well be dead for all the effect you have on me. All your words won't make me give up my estate."

'So the cleric left the Lord of Corresse and went back to Avignon or Catalonia, I'm not sure which. But he did not forget what he had said and about three months later, when the knight was least expecting it, there came to his castle at Corresse, while he was asleep in bed beside his wife, invisible messengers who started bumping and banging all over the castle, so loudly that it seemed they would break everything down. They pounded so hard on the door of the knight's room that his wife, as she lay in bed, was terrified. The knight heard it all but made no remark, not wishing to appear surprised. Also, he was a determined enough man to face anything.

'The knocking and banging went on for a long time in several parts of the castle, and then stopped. Next morning all the household servants assembled and came to their master as he was getting up and said: "My lord, didn't you hear what we heard last night?" The baron pretended to know nothing and said: "No, what did you hear?" Then they told him that something had gone storming through his castle, and knocked over and broken all the crockery in the kitchen. He began to laugh and said that they had been dreaming and it was only the wind. "Before God," said his lady, "I heard it."

'The next night the noise-makers came back and raised a greater commotion than before, banging even more loudly on the door and windows of the knight's room. The knight started up in bed and could not stop himself saying: "Who's that banging at my door at this hour of night?" A voice immediately answered: "It's me, it's me." "Who sent you here?" the knight asked. "The priest from Catalonia whom you have wronged by taking away the dues of his benefice. I shall not leave you in peace until you have restored them and he is satisfied." "You're a good messenger," said the knight. "What is your name?" "My name is Orton." "Orton," said the knight, "serving a cleric will get you nowhere. You will have endless trouble if you believe all he tells you. Now leave him, please, and serve me. I shall always be grateful to you."

'Orton quickly made up his mind, for he found that he liked the knight, and he said: "Do you mean it?" "Yes," said the Lord of Corresse. "Providing you do no harm to anyone in this house, I should like you to work for me, and we shall get on well." "That's all right," said Orton. "I have no power to do harm beyond disturbing you or other people and waking you up when you want to sleep." "Then do as I ask," said the knight, "it will suit us both. And leave that hopeless, miserable cleric. There will be nothing but toil and trouble for you if you stay with him." "Well, since you want me," said Orton, "I'll come to you."

'After that Orton grew so fond of the Lord of Corresse that he constantly came to see him at night and if he found him asleep he tugged at his pillow or gave great bangs on the doors and windows. When it woke the knight he used to say: "Orton, please, do let me sleep," and Orton would say: "No, I won't, not till I've told you the news." The knight's wife was so frightened that her hair stood on end and she hid under the blankets, but the knight would go on to ask: "What

298

news have you got for me and which country have you been to?" Orton would say: "England, or Germany, or Hungary, or some other country. I left there yesterday and such-and-such a thing has happened."

'In this way the Lord of Corresse knew everything that was going on in the world. Their friendship continued for five or six years and the knight could not keep it secret, but mentioned it to the Count of Foix. During the first year, when the Lord of Corresse attended the Count at Orthez or elsewhere, he used to say: "My lord, such-and-such an event has occurred in England, or Scotland, or Germany, or Flanders, or Brabant, or somewhere else," and when the Count found out later that it was true, he was very puzzled to understand how he had known of it. One day he pressed him so hard that the Lord of Corresse told him the whole story, to the Count's delight. "Baron," he said, "keep on good terms with him. I wish I had a messenger like that. He costs you nothing and yet brings you reliable news of everything that happens in the world." "My lord," the knight replied, "I shall take good care of that."

'So Orton went on serving the Lord of Corresse for quite a long time. I do not know whether he had other masters, but two or three times a week he would come at night with the news from the various places he had visited, and the Lord of Corresse would write it to the Count of Foix who was delighted to have it, for he took more interest than almost any other ruler in what was going on in foreign countries. One day when the knight and the Count were chatting good-humouredly about Orton, the Count happened to say: "Baron, have you never actually seen your messenger?" "Good heavens, no, my lord," he answered, "and I've never really pressed him." "No?" said the Count. "That's surprising. If he was as friendly with me as he is with you, I should have asked him to appear to me. Why not try doing it? Then you could tell me what form he takes on – what he looks like. You told me that he speaks Gascon just like you and me." "Yes indeed," said the knight, "he speaks it just as well as you and me. Upon my word, I will have a try at seeing him, now you've suggested it."

'Soon afterwards the Lord of Corresse was in bed as usual, lying beside his wife who by now had grown accustomed to hearing Orton and had lost her fear of him. Orton came and tugged at the pillow, waking the knight from a sound sleep. "Who's that?" he asked. "It's me, of course, Orton." "And where have you come from?" "From Prague in Bohemia. The Roman Emperor is dead." "When did he die?" "The day before yesterday." "How far is it from Prague in Bohemia?" "How far?" he said. "A good sixty days' journey." "And you got here so quickly?" "Yes, of course. I go as fast as the wind, or faster." "Have you got wings?" "No, of course not." "Then how can you travel so fast?" "That is something you do not need to know," said Orton. "Oh, yes," said the knight, "I should very much like to see you, to know what you look like." Orton said again: "You do not need to know. It is enough for you to hear me and know that I bring you sure and certain news." "Come, come, Orton," said the Lord of Corresse, "I should love you better if I had seen you." Orton answered: "Well, since you so much want to see me, look at the first thing you come upon when you get out of bed tomorrow morning. That will be me." "That's good enough," said the Lord of Corresse. "Now go, you are excused for tonight."

'When the Lord of Corresse was preparing to get up next morning, his lady was so frightened that she pretended to feel ill and said that she would spend the day in bed, and when her husband begged her to get up, "No thank you," she said, "I should see Orton. I don't want to, please God, I don't want to see him or meet him." "But I do," said the knight and he got straight out of bed and sat on the edge of it, expecting to see Orton in his true form, but he saw nothing. Then he went and opened the window to let more light into the room, but he still saw nothing of which he could say, "That is Orton."

'That day passed and night fell. When the Lord of Corresse was in bed, Orton came again and began talking in his usual way. "That's enough," said the knight. "You're just a joker. You were to show yourself to me yesterday and you

did nothing of the kind." "But I did!" he said, "I swear I
did!" "You didn't!" "But when you got out of bed," said
Orton, "didn't you see anything?" The Lord of Corresse
thought for a little and then remembered. "Yes," he said,
"while I was sitting on the bed thinking of you, I did see
two long straws twirling and twisting about together on the
floor." "That was me," said Orton. "That was the form I had
taken on." "That's not good enough," said the Lord of
Corresse. "Please take on another shape, in which I can really
see you and recognize you." "If you go on like this I shall get
tired of you and you will lose me. You are asking too much."
"No, no," said the knight, "and you won't get tired of me.
If I could see you just once, I would never ask you again."
"Very well," said Orton, "you shall see me tomorrow. Remember that the first thing you see when you come out of
your room will be me." "That's all right, then," said the
knight. "Now go away for today. You are excused. I want to
get some sleep."

'Orton went away. At nine o'clock the next morning the
Lord of Corresse came out of his room ready dressed and
went along a gallery which gave on to the courtyard. He
looked down there and the first thing he saw was the most
enormous sow he had ever seen, but it was so thin that it
seemed to be nothing but skin and bones and it had great
long teats dangling under it and a long hungry-looking snout.
The knight wondered how it had got there and was by no
means pleased to see it in his courtyard. He called to his
men: "Quick, let the dogs out, I want that sow to be sav-
aged." Servants came up and opened the kennels and set the
dogs on the sow. The sow uttered a loud cry and looked
straight up at the Lord of Corresse as he leaned out of the
gallery. It was not seen again, for it disappeared, and no one
knew where it went to. The knight went back to his room very
thoughtfully, remembering Orton and saying to himself:
"I believe I've seen my messenger. I'm sorry now that I had
the dogs loosed on him. Perhaps I shall never see him again.
He told me several times that if I offended him he would not
come back and I should lose him." He was right. Orton never

returned to the castle and the knight died before the year was out.

'Now I've told you the story of Orton and how willingly for a time he brought the news to the Lord of Corresse.' 'Yes,' I said to the squire who had been telling me the tale, 'you have. But to go back to the reason why you began, is the Count of Foix served by a similar messenger?' 'To tell the truth,' he replied, 'many people in Béarn imagine that he is, for nothing is done in this country – and outside it, too – in which he is really interested, but he knows about it at once, however closely the secret is guarded. That was how it was with the news about the knights and squires from here who lost their lives in Portugal. In any case, the reputation he has for knowing things is of great benefit to him. One could not lose a gold or silver spoon in this castle, or anything else, without him knowing at once.'

Thereupon I took leave of the squire and found other company, among whom I relaxed and amused myself. But I took careful note of the whole story as he told it me, and such as I have related it here.

Early in 1389 Froissart took leave of the Count of Foix and left Béarn. In his following chapters he goes back to describe events which occurred during the two or three previous years, though not always in their exact chronological order.

The French prepared to invade England in both 1385 and 1386. The English were at first uncertain whether England or Calais was to be the object of attack.

Preparations for a French Invasion of England (1386)

THE King of France, with his uncles and his counsellors, were fully informed of the expedition which the Duke of Lancaster was to take to Castile[1] well before it left England, for rumours spread rapidly. They knew that the Spaniards would have to meet an attack, which explained why the Duke of Burgundy had so readily made peace with the people of Ghent, in order to be free to give support to the King of Castile, to whom the French were greatly indebted for a number of reasons. It was due to the King of Castile's seamen and warships that the affairs of France were prospering. Besides that, the young King Charles of France was eager to lead an army of invasion across to England, and in this he had the backing of his knights and squires, and particularly of the Duke of Burgundy, the Constable of France, the Count of Saint-Pol – although he was married to King Richard of England's sister[2] – and the Lord de Coucy. These lords said, and most of the French knights with them: 'Why shouldn't we go over to England for once and have a look at the country and the people? We'll get to know our way about there, just as the English did in their time in France.'

So in that year 1386, both to prevent the Duke of Lancaster's expedition or force it to withdraw from Galicia and Castile, and to threaten the English and see what response they would make, huge preparations were undertaken in France. Taxes were imposed on everyone without exception, in the cities, towns and country districts, to such amounts that more was raised in France in that year than at any other time for the past century.

Great preparations were also made on the sea-coast. Right through the summer until September there was a continual milling of flour and baking of biscuits at Tournay, Lille,

1. See below, p. 328.   2 His half-sister, Matilda Holland.

Douay, Arras, Amiens, Béthune, Saint-Omer and all the towns near to Sluys. It was the intention of the King and his council that the embarkation should take place at Sluys and that from there they should sail to England and ravage the country. To pay for the expedition and have sufficient ships, the rich in France were taxed a quarter or a third of their fortunes, while many smaller men were taxed at more than they possessed to provide the pay of the men-at-arms.

The whole way from the port of Seville in Spain right round to Prussia, there was no big ship at sea which the French could lay their hands on, or had already under their control, which was not reserved for the King and his army. In addition to that, supplies were arriving in Flanders from many places. There were vast amounts of wines, salted meat, hay, oats, barrels of salt, onions, wine-vinegar, biscuits, flour, fats, beaten egg-yolks in barrels, in short everything that could be thought of and which in days to come will seem incredible to those who did not see it . . .

From midsummer on orders were sent to Holland and Zealand, Middelburg, Overyssel, Dordrecht, Schoonhoven, and the other sea-ports or river-ports to commandeer all the big ships which could be used in the enterprise and bring them to Sluys. But when the ships had been bespoken, the Hollanders and Zealanders said: 'If you want us to join you and be in your service, pay us in cash now. Otherwise we shall take no part in it.' They took their money, which was a wise precaution, before they would leave home and harbour. Never, since God created the world, had so many ships and great vessels been seen together as there were that year in the port of Sluys and off the coast between Sluys and Blankenberghe, for by September their number amounted to thirteen hundred and eighty-seven. As you stood at Sluys looking out to sea, you saw a whole forest of masts. Yet this did not include the fleet of the Constable of France, Sir Olivier de Clisson, which was being fitted out at Tréguier in Brittany. To go with it, the Constable was getting carpenters to build the enclosing walls of a town, made entirely of good, strong timber, to be set down in England wherever desired after landing. Inside this the lords could be quartered at night, to avoid the dangers of surprise attacks and to sleep more comfortably and securely. For movement from place to place, this town was so constructed that it could be taken down by loosening the joints, which toothed into each other, and reassembled section by section. There were large numbers of carpenters who had designed and built the thing and knew how it worked. They were kept on at high wages to manipulate it.

Among this armada intended for England, I heard no mention of the Duke of Brittany, who made no appearance or preparations in Flanders, nor of the King's younger brother, the Duke of Touraine, nor of the Count of Alençon or the Count of Blois. But everyone could not go; some had to stay in France to help protect the realm. But anyone who was at Bruges or Damme or Sluys at that time and saw the ships being busily loaded, the trusses of hay being packed in barrels, biscuits put into sacks, and the barrelfuls and so on of onions, garlic, peas, beans, olives, barley, oats, rye, wheat, tallow and wax candles, gaiters, shoes, leg-hose, boots, spurs, knives, axes, hatchets, picks, mattocks, wooden hurdles, boxes of ointment, bandages, dressings, camp-beds, nails and shoes for the horses, bottles of verjuice and vinegar, goblets, mugs, wooden and pewter dishes, candle-sticks, basins, pots, gridirons, cooking utensils, drinking utensils, other utensils and implements and everything that can be thought of to supply the bodily needs of men goi g across the sea – it can be said that the interest and fascination of seeing all this were so great that a man suffering from fever or tooth-ache would have forgotten all his pains as he walked about there. And those French soldiers, to hear them talking, considered England to be already crushed and devastated, all her men killed, and her women and children brought to France and held in slavery. . . .

The great lords vied with one another to make lavish preparations and to embellish their ships with their badges and coats-of-arms. Painters certainly had a prosperous time. They were paid whatever they liked to ask and they refused to give any reductions. Banners, pennants and silken streamers of really surpassing beauty were made. The masts were painted from top to bottom and many, to advertise their wealth and power, had them covered with fine gold-leaf, over which were painted the arms of the lords to whom the ships belonged. I was told in particular that Sir Guy de La Trémoille had his personal ship magnificently decorated and that the devices and paintings which were done on it cost over two thousand francs. The great lords did everything that could possibly be thought of to beautify their ships, and it was all paid for by poor people throughout France, for the taxes levied for this expedition were so great that the richest complained bitterly and the poor tried to escape from them.

All that was being done in France and Flanders, at Bruges, Damme and Sluys, was known in England. Beyond that, exaggerated rumours spread through England, greatly alarming the inhabitants of many places. All over the country, in the towns and cities, religious processions were instituted three times weekly, and observed in a spirit of deep devotion and contrition. Prayers were offered to God to deliver them from this peril. But many thousands of Englishmen desired nothing better than that the French should come. The more light-hearted ones, who were taking it cheerfully and wanted to encourage the pessimists said: 'Let them all come, those French. Not a ballock of them shall get back to France, by God.' Those who were in debt and had no desire to pay up were in particularly good humour, and said to their creditors: 'Just wait. They're minting the money to pay you with in France.' On that assurance they lived and spent lavishly and easily obtained credit. If they were given only meagre fare on credit, they said: 'What's the matter? Surely it's better for us to spend the wealth of this country than for the French to get it and have the enjoyment.' In that way they spent the resources of England recklessly.

There are dissensions in England, but Richard II's council is able to take measures to protect the country. Various commands are set up round the coast and the garrison of Calais is reinforced.

All the ports and harbours from the River Humber round to Cornwall were garrisoned with men-at-arms and archers or reinforced. On all the hills overlooking the sea and opposite the coasts of Flanders and France look-outs were posted, in this manner: they took empty wine-casks from Gascony, filled them with sand and set them on top of one another, and at the very top they fixed platforms on which men stayed day and night keeping watch. They could see twenty miles or more out to sea. Their orders were, if they saw the French fleet coming, to light torches and make big fires on the hills, so as to warn the country and bring all the men together on the sites of the fires. It was decided to let the King of France land unopposed and go inland for three or four days. Then first, before attacking him, they would attack and capture the ships and take or destroy all the supplies. Only then would they tackle the French army, not yet to fight a battle but as a harassing operation. The French would not be able to go foraging, nor would they find anything because the open country would all have been laid waste, and England is a bad country to campaign through on horseback. So they would be starved and in a desperate position.

Such were the plans of the English. Also the bridge at Rochester, which spans a wide river running into the Thames and the sea opposite the Isle of Sheppey, was broken down. The Londoners had this done to make themselves more secure. And it can be said that if the taxation in France imposed on the town-dwellers was harsh and heavy, in England too that year it was crushing, so that the country felt the consequences for a long time after. But people paid gladly in order to be defended with greater vigilance. In England there were a good hundred thousand archers and ten thousand men-at-arms, although the Duke of Lancaster had taken a large force to Castile, as will be described later.

Sir Simon Burley was the governor of Dover Castle, so he often received information about France from men of Calais and English fishermen who continued going to sea in their usual way. To get good catches they often go fishing off Boulogne and outside the harbour of Wissant. They brought news to Sir Simon as he asked them to, for when they met

French fishermen these told them all they knew, and sometimes more. Whether France and England are at war or not,
fishermen at sea would never hurt each other, but are friends
among themselves and helpful when necessary. They buy and
sell their fish between them at sea, when some have a better
catch than the others. If they fought each other there would
be no sea-fish landed and no one would dare to go fishing
without an armed escort.

The Constable of France left Tréguier in Brittany with a
large force of men-at-arms and quantities of supplies. His
whole fleet numbered seventy-two ships all fully laden.
Among them were the ships carrying the wooden town which
was to be set up on land when they reached England. The
Constable's fleet had a favourable wind to begin with, but
when they neared England it became too strong, and the
farther they went the harder it blew. Off Margate, near the
Thames estuary, it strengthened so much that, in spite of all
the sailors could do, their ships became scattered and there
were not twenty sail keeping together. The wind drove several
ships into the Thames and they were captured by the English;
among them were one or two carrying parts of the wooden
town and the craftsmen who had made it. All this was taken
up the Thames to London, to the great joy of the King and the
citizens. Of the rest of the Constable's ships, seven were
carried forward willy-nilly by the wind, loaded with supplies,
to be wrecked off Zealand. However, the Constable himself
and the chief lords reached Sluys after great difficulties and
dangers.

*Because of the dilatoriness of the High Command and various mis-
haps and delays, the French fleet is still waiting at Sluys in December.
The Duke of Berry strongly advises against risking an invasion in
winter. Amid much grumbling, the whole concentration is dispersed
and the enterprise is postponed indefinitely. Froissart puts the cost,
raised in taxes from the Kingdom of France alone, at over three
million francs.*

Trial by Combat (1386–7)

A T that time there was much talk in France, and as far as the most distant parts of the kingdom, of a duel to the death which was to take place in Paris following a decision of the High Court of Paris. The dispute had dragged on for over a year between the two parties, who were a knight called Sir Jean de Carrouges and a squire called Jacques Le Gris, both belonging to the domain and household of Count Pierre d'Alençon, who held the two of them in great regard. Jacques Le Gris in particular was high in the Count's favour. He was especially fond of him and placed great trust in him. He was not a man of very good family, but a squire of humble birth who had risen in the world, favoured by fortune as many people are. But when they are right on top and think themselves secure, fortune flings them back into the mire and they end up lower than they began. Now, as to the mortal combat which ensued and caused such a stir that people came to Paris to see it from many different places, I will describe what led to it, as I was myself informed at the time.

It happened that Sir Jean de Carrouges made plans to go on an expedition overseas – a thing which he had always been fond of doing – to help him in his advancement. Before leaving, he asked for the Count of Alençon's permission and was readily granted it. The knight had married a wife who was young, beautiful, good, sensible and modest in her behaviour. He bid her a loving good-bye, as knights do when they leave for distant lands. He set out, leaving her with her servants in a castle on the border of Le Perche and Alençon, with the name, I believe, of *Argenteuil*.[1] While the knight went journeying on, she remained there, living simply and discreetly.

It then happened – and this was the whole point at issue – that, through a strange, perverse temptation, the devil entered

1. There is no Argenteuil in the region. The castle was probably at Argentan.

the body of Jacques Le Gris, who was still with the Count of Alençon, whose principal counsellor he was. He conceived the idea of committing a great crime, which he had to pay for later; but it could never be proved against him and he never admitted his guilt. His thoughts became fixed upon Sir Jean de Carrouges' wife, who he knew was living almost alone with her servants in the castle of *Argenteuil*. So he left Alençon one day on a good horse and spurred swiftly forward until he reached the castle. The servants welcomed him in, because he and their master both served the same lord and were companions-in-arms. In the same way the lady, not suspecting anything wrong, gave him a friendly reception, led him to her room and showed him a number of her things. Bent on his evil design, Jacques asked the lady to take him to see the keep, saying that that was partly the object of his visit. The lady agreed without question and the two of them went to it alone. Neither man nor maidservant went with them, because since the lady was entertaining him so pleasantly, showing that she had complete faith in his honour, they thought that everything was well.

No sooner had they entered the keep than Jacques Le Gris shut the door behind him. The lady paid little attention to it, thinking that the wind had blown it shut – and Jacques encouraged her to think so. When they were alone there together, Jacques Le Gris, ensnared by the wiles of the Enemy, put his arms round her and said: 'Lady, I swear to you that I love you better than my life, but I must have my will of you.' The lady was astounded and tried to cry out, but the squire stuffed a little glove which he carried into her mouth to silence her, gripped her tight, for he was a strong man, and pushed her down to the floor. He raped her, having his desire of her against her will. When this was done, he said: 'Lady, if you ever mention what has happened, you will be dishonoured. Say nothing and I will keep quiet too for your honour's sake.' The lady, weeping bitterly, replied: 'Ah, you wicked, treacherous man, I will keep quiet, but not for as long as you will need me to.'

She then opened the door of the room in the keep and came down, followed by the squire.

Her people saw that she was distressed and weeping but, having no suspicion that anything was wrong, they thought that he had brought some bad news of her husband or relations, and that this explained her grief.

The young wife shut herself in her room and there gave way to bitter lamentations. Jacques left the castle on his horse and rode back to his master the Count of Alençon. He was present at his levee on the stroke of ten, and he had been seen in the Count's castle at four in the morning. I give these facts in view of the great law-suit which followed later in Paris, during which the point was inquired into by the commissioners of the High Court of Justice. On the day when this miserable thing befell her, the lady of Carrouges stayed in her castle half-dazed, bearing her sorrow as best she could. She revealed nothing to any of her servants, feeling sure that if she did so she was more likely to incur blame than credit. But she fixed firmly in her memory the day and the time when Jacques Le Gris had come to the castle.

Presently her husband, the master of Carrouges, returned home from his journey. His wife greeted him warmly on his arrival, as did all the servants. That day passed, night came, and Sir Jean went to bed. The lady would not come to bed, at which her husband was much surprised and kept asking her to do so. She put him off and walked up and down the room deep in thought. Finally, when all their people were in bed, she came to her husband and, kneeling beside him, told him in pitiful tones of the dreadful thing which had happened to her. At first the knight could not believe it, but she so insisted that he came round and said: 'All right, then, my lady, if the thing happened as you say, I forgive you; but the squire shall die for it in some way to be decided by my friends and yours. And if I find that what you have told me is not true, you shall never live with me again.' The lady maintained and insisted even more strongly that it was absolutely true.

That night passed. The next day Sir Jean had a number of letters written and sent to his wife's closest friends and his own, with the result that soon after they all came to the castle of *Argenteuil*. He welcomed them discreetly and assembled them in a room, where he explained the reason which had caused him to send for them and got his wife to relate the whole happening in detail, to their sheer amazement. He asked for their opinion and was advised to go to his lord the Count of Alençon and tell him the whole story, which he did. The Count, who was extremely fond of Jacques Le Gris, refused to believe him, and appointed a day for the two parties to appear before him. He required the lady who was accusing Jacques Le Gris to be present, in order to describe what had happened in her own words. She came, and many members of her family with her, to the Count of Alençon's court. The proceedings were long and heated, with Jacques Le Gris being accused of the crime both by the knight and by the full account which his wife gave of it. Jacques Le Gris firmly maintained his innocence, saying that there was no truth in the charge and that the lady was accusing him unjustly. He was at a loss, he said in his speech, to know why the lady hated him. He proved clearly, by the evidence of members of the Count's household, that on the day when it happened he had been seen there at four o'clock, and the Count said that at ten o'clock he was attending him in his chamber. He added that it was quite impossible in the time for him to have done what he was accused of doing and ridden the distance there and back, seventy-two miles in four-and-a-half hours.[1] The Count told the lady, in order to support his squire, that she must have dreamt it, and he made a formal order for the charge to be annulled and for no further questions ever to be raised about it. The knight, who possessed great courage and believed his wife, refused to obey this ruling. He went to Paris and laid his case against Jacques Le Gris before the High Court. Jacques responded to his summons and gave securities pledging him to abide by the court's decision.

The proceedings went on for more than a year-and-a-half. The two parties could not be reconciled because the knight

1. Evidently leaving 1½ hours for his visit to the castle. For the distance, the original has '24 leagues'. Alençon is twenty-eight miles from *Argentan* by the modern road, and if the latter town was meant the distance given by Froissart for the double journey is not too far out.

believed absolutely in his wife's account and because the case
had become so notorious that he felt bound to pursue it to
the end. The Count of Alençon was so infuriated by his
obstinacy that there were many times when he would have had
him killed, but for the fact that they had already gone to court.

After much deliberation and argument the court pronounced that, since the lady of Carrouges could not prove
anything against Jacques Le Gris, the matter should be settled
by a duel to the death. All the parties, the knight, the squire
and the knight's lady, were ordered to be present in Paris on
the day appointed, which was to be the first Monday of the
year 1387.

At that time the King of France and his barons had gone to
Sluys with the intention of invading England. When word of
the court's decision reached the King, who already saw that
the invasion would not take place, he said that he would like
to see the duel between the knight and the squire. The Dukes
of Berry, Burgundy and Bourbon, who also wanted to see it,
told the King that it was quite right for him to go. He accordingly sent word to Paris for the combat to be postponed until
he could witness it, and this order was duly obeyed.

The day of the combat arrived at about the beginning of the
year counted as 1387 according to the custom of Rome. The
lists were prepared in St Catherine's Square, behind the
Temple. The King of France was there with his uncles and
vast crowds of people came to watch. At one side of the lists
big stands had been erected, from which the lords could see
the fight between the two champions. These came on to the
field and were armed from head to foot, as was required of
them, and seated each in his separate chair. Sir Jean de
Carrouges was seconded by Count Waleran de Saint-Pol,
and Jacques Le Gris by the Count of Alençon's men. Before
the knight entered the lists, he went over to his wife, who was
sitting clothed in black in a carriage draped entirely in black
also, and said to her: 'Lady, on your evidence I am about to
hazard my life in combat with Jacques Le Gris. You know if
my cause is just and true.' 'My lord,' said the lady, 'it is so. You

can fight confidently. The cause is just.' 'In God's hands be it then,' said the knight. He kissed his wife, pressed her hand, then made the sign of the cross and entered the lists.

The lady remained in the black-draped carriage, praying fervently to God and the Virgin Mary, entreating them humbly to grant her victory on that day in accordance with her right. You will understand that she was in great anxiety and far from certain that her own life was safe, for if her husband got the worst of it, the sentence was that he should be hanged and she burnt without appeal. I do not know – for I never spoke with her – whether she had not often regretted having gone so far with the matter that she and her husband were in such grave danger – and then finally there was nothing for it but to await the outcome.

When the two champions had taken the oath, as is usual before such combats, they were placed opposite each other and told to say why they had come together. They then mounted their horses and sat them very prettily, for both were skilled in arms. The first part of the combat was a joust, in which neither of them was injured. They then dismounted and continued on foot, both fighting very courageously. The first to suffer was Sir Jean de Carrouges, who was wounded in the thigh, to the great alarm of his supporters, but he fought on so stoutly that he felled his opponent and, thrusting his sword into his body, killed him on the spot. He turned and asked whether he had done his duty and was told that he had. Jacques Le Gris's body was delivered to the executioner of Paris, who dragged it to Mountfaucon and hanged it there.

Then Sir Jean de Carrouges went up to the King and kneeled before him. The King made him rise and presented him with a thousand francs, making him also a member of his chamber with a pension of two hundred francs a year for life. After thanking the King and the great nobles, the knight went to his wife and kissed her, then they went together to the Cathedral of Notre-Dame to make their thank-offerings before returning to their house.

Sir Jean de Carrouges did not remain long in France after this, but set off with the younger Lord Boucicaut, son of the great Boucicaut, and Sir Jean Desbordes and Sir Louis de Giac. The four of them were anxious to visit the Holy Sepulchre and the Sultan Amurat, of whom there was much talk in France at the time. With them also was Robin of Boulogne, a squire of honour of the King of France, who in his day made several notable journeys.[1]

1. This was the last known occasion on which the *Parlement* of Paris ordered a trial by combat. It should be added that, according to three other chronicles, Jacques Le Gris was later declared innocent, when a man condemned to death for a different crime confessed to the rape of the Lady of Carrouges. In view, however, of the psychology of the condemned criminal, quite apart from the possibility that the confession was a forced one, this appears by no means conclusive. If, as Froissart says, the Carrouges servants recognized Le Gris when he visited the castle, their mistress's version seems unshakable.

Richard II's First Struggle with his Uncles
(1387–8)

THE King of England's uncles, the Dukes of York and Gloucester, with the Earls of Salisbury, Arundel, Northumberland and Nottingham and the Archbishop of Canterbury,[1] were all allied together against the King and his council. Their discontent was great and they said in private: 'This Duke of Ireland[2] twists the King round his finger and does what he likes in England. The King listens only to bad people, of mean birth in comparison with princes. As long as he has his present council things cannot go right, for a kingdom can never be well governed nor a sovereign properly advised by bad people. It always happens that, when a poor man rises in the world and is honoured by his master, he becomes corrupt and ruins the people and the country. A base man has no idea of what honour means, but wants to grab everything and gobble it up, just like an otter in a pond destroying all the fish it finds there. What good can come of this intimacy between the Duke of Ireland and the King? We know his ancestry and where he came from and we fear that England will be entirely ruled by him, and the King's uncles and blood-relations left aside. That is not a thing to be tolerated.'

'We know who the Earl of Oxford is,' said others. 'He was the son of Earl Aubrey of Oxford,[3] who never had much of a reputation in this country for honour. wisdom, sound judgement or chivalry.'

Such complaints about the Duke of Ireland were widespread in England. What discredited him most was his

1. William Courtenay.
2. Robert de Vere, ninth Earl of Oxford, created Duke of Ireland in 1386.
3. Robert de Vere's father was in fact Thomas, the eighth earl, who is meant here. Aubrey (tenth earl) was his uncle.

treatment of his wife,[1] the daughter of the Lord de Coucy and of the Queen of England's daughter, Madam Isabella who, as you know, was a good and beautiful lady, of the highest and noblest descent possible. But he fell in love with one of the maids-in-waiting of the Queen of England, a German woman, and so worked on Urban VI, who was in Rome and considered himself Pope, that he obtained a divorce from the Lord de Coucy's daughter with no shadow of an excuse except his own presumption and negligence and married that maid of the Queen's.[2] All this was allowed by King Richard, who was so blinkered by the Duke of Ireland that even if he said black was white the King did not contradict him. . . .

The Duke felt himself so secure in the King's favour that he did not believe that anyone could harm him, and a report ran through England that a tax of one noble was to be levied on each hearth, by which the rich [who had several fires in their houses] would make up for the poor. The King's uncles knew that this would be a very great burden, and caused the word to be spread that it would be too damaging to the people and that there were, or should be, large sums of money in the royal treasury, of which an account should be demanded from his mentors.

Richard is obliged, very unwillingly, to call Parliament together to inquire into the management of the funds which have passed through his favourite's hands.

The day of accounting came at Westminster in the presence of the King's uncles and the representatives – prelates, earls, barons and burgesses of the towns. The audit lasted for more than a month. If there were any who could not give a good and honest account, they were punished either physically or financially, and some in both ways. Sir Simon Burley, who had been one of the King's tutors in his youth, was found to show a deficit on that account of 250,000 francs, and was asked where all that money had gone to. He put the responsibility on the Archbishop of York, Alexander Neville, brother of Lord Neville, saying that everything had been done through him and on his advice and through the King's chamberlains,

1. Philippa de Coucy.   2. Agnes Lancecrona.

Sir Robert Tresilian, Sir John Beauchamp, Sir John Salisbury, Sir Nicholas Brembre, Sir John Golafre[1] and others. But these, on being called before the council, denied responsibility and placed it all upon him. The Duke of Ireland said to him: 'I have heard that you are going to be arrested and kept in prison until you repay the sum demanded of you. Don't argue the point, do as they tell you. I will make your peace with them, even if they all swear the contrary. I am to receive 60,000 francs from the Constable of France for the ransom of John of Brittany, which he owes me, as you know. If necessary I will lend it to you to appease the council for the time being. And in the long run the King is supreme. He will pardon you and remit the whole sum, because in the end it must come back to him and no one else.'

Sir Simon Burley trusts in these assurances, but is nevertheless condemned to imprisonment in the Tower until he can make restitution. The King fails to have him released and leaves for the Welsh Marches with the Queen and the Duke of Ireland. His uncles remain in London and the case against Burley is pressed forward.

The common rumour in many parts of England was that for a long time past the Duke of Ireland and Sir Simon Burley had been hoarding up gold and silver and salting it away in Germany. It had come to the knowledge of the King's uncles and the representatives of the English towns that chests and coffers had been taken down secretly at night from Dover Castle to the harbour and then shipped across the sea. It was then said that this had been money collected by the above-named and smuggled fraudulently out of England to other countries, with the result that the realm had been greatly weakened financially. Many deplored this, and said that gold and silver had become so difficult to acquire that trade was stagnating in consequence, and no other explanation of the scarcity could be thought of.

This kind of talk became so general that Sir Simon Burley was gravely prejudiced by it and it was decreed, by the King's uncles and the burgesses acting with them, that he had deserved death on account of the charges against him. What

1. Froissart: Pierre Goulouffre.

told most heavily against him, particularly in the opinion of the common people, was that he had once advised the Archbishop of Canterbury to have the shrine of St Thomas removed from there and taken for safety to Dover Castle – that was when they were expecting the French to invade them. But the common explanation after he had been put in prison was that he meant to steal it and send it abroad.

Such strong accusations were brought against him that none of his answers and protests was of any avail. One day he was brought out from the Tower of London and beheaded in front of it, as a traitor. May God forgive him his misdeeds. I am grieved to write of his shameful death, but I must do so for the truth of the record. But for my part I felt very sorry for him, because in my youth I had found him a very pleasant knight and, in my opinion, a man of sound judgement.

The Archbishop of York, Alexander Neville, is relieved of his post of Treasurer and sent northwards in disgrace. King Richard who, according to Froissart, was established at Bristol, authorizes the Duke of Ireland to raise an army in Wales and the west which he will lead in the King's name against his uncles. To obtain information about the state of things in London, Sir Robert Tresilian is sent there secretly.

He left Bristol, dressed as a poor trader and mounted on a small hackney. Reaching London, he put up at an inn incognito. No one would ever have thought that he was Tresilian, one of the King's chamberlains, for he was dressed not as a gentleman, but as a common fellow. In his first day in London he learnt a great deal about the Duke of York and the Duke of Gloucester and his council, but only things that were common knowledge and nothing more. He heard that there was to be a private meeting at Westminster between the King's uncles and the new council of the realm and he decided to go there secretly and find out what happened at it. He went to Westminster on the day the parliament was to be held in the King's palace and entered a house where ale was sold just outside the palace entrance. He went to an upstairs room looking on to the yard of the palace and stayed there for a long time. He could see those who went in and out, many of whom he knew, but was not noticed himself because of his clothes. After a considerable time a squire of the Duke of Gloucester's, who knew him well, happened to pass before the tavern and looked up and saw him. When Sir Robert saw the squire's face, he immediately recognized him and drew back from the window. The squire had a sudden suspicion and said to himself: 'I feel sure I've seen Tresilian.' He went into the tavern and said to the landlady: 'Tell me, hostess, who's that man drinking up there? Is he by himself, or with friends?' 'Good lord, sir,' the landlady replied, 'I don't know his name, but he is by himself and he's been up there a long time.' Hearing this, the squire went upstairs to have a closer look at him. He greeted him and saw at once that his guess was right, but he covered up and said instead: 'A very good day to you! I'm sorry to have disturbed you, but I thought you might be a farmer of mine from Essex. You're very like him.' 'No,' Sir Robert answered, 'I come from Kent. I'm a tenant of Sir John Holland and the Archbishop of Canterbury's men are nibbling at my land. I should like to make a complaint to Parliament.' The squire said: 'If you will come into the palace down there, I will get you a hearing from the lords and masters of Parliament.' 'Many thanks,' said Sir Robert. 'I won't say no to your offer.'

On this, the squire left him. He ordered a quart of ale, paid for it, then said good-bye to the landlady and went across to the palace, walking through it as far as the approach to the council chamber. He called to an usher, who opened the door. The usher immediately recognized him and said: 'What do you want? The lords are in council.' 'I want to speak to my master the Duke of Gloucester on a matter which concerns him closely, and the whole council too.' Knowing the squire to be a man of standing and importance, the usher let him in and he came before the lords in council. Kneeling before the Duke of Gloucester, he said: 'My lord, I have important news.' 'Important?' said the Duke. 'What is it?' 'My lord,' said the squire, 'I will tell you openly, for it concerns both you and all the gentlemen present. I have seen Sir Robert Tresilian, dressed as a commoner, just outside the palace here, lying up in an ale-house.' 'Tresilian!' said the Duke. 'Yes, my lord, the man himself. You can have him at dinner if you want him.' 'I certainly do want him,' said the Duke. 'He can give us some news about Ireland, and about his master the Duke. Go and fetch him at once, and take enough force with you not to lose him.'

Armed with the Duke's authority, the squire left the council chamber and collected four serjeants-at-arms, to whom he said: 'Follow me at a distance. Then, as soon as I show you a man whom I'm going to look for, lay hands on him and make sure he doesn't get away.' 'Right,' they said.

The squire entered the tavern where Tresilian was and went upstairs to the room where he had left him. Going in and finding him still there, he said: 'Tresilian, you're up to no good in this place. At least, I suppose not. My lord of Glouces-ter has sent for you. He wants to talk to you.' The knight pretended not to understand and tried to wriggle out of it by saying: 'I am not Tresilian. I am one of Sir John Holland's farmers.' 'It's no good,' said the squire. 'Your body is Tresilian's, if your clothes are not.' He signalled to the ser-jeants who were outside the inn door to come and arrest him. They came upstairs, seized him and took him, willy-nilly, to the palace.

As you can well imagine, a huge crowd gathered to see him, for he was well known in London and other parts of England. The Duke of Gloucester was very pleased by his capture and ordered him to be brought in. When he was in his presence, he said: 'Well, Tresilian, what brings you here? What is my lord doing? Where is he?' Seeing that he was definitely recognized and that further concealment was useless, Tresilian answered: 'Of course, my lord. Our lord the King is mostly at Bristol and on the Severn. He's hunting and amusing him-self down there. That was why he sent me here to find out what was happening.' 'What!' said the Duke. 'In a state like that? You have not come as a respectable person, but like a spy and a traitor. If you wanted to find out what was happening, you should have come as a knight and an honest man and brought letters of credence with you. Had you done that, you could have taken back all the information you needed.' 'My lord,' said Tresilian, 'if I have done wrong, forgive me. I was made to do all this.' 'And where is your master, the Duke of Ireland?' 'He is with our lord the King, sir.' 'So?' said the Duke of Gloucester. 'We are informed that he is assembling a large force of men-at-arms, and that so is the King on his behalf. What does he intend to do with them?' 'My lord,' replied Tresilian, 'they are all for an expedition to Ireland.' 'Ireland!' said the Duke. 'Yes, my lord, as God is my witness,' said Tresilian.

The Duke of Gloucester reflected a little and then said: 'Tresilian, Tresilian, your behaviour is neither honest nor creditable. You did a very silly thing to come here, for you are not much liked in London, as we shall show you. You and the others in your party have given a lot of trouble to my brother and me. You have done your best to corrupt and mislead the King and some of the nobles of this country. In addition you have stirred up some of the towns against us. The day has come for you to reap the consequences, since it is only right that you should be paid according to your deserts. Put your affairs in order, for I will touch neither food nor drink as long as you are alive.'

Tresilian was dismayed by these words – and naturally, since no man can be glad to hear his death announced to him in the way the Duke of Gloucester had done. He tried to excuse himself by fine words, pleading several things in mitigation; but all to no purpose, for the Duke was so well informed about him and the other members of the Duke of Ireland's faction that no excuses would serve. Why should I prolong the tale? Tresilian was delivered to the executioner, taken out of Westminster and handed over to those who perform such functions, and there beheaded and then hanged on the King's gibbet by the armpits. So ended Sir Robert Tresilian.

King Richard is infuriated by the news of Tresilian's execution. He presses forward with the assembly of an army in the west. He is advised by Nicholas Brembre, former Mayor of London, that many Londoners would support him but for his absence, which encourages opposition to him. He therefore entrusts the Duke of Ireland with the task of leading his army near to London to test the temper of the citizens. Ireland reaches Oxford with fifteen thousand men marching under the King's banners. The Londoners, however, assure the Dukes of York and Gloucester that they are not afraid of Ireland and will resist him. Men are assembled from the Home Counties.

From Oxford, Ireland sends three knights with a small escort to test reaction in London. They reach the Tower one evening, travelling partly by boat. The Governor of the Tower advises them that London is solidly against them and that they had better stay hidden. Next night they return by barge to Windsor, and thence to Oxford. On receiving their report, the Duke of Ireland grows dubious, feeling uncertain also of the loyalty of his own forces. He finally decides to remain in the field, since he is Constable of England and charged with putting down the rebels; but he asks the King to send him more men.

Gloucester moves towards Oxford, leading a force composed chiefly of London levies. Somewhat hesitantly, the Duke of Ireland comes out to meet him.

Word was brought to the Duke of Gloucester, who was encamped about ten miles from Oxford near a small river which flows into the Thames below Oxford – his men were all along the bank in a fine meadow – that the Duke of Ireland had come out from the city and put his men in battle-order. The news delighted him and he said that he would fight, provided they could get over the Thames. His trumpets sounded the call to strike camp and the army formed up ready for immediate action. They were within two miles of the enemy, if somehow they could find a way to reach them across the river. The Duke sent some of his knights to test the depth of the ford and they found the water as low as had been known for thirty years. These scouts crossed with ease and went on to reconnoitre the enemy's formation. Then they rode back to the Duke of Gloucester and told him: 'Sir, God and the river are on your side today. It is so shallow that it was only up to our horses' bellies in the deepest place. Furthermore, sir, we have seen the Duke of Ireland's dispositions. His men are drawn up in good order. We do not know whether the King is with them, but his banners are there. We saw no other banners except his, showing the arms of France and England.'

The Duke answered: 'God be with us then. We have some share in those arms, my brother and I. Let's ride forward in the name of God and St George, for I want to have a closer look at them.' Everyone advanced eagerly, because they had heard that it would be easy to get over the river. The mounted men quickly reached the bank and crossed, showing the way to the others. Soon their whole army was on the farther side.

Word of this reached the Duke of Ireland, with the knowledge that before long he would be engaged in battle. Anxiety seized him because he knew that, if he were taken prisoner, the Duke of Gloucester would put him to death ignominiously, refusing any offers of ransom. He said to Sir John Golafre and Sir Michael de la Pole: 'I feel no relish for fighting today. If I am captured by the King's uncles, they will give me a shameful death. How the devil did they get across the Thames? It's an unlucky start for us.' 'What do you intend to do, then?' the two knights asked. 'To get away,' said the Duke, 'and let the others escape as best they can.' 'In that case we had better place ourselves on one of the wings,' the two knights went on, 'and so we shall have two strings to our bow. We shall be able to see how our men are doing. If they are fighting well we will stay, for the honour of the King who sent us here. If they are defeated, we will get away across country and have the advantage of being free to ride in whichever direction we choose.'

This course was adopted. The Duke of Ireland took a fresh, strong horse and the knights did the same. They rode round the army looking brave and cheerful, and saying: 'Stand firm, men. We shall win the day, with the help of God and St George, for right is on our side. We are fighting for the King, so our cause is stronger.' So, hiding their intentions and keeping clear of the press, they reached the edge of the army and formed a wing. Then up came the Duke of York, the Duke of Gloucester and the other captains. They came in warlike order with their banners unfurled, amid a great sounding of trumpets. When the King's men saw them, their courage forsook them. They broke formation and began to disperse and take

to their heels. Word had gone round that their commander,
the Duke of Ireland, was running away with his lieutenants.
So they fled in all directions, without attempting to resist.
Meanwhile the Duke and the two knights made off across
country at full gallop. They had no mind to retreat to Oxford,
but to get as far away from it as possible to some place of
safety.

When the Duke of Gloucester saw the disorder in the army
facing him, a twinge of conscience seized him and he decided
not to do his worst against them. He knew that all, or many
of them, had been either forced or incited to come by the
Duke of Ireland. He therefore said to his men: 'The day is
ours, but I forbid you on your lives to kill any man unless he
puts up a defence. And if you come across knights or squires,
take them prisoner and bring them to me.' His orders were
obeyed and there were few killed, except those who died in the
press when they were riding against each other.

In the rout were taken prisoner Sir John Beauchamp, known
as little Beauchamp, and Sir John Salisbury, and handed over
to the Duke of Gloucester, to his great satisfaction. He and his
commanders made their way to Oxford, where they found the
gates open to them and entered unopposed. Those who could
lodged in the town, though they found themselves very
cramped. . . . After two days at Oxford, the Duke disbanded
all his men, telling them to return to their homes and thanking
them for their services to his brother and himself.

*The Duke of Ireland, with John Golafre and Michael de la Pole,
escapes northward and eventually finds his way overseas to Flanders.
John Beauchamp and John Salisbury are beheaded, at Oxford, says
Froissart. After Gloucester's return to London, Nicholas Brembre,
'who had been found and captured in Wales', is beheaded in the capital.*

After the death of Sir Nicholas Brembre, the King's uncles
saw that, since all those whom they hated and wished to remove from the King's council were dead or in exile, so that no
new party could be formed, it was now necessary for the King
and the kingdom to be put back on a sound footing. Although
they had killed or driven out the men mentioned, they did not
want to deprive the King of his sovereignty, but to guide him

along the right road, for his own honour and that of the country. They therefore said to the Archbishop of Canterbury: 'Archbishop, you must go down to Bristol in full state and, when you find the King, explain the measures which have been taken in his kingdom and the present state of affairs. Recommend us to him and tell him plainly, from us, not to credit any different account of the facts. He has swallowed too much false information already, to the dishonour and prejudice of himself and his realm. And tell him that we request him – as do the good people of London – to come back here. He will be made welcome and received with joy. And we will provide him with such counsellors that he will be fully satisfied. . . .'

The Archbishop travels to Bristol and with some difficulty persuades the King to return with him to London. As promised, Richard is given a hearty welcome, to which his response is cold.

It was decided to hold a general assembly of Parliament at Westminster, to which were summoned all the prelates, earls, barons, knights, the councillors of the cities and towns, and all the fief-holders who held or would hold their possessions from the King. The reason was this: the Archbishop of Canterbury had shown in council that, when Richard had been crowned as their sovereign and the oath had been sworn and homage paid to him by his subjects, he had still been under age. By right a king should be twenty-one before he can exercise sovereignty over his territory or rule a kingdom. Before that age, he must be guided by his uncles or other near relations, or by his men. The Archbishop went on to say that, since the King had now come of age, it would be advisable, for greater certainty, for all his vassals to renew their oath to him and recognize him as their sovereign.

This recommendation of the Archbishop's was adopted by the King's uncles and the members of the palace council, and accordingly all the nobles, knights, prelates and leading men of the towns were summoned to London. All came without fail. London and the Palace of Westminster were filled with crowds of people. King Richard went to the chapel of the palace, a fine and noble building, in royal state and wearing the crown. Divine service was taken by the Archbishop of Canterbury, who celebrated a solemn mass. Afterwards he preached a sermon which was listened to with great interest, for he was an excellent preacher.

After mass the King's uncles kissed the King in sign of homage as his vassals and fief-holders, swearing perpetual allegiance to him. Next the earls and barons took the same oath and also the prelates and his dependent land-holders. They did homage in the customary way, with their hands clasped, kissing the King on the lips. It was easy to see by watching this ceremony which ones the King kissed readily and which not. Although he kissed them, they were not all to his liking; but he had to go through with it in order not to go against the ruling of his uncles. However, if he had had the upper hand of them, he would not have done so, but would have exacted vengeance for the execution of Sir Simon Burley and his other knights who had been taken from him and put to death undeservedly. . . .

So England returned to a normal state. But for a long time after the King was not master in his council. It was controlled by his uncles and the barons and prelates named above.[1]

1. The inaccuracies in this section, in the light of modern historical research, are too numerous to list. They bear on the order of events, the various meetings of Parliament, Richard's whereabouts at certain times, the battle near Oxford (Radcot Bridge), the dates and circumstances of the deaths of the King's knights. Burley, Tresilian, Brembre, John Beauchamp and John Salisbury were in fact executed, but all by decision of the so-called Merciless Parliament in 1388, near the end of the story. The general picture so vigorously presented by Froissart remains valid, however, in broad outline.

John of Gaunt's Expedition to Spain (1386-7)

JOHN of Gaunt, Duke of Lancaster, had a claim to the throne of Castile through his second wife Constance, daughter of Peter the Cruel. In 1386 he landed an army in Galicia and captured several towns, including Orense. King John of Portugal, to whom he had married his elder daughter, came to his support. But progress was slow and the Castilians, who were supported by the French, delayed giving battle.

So those two great lords and their armies were in Galicia. They stripped the country of food. The days grew hotter and hotter, until no one dared to go out riding after nine o'clock unless he wanted to be scorched by the sun. The Duke and Duchess and the ladies[1] remained in Orense, but their men were quartered in the country, where there was a great scarcity of everything to provision them and their horses. No grass could grow, nor any other eatable thing, so hard and dry and sunbaked was the earth. Anything that did come up withered quickly because of the excessive summer heat. To get supplies, the English had to send their servants and foragers anything up to sixty miles before they found them. . . .

When the knights and squires saw how dangerous the situation might become, and the shortage of foodstuffs, and the increasing strength of the sun, they began to grumble and their complaints ran through the army: 'This campaign is shaping badly. We stay too long in the same place.' 'True,' said others. 'Two things tell against us particularly. We are taking women with us and they always want to sit about. After one day on the move they need a couple of weeks' rest. That's been a great drag on us so far and will go on being. If we had advanced quickly as soon as we had landed at Corunna, going straight forward from there, we should have done well and have subdued the whole country, with no one attempting to resist us. But the long stops we have made have

1. The Duchess of Lancaster had accompanied the expedition with her daughter and suite.

helped the enemy. They have strengthened their defences and brought men-at-arms from France to guard their towns and castles and block the river-crossings. They will defeat us without giving battle. They don't need to fight us. This Spanish land is not a pleasant one, agreeable to campaign across as France is with all those big villages, that rich country, those cool rivers, lakes and pools, mild and palatable wines to give new strength to fighting men, and that temperate climate. Everything is different here.'

'What was the Duke of Lancaster thinking of,' said others, 'when he planned a big campaign yet brought his wife and daughter with him? It has held us back, all to no purpose. All Spain already knows – and others also – that he and his brother Edmund are married to the heiresses of this country, the daughters of King Peter. As for the campaign and the capture of towns, cities and castles, the ladies are not much help there.'

The English and Portuguese eventually advance together and find a way across the Duero. They approach Medina del Campo, where King Juan of Castile is established, awaiting a further promised reinforcement of French troops under the Duke of Bourbon.

The Duke of Lancaster and the King of Portugal held the country round Medina del Campo, though they would have liked to hold the towns to rest and refresh themselves in them, for whichever way their foragers went they found nothing. Moreover, for fear of attacks and ambushes, they only dared to go out in large companies. When they rode about the district of the Campo and saw from a height or a distance what looked like a large village, they were glad and went towards it in the hope of finding provisions and booty. But when they got there they found only walls and ruined houses, with not a dog or a cat or a cock or a hen or a man or woman among them. Everything had been wrecked and despoiled by the French themselves. So their effort and time were wasted and they went back to their commanders having accomplished nothing. Their horses were lean and weak for lack of proper food, and fortunate indeed when they found grass to eat. They could hardly be ridden, having become so sickly that they died on the road of heat and exhaustion. Like them, some of the greatest lords there were desperately ill with fevers and shivering-fits.

However, a contingent of English knights decide to take the best of the remaining horses and ride over to Villalpando to make an attack on the French force which is garrisoned there under Olivier du Guesclin, the brother of Bertrand, now dead.

After the morning drink one day they left their army and rode, as though foraging, towards Villalpando. They came to the stream which runs below the town and spurred their horses across it. The alarm was given in the town and the report spread through streets and houses that the English were at the barriers. Knights and squires armed themselves briskly and gathered in front of the Constable's house, while grooms saddled the horses and brought them there to their masters. The Constable, Sir Olivier du Guesclin, tried to restrain them from sallying out but could not; they were too eager. Mounted on the finest horses, fresh and in good condition, they went out, thirsting to fight the English. When these had done as they intended by riding up to the town and saw that the French were getting ready to come out at them, they went back across the stream and drew up in good order on a wide stretch of sand which is there. They were about three bowshots away from the stream. At them came the knights and squires of France shouting their battle-cries and gripping their lances. The English wheeled round in a body, lowered their lances and clapped their spurs to their horses. And then, I can tell you, there was a hard, stiff joust and several were stretched on the sand, from both sides. Things would not have ended there, after a single joust, without more fighting when the lance-work was over. But the dust from the loose sand rose beneath the horses' hooves and became so thick that they could not see each other or distinguish friend from foe. Their horses were covered and choked with dust and so were the men, until they could hardly breathe and their mouths were full of sand.

In such conditions they broke off the engagement. The English re-formed to the sound of their rallying cries, while the French did the same and went back to Villalpando. There were no more casualties on either side. The farthest the English got in that day's sally was just three miles beyond Villalpando. Then they returned to their quarters and disarmed. Some bore arms that day for the last time, for sickness seized them, heats, fevers and chills, of which in time they died.

The Duke of Lancaster was at his wits' end and often weighed down by anxiety. He saw his men – the best of them – exhausted and ill and taking to their beds, while he himself felt so weary that he lay in his bed without moving. Yet from time to time he would get up and do his best to seem cheerful, so as not to discourage his men. . . .

The summer wore on and the sun rose higher in the sky and the days became marvellously hot. It was around midsummer, when the sun is in his strength and pride, especially in those countries of Spain and Granada and the kingdoms far from the regions of the north. Since the beginning of April no moisture had descended on the earth, neither rain nor dew, and the grass was burnt brown. The English ate quantities of grapes when they could get them, because they were refreshing and juicy, and then they drank those strong wines of Lisbon and Portugal to quench their thirst. But the more they drank the hotter they became, for the wines burnt their livers and lungs and all the entrails of their stomachs, being quite foreign to their natural diet. The English live on mild-flavoured food and good, heavy ales which keep their bodies humid. Now they had dry, sharp wines and drank copiously to forget their sorrows. The nights there are hot, after the heat of the previous day, but near dawn the air suddenly grows cold. This caught them unawares, for at night they could not bear to have a blanket over them and slept naked because heated by the wine. Then came the morning chill which struck through their whole bodies, giving them sickness and fever and afflicting them with dysentery,[1] of which they inevitably died. It was the same with barons, knights and squires as with humble people.

These are the fortunes of war. It must be said that the Duke

1. The word could not be known to Froissart. More literally, 'the belly-flux'.

of Lancaster in Castile would never have lost so many good men in battle as died of illness in that campaign. He himself nearly died of the epidemic. Sir John Holland, who was acting as Constable of the army, and to whom all arguments and re-criminations were brought and who saw his fellow-soldiers infected with that sickness from which none recovered, heard the mounting complaints of one and all, gentry and com-moners, every day, louder and angrier, running like this: 'Our lord of Lancaster has brought us to Spain to die. Curses on this campaign! He seems to want to make sure that no Englishman in future will ever wish to serve him abroad. He is trying to kick against the pricks. He wants his men to guard the land he has conquered, but who will guard it when they are all dead? He shows no sign of knowing how to conduct a campaign. When he saw that the enemy refused to fight us, why didn't he withdraw in time, to Portugal or somewhere else, and avoid the losses he must suffer – for we shall all die of this beastly plague without striking a blow.'

Lancaster agrees to disband his army and sue for peace. The out-standing problems are the care of the sick and their eventual return to England. Emissaries are sent to King Juan of Castile, who gives them this reply through his Chancellor, the eloquent Bishop of Astorga:

'Knights of England representing the Duke of Lancaster and sent here on his Constable's orders, give ear to this. The King's answer is that, through kindness and pity, he is willing to grant his enemies every favour possible. When you return to your Constable, you will tell him, in the name of the King of Castile, to have it proclaimed throughout his army to the sound of trumpets that this kingdom is open and ready to re-ceive sick and wounded, knights and squires, and their followers; on condition that at the gates of the towns and cities in which they desire to enter or lodge they should lay down all their arms; there they will find men appointed for the task who will lead them to their lodgings; all their names will be written down and taken to the governor of the town, with the object that none who enter shall be allowed to return to Galicia or Portugal for any purpose whatsoever; but shall leave as soon as they are able, after having obtained from His

Majesty the King of Castile a safe-conduct to pass unmolested through the kingdoms of Navarre and France on their way to Calais or any other port or haven which they care to choose, whether on the coast of Brittany, of Saintonge, of La Rochelle, of Normandy, or of Picardy. And the King's stipulation is that all who undertake that journey, knights and squires, to whatever nation they belong, shall not take up arms for the term of six years, for any cause, against the kingdom of Castile. This they will solemnly swear on receiving the safe-conducts they will be given. All that I have now said will be put into unsealed letters which you will take back to your Constable and his companions who have sent you here.'

The terms are accepted by the English.

The news soon spread through the army that the Duke of Lancaster was freely giving leave to all who wished to go. Those who felt weak and ill and desired a change of air went off as quickly as they could, taking leave of the Duke and the Constable. Before they left their accounts were settled. They were paid in good solid cash or else given such generous promises that they were satisfied. They left in their battalions and companies. Some went to Villalpando, some to *Ruelles*,[1] some to *Villelope*,[1] some to Naya, some to Medina del Campo, some to Castrojeriz, others to Sahagún. Everywhere they were well received, were given lodgings, and their names were taken down by the governors of the towns in the way already described. Most of the nobles went to Villalpando because it was garrisoned by foreign mercenaries, Bretons, French, Normans and Poitevins, under the supreme command of Sir Olivier du Guesclin, acting as Constable of Castile. The English still had more confidence in these than in the Spaniards, not without reason. In this manner the Duke of Lancaster's army in Castile was disbanded in that summer and each one fended for himself. . . .

At Villalpando there died three great English barons, important and well-known men. First was Sir Richard Burley, who had been chief Marshal of the Duke's army and, besides him, the Lord of Poynings and Sir Henry Percy, first cousin

1. *Sic* Froissart. Perhaps Roa and Villalón.

of the Earl of Northumberland. In the town of Naya there
died Sir Maubrin de Linières, a very gallant and experienced
knight from Poitou; and, at *Ruelles*, a great Welsh baron,
Lord Talbot. There died in all of the epidemic, in various
places, twelve English barons, at least eighty knights, and
over two hundred squires, all good gentlefolk; and of others,
archers and so forth, more than five hundred. I was assured by
an English knight with whom I talked on his way back from
there through France, Sir Thomas Queensberry [1] by name, that
out of fifteen hundred men-at-arms and a full four thousand
archers whom the Duke of Lancaster had led out from England
not more than half returned, or even fewer. . . .

The sickness attacked no one except the Duke of Lancaster's men. There was no sign of it among the French, and for
that reason there was much grumbling among them and also
among the Spanish, who said: 'The King of Castile has permitted these English to rest and recover in his country and his
towns. But it might prove very costly for us if they started a
fatal epidemic in this country.' Others answered: 'They are
Christians like ourselves. We must have compassion on one
another.'

1. Froissart: Quinebery.

The Battle of Otterburn (Chevy Chase) (1388)

You know how troubled the realm of England had been in the recent past, with King Richard against his uncles, and his uncles against him. As we have already related, the Duke of Ireland received the principal blame for these occurrences, as a consequence of which several knights had been beheaded in England and the Archbishop of York, the brother of Lord Neville, had almost lost his see. By order of the new royal council, controlled by the King's uncles and the Archbishop of Canterbury, Lord Neville, who had guarded the frontier in Northumberland for five years against the Scots, drawing sixteen thousand francs a year from the borough of York and the bishopric of Durham, had been dismissed from his post. His place was taken by the Earl of Northumberland, Henry Percy, who kept the border for eleven thousand francs a year, to the envy and indignation of the Neville family, neighbours and relations of the Percies though they were.

The Scots were well aware of this and their barons and knights decided one day to bring together an army and launch an expedition into England. They knew that the English were divided among themselves and, having received so many buffets from them in the past, they felt that this was the time to give a good one back. To keep their intentions secret, they arranged to hold a festival on the borders of wildest Scotland, in a city called Aberdeen, to which most of the Scottish chiefs went. There it was agreed that in the middle of August of that year 1388 they would all meet, each with his force of men, near the borders of Galloway[1] at a castle deep among the forests called Jedburgh, and on that understanding they dispersed. It should be added that they said nothing to their King about the decision they had come to, but ignored him entirely. They said among themselves that he had no idea of warfare.

1. Froissart: *Galles.* This is his regular name for south-west Scotland, and including part of Cumberland.

The Scottish lords assemble at Jedburgh. Among them are James Earl of Douglas, John Earl of Moray, the Earl of March and Dunbar, William Earl of Fife, John Earl of Sutherland, William Earl of Mar, Sir Archibald Douglas, Sir William and Sir James Lindsay and others.

Never, over the past sixty years, had so many good fighting men been gathered together. They were a full twelve hundred lances and forty thousand men, counting the archers. But the Scots do not trouble much about the use of the bow. Instead, they carry axes on their shoulders and in battle they approach at once. With these axes they deal some very hard blows.

When those lords were all assembled around Jedburgh, they were in high spirits. They said that they would not go home before they had ridden down into England and gone so far that it would be talked of for twenty years to come. In order to decide more exactly which way they would go and how they would proceed, these barons, who were the commanders of all the rest of the people, fixed a day to meet in a church on a moor above the forest of Jedburgh, known locally as *Zedon*.[1]

The English in Northumberland know that the clans are gathering. They had already sent 'heralds and minstrels' to spy on the festival at Aberdeen. They now send another spy to Jedburgh.

This English squire did so well that, without being noticed, he reached the church at *Zedon*, where the Scottish leaders were, and went in among them, as though he were a servant following his master. There he learnt a great deal about their plans and at the end of their conference was ready to get away. He went to the tree to which he had tied his horse, expecting to find it. But it was not there, for some of the Scots are great thieves and one of them had made off with it. He dared not say anything, but set out on foot, booted and spurred. When he had gone about two bow-shots from the church, he passed some Scottish knights who were talking together. The first to notice him said: 'Wonders will never cease. I see a man all

1. Froissart: *Zedon* and *Zoden.* Conjectured by Sir Walter Scott to have been Kirk-Yetholm.

by himself who appears to have lost his horse, and has said ·
nothing about it! I don't see how he can be one of our people.
Now get after him, and see whether I'm right.'

Some squires immediately rode after him and quickly caught
him up. When he saw them on top of him he lost his head and
wished he could just disappear. They surrounded him and
asked him where he came from and where he was going, and
what he had done with his horse. He began to contradict himself and could not answer their questions. They turned him
back, saying that he would have to talk to their leader, and so
he was taken into the church and brought before Earl Douglas
and the others. These at once saw that he was English and
began to interrogate him. They wanted to know who had
sent him, but he was unwilling to say. However, he was pressed
so hard that he revealed everything, for he was told that, if he
would not speak, his head would be cut off without mercy;
but that if he did speak, he need have no fear of death. To
save his life, he admitted that it was the barons of Northumberland who had sent him, in order to discover the strength of
their forces and which way they intended to go. When they
heard this, the Scots were jubilant and felt they would not have
missed capturing him for a thousand marks.

He was then asked where the Northumbrian barons were,
whether there were signs that they were about to take the
field, and which road to Scotland they intended to follow,
the one along the coast through Berwick and Dunbar, or the
higher road through the County of *Montres*[1] leading towards
Stirling. His answer was: 'My lords, since I have to tell the
whole truth, I will do so. When I left them at Newcastle-on-
Tyne, there were no signs yet of their moving out. But they
are equipped and ready to leave from one day to the next. But
when they hear that you are on the move and have crossed the
border, they will not come to meet you directly because they
are not numerous enough to fight the great army which you
are said to have assembled.' 'And what are our numbers said
to be in Northumberland?' asked the Earl of Moray. 'It is said,

1. This name has been conjectured to be Menteith, since Montrose is
impossible.

sir,' the squire replied, 'that you have at least forty thousand
men and twelve hundred lances. So, to counter you, if you
take the Galloway[1] road, they will take the Berwick road, to
reach Dalkeith and Edinburgh through Dunbar. And if you
come down that way, they will make for Carlisle and get into
Scotland through the mountains.'

When the Scottish lords heard this, they fell silent and
looked at one another.

*Their decision is to divide their forces. The main body, with the
supply-train, will make for Carlisle. A smaller force under the Earl
of Douglas, made up of three to four hundred lances and two
thousand archers and 'strong serving-men' (clansmen), all mounted,
will take the Newcastle road.*

When the Earl of Douglas, the Earl of Moray and the Earl
of March and Dunbar, the three leaders, had separated from
the main army, which went on its own way, they prepared to
go towards Newcastle, cross the Tyne by a ford nine miles
from there which they knew well, enter the Bishopric of
Durham, and push on as far as the city. Then they would come
back, burning and wasting the country, and would camp outside Newcastle in the face of the English. They did as they
had planned, moving at a good pace under cover of the terrain
and not stopping to plunder or to attack keep, castle or house.
They entered Lord Percy's lands, crossed the Tyne unimpeded,
and reached the Bishopric of Durham, which is good country.
Once there, they began to make war, killing people, burning
towns and wreaking much destruction.

*The English assemble their forces at Newcastle. Their leader, the
Earl of Northumberland, sends his two sons there, Henry Percy the
younger (Hotspur) and Ralph. He himself remains at Alnwick, with
the idea of cutting off the Scots on their return.*

The three Scottish earls came away from Durham, as they
had intended, and halted outside Newcastle for two days.
There was skirmishing during most of each day. The Earl of
Northumberland's sons, two keen young knights, were always
the first in these skirmishes before the gates and barriers.
There was much skilled fighting with lance and sword and on

1. See p. 335, note.

one occasion there was a long hand-to-hand combat between the Earl of Douglas and Sir Henry Percy. By force of arms the Earl captured Sir Henry's pennon, to his great annoyance and that of the other English, and Douglas said to him: 'I shall take this piece of your trappings back to Scotland and put it up on my castle at Dalkeith, right at the top, so that it can be seen a long way off.' 'By God,' said Sir Henry, 'you shall never get it out of Northumberland. You can count on that, so don't boast about it.' 'All right,' Earl Douglas then said, 'come and get your pennon back tonight. I will plant it in front of my tent and we'll see if you can take it away from there.'

It was now late in the day, so the skirmishing ceased. The Scots withdrew to their camp, disarmed, and had a meal. They had plenty of food, and as much meat as they wanted in particular. They kept good watch that night, expecting to be roused up because of the words which had been exchanged. But they were not disturbed, since Sir Henry's men advised him against it.

The next day the Scots decamped from outside Newcastle and started on the road back to their own country. They came to a place called Ponteland, governed by Sir Raymond Delaval, a good Northumbrian knight. They halted there – it was still early morning – and learnt that the knight was in his castle. They prepared to assault it and attacked with such vigour that they captured the castle and the knight inside it. They burnt down the castle and the town and went on to the town and castle of Otterburn, eight miles from Newcastle,[1] where they halted and took up their quarters.

The castle of Otterburn is assaulted on the next day, but not captured. Most of the Scots are in favour of going on to rejoin their main force at Carlisle, but James Douglas wishes to remain at Otterburn and make another attempt on the castle. The delay will also give Henry Percy a chance to recover his pennon, if he so desires.

1. Elsewhere, Froissart has 'seven miles' and 'six miles' ('English leagues' and 'short leagues'), whereas Otterburn is thirty-two miles from Newcastle by the modern road. The mistake is curious since, as Froissart says later, his description of the battle is based on eye-witness accounts of men who took part in it. These must have ridden the distance, and the considerable discrepancy is hard to explain.

All the others gave in to the Earl of Douglas, both for their own honour and out of regard for him, for he was the greatest among them. They settled down comfortably and peacefully, no one hindering them, and built a large number of shelters from trees and leaves. They protected themselves by making skilful use of some big marshes which are there. On the way in between these marshes, on the Newcastle side, they quartered their serving-men and foragers. They placed all their cattle in the marshland. Then they made great preparations to assault the castle again on the next day, for such was their intention.

English scouts obtain a clear picture of the Scottish movements and numbers. They report to Newcastle that this is not the main army, but a comparatively small force. Henry Percy, who can muster about three times the Scots' numbers, decides to follow them at once without waiting for the considerable force which the Bishop of Durham is bringing up to support him.

Having assembled, they left Newcastle in the late afternoon and set out in good order on the same route which the Scots had taken to Otterburn, seven miles[1] from there along a good road. But they could not move fast because of the foot-soldiers who were with them.

While the Scots were sitting over supper – though many had already gone to bed, for they had had a hard day attacking the castle and meant to get up early to assault it again in the cool of the morning – suddenly the English fell upon their encampment. When they first came to it, they mistook the quarters of the servants, near the entrance, for those of the masters. So they raised their cry of 'Percy! Percy!' and began to break into that part of the camp, which was quite strong. You know what a great commotion there is at such moments, and it was very fortunate for the Scots that the English made their first attack on the serving-men for, although these did not hold out long, it gave the rest of them good warning of what to expect. Their commanders therefore sent up a number of their strongest servants and foot-soldiers to keep the English busy, and meanwhile armed themselves and formed up, every knight and man-at-arms under the banner or pennon of

1. See previous note, p. 339.

their captains, and thence under the earls whom they were to follow, each of whom had his own command. Night was now falling fast, but there was a moon and it was fairly light. It was in August and fine and cloudless, and the air was calm and clear.

When the Scots had formed up noiselessly in the order I have described, they left their encampment. Instead of advancing directly ahead to meet the English face to face, they skirted round the marshes and a hill which was there. They enjoyed the great advantage of having prospected the terrain during the whole of the previous day, when the most experienced among them had discussed it and said: 'If the English tried to surprise us in our quarters, we would go that way, and do this and so on.' It was this that saved them, for it is a great thing for men-at-arms who are exposed to a night attack to know the ground round them thoroughly and to have already concerted their plans.

The English soon overcame the servants who had met their first onrush. But as they went farther into the encampment, they constantly ran into fresh men coming up to fight and hinder them. And suddenly there were Scots on their flank, having come round as I described, who charged down on the English like one man, shouting their battle-cries all together and taking them completely by surprise. The English rallied and closed up, seeking a position on firm ground and shouting: 'Percy!' in reply to the 'Douglas!' of the Scots. A fierce battle began, with prodigious lance-thrusts and men on both sides hurtling to the ground in this first clash. Because the English were in great numbers and eager to beat the enemy, they stood their ground and pushed, driving back the Scots, who were very near to defeat. Earl Douglas, who was young, strong and spirited, and eager to win distinction in arms, ignored the knocks and the danger and had his banner brought forward, shouting 'Douglas! Douglas!' Sir Henry Percy and his brother Ralph, who were so angry with the Earl because of the loss of their pennon outside Newcastle, made towards him, shouting their own cry. Great feats of arms were performed when the two bannerets and their men found themselves face to face. As I said, the English were in such strength and fought so well at this first stage, that they drove the Scots back. Two Scottish knights who were there, called Sir Patrick Hepburn and his son, also named Patrick, fought splendidly alongside their commander's banner. But for them, it would certainly have been taken. But they defended it so stoutly, thrusting and dealing such mighty blows until more of their men could come to the rescue, that they and their heirs are still held in honour for it.

I was told by some who took part in the battle in person, knights and squires on both the English and Scottish sides (for in the year after the battle I met at the Count of Foix's court at Orthez two gallant squires belonging to the Count's domain and family, Jean de Castelnau and Jean de Cantiron, who had been with the English; and also when I was back in Avignon in that same year I met a Scottish knight and two squires of the household of Earl Douglas; I recognized them for what they were and they recognized me by the true facts which I could tell them about their country; for, in my younger days, I, the author of this chronicle, travelled widely about the kingdom of Scotland and spent at least a fortnight in the household of Earl William Douglas, the father of the Earl James of whom I am now speaking, at a castle fifteen miles from Edinburgh called Dalkeith, and I had seen Earl James as a fine-looking boy, and a sister of his called Blanche; so I received my information from both sides, all within the year in which the battle had been fought, and all their accounts agreed) – well, they told me that it was a pretty tough business and as well fought as any battle could be, and I could easily believe them; because English on the one hand and Scots on the other are fine fighters and when they meet in a clash of arms, they don't spare themselves. There is no playing about.

Earl James Douglas saw that his men were falling back, so, to recover the lost ground and show his warlike qualities, he took a two-handed axe and plunged into the thickest of the fight, clearing a way in front of him and breaking into the press. None was so well protected by helm or plate as not to fear the blows he dealt. He went so furiously forward, as though he was a Trojan Hector expecting to win the battle single-handed, that he ran into three lances which pierced him all at the same time, one in the shoulder, one in the chest just above the pit of the stomach, and one in the thigh. He could not avoid these thrusts or parry them and was borne to the ground, very badly wounded. Once down he did not get up again. Some of his knights were following him, but not all. It was too dark and they had only the moon to see by. . . .

The English went on, paying little attention to him, merely supposing they had felled some man-at-arms, because elsewhere the Earl of March and Dunbar and his men were fighting courageously and giving them plenty to think about. In following the Douglas battle-cry, they had come up against the two sons of Percy and there they were, thrusting and striking and slashing. In another place the Earl of Moray with his banner and his men was fighting fiercely, harrying the English they encountered and giving them so much to do that it was almost more than they could manage. . . .

The Earl of Northumberland's sons, Sir Henry and Sir Ralph Percy, were putting all they had into the battle. Near the spot where the Earl of Douglas fell, Sir Ralph Percy came to grief. He advanced so far among the enemy that he was surrounded and severely wounded. Gasping for breath, he was taken prisoner and pledged to ransom by a knight called Sir John Maxwell, belonging to the clan and household of the Earl of Moray. In demanding his parole the Scottish knight asked him who he was, for it was too dark to recognize him. Sir Ralph Percy was so badly hurt that he could do no more; he was growing weaker and weaker through loss of blood. He said: 'I am Ralph Percy.' The Scot said: 'Sir Ralph, rescued or not, I pledge you as my prisoner. I am Maxwell.' 'Right,' said the other, 'I agree. But have me seen to. I am very badly wounded. My chausses and my greaves[1] are full of blood already.'

At that moment the Scottish knight heard the cry of 'Moray! The Earl!' very close at hand and saw the Earl and

1. Pieces of leg-armour.

his banner right beside him. So he said to him: 'Look, my lord, I am giving you Sir Ralph Percy as a prisoner. But have him attended to. He is badly wounded.' Very pleased at this, the Earl told him: 'Maxwell, you have certainly earned your spurs.' He made his men open their ranks and take charge of Sir Ralph, whose wounds they staunched and bandaged. The battle continued to rage fiercely and it was still uncertain who would have the best of it. Many captures and rescues were achieved, not all of which came to light.

Now to go back to the young Earl of Douglas, who had done great deeds that night. When he had fallen, with a great press of fighting-men round him, he could not get to his feet because of the mortal lance-wound he had received. His men were following him as closely as they could, and Sir James Lindsay, a cousin of his, with Sir John and Sir Walter Sinclair and other knights and squires came up to him. They found beside him one of his knights who had kept with him throughout, and a chaplain of his who was there not as a priest but as a worthy man-at-arms, for he had followed him all night through the thick of the battle with an axe in his hand. This doughty warrior was laying about him near the Earl, keeping the English back with the great blows he dealt them with his axe, for which service the Scots were truly grateful. It earned him great renown and in the same year he became archdeacon and canon of Aberdeen. The name of this priest was William of North Berwick. It is a fact that he was a tall, finely built man – and brave, too, to do what he did. Nevertheless, he was severely wounded.

When those knights reached the Earl, they found him in a very bad way, and also the knight I mentioned who had followed him so closely, one Sir Robert Hart, who was lying beside him with five wounds from lances and other weapons. Sir John Sinclair asked the Earl how it went with him. 'Pretty badly,' said the Earl. 'But God be praised, not many of my ancestors have died in their beds. I ask you this: try to avenge me. I know I'm dying, my heart keeps stopping so often. Walter, and you, John Sinclair, raise my banner again' (it was indeed lying on the ground, with the gallant squire who bore it dead beside it; this was *David Colleime*,[1] who had refused to become a knight that day although the Earl had wished to dub him because wherever he fought he had been an outstandingly good squire), 'raise my banner,' he said 'and shout Douglas! And tell neither friend nor foe of the state I am in. If our enemies knew of it they would be encouraged, and our friends would lose heart.'

This is done and the battle continues. The English begin to give ground.

The fighting passed beyond where the Earl of Douglas was lying, now dead. In the final big clash, Sir Henry Percy came face to face with the Lord of Montgomery, a very gallant Scottish knight. They fought each other lustily, untroubled by any others, for every knight and squire on both sides was hotly engaged with an opponent. Sir Henry Percy was handled so severely that he surrendered and pledged himself to be the Lord of Montgomery's prisoner.

The English finally give way and many more are taken prisoner. The rest flee back towards Newcastle.

It should be repeated that the English and Scots, when they meet in battle, fight hard and show great staying-power. They do not spare themselves, but go on to the limits of endurance. They are not like the Germans, who make one attack and then, if they see that they cannot break into the enemy and beat him, all turn back in a body. Not so the English and Scots, who order things differently. They stand their ground in the battle, dauntlessly wielding axes and other weapons for as long as their breath lasts. And when they surrender to each other according to the law of arms, they treat their prisoners well without pressing too hard for money, behaving chivalrously to one another, which the Germans do not. It would be better for a knight to be captured by infidels, out-and-out pagans or Saracens, than by the Germans. These constrain gentlefolk in doubly harsh confinements with iron or wooden fetters, chains and other prison instruments beyond all reason and moderation, by means of which they injure or weaken a man's limbs to extort more money. To tell the truth, the

1. Conjectured to be Campbell.

345

Germans are in many ways outside all reasonable laws and it is surprising that others will associate with them or allow them to practise arms beside them, as the French and English do. These behave chivalrously, and have always done so, but the Germans neither do nor wish to.

Meanwhile, the Bishop of Durham has reached Newcastle with a force composed largely of levies. He sets out from the city late at night in support of the Percies, but turns back after meeting fugitives with news of the defeat. Next day, he feels that honour demands that he should try again.

When the Scottish barons and knights installed at Otterburn received news that the English were approaching, the most experienced of them met together to consult. Several possibilities were discussed but, after full consideration, it was decided to stay where they were and await the outcome, since they could not expect to find a better and stronger place. They had a large number of prisoners, whom they could not take with them unless they were able to move freely, and there were also a number of wounded among both their own men and the prisoners, whom they did not want to leave behind. By now, too, it was broad daylight and a clear morning, so that they had a good view around and ahead of them.

They assembled like the experienced soldiers they were and so positioned themselves that they could only be attacked along a single line of approach. They placed their prisoners on one side and caused all their servants, pages and grooms to be armed, for they had arms in plenty taken from the defeated enemy. This they did to make it appear to the English that their numbers were greater than they really were. They then made their prisoners promise – among them were many knights and squires – that they would remain their prisoners whether rescued or not. After that their buglers were told to blow and they sounded one of the loudest fanfares ever heard.

I should explain that it is the Scottish custom, when their men have gathered like this, for all the foot-soldiers to carry horns slung from their necks like a huntsman's. When they all blow them together, some high, some full, some on a middle note, and the others at their own choice, they make such a noise, with the big drums which they also have, that the sound carries at least four miles by day, and six by night. It gives them a tremendous thrill and strikes terror into their enemies. Their leaders ordered them to play like this and meanwhile drew them up in excellent order, placing the archers and servants at the entry to the encampment in a strong posture of defence.

When the Bishop of Durham and his force, consisting of quite ten thousand men of one kind or another, commonfolk and levies – there were few gentry, since these had already gone with Sir Henry Percy – were about three miles from Otterburn, the Scots began to blow their horns and bang their drums, so that it sounded as though the devils of hell were racketing there with them. The approaching force, knowing nothing of this Scottish practice, were thoroughly scared. The din and horn-blowing went on for a long time, and then stopped. When the English came within about one mile of them, they again began to sound their horns as loud and long as before, and then stopped. The Bishop approached with his men in battle-order and halted in full view of the Scots some two bow-shots away. Once again the Scots blew their horns loud and clear and then stopped, but the echo went rolling round for a considerable time. The Bishop of Durham stood there looking at them and noting how they were drawn up, with their flanks protected and themselves closely massed in an order and position which gave them a great advantage. He consulted with a few knights who were there as to what they should do. I understand that, having considered and appreciated the situation, they decided not to launch an attack, and turned back without taking action. It was clear to them that they had more to lose than to gain.

I was told by those on the Scottish side who were at that battle fought between Newcastle and Otterburn on 19 August,[1] 1388, that one thousand and forty of the English of various ranks were taken prisoner, and eighteen hundred and sixty killed, on the field or in the pursuit, with more than a thousand

1. According to other sources, 5 August.

wounded. Of the Scots, about a hundred were killed and two hundred taken prisoner in the pursuit when the English were retreating. If these saw an opportunity, they turned back and fought with their pursuers. The only Scots to be captured were taken in this way, not in the battle.

You can judge what an outstanding and hard-fought battle this was by the number who were killed and captured on both sides, though one came off worse than the other.

BOOK FOUR

(1389–1400)

Queen Isabella's Entry into Paris (1389)

FOUR years after her marriage to Charles VI, a ceremonious reception in the capital was arranged for the young Queen. Froissart was an eye-witness of the festivities he describes.

On Sunday, 20 August 1389, there were such crowds of people in Paris and its outskirts that it was wonderful to see them. In the afternoon of that day the great ladies who were to accompany the Queen assembled in the town of Saint-Denis, and with them the nobles who were to escort their litters and that of the Queen. There were also twelve hundred citizens of Paris, all drawn up on horseback on the two sides of the road and dressed uniformly in tunics of green and crimson silk. The first to enter Paris were Queen Jeanne and her daughter the Duchess of Orléans.[1] They travelled in covered litters with a large escort of gentlemen. Passing along the Rue Saint-Denis, they came to the Palace, where the King was awaiting them. They went no farther on that day.

Then the Queen of France set out with the other ladies: the Duchess of Berry, the Duchess of Burgundy, the Duchess of Touraine, the Duchess of Bar, the Countess of Nevers, the Lady de Coucy and all the others, in order of precedence. Their litters were all similar, and so richly decorated that nothing was lacking. The Duchess of Touraine, however, had no litter, to distinguish her from the others, but was mounted on a palfrey with very rich trappings and rode at a walking-pace on one side of the road. The horses drawing the litters and the nobles accompanying them all went at a walk.

The Queen's escort was headed by the Duke of Touraine and the Duke of Bourbon. After them came the Dukes of

1. *Sic* Froissart, but Jeanne de Bourbon, the Queen Mother, had died in 1377 and he can only be referring to the young King's step-great-grandmother, Blanche de Navarre, widow of Philip VI, who was still alive and took an active part in organizing the ceremonial. The then Duchess of Orléans, Blanche de France, was not her daughter but her step-daughter-in-law.

Berry and Burgundy, one riding on each side, while Sir Pierre
de Navarre and the Count of Ostrevant brought up the rear.
The Queen's litter was an open one with extremely rich
decorations.

[Next came the various ladies of royal blood, with their
escorts.] Of the other ladies who followed them, in covered
carriages or on palfreys, there is no need to speak, nor of the
knights who rode behind them. But I should say that the
serjeants-at-arms and the King's officers had hard work to
clear a way through the crowds. The streets were so thronged
that one might have thought that the whole population had
been summoned out.

At the first Gate of Saint-Denis, which is the entry to Paris
and is called the Bastide, there was the representation of a
starry sky, and in this small children dressed as angels sang
softly and harmoniously. Among them, acted by living people,
was a person representing Our Lady, holding a baby in her
arms. The baby was playing with a little mill made out of a
large walnut. The starry canopy was high and richly emblazoned with the arms of France and Bavaria, with a shining
gold sun which darted out its beams. This gleaming sun was
the King's emblem for the festivities and the jousts. The Queen
and the ladies looked at these things with great pleasure as they
came through the gate, and so did everyone else when they
passed by there.

After seeing this, the Queen and the ladies moved on slowly
to the fountain in the Rue Saint-Denis, which was draped with
a fine azure cloth embroidered with golden fleurs-de-lys, while
the pillars surrounding it were decorated with the arms of
some of the principal nobles of France. From the fountain
flowed streams of excellent honied and spiced wine, and all
round it stood young girls very richly dressed, wearing handsome golden hats and singing very tunefully. It was a sweet
and delightful thing to hear. In their hands they held cups and
goblets of gold, in which they offered wine to all who wished to
drink. When she came up to them, the Queen halted to look
at them and expressed her pleasure at the sight, as did all the
others who saw them.

Next, outside the Church of the Trinity, a raised platform had been set up overlooking the street. On it was a castle, and disposed along the platform was the tournament of King Saladin, with all the participants, the Christians at one end and the Saracens at the other. There were men impersonating all the famous knights who had fought at Saladin's tournament equipped with the arms and armour which were used at that time.[1] A little way from them was a person representing the King of France, with the twelve peers of France round him all wearing their arms. As the Queen's litter came opposite the platform, King Richard (Lionheart) stepped forward from among his companions, went up to the King of France, and asked permission to attack the Saracens. When it had been given, he went back to his twelve companions who drew up in battle order and immediately moved to the attack of Saladin and his Saracens. A fierce mock battle took place, which lasted for some time and delighted the spectators.

The procession then passed on to the second Gate of Saint-Denis, where a castle had been set up, as at the first gate, and a heaven full of stars with a representation of God the Father, the Son and the Holy Spirit, sitting there in majesty. In this heaven young choir-boys dressed as angels were singing very sweetly. As the Queen passed beneath it in her litter, the gates of paradise opened and two angels came out and began to descend. They held in their hands a magnificent crown of gold set with precious stones, and this they set gently on the Queen's head, at the same time singing these lines:

> Lady with the lilied gown,
> Queen you are of Paris town,
> Of France and all this fair countrie:
> Now back to paradise go we.

After this, the lords and ladies saw on the right-hand side of their route, in front of the Chapel of Saint-Jacques, another platform covered with finely woven cloth and curtained like a

---

1. Saladin's tournament was a mock battle, evidently traditional in Froissart's time, representing a perhaps legendary feat of arms by Richard Cœur de Lion and twelve knights during the Third Crusade.

private room. In it were men playing an organ very melo-
diously. And the whole of the Grand'Rue Saint-Denis was
roofed over with camlet and silk, as sumptuously as though
cloth could be had for nothing or as though this had been
Alexandria or Damascus.

And I, the author of this book, who witnessed all these
things myself, could only wonder where they had come from
when I saw them in such abundance. All the houses on both
sides of the Grand'Rue Saint-Denis as far as the Châtelet, and
indeed down to the Grand Pont de Paris, were covered and
hung with tapestries depicting various scenes, which it was
pleasant and entertaining to look at. And so, at walking-pace,
the ladies in their litters and the lords who escorted them came
slowly to the gate of the Châtelet. There they halted to see
another magnificent spectacle. Before the gate of the Châtelet
a wooden castle with watchmen's turrets had been set up,
built strongly enough to last for forty years. At each of the
look-out slits was a man-at-arms in full armour and inside the
castle was a bed curtained and hung as richly as if it had belonged to the King's own chamber. This bed was called the
bed of justice, and on it, represented by a living person, lay
our lady St Anne.

In the courtyard of the castle, which was extremely spacious,
there was a rabbit-warren with great heaps of branches and
foliage, and inside those a large number of hares, rabbits and
birds which kept flying out and going back again, for fear of
the crowd. Then from among the foliage, on the side from
which the procession was coming, a big white stag came out
and made towards the bed of justice. From the other side
came excellent imitations of a lion and an eagle, which advanced fiercely towards the stag and the bed. Then there
appeared from among the branches a dozen young maidens,
wearing golden caps and carrying drawn swords in their
hands. They placed themselves between the stag and the
eagle and the lion, and showed that they intended to protect the
stag and the bed of justice with their swords. The Queen and
the lords and ladies watched this scene with delight, then went
on towards the Grand Pont, which was decorated so mag-

nificently that it could not have been done better. It was draped
with red and green silken cloth and covered with a starry
canopy. The streets were hung and decorated right up to the
Cathedral of Notre-Dame. When the ladies had crossed the
bridge and were approaching Notre-Dame, it was already
late, for ever since they had set out from Saint-Denis the
litters and their escorts had moved only at walking-pace.

Before the Queen entered the Cathedral, she saw another
sight which gave her great pleasure, as it did to all who witnessed it. It was this:

A full month before the Queen's entry into Paris, a skilful
master engineer from Geneva had fastened a rope to the top
of the highest tower of Notre-Dame. This rope, which was of
great length, passed high above the roofs and was fixed at the
other end to the tallest house on the Pont Saint-Michel. As the
Queen and the other ladies came along the Grand'Rue
Notre-Dame, this master, holding two lighted tapers in his
hands (for it was now dark), came off the platform which he
had built on the Cathedral tower and sat on the rope. Then he
walked along it above the street, singing as he went, and all
who saw him wondered with amazement how he could do it.
Still holding the two lighted tapers, which could be seen all
over Paris and for several miles beyond, he performed all
kinds of acrobatic tricks, winning much applause for his skill
and agility.

In the square in front of the Cathedral the Bishop of Paris
was waiting in his ceremonial vestments, together with the
whole body of the clergy. The Queen descended from her
litter, aided by the four Dukes who were with her: Berry,
Burgundy, Touraine and Bourbon. Similarly the other ladies
were helped down from their litters, and those who were on
horseback from their palfreys. They then moved into the
Cathedral in order of precedence, headed by the Bishop and
clergy singing the praises of God and the Virgin loud and
clear.

The Queen was escorted through the church and the choir
up to the high altar, where she knelt down and said prayers
of her own choice, and offered to the treasury of Notre-Dame

four cloths of gold and the crown which the angels had placed on her head as she entered Paris. Immediately after, Sir Jean de La Rivière and Sir Jean Le Mercier offered her a considerably richer crown which they held in readiness, and this was placed on her head by the Bishop of Paris and the four dukes of her escort.

When this had been done, the procession moved back through the Cathedral, and the Queen and the ladies were helped up again into their litters. Around them now were more than five hundred tapers, since it was night. In this state they were led back to the Palace where the King was waiting for them, with Queen Jeanne and her daughter the Duchess of Orléans.[1] Here the ladies were taken, in order of rank, to the rooms reserved for them, but the lords did not go home until after the dancing.

On the next day, which was Monday, the King gave a dinner at the Palace for the ladies, of whom there were a great number. But first the Queen was escorted by the four dukes already named to high mass in the Sainte-Chapelle of the Palace. During mass she was consecrated and anointed, as a Queen of France should be. The Archbishop of Rouen, who at that date was Guillaume de Vienne, officiated.

After mass had been solemnly sung, the King and Queen went back to their rooms in the Palace, and all the ladies retired to theirs. Soon afterwards, the King and Queen entered the banqueting-hall, followed by the ladies.

I should say that the great marble table which is always in the Palace and is never moved had been covered with an oak top four inches thick, on which the dinner was laid. Behind this great table, against one of the pillars, was the King's sideboard, large, handsome and well arranged, covered with gold and silver plate. Many an eye looked covetously at it on

---

1. See note, p. 351. According to the *Grandes Chroniques de France*, the young King had gone out *incognito* earlier in the day to watch his wife's entry. Mingling with the crowd, he had received some hard blows from the sticks of police-sergeants trying to keep the way clear. He took it in good part.

that day. In front of the King's table was a stout wooden barrier with three openings guarded by serjeants-at-arms, royal ushers and mace-bearers, whose duty it was to see that none came through except the serving-men. For you must know that the crowd in the hall was so dense that it was very difficult to move. There were numbers of entertainers, each showing their skill in their different arts. The King, the prelates and the ladies washed their hands. They took their places at table, in this order: at the King's high table, the Bishop of Noyon was at one end, then the Bishop of Langres, then, next to the King, the Archbishop of Rouen. The King wore an open surcoat of crimson velvet lined with ermine and had a very rich gold crown on his head. Next to the King, at a slight distance, sat the Queen, also wearing a rich gold crown. Next to her sat the King of Armenia, then the Duchess of Berry, then the Duchess of Burgundy, then the Duchess of Touraine, then Madame de Nevers, then Madame de Bar, then the Lady de Coucy, then Mademoiselle Marie d'Harcourt. There were no others at the King's high table, except, right at the lower end, the Lady de Sully, wife of Sir Guy de La Trémoille.

At two other tables, running right round the sides of the hall, sat over five hundred other ladies, but the crowd round the tables was so great that they could only be served with the greatest difficulty. Of the courses, which were abundant and excellently prepared, I need not speak. But I will say something of the interludes which were performed. They could not have been better planned, and they would have provided a delightful entertainment for the King and the ladies if those who had undertaken to perform had been able to do so.

In the middle of the great hall a castle had been set up, twenty feet square and forty feet high. It had a tower at each of the four corners and a much higher one in the middle. The castle represented the city of Troy, and the middle tower the citadel of Ilium. On it were pennons bearing the arms of the Trojans, such as King Priam, the knightly Hector his son and his other children, as well as the kings and princes who were besieged in Troy with them. This castle moved on wheels which turned very ingeniously inside it. Other men came to attack the castle in an assault-tower which was also mounted on ingeniously hidden wheels, with none of the mechanism showing. On this were the arms of the kings of Greece and other countries who once laid siege to Troy. There was also, moving in support of them, a beautifully made model ship, on which there must have been a hundred men-at-arms. The three things, castle, assault-tower and ship, moved about thanks to the skilful mechanism of the wheels. The men on the tower and the ship made a fierce attack on one side of the castle, and the men in the castle defended it stoutly. But the entertainment could not last long because of the great crush of people round it. Some were made ill by the heat, or fainted in the crowd. A table near the door of the parliament chamber was overturned by force. The ladies who were sitting at it had to get up hurriedly, without ceremony. The great heat and the stink of the crowd almost caused the Queen to faint, and a window which was behind her had to be broken to let in the air. The Lady de Coucy was also seriously affected. The King saw what was happening and ordered the performance to stop. This was done and the tables were quickly cleared and taken down, to give the ladies more room. The wine and spices were served hurriedly and, as soon as the King and Queen had gone to their apartments, everyone else left also.

Now I would like to say something of the gifts which the Parisians presented on the Tuesday to the Queen of France and the Duchess of Touraine. The Duchess had lately arrived in France from her native Lombardy, for she was the daughter of the Lord of Milan and had married Duke Louis of Touraine this same year. Since this young lady, whose name was Valentine, had never been to Paris until she entered it in the company of the Queen, the citizens rightly owed her a warm welcome.

At twelve o'clock on the Tuesday about forty of the most prominent citizens of Paris, all dressed identically, came to the Hôtel de Saint-Pol [a royal residence on the Seine to which the King had moved the previous evening], bringing the Queen's present through the streets of Paris. It was carried on a litter of beautiful workmanship by two strong men disguised as savages. The litter had a canopy of fine silk crêpe, through which could be seen the treasures which it contained. When the citizens reached the Hôtel de Saint-Pol, they went at once to the King's room, which was open and ready for their reception. They were expected, and those who bring gifts can always be sure of a welcome. They placed the litter on two trestles in the middle of the room, then knelt before the King, saying:

'Most dear and noble sire, to celebrate the joyous arrival of your Queen, your burgesses of Paris offer you all the precious objects on this litter.'

'Many thanks, good people,' replied the King. 'It is a handsome and costly present.'

The burgesses rose to their feet and stepped back. Then, with the King's permission, they left him. When they had gone, the King said to Sir Guillaume des Bordes and to Montaigu, who were with him: 'Let us have a closer look and see what the presents are.'

They went up to the litter and looked into it. This is what it contained: there were four gold pots, four large gold goblets, four gold salt-cellars, twelve gold cups, twelve gold bowls and six gold dishes. The whole of this plate weighed seventy-five pounds in solid gold.

Meanwhile other citizens of Paris, richly dressed all in similar clothes, waited on the Queen, taking her present on a litter which was carried to her room and commending the city and its inhabitants to her. The present consisted of a ship made of gold, two large gold flagons, two gold comfitdishes, two gold salt-cellars, six gold pots, six gold goblets, twelve silver lamps, two dozen silver bowls, six large silver dishes, two silver basins. The whole, both gold and silver, weighed a hundred and fifty pounds. The present was carried into the Queen's room on a litter, as I said, by two men, one of them dressed as a bear and the other as a unicorn.

The third present was taken in a similar way to the Duchess of Touraine by two men disguised as Moors, with blackened faces, rich costumes and white cloths wrapped round their heads, as though they had been Saracens or Tartars. . . . The Duchess was presented with a gold ship, a large gold pot, two gold comfit-dishes, two large gold plates, two gold salt-cellars, six silver pots, six silver dishes, two dozen silver bowls, two dozen silver salt-cellars and two dozen silver cups. The whole, counting the gold and silver together, weighed one hundred pounds. The Duchess was greatly pleased with the gift – and naturally, for it was handsome and costly. She expressed grateful and appropriate thanks to the burgesses who presented it to her, and to the city of Paris which had contributed to buy it.

Such were the gifts presented on that Tuesday to the King, the Queen and the Duchess of Touraine. Their great value was a sign of the wealth and power of the Parisians, for I, the author of this chronicle, who saw them, was told that their cost had amounted in all to more than sixty thousand gold crowns.

A Royal Visitation (1389)

In 1389 the young King Charles VI goes on an official tour of the south of France. Having passed through Burgundy, he visits Pope Clement at Avignon, then travels through his domains in Languedoc. This region has been harshly exploited in the past by the royal dukes of Anjou and Berry and one object of the King's visit is to investigate the complaints of extortion which have been brought to him. His route takes him from Avignon to Nîmes, Lunel and Montpellier.

The King stayed for more than twelve days in Montpellier. All that he saw there, the aspect of the town and of the married ladies and the young ladies, the style they lived in and the amusements which were provided for him and his court, were very greatly to his liking. To tell the truth, the King was still completing his education, for at that time he was young and light-hearted. So he danced and danced the whole night long with the lively ladies of Montpellier. He gave splendid banquets and suppers for them and presented them with gold rings and clasps, to each according to his estimation of her worth. He did so much that he won them over completely, the older with the younger. And some of them would have wished him to stay longer than he did, for every day and night there were parties, dancing and entertainments, and always more to come.

The King enjoyed himself for about a fortnight at Montpellier, while he and his councillors went very thoroughly into the affairs of the town, for that was the main object of his visit. When he had put everything in order with the help of his inner council and had removed several injustices by which the inhabitants had been oppressed, he took affectionate leave of the ladies and set out one morning for Lymous, where he dined, and then lodged for the night at Saint-Hubert. After his morning drink the next day he went on to Béziers, where he received an enthusiastic welcome. The inhabitants of that

361

town and of neighbouring places – Pézenas, Capestang, Narbonne – were awaiting him eagerly in order to lay complaints before him in person against an official of the Duke of Berry called Betisac who had stripped the surrounding districts of everything he had been able to lay hands on. Ever since the royal party had left Avignon, this Betisac had been riding in the company of the King's councillors, who never hinted that they were contemplating his utter destruction. They might have said: 'Betisac, be on your guard, for the King has received grave and bitter complaints against you and strict inquiries are going to be made.' Instead, they welcomed him among them and laughed and joked with him, promising him many honours. He had none of these, as you shall shortly hear.

The King spent three days at Béziers in revels and parties with the ladies before Betisac was in any way accused or even summoned. But the examiners whom the royal council had appointed were inquiring secretly into his affairs. They came upon several damning charges against him which could not be overlooked. So on the fourth day of the King's visit he was called before the council sitting *in camera* and was told: 'Betisac, look at these accusations and answer them.' He was shown a large number of written complaints which had been brought to Béziers and presented to the King in the form of petitions. All spoke loudly of Betisac's scandalous administration and of the impositions and extortions he had inflicted on the people. For some he had good and reasonable answers, for others not. Of the latter he said: 'I have no knowledge of that. Ask the Seneschals of Beaucaire and Carcassonne and the Chancellor of Berry.'

Finally he was told that he must remain under arrest for the time being until matters were cleared up. He had no choice but to obey. As soon as he was in prison, the examiners went to his house and took possession of all the documents and accounts relating to his dealings in the past. They went through them very thoroughly and found that they referred to sums of money levied in the King's estates and domains, to such large amounts that the councillors were amazed when they were read out to them. Betisac was brought before them again. His papers were shown to him and he was asked whether all the sums of money recorded as having been levied in his time in the domains in question were exact, and what had been done with them. He replied: 'The figures are exact. The whole amount has been paid to my lord of Berry, after passing through my hands and those of his treasurers. I have proper receipts for all the sums paid in such-and-such a place in my house.'

They sent there again, and the receipts were brought and read to the council. They corresponded closely enough to the sums levied. The examiners and the council were perplexed and embarrassed. Sending Betisac back into nominal custody, they discussed the matter and said:

'Betisac is cleared of all the charges which have been brought against him. He has shown that the levies of which the people complain have gone in full to my lord of Berry. What has it to do with Betisac if they have been squandered or misused?'

Rightly considered, there were no flaws in Betisac's defence, for the Duke of Berry was the most rapacious of men and did not care how money was raised, so long as he got it. When he had funds before him he wasted them on petty things, like many lords now and in the past. The King's councillors could not see any reasons for condemning Betisac to death; at least, some could not, but there were a certain number who argued thus: 'Betisac has practised so many cruel extortions and has impoverished so many communities to satisfy the Duke of Berry that the blood of these unhappy people cries out against him and demands his death. Since he was in the confidence of the Duke of Berry and knew of the people's poverty, he ought to have quietly remonstrated with him. If the Duke had refused to listen, he should have come before the King and his council and told them of the people's misery and of the way the Duke was treating them. Measures would have been taken, while Betisac would have been fully exonerated of the misdeeds with which he is charged now.'

So Betisac was brought again before the council sitting *in camera*. They questioned him very closely to discover what had happened to all the money he had handled, for the total was found to amount to three million francs. His reply was: 'My lords, it is impossible for me to know exactly. The Duke spent a great deal on buildings and repairs to his castles and houses, on the purchase of estates from the Count of Boulogne and the Count of Étampes, and on jewelry. As you know, he bought such things very freely. Also, he spent money to maintain the great state in which he always lived, and then he gave to Thibault and Morinot and his servants round him, so that they have all become rich.'

'And you yourself, Betisac,' said the council. 'You have been well rewarded for your labours and services, since you have had a hundred thousand francs for your own pocket.'

'My lords,' replied Betisac, 'what I have had was with my lord of Berry's full consent, for he likes his servants to grow rich.'

Then the council answered as one man: 'Ah, Betisac, that was a rash thing to say. It is neither right nor reasonable to grow rich on ill-gotten gains. You must go back to prison while we deliberate on what you have told us. You will await the decision of the King, before whom we shall lay all you have said in your defence.'

'My lords,' said Betisac, 'may it rest in God's hands.'

He was taken back to prison and left there, without appearing again before the council, for a full four days.

When news of the inquiry and of Betisac's imprisonment began to spread, and with it the rumour that any man who had a grievance against him was to come forward, people from the surrounding country flocked into Béziers and, asking their way to the King's quarters, lodged grave and bitter accusations against Betisac. Some complained that he had wrongfully deprived them of their inheritances, others that he had misused their wives and daughters. I must say that, when so many new charges were brought against him, the councillors grew weary of hearing them, for the growing number of complaints showed how fiercely the people hated him. Yet, considered rightly, he had earned this hatred by carrying out the wishes of the Duke of Berry and filling his master's purse. The councillors did not know what to do, since two knights had been sent by the Duke, the Lord of Nantouillet and Sir Pierre Mespin, bearing letters of credence to the King. These knights took responsibility, on the Duke's behalf, for all that Betisac had done in the past, and the Duke called upon the King and his council to hand over his man and treasurer to him.

The King now hated Betisac because of the outcry and the various infamous reports which were current about him. He and his brother were anxious that he should die, saying that he well deserved to. Yet the council dared not condemn him for fear of angering the Duke. They said to the King:

'Sire, since my lord of Berry takes responsibility for all Betisac's acts, whatever they were, we cannot see that he has justly deserved death. At the time when he was at work in this region, imposing taxes and levying tolls, my lord of Berry, on whose behalf he was acting, had sovereign authority here, just as you have now. But one thing could be done to punish the crimes of which he is accused. We could seize all his goods and rents, reducing him to the state he was in when my lord first appointed him, and use them to make restitution to the poor people in those districts which he has exploited most.'

In short, Betisac was on the point of being set free, though at the price of losing his fortune, when events took a new turn.

I cannot be certain without having known the man whether he was as he described himself, but he now declared that he had long been a heretic and was guilty of a most extraordinary and deplorable thing. According to the account which I heard, some men came to visit him by night and said, in order to frighten him:

'Betisac, your case is going very badly. The King, his brother and his uncle the Duke of Bourbon are so mortally angry with you because of the many complaints which have been made against your harsh administration of Languedoc that all three condemn you to be hanged. You cannot escape by giving up your possessions. They have been offered to the King, but his reply was that your fortune is his and your person also, and you will not be left in this prison much longer. We know what we are saying, for you are to be taken out tomorrow, and by all appearances you will be sentenced to death.'

Betisac was greatly alarmed when he heard this. He said to those who were speaking to him:

'Ah, Holy Virgin! Can nothing be done to prevent this?'

'Yes,' they said. 'Tomorrow morning say that you wish to be heard by the King's council. Either they will come to you here or they will send for you. When you are before them, say: "My lords, I fear I have offended God greatly, and it is because of His anger that this misfortune has befallen me." They will ask you in what way you have offended. You will say that you have long erred against the faith and that you firmly hold a certain opinion. When the Bishop of Béziers hears this, he will claim you as his prisoner. You will immediately be handed over to him, because the examination of such cases belongs to the Church. You will be sent before the Pope in Avignon, but once you are there no one will bring a charge against you, for fear of my lord of Berry. The Pope himself would not dare to cross him. If you do as we suggest, neither you nor your fortune will suffer. But if you stay in your present situation and have not got out of it by tomorrow, you will be hanged. The King hates you because of the public outcry against you.'

Betisac believed these deceitful arguments, for when a man goes in fear of death he hardly knows what he is doing. He answered: 'You are true friends to give me such sound advice. May God reward you. The time will yet come when I shall be able to show you my gratitude.'

They went away, leaving Betisac in prison.

When morning came, he called the gaoler and said: 'Friend, I must ask you to send for so-and-so and so-and-so,' (naming the men who were investigating his case). 'Certainly,' replied the gaoler. The examiners were told that Betisac was asking for them. They went to the prison, perhaps already knowing what he intended to tell them. When they arrived, they asked: 'What is it that you have to say to us?' He replied: 'Noble sirs, I have been looking into my acts and conscience, and I fear that I have greatly offended against God. I cannot believe that there is such a thing as the Trinity, or that the Son of God ever abased himself so low as to come down from heaven into the mortal body of a woman. And I believe and declare that our soul ceases to exist when we die.'

'Now, by the Holy Virgin,' said the examiners, 'you err very gravely against the Church. Your words call for the fire. Think what you are saying.'

'I do not know,' replied Betisac, 'whether my words call for fire or for water. But I have held these opinions since I reached the age of understanding, and shall hold them till the end.'

The examiners refused to hear anything more for the moment, and perhaps they were delighted by what they had already heard. They gave strict orders to the gaoler to allow no one in to speak to Betisac, so that he should have no opportunity of retracting, then they went to the King's councillors to tell them the news. When the councillors heard it, they waited on the King, who was just rising from bed. The King was astonished and said:

'It is our will that he should die. He is an evil man, a heretic and a robber. Our will is that he should be burnt and hanged, for then he will have his deserts. He shall certainly not be pardoned or spared to please our fine uncle of Berry.'

It became known in the city of Béziers and the surrounding districts that Betisac had confessed of his own free will that he was a heretic and had long held the opinion of the Bulgars,[1] and that the King intended to have him hanged and burnt. Béziers was filled with rejoicing crowds, so greatly was the man detested. The two knights who had been sent to claim him for the Duke of Berry heard the news. They were astonished and did not know what to make of it. Sir Pierre Mespin reflected and said: 'My lord of Nantouillet, I fear that Betisac has been betrayed. Someone must have secretly advised him to say this horrible thing, giving him to understand that he will be handed over to the Church and sent to Avignon. The fool! He has been badly misled. We can hear people saying what the King means to do with him. We must go at once to the prison and get him to change his plea.'

The two knights left their hostelry and went to the prison, where they told the gaoler that they wished to speak to Betisac. The gaoler made excuses, saying: 'Sirs, I have received strict orders from the King – and so have these four serjeants-at-arms who have been sent here under special instructions – to allow no one to see him, on pain of death. We dare not go against the King's orders.'

The knights saw at once that there was nothing more they could do and that Betisac was lost. They returned to their hostelry, called for their bill, paid it, then mounted their horses and rode back to the Duke of Berry.

The end of Betisac was this. The next day on the stroke of ten he was taken from the prison to the Bishop's palace where the Bishop's legal officers were assembled, together with all those of the King. The Bailiff of Béziers handed over his prisoner to the Bishop's people with these words:

'This is Betisac. We deliver him to you as a Bulgar and a heretic, and a rebel against the faith. If he were not a clerk in holy orders we should have dealt with him as his acts deserve.'

1. *Bulgares* or *Bougres*, whence buggers through the accusation of sodomy: name given to the Albigenses of south-west France. Though savagely suppressed in the Albigensian Crusade of the previous century, the heresy persisted in the local background. Its adherents were Manicheists. They denied the divinity of Jesus and the doctrine of the Trinity and rejected baptism by water. Believing that the Kingdom of Heaven is in this world, they also denied the immortality of the soul.

The ecclesiastical judge asked him if he was such as the Bailiff described him and if he was prepared to admit the fact in public. Thinking that it was in his own interest and that his confession would save him, Betisac answered: 'Yes.' He was asked the same question three times, and three times he admitted his guilt for all to hear. It is strange that a man should be so deceived and deluded, for if he had kept his mouth shut except about the charges on which he had been arrested, no harm would have come to him and the Duke of Berry's warrant would have set him free. But it must be supposed that Fortune played him this trick, so that when he thought he was most securely seated on top of her wheel, she spun him down into the mud – as she has done to thousands of others since the world began.

He was delivered back by the ecclesiastical judge into the hands of the Bailiff, who exercised temporal authority for the King, and the Bailiff immediately had him taken to the square outside the palace. Betisac was hustled so fast that he had no chance of arguing or recanting, and when he saw the fire prepared in the square and found himself in the hands of the executioner he was struck dumb with terror, seeing clearly that he had been betrayed. At last he cried out that he wanted to be heard, but no attention was paid to him. He was told: 'Betisac, it is decreed that you shall die. Your evil acts have brought you to this evil end.'

They hustled him on. The fire was ready. A gibbet had been set up in the square, and at the foot of it a stake with a heavy iron chain. Another chain hung from the top of the gibbet with an iron collar attached. This collar, which opened on a hinge, was put round his neck, then fastened and hauled upwards so that he should last longer. The first chain was wound round him to bind him more tightly to the stake. He was screaming and shouting: 'Duke of Berry, I am being wronged! They are killing me without cause!'

As soon as he was secured to the stake, great heaps of faggots were piled against it and set on fire. They flamed up immediately. So was Betisac hanged and burnt, and the King of France could have seen him from his window if he wanted to.

By Betisac's miserable end the people were avenged on
him. It is true that he had done them great harm by his extortions in the time when he administered Languedoc.

After Béziers, the King visits Carcassonne, Narbonne and other
places, before coming to Toulouse. Here he is joined by Gaston
Phoebus of Foix, travelling in almost royal state. The Count does
homage to the King of France and tries to settle the succession of part
of his domains on his bastard son Yvain, in return for a promised
legacy of 100,000 francs to the King. He is given a guarded answer.

Acting on the advice which he had received, the King said
this to the Count and barons of Foix:

'I hold in my hand the homage made for the domain of
Foix, and if it should happen that in our time the title becomes
vacant through the death of our cousin the Count of Foix, we
will then decide the matter so justly, according to the best
advice we are given, that Yvain de Foix and all the men of
Foix will be contented.'

This assurance was quite satisfactory to the Count of Foix
and the barons and knights of Foix who were present there.

Soon afterwards, it was decided that the King should leave
Toulouse and make his way back to France. All his followers
made their arrangements accordingly, while the Archbishop
of Toulouse, the citizens and the ladies of the place went to
take their leave of him. He left the city one morning after his
drink and lodged that night at Castelnaudery, then pressed on
until he reached Montpellier, where he had a joyous welcome.
He relaxed there for three days, for this was the town which
had pleased him so much, with its maids and its ladies; yet he
very much wanted to get back to Paris and see the Queen.
It so happened that, while chatting idly with his brother, the
Duke of Touraine, he said: 'Brother, I wish that I and you
were in Paris at this moment, leaving all our followers here,
just as they are. I feel a great desire to see the Queen, and you
no doubt to see your duchess.' 'Sire,' replied the Duke, 'we
aren't in Paris. It's too far off to get there just by wishing it.'
'You are right,' said the King. 'Yet I have an idea that I could
soon really be there if I wanted to.' 'By hard riding, then,'

said the Duke. 'That's the only way. So could I, but it would be a horse that would take me.' 'All right,' said the King. 'Which of us will get there first, I or you? Let's have a bet on it.' 'It's a bargain,' said the Duke, who was quite ready to exert himself to win the King's money.

They made a wager of five thousand francs on which of them would reach Paris first, both to start at the same time on the next day. Each was to take only one servant with him, or a knight in place of a servant, for that was how it turned out. No one raised objections to the wager, and they both got on their horses as arranged. With the King was the Lord of Garencières as his sole attendant. The Duke of Touraine had the Lord of La Viefville with him. Those four keen young men continued riding night and day or, when they felt like it, had themselves taken on in carriages to give themselves a rest. Of course they made several changes of horses.

So the King of France and his brother of Touraine rode forward with all their energy, each striving to win the other's money. Think of the discomforts those two rich lords endured through sheer youthful spirits, for they had left all their household establishments behind. The King took four-and-a-half days to reach Paris, and the Duke of Touraine only four-and-a-third; they were as close to each other as that. The Duke won the bet because the King rested for about eight hours one night at Troyes, while the Duke went down the Seine by boat as far as Melun, and from there to Paris on horseback. He went to the Hôtel de Saint-Pol, where the Queen and his own wife were, and asked for news of the King, not knowing whether he had arrived ahead of him or not. When he learnt that he was not there yet, he was very pleased indeed and said to the Queen: 'Madam, you will soon be hearing something of him.' He was quite right, for not long after the King came in too. When his brother saw him, he went to meet him and said: 'Sire, I've won the bet. Have the money paid to me.' 'Yes, you have won,' said the King. 'You shall be paid.'

Then they described their whole journey to the ladies, saying where they had started from and how, in four-and-a-half days, they had come all that way from Montpellier, which is a good four hundred and fifty miles from Paris. The ladies treated the whole thing as a joke, but they did realize that it was a great feat of endurance, such as only the young in body and heart would have attempted. I should add that the Duke of Touraine insisted on being paid in hard cash.

Tournament at Saint-Inglevert (1390)

WHILE *Charles VI was in the south of France, three French knights, Boucicaut the younger, Regnault de Roye and Jean de Sempy, had issued a challenge inviting all comers to meet them in a friendly trial of arms near Calais. The challenge was directed particularly at England, with which country a three-year truce had recently been concluded. Part of the formal invitation ran:*

'... and we beg all those noble knights and foreign squires who are willing to come not to imagine for a moment that we are doing this out of pride, hatred or malice, but in order to have the honour of their company and to get to know them better, a thing which we desire with our whole hearts. And none of our shields shall be covered with iron or steel, nor shall the shields of those who come to joust against us. Nor shall there be any other unfair advantage, fraud, trickery or evil design, nor anything not approved by those appointed by both sides to guard the lists.'

At the beginning of the merry month of May, the three young knights of France named above were fully prepared for the trial of arms they were to hold at Saint-Inglevert and which had been announced in France, England and Scotland. They came first to Boulogne-sur-mer, where they stayed for a certain number of days, and then went on to the Abbey of Saint-Inglevert. There they were delighted to learn that a large number of knights and squires had come across from England to Calais. In order to hurry things forward and let the English know they were ready, they had three large and luxurious crimson tents set up in due form at a spot between Calais and Saint-Inglevert. At the entrance to each tent were hung two shields emblazoned with the arms of the particular knight, one a shield of peace and the other a shield of war.[1]

1. The 'peace' arms sometimes used in tournaments were lighter and less lethal than those used in actual war. This applied particularly to the

373

The understanding was that whoever wished to run a course against any of them should touch one of the shields, or send someone to touch it, or both shields if he liked. He would then be provided with the opponent and the choice of joust he had asked for. . . .

On 21 May, in accordance with the proclamation which had been made, the three French knights were in readiness, with their horses saddled and equipped, as the rules of the tournament required. On the same day, all those knights and squires who wished to joust, or to watch the jousting, set out from Calais and rode to the appointed spot, where they drew up on one side of the lists. It was a wide and spacious stretch of ground with a level surface of good grass.

Sir John Holland (Earl of Huntingdon) began by sending one of his squires to knock on the war shield of my lord Boucicaut. Boucicaut came out of his tent in full armour, mounted his horse, and took up a shield and then a stout lance with a good steel point. The two knights rode to their separate ends and, having eyed each other carefully, they clapped spurs to their horses and came together at full speed. Boucicaut hit the Earl of Huntingdon in such a way that he pierced his shield and slid the point of his lance right over his arm without wounding him. Both knights rode on and stopped neatly at the end of their course. This joust was much admired. At the second lance they hit each other slightly, but did no damage, and at the third the horses refused.

The Earl of Huntingdon, who was jousting with relish and had warmed to the work, rode back to his mark and waited for Boucicaut to take up his lance again; but he did not do so and made it clear that he had finished jousting for that day so far as the Earl was concerned. Seeing this, the Earl sent a squire to knock on the war shield of the Lord of Sempy. He, who would never have refused a challenge, immediately came out of his tent, mounted his horse and took up his shield and lance.

_____

lance, which in its 'peace' form had a head consisting of three blunt prongs in place of the sharp-pointed blade of the war lance.

When the Earl saw that he was ready and eager to joust, he clapped his spurs to his horse, while Sempy did the same. They lowered their lances and came straight at one another, but just as they met, the horses crossed. They hit each other nevertheless, but because of the unfortunate crossing, the Earl was unhelmed. He returned to his own men and was quickly rehelmed and handed his lance. The two knights spurred forward and met this time with straight lances, hitting each other clean and hard on their shields. Both were nearly knocked to the ground, but they gripped their horses with their legs and stayed on. Each went back to his own end to rest a little and get his breath back. Sir John Holland, always eager to perform with honour in the lists, took up his lance again and gripped his shield tight and spurred his horse on. When Sempy saw him coming, he did not hold back but rode towards him in the straightest possible line. The two knights hit each other with their war lances on the steel helms, striking them so clean and hard that sparks flew from them. In this clash Sempy was unhelmed. The two knights passed very briskly on, then rode back each to his own end.

This joust was very highly applauded, and both French and English said that all three knights, the Earl of Huntingdon, my lord Boucicaut and the Lord Sempy, had jousted admirably, without either sparing themselves or causing each other an injury. The Earl of Huntingdon asked to be allowed to run another lance for the love of his lady, but this was not permitted him.

Froissart goes on to describe the whole of the rest of the tournament, encounter by encounter and lance by lance, using very similar terms throughout. In the four days over which the jousts lasted, more than forty challengers measured themselves against the three French knights, who remained unbeaten. In all one hundred and thirty-six lances are described, of which the following are a small further selection.

Next, a gallant knight of great spirit, John of Beaumont in England, came forward and sent a squire to rap on my lord Boucicaut's shield. That knight was not slow to respond, for he was already mounted on his horse, having jousted a short time before with Sir Lewis Clifford. He took his shield and his lance and placed himself in position for jousting. The two knights spurred their horses hotly forward and came at each other. Lord Beaumont did not handle his lance well and struck Boucicaut a glancing blow, but Boucicaut struck him squarely on the middle of his shield and knocked him off his horse and then passed on. The English knight got up and, with the help of his men, was put back on his horse. The Lord Sempy then came forward to joust with him. They ran two lances very prettily without hurting one another.

Next came forward Sir Godfrey Seton, a gallant knight and a good jouster. He showed plainly, by the way he sat on his horse holding his lance, that he was eager to joust. He sent one of his squires to rap on the war shield of Sir Regnault de Roye. That knight responded, for he was ready mounted on his horse, with his shield at his neck. He took his lance and put himself in good jousting posture. The two knights spurred forward simultaneously and came together as squarely as they knew how, striking a violent blow on each other's shields. Their lances were stout and did not break, but curved up, and the powerful thrusts by strong arms stopped the horses dead in their tracks. Both knights then went back to their own ends, without dropping their lances, which they carried freely in front of them before putting them again in the rests. Then they spurred their horses, which were good, strong and tough. They came again at each other, but crossed just as they met, through the fault of the horses, not of the riders. As they passed by each other to ride round to their own ends again, they dropped their lances. They were picked up by ready hands and given back to them. When they had them, they put them in the rests and spurred their horses, showing that they did not mean to spare themselves, for they had warmed to the work. The English knight hit Sir Regnault de Roye very hard near the top of his helm, but did no other damage to him; Sir Regnault hit him on the shield with such a firm, powerful thrust, delivered with so strong an arm – for he was one of the strongest and toughest jousters in France at that time and also he was truly in love with a gay and beautiful young lady, and this contributed greatly to his success in all his undertakings – that his lance pierced the left-hand side of the English knight's shield and went straight into his arm. As it did so, the lance broke, the longer part falling to the ground and the shorter part remaining in the shield with the steel point in the arm. Nevertheless, the Englishman completed his ride round and came back very briskly to his own end. His friends attended to him. The lance head was pulled out and the wound staunched and bound up, while Sir Regnault de Roye went back to his people and waited there, leaning on another lance which they had given him.

For this joust Sir Regnault was greatly admired by his own side, and equally by the English. Although he had wounded the other knight, not a single abusive remark was made to him, for such are the hazards of arms. One man comes off well, the other badly. And also they were jousting with the full armament.

An English squire and good jouster called John Savage came forward; he was a squire of honour of the bodyguard of the Earl of Huntingdon. He sent a man to rap on the war shield of Sir Regnault. The knight, who was waiting ready armed inside his tent, came out eager to joust and mounted his horse. His shield was buckled on, he took his lance and placed it in the rest. Both men spurred at full speed towards each other until they met. They hit each other full on the centre of their shields, with such force that one or both must have fallen if the shields had not split.

This was a fine and dangerous encounter, although the jousters suffered no injury. After piercing the shields, their lances glanced off sideways, breaking off about one foot from the blades, which remained fixed in the shields, while the two men passed on with the broken shafts. The onlookers feared that they had wounded each other badly, and each side hurried to their man, but were glad to find that neither had suffered harm. They were told that they had done enough for that day, but John Savage was not satisfied by this, saying that

377

he had not crossed the sea merely to run one lance. When this remark was repeated to Sir Regnault de Roye, he said 'He is quite right. It is proper for him to be fully satisfied either by me or my companions-in-arms.' They were got ready again and given new shields and lances. When each was in position on his mark, they eyed one another and clapped spurs to their horses simultaneously. They lowered their lances as they approached and expected to meet squarely, but were prevented by their horses running across. So they missed with their second lance, to their great annoyance, and returned each to his own end. Their lances, which they had thrown down in disgust, were handed back to them, and they put them in the rests, looked carefully at one another and spurred their horses forward. This time they hit each other on the helms, straight on the eye-slits; the points caught there in such a way that they unhelmed each other as they rode past. It was a fine thrust which all admired. Each returned to his own end. The English went up to John Savage and told him once more that he had done enough for that day and could leave off with honour, and that others besides himself must be given a chance to practise arms. He yielded to this advice, put down his shield and lance and, getting off his courser, mounted a rounsey to watch the others jousting.

Next there came foward a knight from Bohemia, belonging to the Queen of England's personal guard, whose name was Herr Hans. He was considered a good jouster, strong and tough. His arms were argent, three gryphons' feet sable with azure claws. When he came into the lists, he was asked which of the three knights he wished to joust against. He said, Boucicaut. An English squire was sent, as the rules required, to knock on my lord Boucicaut's war shield. This knight, being ready armed and mounted, duly responded to the challenge. His shield was buckled on, he took his lance and placed it in the rest, and looked carefully at the Bohemian knight, who was also in jousting posture with his shield at his neck and his lance in his hand. They spurred their horses hard forward and came together, expecting to hit each other squarely, but this they failed to do. The Bohemian knight dealt a foul blow which was strongly condemned, for he struck my lord Boucicaut's helm with an ugly sideways thrust before riding on. The English saw clearly that he was at fault and knew that he had forfeited his horse and armour if the French insisted on it. The French and English held a long discussion together about that improper thrust, but finally the three knights excused him, from a desire to please the English.

Herr Hans begged to be allowed to run just one more lance and was asked whom he wished to challenge. He sent a squire to rap on the war shield of Sir Regnault de Roye. This knight, who was in his tent and had not yet jousted that day, came out fully armed and said that he would be glad to satisfy him, since such was the agreed procedure. His shield was buckled on, his lance was handed to him. He took it and put it in the rest and looked long and carefully ahead of him, so as to hit the Bohemian fair and square. Both spurred their horses. As they neared each other, they lowered their lances and struck one another full on their shields. Sir Regnault de Roye, who was one of the strongest and toughest jousters in France at that time, hit him so hard that he lifted him right out of the saddle and sent him flying to the ground with such force that they thought he was killed. The French knight passed on and rode round to return to his mark. Herr Hans's men got him up with great difficulty and took him back among them. The English were very pleased that he had suffered this defeat, because of the unchivalrous way in which he had jousted on his first course. And need I say that he had no mind to joust again that day?[1]

1. The passages given above cover nearly all the incidents and variations of the joust as described by Froissart. A few additional details are contained in these extracts:

As they were nearing each other, both horses swerved away, preventing them from hitting each other with a full thrust. (Sempy and John Russell.)

My lord Boucicaut broke his lance, but the English knight kept his intact and used it well, for he knocked off Boucicaut's helm so violently that the blood gushed from his nose. My lord Boucicaut retired to his tent and did no more jousting that day, for it was getting towards evening. (Boucicaut and Sherborne.)

The jousts ended for that day (Thursday) and no one else came forward from the English side. So the Earl of Huntingdon, the Earl Marshal, Sir Lewis Clifford, Lord Beaumont, Sir John Clynton, Sir Jean d'Aubrecicourt, Sir Thomas Sherborne and all the knights who had jousted during the four days went in a company to the French knights and thanked them warmly for the sport they had had, saying:

'All the knights and squires in our company who wish to joust have done so, so we take our leave of you, for we are returning to Calais and thence to England. We are well aware that anyone else wishing to make a trial of arms against you will find you here for the remainder of the thirty days mentioned in your challenge. Once we are back in England, we assure you that we will inform all the knights and squires whom we meet of this tournament and will request them to come and find you here.'

'Many thanks,' the three knights replied, 'they will be cordially welcomed and provided with a trial of arms, as you have been. And with that we thank you greatly for the courtesy which you have shown us.'

On that peaceful and friendly note the English left the French at the lists of Saint-Inglevert and went back to Calais.

It may be added that, after the English company had taken leave of the French knights, the King of France and the Lord of Garencières, who had been present at the jousts *incognito*,

---

Sempy unhelmed him so violently that the buckle to which the helm was attached behind broke, and it fell on the grass. (Sempy and Blaket.)

The thrusts were good and much admired, for both were unhelmed, only their caps remaining on their heads. (Boucicaut and William Mascley.)

The force of the thrusts which they delivered on each other's shields lifted their horses' forelegs from the ground and both knights reeled in the saddle. Nevertheless, they rode on. . . . (R. de Roye and Jean d'Aubrecicourt.)

Swinnerton did very well not to fall off. It was quite surprising, for Sir Regnault hit him in such a way that he forced his spine right back on to his horse's crupper. He straightened up very nimbly as they passed by, but lost his lance. (R. de Roye and Swinnerton.)

went back for the night to Marquise. Early the next day, Friday, they left there to return to France, riding continually until they reached Creil on the river Oise, where the Queen of France was staying. Very few people except his personal attendants knew where the King had been.

The Duke of Touraine in Trouble (*1391*)

THE Duke of Touraine at that time so doted on Sir Pierre de Craon that he treated him as his most intimate companion, dressed him in clothes similar to his own, took him with him wherever he went, and told him all his secrets. The Duke was still a susceptible young man, very fond of the company of ladies and girls, and very willing to amuse himself with them. In particular, I was told, he fell violently in love with a beautiful Parisian lady, young and gay. His attachment became known and his secret was revealed in such a way that the affair led him into serious trouble. The Duke could think of no one to blame for this except Sir Pierre de Craon, since he had confided in him about everything and had taken him secretly with him when he had a meeting with the young lady. The Duke, who was very much in love with her, seems to have promised her a thousand gold crowns if she would go to bed with him. The lady refused them, saying that she did not love the Duke for his money, but had been attracted to him by true affection, and that, 'thank God, she would not sell her honour for gold or silver'. All this conversation, these secrets and promises, came to the ears of the Duchess of Touraine,[1] who immediately sent for the young lady and had her brought to her private room. When she came in, she addressed her by her name and said very angrily: 'Well, so you're trying to make trouble between the Duke and me!' The young lady was dumbfounded and answered, weeping, 'No, no, madam, I swear to God! I am not trying to. I would never dare to think of such a thing.' 'But that's how it is,' the Duchess went on. 'I know everything about it. The Duke loves you and you love him, and things have gone so far that in such-and-such a place (which she named), he promised you a thousand gold crowns to go to bed with him. You refused them. That was wise of you, and this time I forgive you. But I forbid you,

1. Valentina Visconti, daughter of the ruler of Milan.

382

if you value your life, to have any more dealings with him. Just send him packing.'

The young lady, feeling the truth of this accusation and the danger she was in, replied: 'Of course, madam, I will get rid of him as soon as I can and will make sure that you never hear of anything else to displease you.' On this understanding the Duchess dismissed her and she went back to her house.

Soon afterwards the Duke, in ignorance of all this and still very much in love with the lady, went to some place where she also was. When she saw him, she avoided him and showed no signs of love, but quite the contrary. She dared not show her feelings, and also she had given the Duchess her sworn promise. The Duke was very puzzled by her behaviour and insisted on knowing the reason for it. The young lady answered amid tears: 'My lord, either you have been telling Madame de Touraine about that offer you once made me, or someone else has done it for you. Think carefully who you have confided in, for I have been threatened with most dire consequences by Madame de Touraine herself. I have promised faithfully that, except on this one occasion, I will have no more conversations with you, so that she shall have no further cause for jealousy.'

The Duke was both angry and perplexed to hear this, and said: 'My dear lady, I swear to you on my honour that I would rather lose a hundred thousand francs than tell that to the Duchess. But, since you have given a promise, keep it, and I will try at all costs to get to the bottom of this and find out who can have disclosed our secrets.'

With this assurance, the Duke turned away from the young lady and left her in peace, hiding his displeasure for the time being. He possessed a cool and controlled manner and could disguise his feelings, but he was thinking hard about the matter. That evening he went to his wife the Duchess and had supper with her, and gave a greater show of affection than he had ever done before. He succeeded, by kind and coaxing words, in persuading her to reveal her secrets and admit that she had found out about him from Sir Pierre de Craon. At the time he affected to treat it lightly and said little more about it.

That night passed. The next morning, on the stroke of nine,

he got on his horse and left the Hôtel de Saint-Pol for the Louvre, where his brother the King was about to go to mass. The King, who was extremely fond of him, greeted him affectionately, but he noticed, from the Duke's behaviour, that he was very disturbed. 'Well, brother,' he said to him. 'What is the matter? You look worried.' 'Sire,' he replied, 'I have good reason to be.' 'Why?' the King asked. 'We wish to know the cause.'

Holding nothing back, the Duke related the whole affair to him in detail, complaining bitterly of Sir Pierre de Craon's behaviour, and saying: 'Sire, I swear by my loyalty to you that, if it would not reflect on my honour after showing him such great favours, I would have him killed.' 'You must not do that,' said the King, 'but I will have him told by my most trusty servants to leave my household, because I no longer require his services. At the same time you will turn him out of yours.' 'That is exactly what I mean to do,' said the Duke, feeling more or less satisfied by the King's reply.

On that same day Sir Pierre de Craon was told by the Lord de La Rivière and Sir Jean Le Mercier, speaking in the King's name, that his services were no longer required in the royal household and that he should seek advancement elsewhere. He was told the same thing by Sir Jean de Bueil and the Lord of Herbault, Seneschal of Touraine. Finding himself dismissed like this, he was thoroughly crestfallen, and then bitterly resentful. He was unable to imagine the reason, for none had been given him. He did indeed try to come before the King and the Duke, to ask in what way he could have offended them, but was told that neither was willing to see him. Realizing that he had been cornered, he made his arrangements and left Paris with a heavy heart. He went first to a castle he possessed in Anjou, called Sablé, where he stayed for a time. He was very depressed, for now he had been expelled from the royal household, the Touraine household, and the household of the Queen of Naples and Jerusalem.[1]

1. The widow of the King's uncle, the Duke of Anjou, to whom P. de Craon had first been attached. The title had been assigned to the Anjou family by Queen Joanna of Naples. See above, pp. 209–10.

Since these three courts were closed to him, he decided to go to his cousin, the Duke of Brittany, and tell him all that had happened. Arriving at Vannes, he was welcomed by the Duke, who already knew most of the story. He related the whole business to him again word for word, describing how he had been treated. When the Duke of Brittany had heard his account, his comment was: 'Console yourself, cousin. All this has been brewed up against you by Clisson.'[1]

1. Olivier de Clisson, Constable of France, opposed to P. de Craon and an enemy of the Duke of Brittany, whom he had once served.

The Death of the Count of Foix (1391)

In that same year the noble and gallant Count of Foix died, in rather a strange way. I will describe how it happened.

It should be said that of all the pleasures of this world he particularly loved hunting with hounds, and constantly maintained more than sixteen hundred of them for his use. At that time the Count was at Orthez in Béarn and had gone out hunting in the woods of Sauveterre on the road to Pamplona in Navarre. On the day of his death he had spent the whole morning until noon in pursuit of a bear, which was finally caught. By the time it had been killed and cut up, it was mid-afternoon. He asked his men where dinner had been prepared for them, and was told at the Hospice of Orion about five miles from Orthez. 'Good,' he said, 'let's go and eat there. Then in the cool of the evening we will ride on to Orthez.'

They proceeded to do as he said and rode slowly into the village mentioned. The Count dismounted before the inn, followed by his people. He went into the room prepared for him and found it strewn with freshly cut greenery and all the walls covered with green branches to make the place cooler and more fragrant, for the air outside was stiflingly hot, as is usual in August. When he got into this cool, fresh room, he said: 'This greenstuff makes me feel much better. It's been a dreadfully hot day.' He sat down on a chair and chatted a little with Sir Espan de Lyon, talking about the hounds and which of them had done best. While he was talking, his bastard son Yvain came in with Sir Pierre de Gabaston; the tables were ready laid in the same room. He called for water to wash in and two squires, Raymonnet de Lanne and Raymonnet de Caupenne, came forward with it. Arnauton d'Espagne took the silver basin and another knight called Sir Thibault took the towel. The Count rose from his seat and stretched out his hands to be washed. As soon as the cold water fell on his fingers, which were well-shaped, long and straight, his face turned white, his heart throbbed violently, his legs failed him, and he fell back on to the chair, exclaiming: 'I am dying. Lord God have mercy!' These were the last words he spoke, though he did not die at once, but fell into a state of pain and shivering.

The knights and his son, who were watching him in dismay, lifted him in their arms and carried him very gently to a bed, on which they laid him and covered him. They thought that he had simply had a fainting-fit. The two squires who had brought the water, in order not to be suspected of having poisoned him, went to the wash-basin and said: 'This was the water! We tested it in the presence of all of you. We will do so again.' And they did so, until all were satisfied. Bread, water, spices and other restoratives were put into his mouth, but all to no effect. Within half-an-hour he was dead, having given up his soul very quietly. May God have mercy upon him!

It need hardly be said that all those present were grieved and appalled beyond measure. They shut the door tight so that no one in the inn should see what had happened or know that the gallant Count was dead. The knights looked at his son Yvain, as he stood there lamenting and wringing his hands, and said to him: 'Yvain, it's all over. You have lost your gallant father. We know that he loved you above everyone else. Now act quickly. Get your horse and ride to Orthez. Take possession of the castle and the treasure inside it, before anyone else gets there or my lord's death is known.'

This persuaded Sir Yvain and he said:

'Sirs, I thank you. You have done me a generous service for which I shall yet reward you. But give me my father's tokens, because I shall not be able to get into the castle without them.'

'That is true,' they replied. 'Here they are.' He took them. They were a ring which the Count of Foix wore on his finger and a little knife with a long blade with which he sometimes cut up his food at table. These and none others were the tokens known to the gate-keeper of Orthez castle. Unless he was shown them he would never open the gate.

Sir Yvain de Foix set out from the Hospice of Orion with two companions only and rode fast to Orthez. No news of his father's death had reached the town. He rode through the length of it without speaking to anyone, and no one took much notice of him. He came to the castle and called to the gate-keeper, who answered: 'What do you want, my lord Yvain? Where is my lord?' 'He is at the Hospice,' said Yvain. 'He has sent me to get some things from his room and take them back to him. To prove that that is true, look at these. Here are his ring and his knife.' The gate-keeper looked through a window and recognized the tokens. He opened the wicket-gate and Yvain went in with one companion, while the servant stayed with the horses or took them to the stable.

When Sir Yvain was inside, he said to the gate-keeper: 'Lock the door.' He did so. When it was locked, Sir Yvain seized the keys and said to him: 'If you utter a word you're a dead man.' The gate-keeper was astounded and asked why. 'Because,' said Yvain, 'my father has died and I want to take possession of his treasures before anyone else comes.' The gate-keeper obeyed, having no choice, and because he would just as soon have Sir Yvain reap the advantage as another. Sir Yvain knew where the Count's treasure was kept and he went towards it. It was in a big tower which had three pairs of heavy doors secured with iron bars, each of which had to be opened with different keys. These keys did not come to his hand, for they were kept in a casket made of tempered steel and locked with a little steel key. The Count used to carry this key on him when he went riding outside Orthez, and it was found in a silk tunic which he wore over his shirt, by the knights watching the body, after Yvain had left the Hospice. When they saw it, they were puzzled to know what the little key was for. But the Count's chaplain who was there, and who knew all his master's secrets because he was high in his confidence and had been taken alone with him on the visits he made to his treasury, said on seeing it: 'Sir Yvain has made a wasted journey. Without that key he cannot get to the treasure, for it unlocks a small steel box containing all the keys of the treasury.'

The knights were dismayed to hear this and said to the chaplain, whose name was Master Nicholas: 'You would do well to take it to him. It would be much better for Sir Yvain to be in possession of the treasure than someone else. He is a good knight, and our lord the Count, to whom God be merciful, was very attached to him.' 'Since that is how you feel,' said the chaplain, 'I will gladly do so.'

He took the key, got on his horse and set out for the castle of Orthez, where Sir Yvain was desperately searching for the keys and vainly trying to devise some way of breaking the iron fastenings of the doors in the tower, for they were very strong and he lacked the necessary tools to do it with. While this was going on and Master Nicholas was hurrying to join him, the rumour reached Orthez by some means or other, perhaps through women or servants from the Hospice of Orion, that their lord the Count was dead. It was bitter news, for he was greatly beloved by everyone. The whole town began to stir and the people to collect in the main square and talk among themselves. Some said that they had seen Sir Yvain passing by all alone. 'We saw Sir Yvain come and ride through the town and go towards the castle. It was easy to tell by his face that something was wrong.' Others took it up: 'Yes, something must have happened. He never used to ride back ahead of his father.' While the people were gathering and murmuring in the square, along came the chaplain and landed right in the middle of them. They swarmed round him to get the news, asking: 'Master Nicholas, how is my lord? They are saying that he is dead. Is it true?' 'No,' said the chaplain, 'but he is very ill. I've come to get something to make him better, and then I shall go back to him with it.' So saying, he left them and reached the castle, where Sir Yvain was overjoyed to see him, for without the key which he brought he could never have entered the treasury tower.

Now this is what the people of the town did: they began to grow very suspicious about the Count's fate and said among themselves: 'It is night now, but there has been no definite news of my lord, no sign of steward or clerks or officers: yet Sir Yvain and his chaplain, who knew all his secrets, have gone into the castle. Let us place a guard over the castle for tonight and tomorrow we shall know more about things. And let us send secretly to the Hospice to find out what is happening, for we know that most of my lord's treasure is in the castle. If it were stolen or removed by some trickery, we should be held responsible and would get the blame, so we must provide against that.'

They all agreed on this and had you been there you would have seen the men of Orthez rousing up, flocking towards the castle, assembling in the open space in front of it, while their leaders set guards over all the town gates, so that none could enter or leave without permission. There they stayed until morning, when the news of the Count's death became known for certain. The whole town was filled with lamentations, for he was much beloved there. The guard was strengthened at every point and all the rest of the townsmen went with their weapons to the space before the castle.

When Sir Yvain de Foix saw them from inside and realized that they knew the truth about his father's death, he said to the chaplain: 'Master Nicholas, I have failed in my plan. These men of Orthez have woken up to it and I cannot get out of here without their permission. More and more of them are flocking into the square down there. I shall have to make myself small before them. It's no good trying to use force.' 'Quite right,' said the chaplain, 'you will gain more by soft words than by proud ones. Go and talk to them, and speak prudently.'

Yvain addresses the citizens from the tower, appealing to them to support his claim to part of an inheritance which will be divided and may well be in dispute. They consent to do what is in their power to see that justice is done him, and are admitted into the castle.

On that same day the body of Count Gaston of Foix was brought to Orthez and put in a coffin. Everyone, men, women and children, wept bitterly at the sight of it when it was carried into the town. They recalled amid their lamentations the sterling qualities of the man, his noble life, his princely state and governance, his wisdom and sound judgement, his prowess in war, his generosity and the peace and prosperity in which they had lived during the years he ruled over them, when neither French nor English would have dared to offend them. And they said: 'How things will turn against us now! How fiercely will our neighbours war on us! We have lived in a land of peace and liberty, but now it will be a land of misery and servitude, for none will protect our rights, none will stand up to defend us. Ah Gaston, splendid boy, why did you ever anger your father? If you were with us still, who had such promising beginnings, how greatly should we be comforted! But we lost you too young and your father has stayed too short a time with us. He was a man of only sixty-three, no great age for a prince who was strong in body and stout at heart, who lived at his ease and satisfied his desires. Disconsolate land of Béarn deprived of a true-born heir, what will become of you now? Never again will you see the like of the noble and chivalrous Count of Foix!'

Charles VI Goes Mad (1392)

AFTER his disgrace at court (p. 384 above), Pierre de Craon schemes to take revenge on the man he holds responsible, Olivier de Clisson, Constable of France and favourite of the King. But his attempt to assassinate him one night in the streets of Paris fails and he flees back to the protection of the Duke of Brittany. Enraged by this attack on his favourite, Charles VI insists on leading a punitive expedition against the Duke.

It was fearfully hot on the day when the King left Le Mans, as was to be expected, for it was in August, when the sun is naturally at its greatest strength. It should also be said, to help understand what happened, that while at Le Mans the King had been overloaded with councils. Apart from this unforeseen work, he was not at all well and had not been so all the year, but had been suffering from head-pains, eating and drinking little, and almost every day afflicted with heats and fevers. He was disposed to these, by the nature of his constitution, and very harmful to him they were. In addition, the attack on his Constable had plunged him into a state of melancholy and anxiety. His doctors were well aware of all this, as were his uncles, but they could do nothing to improve matters because he refused even to listen to their advice against going to Brittany.

I was told – and such was my information – that as he was riding through the forest of Le Mans, he was given a solemn warning which ought to have caused him to reflect and to call his council together before going farther. There suddenly came towards him a man with bare head and feet dressed in a mean smock of white homespun and looking more nearly mad than sane. He dashed out from between two trees, boldly seized the reins of the King's horse, stopped him short and said: 'King, ride forward no farther. Turn back, for you are betrayed.' These words struck home into the King's mind, which was already weakened, and afterwards had a very much worse effect, for his spirits sank and his blood ran cold.

At this, men-at-arms came up and beat savagely on the man's hands, which were holding the reins, so that he let go and was left behind; and they paid no more attention to his words than to those of a madman. This was madness indeed, in many people's opinion. They ought at least to have spent a little time on the man, finding out something about him and questioning him to try to discover whether he was sane or insane and what had made him utter that warning, and where it came from. None of this was done and they simply left him behind. No one knows what became of him and he was never seen again by anyone who recognized him, but those who were near the King at the time certainly heard him speak the words.

The King and his troop went on. It was about twelve o'clock when they cleared the forest and came to a fine open stretch of sandy heaths. The sun was dazzlingly bright, blazing down in its full strength. Its beams shone with such force that they penetrated everything. The sand was hot underfoot and the horses were sweating. No one was so fit or so hardened to campaigning as not to be affected by the heat. The chief lords rode separately, each with his company. The King was some little distance from the others so as to get less dust. The Dukes of Berry and Burgundy rode talking together about a hundred yards away from him on the left. The other lords, the Count de la Marche, Lord Charles d'Albret, Lord Philippe d'Artois, Lords Henri and Philippe de Bar, Lord Pierre de Navarre, were all riding with their own troops of men. The Duke of Bourbon, the Lord de Coucy, Sir Charles de Hangest and the Baron d'Ivry were in other companies, all separate from the King's troop. They were chatting among themselves, with no premonition of what was suddenly to befall the head of the whole company, the very person of the King. In such ways are made manifest God's works and his terrible scourges, greatly to be feared of all creatures. Many examples are to be found in the Old and New Testaments. Was there not Nebuchadnezzar, King of Assyria, who reigned for a time in such might that there was no whisper of another higher than him? And suddenly, at the height of his power and glory, the King of Kings, God, Lord of Heaven and earth and maker and disposer of all things, so visited him that he lost his reason and his kingdom, and remained in that state for seven years. He lived on acorns and crab-apples, with the tastes and appetite of a swine. And when he had done penance, God restored his memory to him and he said to the prophet Daniel that above the God of Israel there is no other God. In plainer words and in the light of truth, God the Father, the Son and the Holy Ghost, three in one name and all of one substance, was, is and ever shall be as mighty to manifest His works as heretofore, and none should wonder or be amazed at anything He may do.

To return to the subject which prompted me to write those words, a strange influence from the heavens descended that day upon the King of France, and many say that it was his own fault. Because of his bodily constitution and the state of health he was in, as these were known to his doctors, who were precisely the people who should know, he ought not to have ridden out on so hot a day; perhaps in the morning or the cool of the evening, but not at that hour. For this, those on whose guidance and advice he most relied at that time were blamed and discredited.

So the King of France was riding in the sun over the sandy plain, on the hottest August day that has ever been known before or since. He was wearing a black velvet jerkin, which made him very hot, and had on his head a plain scarlet hat and a string of large milky pearls which the Queen had given him when he said good-bye to her. Behind him was riding a page who wore a Montauban helmet of burnished steel which glittered in the sun. Behind him came another page carrying a gilded lance on which was fixed a silk banner, the distinguishing mark of the King. The lance had a broad head of fine, gleaming steel; it was one of a dozen which the Lord de La Rivière had had forged when he was at Toulouse. He had presented all twelve to the King, who had given three to the Duke of Orléans and three to the Duke of Bourbon.

Then, as they were all riding along like this, the page carrying the lance forgot what he was about or dozed off, as boys and pages do through carelessness, and allowed the blade of the lance to fall forward on to the helmet which the other page was wearing. There was a loud clang of steel, and the King, who was so close that they were riding on his horse's heels, gave a sudden start. His mind reeled, for his thoughts were still running on the words which the madman or the wise man had said to him in the forest, and he imagined that a great host of his enemies were coming to kill him. Under this delusion, his weakened mind caused him to run amok. He spurred his horse forward, then drew his sword and wheeled round on to his pages, no longer recognizing them or anyone else. He thought he was in a battle surrounded by the enemy and, raising his sword to bring it down on anyone who was in the way, he shouted: 'Attack! Attack the traitors!'

The pages saw the King's fury and took fright, not without reason. They thought it was their carelessness which had made him angry, so they spurred their horses aside to avoid him. The Duke of Orléans[1] was not far off. The King rode up to him brandishing his sword. He had lost all recollection of who people were and could not recognize his own brother or his uncles. When he saw him coming at him with drawn sword, the Duke was naturally afraid and spurred hurriedly away, with the King after him. The Duke of Burgundy was riding on the flank when, startled by the cries of the pages and the pounding of the horses' hooves, he looked across and saw the King chasing his brother with the naked sword. He was horror-struck and called out: 'Ho! Disaster has overtaken us! The King's gone out of his mind! After him, in God's name! Catch him!' And then: 'Fly, nephew, fly! The King means to kill you!' It was certain that the Duke of Orléans felt far from reassured and he was fleeing in earnest as fast as his horse could carry him, with knights and squires after them both. Everyone began shouting and turning their

1. Previously the Duke of Touraine. He had been created Duke of Orléans in that year, 1392.

horses in that direction. Those who were farther off, riding on the flanks, thought they were chasing a wolf or a hare, until they learnt the truth, that something was wrong with the King. However, the Duke of Orléans escaped by turning and twisting, and also people came to his help. Knights, squires and men-at-arms formed a circle right round the King, allowing him to tire himself out against them. The longer he raged about, the weaker he grew. When he came at any of them, knights or squires, they simply let themselves fall under his blows. I did not hear that any were killed in that affair, but he struck down quite a number, for none defended himself. Finally, when he was quite exhausted, and his horse as well, and both of them were drenched in sweat, a Norman knight called Sir Guillaume Martel, who was his chamberlain and of whom he was very fond, came up behind him and flung his arms round the King as he still waved his sword, and gripped him tight. While he was being held, all the others came up. His sword was taken from him and he was lifted from his horse and laid very gently on the ground and stripped of his jerkin to cool him. His three uncles and his brother went to him, but he had lost all recollection of them and gave no sign of affection or recognition. His eyes were rolling very strangely, nor did he speak to anyone.

The expedition against the Duke of Brittany is at once called off. The King is taken back to Le Mans in a litter.

That evening the doctors were very busy and the great lords very troubled. Tongues began to wag and various opinions were put forward. Some, who were ready to believe the worst, said that the King had been drugged and bewitched when he set out from Le Mans that morning, in order to bring disaster and dishonour on the realm of France. This rumour was so persistent that it came to the ears of the King's blood-relations and they began to discuss it among themselves. 'You and you, listen, if you will, to this widespread rumour about the people who are responsible for the King's welfare. It is being said that he has been drugged or put under a spell. We must find out how that could have been done and where and when.' 'How can we find out?' 'From the doctors,' some said. 'They must know. They are familiar with his constitution and temperament.'

The doctors were sent for and closely questioned by the Duke of Burgundy. Their reply was that the King had been sickening for this illness for some time past. 'We knew very well that this weakness of the head had been troubling him seriously and that, sooner or later, it was bound to break out.' The Duke of Burgundy then said: 'That explanation clears you entirely, but he was so set on going on this expedition that he would not listen to us, or to you. It is a thousand pities that it was ever mooted, for it has brought him nothing but discredit. It would have been better if Clisson and all his following had been killed than that the King should have developed this illness. It will set tongues wagging all over the country, because the King is still a young man. And we, his uncles and blood-relations, whose duty is to direct and advise him, will receive the blame, although it was not our fault. Now tell us,' the Duke of Burgundy went on, 'this morning, before he mounted his horse, were you at his breakfast?' 'Indeed we were,' said the doctors. 'And what sort of meal did he make?' 'He hardly ate or drank anything, he seemed to be lost in thought.' 'And who was the last to serve him with wine?' asked the Duke. 'We do not know,' said the doctors. 'As soon as the table was cleared we left to get ready for riding. Find out from the butlers or his chamberlains.'

They sent for Robert de Tanques, a squire from Picardy who was the head wine-steward. When he came, he was asked who had poured out the King's last glass of wine. 'My lords,' he told them, 'Sir Hélion de Neilhac.' That knight was sent for and asked from where he had got the wine which the King drank in his room just before he left. His answer was: 'My lords, Robert de Tanques here brought it in and tasted it, and so did I, in front of the King.' 'That's true,' said Robert de Tanques, 'but there can be no cause for doubt or suspicion about this, because there is still some of the same wine in the royal bottles and we will readily drink some and test it before you.' Then the Duke of Berry said: 'We are arguing and racking our brains for nothing. If the King has been poisoned or bewitched, it is only by evil counsels. This is not a fit time to discuss the matter. Let us leave it in suspense until later.'

The next day, the King's uncles went to visit him and heard that he was very weak. They asked how he had slept. His attendants said, hardly at all; he did not seem able to get any rest. 'Bad news,' said the Duke of Burgundy. All three uncles went up to the King's bed, where the Duke of Orléans was already, and asked him how he felt. The King said nothing, but looked at them strangely and did not recognize them. They were perplexed and said to each other: 'There is nothing we can do here. He is in a very bad way. We are doing him more harm than good. We will leave him in charge of his doctors and attendants, they will look after him. Our task is to consider how to order the realm, for there must be government and administration. Otherwise there would be trouble.' 'Brother,' said Burgundy to Berry, 'we must get back to Paris and arrange for the King to be taken there by comfortable and easy stages. We can attend to him better there than in this distant province. Once we are in Paris, we will assemble the whole council of France and it will be decided how the kingdom is to be managed and who will be responsible for its administration, whether our dear nephew of Orléans, or us.' 'Quite right,' said the Duke of Berry. 'Now we must decide on the most suitable and healthy place to take him to, to give him the best chance of a quick recovery.' It was then agreed that he should be quietly taken straight to the Castle of Creil, which lies in pleasant country on the River Oise and where the air is good.

News of the French King's illness spread far and wide, and though some were grieved by it, you can well imagine that the Duke of Brittany and Sir Pierre de Craon were not among them. Their tears were soon dry, for they knew how much he hated them.

When the Pope in Rome, Boniface, and his cardinals heard the news, they also rejoiced at it and assembled in consistory. They said that their greatest enemy, the King of France, had been beaten by rods of wrath when God clouded his mind, and that this influence had been rained down from heaven to chastise him; he had inclined too much to the anti-Pope in Avignon, and this bitter scourge had been sent upon him to divide his kingdom. They felt that their cause would now be strengthened. Everything considered and on a reasonable view, this really was a serious warning, and one which Pope Clement and the cardinals of Avignon might well have taken to heart. But they ignored it, except insofar as it affected the prestige of the King and the kingdom. Their conclusion was that one could hardly expect anything else of a king who was young and headstrong, because he had been allowed to be over-active and too little care had been taken of him. He had indulged to excess in riding night and day and in tiring his body and mind in all kinds of labours far beyond what was reasonable. Those who had directed him in the past were to be blamed for it and no one else, for it was plainly their fault. If, during his childhood and youth, they had laid down a reasonable rule of life for him, and had kept him to it under the supervision of his uncles, this outbreak of illness would never have occurred. 'But in spite of that, he has a fund of sound reason, for he promised the Pope and gave his royal word that he would so order things that the anti-Pope in Rome and his cardinals would be destroyed by force, the schism of the Church would be healed, and the present troubles remedied. But he has done none of this. Rather he has consistently gone against his word and oath, whereby God is offended. As a solemn warning, He has struck him with this scourge of madness, and that, on any reasonable view, supports our case. If he recovers his sanity, as may well happen, we must send wise and capable legates to him, who will point out his failure to keep his promises, so that he shall not be unaware of it through any neglect of ours.'

Such were the arguments and suggestions of the Pope and cardinals at Avignon. They alleged that he had fully deserved to be afflicted by this illness, having brought it upon himself, and they fastened the whole blame upon him, his guardians and his inner council. Independently of them, many other people in France thought the same thing. Envoys were sent to a town called Haspres, situated in Hainault between Cambrai and Valenciennes, where there is a church dependent on the Abbey of Saint-Vaast of Arras, in which Saint Achar is revered. The body of this holy saint lies in a sumptuous silver shrine and attracts pilgrims and suppliants from many places whenever the outbreaks of madness and possession are particularly severe. In honour of the saint, they had a man made in wax in the resemblance of the King of France and sent it there with a large and splendid candle. These were offered with humble devotion to the saint's body, in order that it should intercede with God for the King's cruel affliction to be relieved. Very wide interest was aroused and a similar offering was made to Saint Hermer of Renaix, which saint has merit to cure all kinds of frenzy. To all other places known to have bodies of male or female saints possessing the merit and virtue by the grace of God to cure cases of madness and possession, the King's offering was sent in due and pious form.

Meanwhile a famous doctor, one Guillaume de Harselly, has been summoned on the recommendation of his patron, Enguerrand de Coucy. The case is entrusted to him.

Master Guillaume de Harselly, who was in charge of the King, remained quietly with him at Creil, treating him skilfully and successfully. The case brought him much honour and advantage, as little by little he restored him to health. First, he removed the heats and fevers and restored his appetite for food and drink. He enabled him to relax and sleep and to recover his awareness of things around him. But he was still very weak, so gradually, to get him into the fresh air, he persuaded him to ride and go out hunting and hawking.

When it became known that the King was rapidly recovering his health, reason and memory, all conditions of people rejoiced at the news and gave humble and hearty thanks to God for it. The King, still at Creil, asked to see his wife the Queen and his son the Dauphin. They both went there and were given a joyful welcome. So little by little, by the grace of God, the King was restored to full health. When

Master Guillaume de Harselly saw it, he was delighted – and rightly so, for he had effected a notable cure. He handed the King over to his brother of Orléans and his uncles of Berry, Burgundy and Bourbon with the words: 'Thanks be to God, the King is in sound condition. I return him into your hands. Care should be taken not to agitate or depress him, for his spirits are still a little unstable, but they will gradually grow stronger. Amusements, relaxations, sports and pastimes within reason are more beneficial to him than anything else. Try to burden him the least possible with affairs of state. His mind is still weak and sensitive, and will be all this year, for he has undergone a very severe illness.'

It was proposed that this Master Guillaume should be retained in the King's service in return for a salary high enough to content him; since that is the aim which doctors always pursue, to get large payments and profits from the lords and ladies they attend. So he was urgently requested to stay, but he made vehement excuses, saying that he was now an old man, feeble and useless, unable to endure the routine of the court, and that in short he wished to go back to his native place. When they saw that persuasion was useless they did not want to upset him and he was given leave to go. On his departure he was given a thousand gold crowns and was put on the books as entitled to four horses at any time when he cared to come to court. I do not think he ever did come back, because soon after he reached the city of Laon, where he usually lived, he died a very rich man. He was found to possess at least thirty thousand francs in cash, yet in his day he had been the meanest and stingiest person ever known. His only pleasure in life had been to amass great piles of florins. There were days when he hardly spent a penny of his own, but went round getting free meals and drinks wherever he could. All doctors suffer from such weaknesses.

Froissart Revisits England (1395)

Now the fact is that I, Sir[1] Jean Froissart, at that date treasurer and canon of Chimay in the County of Hainault and the
diocese of Liège, was filled with a strong desire to revisit
England, when, having been at Abbeville, I saw that a truce
had been concluded between England and France, their allies
and dependent territories, for the term of four years on land
and sea. Several reasons prompted me to undertake the journey. The first was that in my youth I had been brought up in
the court and household of the noble King Edward of happy
memory and the noble Queen Philippa, his wife, and among
their children and the barons of England, who were living
there at that time; and I had been treated by them with all
honour, friendliness, generosity and courtesy. So I wanted
to see the country again, and I had a feeling that if I did see it
I should live the longer for it, for I had not been there for a
full twenty-seven years, and if I did not find the same lords
whom I had known at the date of my departure, I should meet
their successors and that would be a real consolation to me.
Also I could confirm the accounts of their doings about which
I had written so much. I spoke of this to my dear patrons who
were then reigning, to Duke Albert of Bavaria, Count of
Hainault, Holland and Zealand and Lord of Friesland, and his
son Lord William, at that time Count of Ostrevant, and to my
very dear and honoured Lady Jeanne, Duchess of Brabant
and Luxemburg, and my dear and powerful lord, Enguerrand
de Coucy, and also to that gallant gentleman the Chevalier de
Gommegnies whom I had known at the English court when
he and I were both young; and so too I had known the Lord de
Coucy and all the other French nobles who had been kept in

---

1. Froissart never held the knighthood which this title (*sire*) implies,
but he felt morally entitled to it. Elsewhere he writes: 'Those who wish to
please me will call me *sir*.'

London as hostages for the ransom of King John of France, as is recorded in our chronicle many pages back.

The three great lords I have named and the Chevalier de Gommegnies and Madame de Brabant approved of my plan when I mentioned it to them and all gave me letters of introduction to the King and his uncles, except for my lord de Coucy, who dared not give one because he was French, but wrote to his daughter,[1] who at the time had the title of Duchess of Ireland. As a preparation for my visit, I had brought together all the writings on love and morality which I had composed over thirty-four years by the grace of God and of Love, and had had them copied, engrossed and illuminated. This much increased my desire to go to England and see King Richard, the son of the noble and powerful Prince of Wales and of Aquitaine, for I had not seen him since he had been baptized in the cathedral at Bordeaux, where I was in those days. I had intended to go on the expedition to Spain with the Prince and the other lords, but when we were at Dax the Prince sent me back to England to be with his mother the Queen. So I was eager to see this King Richard and his noble uncles, and I had with me this very fine book, nicely decorated, bound in velvet with studs and clasps of silver gilt, which I meant to present to the King by way of introducing myself. In my enthusiasm for the journey I found all these preparations easy, for when one undertakes a thing gladly the effort seems to cost nothing. I provided myself with horses and travelling necessities and, crossing from Calais, arrived at Dover on the twelfth of July (1395). But when I reached Dover, I found no one with whom I had been acquainted in the days when I lived in England. The hostelries and houses were all repopulated with strange people and the little children had grown into men and women who didn't know me, as I didn't know them.

I stayed there for that afternoon and one night, to rest myself and my horses. That was on a Tuesday; on the Wednesday I reached Canterbury at just about nine o'clock and went

1. Philippa de Coucy, married Robert de Vere, Duke of Ireland. See above, p. 317.

to see the shrine of St Thomas and the tomb of the Prince of Wales, who is buried there in great pomp. I heard high mass and made my offering to the holy relics, then went back for dinner at my hostelry. I learnt that the King was coming on pilgrimage on the Thursday. He was back from Ireland where he had been campaigning for about nine months and was anxious to visit the cathedral of St Thomas of Canterbury, both out of reverence for the honoured body of the saint and because his father's tomb is there. So I decided to await him, which I did.

The next day he came in great state, accompanied by numerous lords and ladies. I mingled with them and everything seemed strange to me. I knew not a soul, for things had changed greatly in England over the past twenty-eight years. The King had none of his uncles with him. The Duke of Lancaster was in Aquitaine and the Dukes of York and Gloucester somewhere else. So I felt completely lost at first. If only I could have come across a certain old knight, who had been one of the knights of King Edward's chamber and had become a member of King Richard's privy council, I should have felt comforted and would have gone up to him. His name was Sir Richard Stury. I inquired if he was still alive, and was told that he was, but that he was not there, having stayed in London. Then I thought of approaching Sir Thomas Percy, Steward of the Royal Household, who was there. I made myself known to him and found him most affable and courteous. He offered to present me and my letters to the King. I was delighted by this offer, for one has to have some connexions before one can approach such a mighty prince as the King of England. He even went to the King's chamber to see if it was a suitable moment, but he found that the King had retired to sleep, so told me to go back to my hostelry. I did this and, when the King had had his sleep, I went back to the Archbishop's palace in which he was staying and found Sir Thomas Percy giving orders to his people to move off, for the King had decided to go back for the night to Ospringe, from which he had come that morning. He advised me not to announce my arrival just yet, but to join the company round the King, saying that he would see that I was properly lodged, until such time as the King had settled with his entire household in the place to which he was going. This was a delightful castle called Leeds, in the County of Kent.

I made my arrangements accordingly and set out. At Ospringe I was lodged quite by chance in a house in which the High Steward had also placed a gallant English knight belonging to the King's chamber. He had stayed behind there when the King had left in the morning for Canterbury because of a slight headache which had come on during the night. Seeing that I was a foreigner and a Frenchman – for they consider all people whose language is Northern French as Frenchmen, whatever country or nation they belong to – this knight, whose name was Sir William de Lisle, made friends with me and I with him, for the gentry of England are particularly courteous and easy to get to know and to talk to. He asked me about my position and my business, and I told him a sufficient amount and added all the advice which Sir Thomas Percy had given me. He said that that was the very best course to follow and told me that by dinner-time on Friday the King would be at Leeds, where his uncle the Duke of York was to come to join him.

This was excellent news for me, because I had letters of introduction to the Duke and also because he had seen me in the household of the noble King Edward his father, in the days when we were both young. This I felt would give me wider connexions in the household of King Richard.

On the Friday morning Sir William de Lisle and I set out for Leeds Castle, riding together. On the way I asked him whether he had been on the Irish expedition with the King. He said he had. I then asked him about the place called St Patrick's Hole, and whether the stories told about it were true. He said they were and that when the King was in Dublin he and another English knight had been to it and had spent the whole night there, from sunset to sunrise. So I questioned him about the wonders and strange things which people say are to be seen there, and inquired whether there was anything in it. His answer was this: 'When I and my friend had passed through the gate of the cavern, which is called St Patrick's Purgatory, and had gone down three or four steps – for it is like going down to a cellar – a kind of heaviness came over us. We sat down on the stone steps and, as soon as we had done that, we were overcome by a strong desire to sleep, and we slept the whole night through.' I asked him whether, as they slept, they knew where they were and what visions came to them. He told me that they launched out in their sleep into strange dreams and great imaginings and saw, they felt, very many more things than they would have done in their own beds at home. Of this they were quite sure. 'But when we woke in the morning and they opened the gate for us, as we had arranged, we came out and could not remember a single thing we had seen. We considered it had all been a delusion.'

I asked him no more about this subject, but stopped, for I should have liked to question him about the expedition to Ireland and set him talking about that. But other knights with their followers rode up to speak to him, so I dropped the conversation. We rode as far as Leeds Castle, to which the King came with all his retinue and where I found my lord Edmund, Duke of York. I made myself known to him and gave him the letters from his cousin the Count of Hainault and from the Count of Ostrevant. The Duke seemed to remember me fairly well and gave me a warm welcome, saying: 'Sir John, keep near me and stay among my men. We will show you every kindness and consideration. That is your due for the sake of old times and of our royal mother to whom you were attached. We have not forgotten it.' I thanked him sincerely for saying this. So I was helped forward, both by him and by Sir Thomas Percy and Sir William de Lisle, and was taken into the chamber of the King and presented to him by his uncle of York. King Richard received me cheerfully and graciously, took all the letters which I offered him, and read them attentively. When he had done so, he told me that I had done well to come and that, as I had been of the household of his grandparents the King and Queen, I still belonged to the household of the King of England. On that day I did not show him

the book which I had brought for him, for Sir Thomas Percy
said the time was not yet ripe, since he was too busy with
affairs of state. He was in the middle of deliberating two great
matters.

*These are, first, the complaint brought by a delegation of Gascon
barons against the royal decision to transfer the crown domains of
Aquitaine to the Duke of Lancaster. They wish to retain their
direct allegiance to the King, but their request is not granted. The
second question is that of the King's re-marriage. Froissart is informed of these matters by his old friend, Sir Richard Stury, whom
he meets again when the court moves on to Eltham, and by Sir Jean
de Grailly, illegitimate son of the Captal de Buch.*

'Now let's leave the Gascon question for the time being,'
said Sir Jean de Grailly, 'and speak of the second and the
King's personal desires. I feel fairly sure, according to what I
see and hear, that King Richard would like to get married
again. He has made soundings in several places, but no wife
has been found for him. If the Duke of Burgundy or the
Count of Hainault had marriageable daughters, he would be
glad to consider them, but they have none who are not already
allotted. It was mentioned to him that the King of Navarre
had sisters and daughters, but he is not interested in them.
His uncle the Duke of Gloucester has a daughter quite old
enough to embark on marriage, but the King will have none
of her and says she is too closely related to him, being his
cousin german. He is attracted to the daughter of the King of
France and to no one else, and it has caused some dismay in
this country that he should wish to marry his adversary's
daughter. It does him no good with his people, but he takes
no notice. He makes it clear, as he has always done, that he
would rather make war elsewhere than on France, desiring –
as we already know of him by past experience – that there
should be a lasting peace between him and the King of France
and their two countries. He says that the war has gone on
too long between him and his ancestors and the French, that
too many brave men have been killed in it, too many evil
deeds perpetrated, and too many Christian people destroyed
or ruined, to the detriment of the Christian faith. In an attempt

to change the King's mind – for the English do not find it agreeable for him to marry a Frenchwoman – he was told that the French King's daughter, whom he has in view, is too young, and that for another five or six years she could be no wife to him. His answer was that God will provide, that she will grow older, and that he would much rather she was too young than too old. The reason he gives in support of his desires and ideas is that if he marries her young, he can form her according to his wishes and guide and train her in English ways; and he says that he is still young enough to wait until the lady is of age.'

The deliberations and councils having been concluded, the moment comes for Froissart to present his book.

So it happened, on the Sunday after all the counsellors had left for their homes in London or elsewhere, except for the Duke of York and Sir Richard Stury who remained with the King, that these two, with Sir Thomas Percy, spoke to the King of my affairs and the King asked to see the book which I had brought. I took it to his chamber, for I had it ready with me, and laid it on his bed. He opened it and looked inside and it pleased him greatly. Well it might, for it was illuminated, nicely written and illustrated, with a cover of crimson velvet with ten studs of silver gilt and golden roses in the middle and two large gilded clasps richly worked at their centres with golden rose-trees. The King asked me what it was about and I told him: 'About love!' He was delighted by this answer and dipped into the book in several places and read, for he spoke and read French very well. Then he gave it to one of his knights, called Sir Richard Credon, to take into his private room and was more cordial than ever towards me.

The English in Ireland (1394-5)

ON the same Sunday when the King accepted my book with such appreciation, there was an English squire present called Henry Crystede,[1] a very worthy and serious man who spoke French quite well. He made friends with me because he had seen how warmly the King and the great lords received me and he had also seen the book I had presented. He supposed, as I gathered from his words, that I was a historian – and indeed Sir Richard Stury had said as much to him – and he told me what I will now set down.

'Sir John,' said Henry Crystede, 'have you met anyone in this country or at the court who has told you about the expedition which our lord the King made this year to Ireland and the way in which four Irish kings, great lords in their own land, came to do homage to him?'

'No,' I said, in order to encourage him to go on.

'Then I will tell you,' said the squire, who appeared to be a man of about fifty, 'so that, when you go back to your own country and have the time and inclination to do so, you can put it on permanent record.'

'Thank you, indeed,' I said, feeling delighted by his words.

Then Henry Crystede began to talk, and said this:

'No English king within memory has led so large an army to Ireland as the King did this season, when he maintained himself on the Irish frontier for nine months at very great expense. The whole cost was willingly borne by the country, and the merchants of the English cities and towns felt that the money had been well spent when they saw the King returning

1. He appears only to be known from this chapter of Froissart's, in which he is called 'Henry Crystède'. The main authorities render this as 'Christede or Castide' (E. Curtis, *Richard II in Ireland, 1394-95*) and 'Castide' (J. O'Donovan, *Annals of the Four Masters*, Vol. IV). He has been almost certainly identified as the King's Esquire Henry Kyrkestede in *The Stranger as Historian*, a recent unpublished paper by Kenneth Clear of Dublin.

with honour from the campaign, having employed none but gentry and archers in his war. He had with him easily four thousand knights and squires and thirty thousand archers, all of whom were well and punctually paid week by week, so that all were satisfied. I must tell you, to give you a clearer idea of the campaign, that Ireland is one of the most difficult countries in the world to fight against and subdue, for it is a strange, wild place consisting of tall forests, great stretches of water, bogs and uninhabitable regions. It is hard to find a way of making war on the Irish effectively for, unless they choose, there is no one there to fight and there are no towns to be found. The Irish hide in the woods and forests, where they live in holes dug under trees, or in bushes and thickets, like wild animals. When they learn that you have entered their territory to make war on them, they come together in various places by different paths, so that it is impossible to reach them. But they, if they see they have the advantage, can attack the enemy as it suits them, for they know the country backwards and are skilled fighters. No mounted man-at-arms, however good his horse, can ride so fast that they cannot catch him. They spring out of the ground on to the horse's back and seize the rider from behind and pull him off, for they are very strong in the arm. Or else they stay up behind him and hold him in so tight a grip that he cannot defend himself. They carry sharp knives, with a big double-edged blade, like the head of a throwing-spear, with which they kill their enemies. And they never leave a man for dead until they have cut his throat like a sheep and slit open his belly to remove the heart, which they take away. Some, who know their ways, say that they eat it with great relish. They take no man for ransom, and when they see that they are getting the worst of a fight, they scatter and take cover in thickets and bushes and under the ground. So they disappear and it is impossible to know where they have gone to.

'Even Sir William of Windsor, who had longer experience of campaigning on the Irish border than any other English knight, never succeeded in learning the lie of the country or in understanding the mentality of the Irish, who are very dour people, proud and uncouth, slow-thinking and hard to get to know or make friends with. They have no respect for pleasant manners or for any gentleman, for, although their country is ruled by kings, of whom there are a large number, they will have nothing to do with courtly behaviour, but cling to the rough ways in which they have been brought up.

'Yet it is true that four Irish kings, among the most powerful in the country, were persuaded to do homage to the King of England by peaceful means, not by battle or compulsion, and it was the Earl of Ormonde, whose territory borders theirs, who had most to do with it. He induced them to go to Dublin, where our lord the King then was and where they made submission to him and the crown of England. That is why the King and the whole realm consider the expedition to have been so brilliant and noteworthy. Even King Edward, of happy memory, never had so much success against them as King Richard has had. There is much honour in it, but the gain is small, since these kings are the most uncouth people you could imagine. I will tell you something of that and you will be able to compare them with other nationalities. I know about it from personal experience, for I was in charge of them for about a month at Dublin, on the instructions of our lord the King and his council, with the idea of introducing and accustoming them to English ways. That was because I can speak their language as well as I can speak French and English. I was brought up in Ireland and Earl Thomas of Ormonde, the father of the present Earl, kept me in his household and was very fond of me because I was a good horseman.

'It happened once that the old Earl I have just mentioned was sent to the Irish border to make war on them, with three hundred lances and a thousand archers. The English have always had war with them in order to keep them down. Well, the Earl of Ormonde was leading this expedition against them and on that particular day he had mounted me on a fast and beautifully trained horse and I was riding beside him. The Irish had laid an ambush and when we came up to it they sprang out at us and began to hurl their javelins, while the archers on our side shot back at them. The Irish could not stand their fire, for their armour is very simple, and they retreated. My master the Earl began to pursue them, while I followed him closely on my fine horse. But in the pursuit the horse took fright and bolted, carrying me so far into the Irish that our people could not rescue me. As I passed among them, one of them, showing immense agility, took a running leap up behind me and flung his arms round my body. Instead of attacking me with any weapon, he turned the horse aside, and we rode like that, the horse, him and me, for a good two hours until we reached a very remote spot covered with thick bushes. There he rejoined his men who had come to put themselves in safety among the bushes, where the English could never have followed them. He was obviously very pleased with my capture and he took me to where he lived, in a fortified house and town surrounded by woods and stockades and stagnant waters, of which the name is Herpelipin.[1] The gentleman who had captured me was called Brin Costerec.[1] He was a finely built man. I inquired after him from the kings I was with lately and was told that he is still alive, though very old. This Brin Costerec kept me with him for seven years and gave me one of his daughters in marriage. I had two daughters with her. Now I will tell you how I was set free.

'In the seventh year of my living among the Irish, one of their kings, called Arthur McMorrough, King of Leinster, led an army against Lionel Duke of Clarence, the son of King Edward of England, and Sir William of Windsor. The Irish and the English met at a place fairly near the city of Leinster and fought a battle in which some were killed on both sides or taken prisoner. The English won the day and the Irish had to flee, King Arthur McMorrough among them. My wife's father was taken prisoner riding the horse he had won from me. The horse was recognized by the English and particularly by the Earl of Ormonde's men, and from this and what Brin Costerec told them they learnt that I was alive and living quite

1. *Sic* Froissart.

honourably in his manor at Herpelipin, with one of his daughters as my wife. . . .

'It was proposed to him that, if he wanted his freedom, he should send me back to the English commanders, free of all obligations, with my wife and children. He was most unwilling to make this bargain, for he was very fond of me, and of his daughter, and of our children. But when he saw that there was no other way out, he agreed, but stipulated that my elder daughter should remain with him. So I came to England with my wife and second daughter, and was given a place to live in near Bristol, on the Severn. Both my girls are married. The one in Ireland has three sons and two daughters. The one I brought back with me has four sons and two daughters. And because the Irish language comes as easily to my tongue as English – for I have always gone on speaking it with my wife and have started my grandchildren on learning it as well as I have been able – I was appointed by the King and the great nobles of England to persuade, direct and guide in the ways of reason and the customs of this country those four Irish kings who have made their submission to the English crown and have sworn to observe it for ever. But I must say that those four kings, whom I initiated and instructed to the best of my ability, did prove to be very uncouth and gross-minded people. I had the greatest difficulty in polishing them and moderating their language and characters. And even so, if they have made some progress, it is not very much. On many occasions they still slip back into their rough ways.

'The mission that was entrusted to me was based on the King's expressed wish that in behaviour, bearing and dress they should conform to the English pattern, because he wished to dub them knights. As a beginning, they were allotted a fine, big house in the city of Dublin, for themselves and their followers. I was instructed to live with them, never leaving them or going out, except in case of absolute necessity. I spent the first three or four days in their company, so as to get to know them, and they me, without contradicting anything they wished to do. I saw those kings behaving at table in a way which was not at all seemly, and I said to my-self that I would change that. When they had sat down and were served with the first course, they would get their minstrels and their principal servants to sit with them and eat off their plates and drink from their goblets. They told me that such was the custom of the country. Except for their beds, they had everything in common. I allowed all this for three days, but on the fourth I had the tables in the hall arranged and laid in the correct manner. The four kings were seated at the high table, the minstrels at a table well away from theirs, and the servants at another. This appeared to make them very angry. They looked at each other and refused to eat, saying that it was a breach of the excellent custom in which they had been brought up. I answered, laughingly in order to placate them, that their previous arrangement was not a reasonable one and that they would have to abandon it and adopt the English usage, for those were my instructions and what the King and his council had appointed me to do.

'On hearing this, they agreed to it, since they had made sub-mission to the King of England, and they respected my ar-rangements quite meekly, for as long as I was with them. They had another custom of which I already knew, for it is quite general in their country: they do not wear breeches. So I had a large quantity of linen drawers made and had them sent to the kings and their servants. I taught them to wear them and during the time I spent with them I cured them of many boorish and unseemly habits, both in dress and in other things. At first it seemed too great a change for them to wear silk robes trimmed with miniver and squirrel, for previously they had felt well enough dressed in an Irish cloak; and they rode on the kind of saddles used for pack-horses, without stirrups. It was only with great difficulty that I got them to ride on the kind of saddles we have.

'Once I asked them about their faith, and what they believed in, but they were not at all pleased by the question and I had to stop. They said that they believed in God and the Trinity, just the same as us, with no difference whatever. I asked them

which pope they inclined to. They replied: "To the one in
Rome, with no compromise." I asked them if they were willing to enter the order of chivalry, saying that the King of
England wished to knight them, as is the custom in France
and England and other countries. They replied that they were
knights already and that that should be quite good enough.
I asked how and where they had been made knights. They explained that in Ireland a king knights his son at the age of
seven; and that, if the father is dead, his nearest blood-rela-
tion does it. The young aspirant has to joust with light lances,
such as he can easily hold, against a shield set up in a meadow
on a post. The more lances he breaks, the greater the honour
for him. "By means of such tests knights are made very young
in our country, and especially all the sons of kings." Although
I was questioning them about it, I already knew all the procedure. So I said no more on the subject, except to tell them
that the knighthood which they had received in their youth
was not enough for the King of England, but that he would
give them a different kind. They asked what it would be and I
said that it would be in church, which was the most honourable way possible. They accepted my explanation fairly
readily.

'About two days before our king intended to make them
knights, they were visited by the Earl of Ormonde, who
knows their language well because some of his lands lie along
the Irish border. He had been sent to the house we occupied
with a mandate from the King and his council, to give him
greater authority in their sight. He began speaking to them
as affably and courteously as he knew how and asked them
what opinion they had formed of me. They all replied very
pleasantly and sensibly: "He has explained and taught
us the doctrine and usage of this country. We ought to be
grateful to him, and so we are." The Earl of Ormonde
liked this answer, for it was a reasonable one, and from one
thing to another he came to speak of the order of chivalry
which they were to receive. He expounded point by point
and article by article the manner in which a knight should
conduct himself and the virtues and obligations of chivalry,

and explained how those who undertook them entered the order.

'All the Earl said was greatly to the liking of those four Irish kings, whose names I have not yet given you, but I will do so. The first was the great O'Neill, King of Meath; the second O'Brien of Thomond; the third Arthur McMorrough, King of Leinster; the fourth O'Conor, King of Connaught and Erp.

'They were knighted by the hand of King Richard of England in the cathedral church of Dublin, which is consecrated to St John Baptist, on Lady Day in March, which this year was a Thursday. During the whole of the Wednesday night they kept vigil in the cathedral and at mass next morning, with great solemnity, they were made knights, and with them Sir Thomas Ourghem, Sir Jonathan of Pado and his cousin Sir John of Pado. The four kings were dressed in rich robes, as befitted their rank, and they sat that day at the table of King Richard of England. It must be said that they were thoroughly stared at by the English and others who were present, and not without reason, for they were foreign and different in appearance from the English and other nationalities, and people are naturally curious to see some new thing. It was certainly a great novelty to see those four kings of Ireland and you would have thought the same if you had been there.'

'Yes, Henry,' I said, 'I can well believe you, and I would have given a lot to see it. At the time all my preparations had been made to come to England and I should have come, but for the news of the death of Queen Anne of England,[1] which made me put off my journey for the time being.'

Later, we took leave of each other and I went at once to find the March Herald. I said to him: 'March, tell me what are the arms of Henry Crystede, for I found him most friendly and obliging and he kindly described to me the King's expedition to Ireland and the condition of those four Irish kings

1. Richard II's first wife, Anne of Bohemia, died summer 1394.

whom he had, he says, under his guidance for over a fortnight.' March replied: 'His arms are a chevron gules on a field argent, with three besants gules, two above the chevron and one below.'

All these things I put down in writing, in order not to forget them.

Two Marriages (1395-6)

THE Earl Marshal, the Earl of Rutland and the English ambassadors spent about three weeks in Paris at the Court of France where they were very cordially received and lavishly entertained. The negotiations went so well that a marriage-agreement, which was the object of their visit, was concluded between the King of England and Isabella, the eldest daughter of King Charles of France. She was affianced and married by procuration to the Earl Marshal, in the King of England's name, and henceforward the lady had the title of Queen of England. At that time, I was told, it was a pleasure to see her, young though she was, for she well knew how to behave as a queen.

Around that time the Duke of Lancaster entered into a third marriage with a lady who had been the daughter of a knight of Hainault called Sir Paon de Ruet, in his day one of the knights of good Queen Philippa of England, who had loved the Hainaulters because she was of their nation. This lady, whom the Duke of Lancaster now married, was called Catherine;[1] in her youth she had been placed in the household of the Duke and Duchess Blanche of Lancaster. After Duchess Blanche had passed away and also Madam Constance of Castile, daughter of King Peter of Spain, whom the Duke of Lancaster married as his second wife and by whom he had that daughter who became Queen of Spain – when, then, this second Duchess Constance had died, the Duke of Lancaster had maintained this lady, Catherine de Ruet, who for her part had become married to an English knight. Both during and after the knight's lifetime, Duke John of Lancaster had always loved and maintained this lady Catherine, by whom he had three children, two sons and a daughter. The elder

1. Better known as Catherine Swynford. Her sister, Philippa de Ruet, or Roet, married Geoffrey Chaucer.

son was named John, otherwise Beaufort of Lancaster, and
was a great favourite with his father. The other's name was
Henry;[1] his father the Duke sent him to the school at Oxford
and made a great jurist of him. This learned man was later
Bishop of Lincoln, which is the noblest and richest diocese in
the whole of England. Out of love for his children, the Duke
of Lancaster married their mother, Madam Catherine de
Ruet, which caused much astonishment in France and England, for she was of humble birth compared to the other two
ladies, Duchess Blanche and Duchess Constance, whom the
Duke had had as his wives before her.

When the news of this marriage to Catherine de Ruet
reached the great ladies of England, such as the Duchess of
Gloucester, the Countess of Derby, the Countess of Arundel
and other ladies with royal blood in their veins, they were surprised and shocked, considering it scandalous, and said: 'The
Duke of Lancaster has quite disgraced himself by marrying
his concubine. And since she has got so far, it will mean that
she will rank as the second lady in England. What a disgrace-
ful reception for the new Queen of England when she comes.'

They went on to say: 'We will leave her to do the honours
all by herself. We will not go to any place where she may be.
It would really demean us too much if that kind of duchess,
who comes of humble stock and was the Duke's concubine
for a very long time, inside and outside his marriages, were to
take precedence over us. Our hearts would burst with vexation, and rightly so.'

The two who had most to say about this were the Duke
and Duchess of Gloucester. They considered that the Duke of
Lancaster had overstepped all bounds when he took his
concubine to wife and said they would never recognize her
marriage or call her lady or sister. The Duke of York soon
got over it, for he was most often in the company of the King
and his brother of Lancaster. The Duke of Gloucester was of
different stuff, for he respected no one's opinions, although he
was the youngest of all the brothers [the King's uncles]. He
was inclined by nature to be proud and overbearing and he

1. Froissart has 'Thomas' mistakenly.

was always in disagreement at the King's councils, unless they went exactly as he liked.

This Catherine de Ruet remained Duchess of Lancaster for the rest of her life. She was the second lady in England and elsewhere after the Queen and she had a perfect knowledge of court etiquette because she had been brought up in it continually since her youth. She loved the Duke of Lancaster and the children she had with him, and she showed it in life and in death.

The Downfall of Richard II (1397-1400)

THE MURDER OF GLOUCESTER

Now I must say something about Thomas, Duke of Gloucester, the youngest son of King Edward III, in connexion with his constant and heartfelt dislike of the French. He was rather pleased than sorry to hear of the defeat which they had suffered in Hungary[1] and, having with him a knight called John Lackinghay, the chief and most intimate of his counsellors, he confided in him and said:

'Those frivolous French got themselves thoroughly smashed up in Hungary and Turkey. Foreign knights and squires who go and fight for them don't know what they are doing, they couldn't be worse advised. They are so overbrimming with conceit that they never bring any of their enterprises to a successful conclusion. That was proved often enough in the wars my royal father and my brother the Prince of Wales had with them. They could never capture a castle or win a battle against us. I don't know why we have this truce with them, for if we started the war again – and we have a perfectly good reason for doing so – we should make hay of them. Particularly at this moment, when all the best of their knights are dead or prisoners. And the people of this country want war. They can't live decently without it, peace is no good to them. By God, Lackinghay, if I live a couple of years longer in good health, the war will be renewed. I won't be bound by treaties and pacts and promises – the French never kept any of theirs in the past. They used fraud and trickery exactly as it suited them to steal back the domains in Aquitaine which had been made over to my royal father by an absolutely binding peace treaty. I pointed that out several times at the various meetings we had with them outside Calais. But

1. During a 'crusade' against the Ottoman Turks in which a strong French contingent had participated and had suffered a disastrous defeat at Nicopolis (1396).

they answered me in such smooth and flowery language that
somehow they always managed to fall on their feet and I could
never persuade the King or my brothers to believe me. Now,
if there was a strong king in England today who really wanted
a war to recover his rightful possessions, he could find a
hundred thousand archers and six thousand men-at-arms all
eager to follow him over the sea and risk everything in his
service. But there isn't one. England hasn't a king who wants
war or enjoys fighting. If she had, things would be different. . . .

'I am the youngest of King Edward's sons,' the Duke of
Gloucester went on, 'but if I was listened to I would be the
first to renew the wars and put a stop to the encroachments we
have suffered and are still suffering every day, thanks to our
simplicity and slackness. I mean particularly the slackness of
our leader the King, who has just allied himself by marriage
with his principal enemy. That's hardly a sign that he wants
to fight him. No, he's too fat in the arse and only interested in
eating and drinking. That's no life for a fighting man, who
ought to be hard and lean and bent on glory. I still remember
my last campaign in France. I suppose I had two thousand
lances and eight thousand archers with me. We sliced right
through the kingdom of France, moving out and across from
Calais, and we never found anyone who dared come out and
fight us. . . .

'Things cannot go on like this,' the Duke continued. 'He's
raising such heavy taxes from the merchants that they're
growing restless, and no one knows where the money goes
to. I know he spends plenty, but it's on silly and futile things,
and his people have to pay the bill. There will soon be serious
trouble in this country. The people are beginning to grumble
and say that they won't stand it much longer. He's letting it
be known, since there is a truce now with France, that he
thinks of leading an expedition to Ireland and employing his
knights and archers that way. He's been there before and
gained very little, for Ireland is not a place where there's
anything worth winning. The Irish are a poor and nasty
people, with a miserable country that is quite uninhabitable.

Even if the whole of it were conquered one year, they'd get it back the next. Yes, my good Lackinghay, all that I'm telling you is absolute fact.'

In conversation with his knight, the Duke of Gloucester used foolish words like these, and others still worse, as was disclosed later. He had conceived such a hatred for the King that he could find nothing to say in his favour. In spite of the fact that, with his brother, the Duke of Lancaster, he was the greatest man in England and ought to have taken a leading part in the government of the realm, he showed no interest in it. When the King sent for him, he went if it suited him, but more often he stayed away. If he did go, he was the last to arrive and the first to leave. As soon as he had given his opinion, he insisted on its being accepted without question, then took his leave immediately and mounted his horse to ride back to Pleshey, a place in Essex thirty miles from London where he owned a fine castle. It was there that he spent most of his time.

The Duke worked in all kinds of subtle and secret ways to win over the Londoners to him, feeling that, if he had them on his side, the rest of England would be his also. He had a great-nephew, the son of the daughter of an elder brother of his called Lionel, who had been Duke of Clarence and had been married in Lombardy to the daughter of Galeazzo, Lord of Milan, and had died at Asti in Piedmont. The Duke of Gloucester would have liked to see this great-nephew of his, whose name was John,[1] Earl of March, on the throne of England, in place of King Richard, who he said was unworthy to reign. He made this clear to those in whom he was rash enough to confide and he arranged for the Earl of March to come and visit him. When he was there, he revealed all his most secret ambitions to him, saying that he himself had been chosen to appoint a new king for England and that Richard would be shut up, and his wife with him. There would be sufficient provision for their eating and drinking as long as they lived. He entreated the Earl of March to agree to this and

1. In fact Roger (Roger Mortimer).

to rely on his word, saying that he could make it good and that he already had the support of the Earl of Arundel, Sir William and Sir John Arundel, the Earl of Warwick and numerous other barons and prelates.

The proposition dismays the young Earl of March, but he prevaricates, saying he needs time to think it over. Having sworn to observe secrecy, he leaves for Ireland and has no more dealings with Gloucester.

The Duke then stirs up the merchants of London, urging them to ask to be relieved of taxation originally imposed to meet the expenses of the wars, but now squandered on King Richard's entertainments. Together with the councillors of several other towns, they petition the King for relief but are temporarily placated by the Dukes of York and Lancaster, and summoned to attend a parliament at Westminster. Here again, Lancaster speaks for the King:

'It is my Sovereign's pleasure, men of London, that I should reply specifically to your demands, and I do this on the instructions of the King and his council and in accordance with the will of the prelates and nobility of his realm. You are aware that, in order to avert greater evils and provide safeguards against certain dangers, it was decided and unanimously agreed by you and the councils of all the cities and large towns in England that a tax of thirteen per cent should be levied on sellers of goods – in the form which has now been current for about six years.

'In consideration of this the King granted you a number of concessions, which he does not wish to withdraw, but on the contrary increase and amplify progressively, provided you are deserving of them. But should you prove rebellious and refractory to an undertaking which you willingly entered into, he annuls everything he has conceded. And here present are the nobles, prelates and holders of fiefs, bound by oath to the King, and he to them, to aid each other mutually in the maintenance of all measures lawfully decreed and established in the best interests of all, to the execution of which oath they have subscribed in full knowledge. Take note of this and remember that the King's establishment is large and powerful. If it has increased in some ways, it has diminished in others. His rents and other sources of revenue yield him less than in the past, and he and his officers had to bear heavy expenses when war was renewed with France. Then great expenditure was incurred by the emissaries who went over to negotiate with the French. The preliminaries to the King's marriage have also been very costly. And, although there is now a truce between the two countries, much money has to be spent on the garrisons of the castles and towns which owe allegiance to the King, whether in Gascony or the districts of Bordeaux, Bayonne and Bigorre, or those of Guines and Calais, as well as all our coastal area, which has to be guarded with its ports and havens.

'On the other side, the whole of the Scottish border, with its roads and passes, requires guarding, and so does the frontier in Ireland, which is a lengthy one. All these things and many others relating to the royal establishment and the prestige of England cost large sums of money every year. The nobles and prelates of the realm know and understand this better than you, who are busy with your manufacturing and your merchandizing. Be thankful that you have peace and remember that no one pays unless he has the means and is doing business. Foreigners have to pay considerably more than you in this country. You get off much more lightly than they do in France and Lombardy and other places to which quite possibly you send your goods, for they are taxed and re-taxed two or three times a year, while you are subject to a reasonable assessment based on the amount of trade you do.'

The London merchants meekly submit. The Duke of Gloucester, who has attended the parliament, keeps silent and returns to his seat at Pleshey.

Soon after, the Comte de Saint-Pol arrives from France on a goodwill mission to Richard and his infant queen. Informed of the dangers threatening the King, he advises him to take action before it is too late.

I was informed that, about a month after the Count of Saint-Pol had returned to France, a report spread through England which was highly detrimental to the King. The general rumour was that the Count had come over to discuss some way of giving Calais back to the French. No single question could have disturbed the English people more thoroughly than this. The consequence was that the Londoners went to see the Duke of Gloucester at Pleshey. The Duke neither calmed them nor denied the rumours, but made the most he could of them by saying: 'It's extremely likely. The French wouldn't mind if he took all their King's daughters, provided they became masters of Calais.'

Depressed by this reply, the Londoners said that they would go and speak to the King and tell him squarely how disturbed opinion was. 'Certainly,' said the Duke. 'Speak out loud and pointedly, and don't be shy about it. Listen carefully to what he says in reply and then you will be able to tell me about it when I next see you. I will advise you according to the answer he gives. It's highly probable that some crooked business is afoot. The Earl Marshal, who is captain and governor of Calais, has already been twice into France and stayed in Paris, and he had more to do with arranging the marriage with the French King's daughter than anyone else. The French are very clever at laying their plans far ahead and slowly nearing their aim. And they give big promises and rewards if it helps them to gain their ends.'

With the Duke's encouragement, the men of London went one day to Eltham to see the King. With him at that time were his two half-brothers, the Earls of Kent and Huntingdon, the Earl of Salisbury, the Archbishop of Canterbury, his confessor the Archbishop of Dublin, Sir Thomas Percy, Sir William de Lisle, Sir Richard Credon, Sir John Golafre and several knights of his household. The Londoners explained the reason for their visit, putting it in very respectful and temperate terms, and they told him of the scandalous rumour which was spreading through England.

The King assures them that Saint-Pol's visit was a purely friendly one, with no ulterior motive. Lord Salisbury also speaks out to condemn the disseminators of idle rumours. These could easily lead to a popular rising, with harmful consequences for them all. Largely reassured, the Londoners leave, but Richard remains shaken by the episode and begins to distrust all his uncles, though his chief fear is of Gloucester. Soon after, he receives information, considered reliable, of the plot to seize the Queen and himself and put them under guard. The country is to be governed temporarily by Lancaster, York, Gloucester and Arundel, each taking a different region. A pretext is to be found for ending the truce with France and for sending the infant Queen back to her father if she so chooses.

If the King of France wished to have his daughter back, she was still very young and aged only eight and a half, so she could well wait until she reached womanhood. When she was twelve she might quite possibly regret her marriage, for she had been married to Richard in all innocence, and it had been an unjust step to break off her match with the heir of Brittany. If, however, she chose to stay and observe the present marriage arrangements, she would remain Queen of England and would have her dowry. But she should never be deflowered by the King of England; and, if he died before she reached the age, they would examine the question of sending her back to France.

Unrest grows in the country, and with it Richard's anxiety. He appeals to his uncles of Lancaster and York to give him their advice and support.

They said to him: 'Sire, be patient and leave things to time. We know that our brother Gloucester is the most unruly man in England, and the rashest. But he is only one man and can achieve nothing by himself. If he is working on one side, we will work on the other. As long as you will allow us to advise you, you will take no notice of our brother. He sometimes says all kinds of things which are quite baseless. He alone, or his intimates, cannot break the truce with France, and as for shutting you up in a castle or separating you from your wife, the Queen, we will never allow such things to happen. He is deluding himself when he talks in that way. So be reassured, matters will right themselves. What one sometimes thinks or says is not the same as what one actually does.'

With such arguments the Dukes of Lancaster and York calmed their nephew Richard of England.

Seeing, however, that the affairs of the realm were beginning to go badly and that a great feud was growing up between the King and Gloucester, they did not wish to be involved. Taking leave of the King for a time, they left the court with the whole of their families and withdrew each to his own place. The Duke of Lancaster took his wife, Catherine Ruet,[1] who for some time had been a companion to the young Queen, and took the opportunity to go hunting stags and deer, as the custom is in England. The King remained with his followers in the London region. Later his two uncles bitterly regretted having left him, for soon after their departure things happened which caused deep disquiet in the whole of England and which would not have occurred if they had stayed. They would have given very different advice from that which the King now received from his followers.

Richard's intimates work on his fear of Gloucester, which some of them share. They stress the charges brought against him by popular rumour, particularly those of being a weak and cowardly sovereign.

King Richard noted all these things which were said to him in the privacy of his chamber and took them so much to heart (he was apprehensive by nature) that, shortly after the Duke of Lancaster and York had gone away, he decided upon a bold and daring move. He had reflected that it was better to destroy than to be destroyed and that speedy action could prevent his uncle from ever being a threat to him again. Since he could not carry out his plans without help, he confided in the man whom he trusted most, his cousin the Earl Marshal, Earl of Nottingham, telling him exactly what he wanted done. The Earl Marshal, who preferred the King to the Duke of Gloucester, having received many favours from him, revealed the King's plans to no one, except to those whose assistance he required, for he also could not act alone. What had been agreed between them will become clear as you read on.

On the pretext of hunting deer, the King went to a manor in Essex called Havering-atte-Bower, twenty miles from London and about the same distance from Pleshey, where the Duke now lived almost permanently. One afternoon the King left Havering-atte-Bower with only a part of his retinue, hav-

1. Catherine Swynford.

ing left the others at Eltham with the Queen, and reached Pleshey at about five o'clock. It was a very fine, hot day with no one keeping watch, and he entered the castle unnoticed, until someone shouted: 'The King is here!' The Duke of Gloucester had already finished supper, for he was a sparing eater and did not linger over his meals. He came out to meet the King in the courtyard of the castle, receiving him with all the forms of respect due to the sovereign, which he well knew how to pay. The Duchess and her children who were there did the same. Then the King went into the hall and from there into the chamber. A table was set for him and he ate a little. He had already said to the Duke: 'Uncle, have some of your horses saddled – not all, but half-a-dozen – I want you to come back to London with me. I have a meeting with the Londoners tomorrow at which my uncles of Lancaster and York will certainly be present, and I shall want your advice on how to deal with a request they are bringing to me. Tell your steward that the rest of your people must follow tomorrow and join you in London then.'

The Duke, who had no suspicions, readily agreed. The King soon finished eating and got up. Everyone was ready; the King took leave of the Duchess and her children and mounted his horse, as did the Duke, taking with him from Pleshey only four squires and four servants. They took the *Bondelay*[1] road to have an easier ride and avoid Brentwood and other towns and they travelled fast, for the King pretended to be in a hurry to reach London. He and his uncle chatted together as they rode and made such progress that soon they came near to Stratford and the Thames. There, in a narrow place, the Earl Marshal was waiting in ambush. When the King had almost reached the spot, he left his uncle's side and galloped ahead of him. The Earl Marshal appeared with a number of men on horseback and, going up to the Duke of Gloucester, said: 'I arrest you in the King's name.' The Duke was astounded and saw clearly that he had been betrayed and began to shout after the King. . . .

Richard, on whose orders all this was being done, affected

1. *Sic* Froissart. Perhaps Billericay.

not to hear, but rode straight on and came that night to the Tower of London.

His uncle of Gloucester had a very different lodging, for in spite of his protests, he was forced into a barge on the Thames and transferred from that to a ship which lay at anchor in the middle of the river. The Earl Marshal and his men also went on board and they sailed down the river, reaching Calais late the next day with the help of a following wind. Only the King's officers in Calais, of which the Earl Marshal was the governor, knew about their arrival. . . .

Early the next morning the King left the Tower of London for Eltham, where he remained. In the evening of the same day the Earls of Arundel and Warwick were taken to the Tower and imprisoned there, to the amazement of London and the rest of England. Many strong protests were raised, but no one dared to go against the King's orders for fear of incurring his anger.

The people console themselves with the thought that Lancaster and York will restrain the King. Meanwhile, the Duchess of Gloucester has appealed directly to the two dukes. They send her reassuring answers and remain passive.

When the Duke of Gloucester had been taken into the castle of Calais and found himself shut in there and deprived of his attendants, he began to feel very afraid. He said to the Earl Marshal: 'Why have I been spirited out of England and brought here? You seem to be treating me as a prisoner. Let me take a walk through the town and see the fortifications and the people and the sentries.' 'Sir,' replied the Earl Marshal, 'I dare not do as you ask, for my life is answerable for your safe-keeping. My lord the King is a little displeased with you at the moment. He wishes you to stay here and put up with our company for a time. You will do that until I receive further instructions, which I hope will be soon. As for your own displeasure, I am very sorry about it and I wish I could relieve it. But I have my oath to the King, which I am bound in honour to obey.'

That was all the Duke could get from him and concluding,

from other signs that he noticed one day, that his life was in danger, he asked a priest who had already sung mass for him to hear his confession. He confessed at some length, kneeling before the altar in a pious frame of mind, devout and contrite. He prayed and asked God's mercy for all the things he had done and repented of all his sins. It was indeed high time for him to purge his conscience, for death was even nearer to him than he thought.

According to my information, just at the hour when the tables were laid for dinner in the castle of Calais and he was about to wash his hands, four men rushed out from a room and, twisting a towel round his neck, pulled so hard on the two ends that he staggered to the floor. There they finished strangling him, closed his eyes and carried him, now dead, to a bed on which they undressed his body. They placed him between two sheets, put a pillow under his head and covered him with fur mantles. Leaving the room, they went back into the hall, ready primed with their story, and said this: that the Duke had had an apoplectic fit while he was washing his hands and had been carried to his bed with great difficulty. This version was given out in the castle and the town. Some believed it, but others not.

Two days later, Gloucester is reported to be dead. The Earl Marshal and all the English officers in Calais put on mourning. The reaction in France is one of relief. In England, opinions are divided.

After the Duke's death at Calais, he was given an honourable embalmment and put in a lead coffin with a wooden casing and so sent by sea to England. The ship carrying him anchored under Hadleigh castle, on the Thames, and from there the body was conveyed very simply to Pleshey and placed in the church of the Holy Trinity which the Duke himself had founded, appointing twelve canons to perform the divine services; and there he was buried.

It may be said that the Duchess of Gloucester, with her son Humphrey and her two daughters, were naturally deeply distressed when their husband and father was brought home dead, and the Duchess had to suffer another blow when the King had her uncle, Earl Richard of Arundel, publicly beheaded in Cheapside, London. None of the great barons dared to thwart the King or dissuade him from doing this. King Richard was present at the execution and it was carried out by the Earl Marshal, who was married to Lord Arundel's daughter and who himself blindfolded him.

The Earl of Warwick was in great danger of being beheaded also, but the Earl of Salisbury, who was high in the King's favour, interceded for him, as did other nobles and prelates, with such strong arguments that the King granted their request.

Warwick is reprieved, on Salisbury's plea, and banished for life to a comfortable exile in the Isle of Wight.[1] *The Dukes of Lancaster and York, highly alarmed by the death of their brother Gloucester, now bestir themselves and come to London.*

At that date King Richard, who was established at Eltham, summoned to him all those who held fiefs from him and owed him homage. He assembled and maintained more than ten thousand archers round London and in the counties of Kent and Sussex. He had with him his half-brother, Sir John Holland, the Earl Marshal, the Earl of Salisbury and many of the English knights and barons, and he sent orders to the Londoners that they were not to harbour the Duke of Lancaster. They replied that they knew nothing against the Duke to make him unacceptable. Lancaster therefore remained in London, with his son the Earl of Derby, and also the Duke of York, whose son, the Earl of Rutland, was on intimate terms with the King. With the Earl Marshal, the King loved him beyond reason.

Rutland mediates between King Richard and Lancaster, who reflects that a breach with Richard and hence with the French, who would support him, might prove harmful to his two daughters, who are married to the Kings of Spain and Portugal. He is persuaded grudgingly to make peace with Richard and receives his promise to act in future only on his advice. The promise is never observed.

So King Richard was reconciled with his uncles over the death of the Duke of Gloucester and went on to rule more harshly than before. He moved his establishment to Essex,

1. This seems to have been a mistake of Froissart's. Warwick was banished to the Isle of Man.

formerly the domain of the Duke of Gloucester and which ought to have gone to his heir, Humphrey. But the King took freehold possession of it all. The rule in England is that the King has custody of the inheritances of all minors who lose their fathers and that the inheritances are returned to them when they are twenty-one. King Richard made himself the trustee of his young cousin, Gloucester's heir, and took over all his lands and possessions for his own benefit. He obliged young Humphrey to live in his household, and the Duchess and her two daughters in that of the Queen. He removed from Humphrey the hereditary office of Constable of England, which his father had held in his lifetime, and gave it to his cousin the Earl of Rutland. He began to reign with greater pomp than any English king before him; none had come within a hundred thousand nobles yearly of the amount he now spent. He likewise brought to his court the heir of the Earl of Arundel, whom he had had beheaded in London, as already related. Because one of the Duke of Gloucester's knights called Corbet spoke too freely one day about the King and his council, he had him seized and beheaded. Sir John Lacking-hay was also in great danger, but when he saw that things were going against him, he tried to put a smooth face on it, left the service of his lady the Duchess of Gloucester, and went to live elsewhere.

In those days, not even the greatest in England dared to criticize the King's acts or intentions. He had his private circle of advisers, the knights of his chamber, who persuaded him to do everything they wanted. And the King kept in his pay a retinue of two thousand archers who guarded him day and night, for he felt by no means safe from his uncles or from the family of the Earl of Arundel.

THE CHALLENGE AND BOLINGBROKE'S BANISHMENT

It was only too true that the Duke of Gloucester's death had greatly disturbed several of the great lords of England, some of whom talked and complained confidentially among themselves. But the King had so subdued them that none dared to show his dissatisfaction openly, for Richard had had the word spread throughout England that anyone who spoke in favour of either the Duke of Gloucester or the Earl of Arundel would be branded as false, miscreant and a traitor and would incur his extreme anger. Such threats had imposed silence on many people who were in strong disagreement with his recent actions.

In these circumstances the Earl of Derby and the Earl Marshal were having a conversation on various matters and, from one thing to another, came to speaking about the King and his council in which he placed so much trust. The Earl Marshal took particular notice of a remark made with the best intentions by the Earl of Derby, who meant it as a confidential opinion and never thought that it would be repeated. There was nothing disloyal or excessive about his words, which were these: 'Well, good cousin, what does our cousin the King think he is doing? Does he want to drive all the nobles out of England? There will be none left soon. He shows clearly that he has no desire to increase his country's power.' The Earl Marshal made no reply, but affected to ignore a remark which he thought was highly offensive to the King. However, he could not keep it to himself, feeling that the Earl of Derby was on the point of stirring up trouble in England, with the support of the Londoners who loved him greatly. He decided – since the devil was no doubt working on his mind and what must be, must be – that the Earl of Derby's words must be repeated to the King in such a public way, and in the presence of so many of the nobility, that an open scandal would be unavoidable. So soon afterwards he went to the King and, thinking to please him and enter his good graces, he said: 'My lord, all your enemies and ill-wishers are not yet dead or out of England.' 'What do you mean by that, cousin?' said the King, changing colour. 'I know what I mean,' replied the Earl Marshal, 'but for the moment I will say no more. But in order to deal promptly and effectively with the matter, you should hold a solemn feast this coming Easter and summon to it all the members of your family who are in England, not forgetting to invite the Earl of Derby, and then you will hear some very peculiar things which you do not suspect at present. They touch you closely.'

The King became very thoughtful when he heard this and asked the Earl Marshal to be more explicit, assuring him that whatever he told him would remain secret. I do not know whether he said more then, but if he did the King gave no outward sign of it and allowed the Earl Marshal to proceed with his intention, with the results which I will describe. The King announced a solemn festival at Eltham, to be held on Palm Sunday, to which all his kindred were invited. He particularly urged his uncles of Lancaster and York to come with their children, and they, suspecting nothing amiss, appeared with their full retinues.

After dinner on the day of the festival the King retired to his robing-room with his uncles and the other nobles. He had not been there long when the Earl Marshal, his plan fully prepared, came and knelt before him, saying: 'Beloved sire and mighty King, I am your kinsman and liegeman and Marshal of England. I am closely bound to you by word and oath. I have sworn with my hand in yours never to be in any place or company where evil is spoken against your royal majesty. If I were, and concealed it in any way whatsoever, I would rightly be called false, miscreant and a traitor,[1] which thing I will never tolerate, but rather will do my duty to you in all circumstances.'

The King looked at him fixedly and said: 'Why do you say this, Earl Marshal? We wish to know.'

'My very dear and mighty lord,' replied the Earl, 'I will tell you because I cannot suffer or conceal a thing which may be prejudicial to you. Call out the Earl of Derby and I will

1. This phrase, used four times by Froissart ('*faux, mauvais et traitre*'), was evidently the formula of indictment. To justify 'miscreant' for the second term in English, see Shakespeare, *Richard II*, I, i, which also contains a choice of other injurious epithets: 'Thou art a traitor and a miscreant ... foul traitor ... a slanderous coward and a villain ... false traitor and injurious villain ... false Mowbray ... There I throw my gage.' In Shakespeare, as historically, the challenge was made by Derby.

speak openly.' The Earl of Derby was called forward by the King, and the Earl Marshal, who had spoken on his knees, was told to stand up.

When the Earl of Derby had come forward in all innocence, the Earl Marshal said to him:

'Lord Derby, I maintain that you thought and spoke what you ought not to have done against your natural lord and master, the King of England, in saying that he is unworthy of ruling land or kingdom, since without forms of justice or consultation with his men, he unsettles his realm and with no shadow of justification drives out from it the gallant men who would help him to protect and uphold it: wherefore I offer you my gage and am ready to prove by my body against yours that you are false, miscreant and a traitor.'

The Earl of Derby was astounded by these words and drew back, standing very stiffly for some time without speaking or consulting his father or his men on what he ought to say in reply. When he had reflected a little, he stepped forward with his hat in his hand and, coming before the King and the Earl Marshal, he said: 'Earl Marshal, I say that you are false, miscreant and a traitor. All that I will prove by my body against yours and here is my glove.' Upon which the Earl Marshal, noting the challenge and being clearly willing to fight the Earl, picked up the glove and said: 'Lord Derby, I call the King and all these lords to witness your words. I shall turn your word to derision and prove mine true.'

Both earls then drew back among their followers; the ceremony of serving wine and sweetmeats was abandoned, for the King showed signs of extreme displeasure. He went into his private room and shut himself in there. His two uncles remained outside with all their children and the Earls of Salisbury and Huntingdon. Shortly afterwards the King called the last two in to him and asked them what was the best thing to do. They answered, 'Sire, send for your Constable and then we will tell you.' The Earl of Rutland, Constable of England, was summoned and, when he entered, was told: 'Constable, go out to the Earl of Derby and the Earl Marshal, and make them give assurances that neither will leave England without the King's permission.' The Constable did as he was instructed, then went back to the King's room.

As you can well imagine, the whole court was in a state of confusion and many of the nobles and knights were greatly disturbed, privately blaming the Earl Marshal. But he could not take back what he had said and he appeared to have no thought of doing so. He was far too great and haughty, with a heart full of pride and presumption. So the various lords left, each returning to his own house.

The Duke of Lancaster, though outwardly calm, was greatly upset by the words that had been exchanged. He felt that the King ought not to have taken them in the way he did, but should have passed them over. This was also the opinion of the majority of the English barons. The Earl of Derby took up his residence in London, where he had his palace. His guarantors were his father, his uncle the Duke of York, the Earl of Northumberland and many other prominent lords, for he was greatly liked in England. The Earl Marshal was sent to the Tower of London and took up residence there, and the two earls made lavish preparations for the combat. Lord Derby sent messengers urgently to the Duke of Milan in Lombardy to obtain armour of his size and choice. The Duke welcomed his request and allowed a knight whom the Earl had sent, a certain Sir Francis, to make a choice among his entire collection of armour. Not content with that, after the knight had inspected the plate and mail and picked out all the pieces he wanted, the Duke of Milan, inspired by sheer generosity and the desire to please the Earl, sent four of the best armourers in Lombardy back to England with the knight to ensure that the Earl of Derby was fitted to his exact size. The Earl Marshal, for his part, sent to places in Germany, where he thought his friends would help him and defray his expenses, and he also equipped himself lavishly for the day. The whole business proved very costly to the two noblemen, each striving to outdo the other. In particular, the Earl of Derby spent much more on his preparations than the Earl Marshal on his. I must say that, when the Earl Marshal first embarked on the affair, he expected stronger support and assistance from the King than he received. But those who were near to Richard advised him thus: 'Sire, you should not intervene too openly in this business. Say nothing and let them get on with it; they will manage all right. The Earl of Derby is extraordinarily popular in this country, especially among the Londoners, and if they saw you taking sides with the Earl Marshal against him, you would lose their favour entirely.' King Richard saw the force of these arguments and realized that they were sound. He therefore hid his hand as far as he could and left the two to provide themselves with arms and trappings on their own account.

Nevertheless, public opinion is critical of Richard's inaction. It is felt that he should have used his authority to stifle the affair. Lancaster deplores the matter in private but is too proud to approach the King, since his son's honour is involved. The Londoners and some of the nobles express their strong support of Derby, saying that he has a better claim to the throne than Richard, who was imposed upon them by his grandfather, Edward III. Richard again consults his inner council and receives advice which he proceeds to follow.

A short time after the King had held this council, he summoned many of the prelates and great barons of England to Eltham. When they were assembled, he acted on the advice he had been given and called before him the Dukes of Lancaster and York, the Earls of Northumberland and Salisbury, his half-brother the Earl of Huntingdon, and the other great lords of his kingdom who had come to witness the combat. The Earl of Derby and the Earl Marshal were at Eltham also, each with his followers and an apartment of his own. They were forbidden to meet, the King letting it be known that he wished to stand between them and that he was highly displeased by all they had said and done, which were not things to be easily forgiven. He then sent the Constable and the Steward of England with four other noblemen to obtain a promise from the two adversaries that they would obey any order that the King gave them. Both pledged themselves to do so and their promise was reported to the King in the presence of the whole court. The King then said:

'I proclaim and command that the Earl Marshal, on the grounds that he has sown dissension in this country and uttered words of which there is no other evidence but his own account of them, shall put his affairs in order and leave the kingdom for any place or land where he pleases to live, this banishment being perpetual with no hope of return. Next, I proclaim and command that our cousin the Earl of Derby, on the grounds that he has angered us and is in some part the cause of the Earl Marshal's offence and punishment, shall prepare to leave the kingdom within fifteen days and go to whatever place he chooses. The length of his banishment is ten years, unless we recall him. In his case we may exercise our power of recall or remission at any time which may seem good to us.'

This sentence was received with fair satisfaction by the lords who were present.

The Earl Marshal, having banked funds for his use with the Lombards in Bruges, leaves for Calais, of which he had once been the governor. From there he makes his way to Cologne. Derby takes formal leave of the King, who remits four years of his exile as had previously been planned. Amid the lamentations of the citizens of London, he also leaves for Calais. Declining the invitation of the Count of Ostrevant to come to Hainault, he goes on to Paris, where he is welcomed by the French royal family. In February 1399, his father dies. Far from taking this opportunity to recall and pardon him, Richard seizes the Lancastrian estates. This makes little difference to the favour which Derby enjoys in France.

As a matter of fact, the King of France never for a moment had unfavourable thoughts about him, and neither had his brother or his uncles. They had great love and respect for the Earl of Derby and wanted to have him with them even more; and very good company he was to them. They considered the point that he was a widower and free to re-marry, and that the Duke of Berry had a daughter, already widowed twice but still young, called Marie. She had been married to Louis de Blois, who had died young, and then to Lord Philip of Artois, Count of Eu, who had died on the way back from Hungary. Marie de Berry would have been about twenty-three at that date. Her marriage with the Earl of Derby had been

considered and negotiated and was on the point of being concluded, for it was well known that the Earl was heir to great
estates in England. Moreover, the King of France was influenced by the thought of his daughter, the young Queen of
England. It was felt by him and other French lords that two
great ladies such as they were and so closely related would be
excellent company for each other, and also that the marriage
would draw the two countries closer in peace and friendship.
Those who held this opinion were quite right, but the match
came to nothing. It was fated to be broken off, thanks to the
intervention of King Richard and his council.

*Richard sends the Earl of Salisbury to Paris to inform the French
of his displeasure at the prospect. The marriage project is dropped.*

RICHARD LOSES CONTROL

Not long after the Earl of Salisbury's return to England, King
Richard had it announced throughout his kingdom and as far
as Scotland that a tournament was to be held at Windsor, in
which forty home knights and forty squires would challenge
all comers. They were to be clothed in green with the device
of a white falcon. The Queen was to be there, accompanied
by a large suite of ladies. The feast was held. The Queen came
in full state, but very few lords attended, for at least two-
thirds of the English knights and squires were strongly hostile
to the King, not only because of the banishment of the Earl of
Derby and the wrong done to his children, but also because of
the murder of the Duke of Gloucester at Calais and the execution of the Earl of Arundel in London, so that none of the
families of those nobles came to the feast. There was almost
no one there.

At that feast the King made arrangements to go to Ireland
to find a use for his time and his men. He left Queen Isabella
and all her court at Windsor and set out for Bristol. There and
in the surrounding country he assembled his expedition and
supplies. He had at least two thousand lances of knights and
squires and ten thousand archers. When the Londoners heard
where he was going they began to murmur together and make

predictions. 'Richard of Bordeaux is off to Bristol and Ireland,' they said. 'He's going to his destruction. He'll never come back in peace, any more than his ancestor King Edward, who ruled so badly that he paid for it, relying too much on the advice of Lord Despenser. Richard of Bordeaux also has had such bad and feeble counsellors that it cannot be concealed or endured much longer, and he'll have to pay for it, too.'

Richard summons the Percies of Northumberland, whose loyalty has become suspect, to join his Irish expedition. They refuse and receive a sentence of banishment which is not enforced.

King Richard and his counsellors had so many things to do in a short time that they had no opportunity of dealing with the Earl of Northumberland nor of telling him: 'You will clear out of England or we will clear you out by force.' They had to drop the matter and, soon after, to change all their plans.

While the King and his following were at Bristol, the population of England in general began to stir and engage in internal strife. All the courts of justice were closed, to the dismay of honest men who asked only for tranquillity and fair dealing, with the payment of their lawful debts. They began to be attacked by a class of people who roamed the country in troops and gangs. Merchants dared not ride about upon their business for fear of being robbed, and they did not know to whom to turn for protection or justice. Such things were most disagreeable to the English people and contrary to their habits and customs, for in England every man, whether merchant or farmer, had grown used to living and trading pacifically, and the farmers to living quietly and well off their land, according to the produce of the season, but now just the opposite was happening.

First, when traders travelled from one town to another, any money that they carried in their purses was snatched from them and they were left with nothing. The farmers were robbed of their corn, oxen, cows, pigs and sheep and were afraid to say anything about it. Such misdeeds began to multiply rapidly, until complaints and lamentations were heard all over England and honest people were saying: 'Things have

changed very much for the worse since the death of good
King Edward of happy memory. In his time justice reigned
and was properly enforced. No man, however bold, dared to
take a sheep or a hen without paying for it. Now our things
are taken from us by force and we dare not complain. If this
state of affairs goes on for long, England will be ruined, for no
one tries to stop it and the King is useless. His only concern is
to enjoy himself in idle shows and he seems not to care how
things are going, so long as he gets his own way. Something
must be done about it, or our enemies will begin to crow over
us. Now this King Richard has sent his brother, the Earl of
Huntingdon, to Calais. How easy it would be for him to make
some crooked secret pact with the French and give back
Calais to them. If that did happen, we English would feel
utterly beaten and humiliated; and rightly, for we should have
lost the key to the kingdom of France.'

These kinds of complaints and misgivings were echoed in
many parts of the country and the prelates and men of substance went to live in London for greater security. The families of the men whom Richard had killed or banished were
glad at the troubles which had arisen and only hoped that they
would increase. The citizens of London, who are rich and
powerful, and draw their living chiefly from merchandise sent
over land and sea, which enables them to live in great prosperity, are the real leaders of the kingdom, without whom the
rest of the country would neither dare nor be able to do anything; these saw that the situation might quickly become disastrous unless something was done to remedy it.

THE RETURN OF BOLINGBROKE

*The Londoners hold a secret meeting, 'with certain prelates and
knights', at which it is decided to offer the crown to the Earl of Derby.
The mission of taking the offer to Derby in Paris is confided to the
Archbishop of Canterbury, Thomas Arundel.*

The Archbishop, accompanied by only six others, boarded
a ship in the port of London and crossed over safely to Sluys
in Flanders. From there he went to Ardenburg, Ghent,

Oudenarde, Ath in Brabant, then Condé on the Scheldt, and then Valenciennes, where he put up at the hostelry of the Swan in the Market Place. He stayed there for three days, resting from his journey. He was not travelling as Archbishop of Canterbury, but as a pilgrim monk, and he revealed his identity and his plans to no one. From Valenciennes he took with him a guide familiar with the road to Paris, giving out that he was on a pilgrimage to Saint-Maur-des-Fossés. He travelled on until he came to where the Earl of Derby was then living. I think it was in the mansion known as Winchester,[1] lying outside Paris towards Saint-Denis.

When the Earl of Derby saw the Archbishop of Canterbury coming towards him, his heart leapt within him and his spirits rose. All those around him experienced the same exultation, imagining at once that he had brought some message from England. The Archbishop did not at first disclose his purpose, but prudently kept his mission secret. He said, for public hearing, that he was going on a pilgrimage to Saint-Maur-des-Fossés, and this convinced and satisfied the Earl's household. When the Archbishop saw that the moment had come to speak of his real purpose, he took the Earl of Derby aside and went alone with him into a private room. There he described to him the troubled state of England, the violence and destruction which were taking place in many parts of the country, recalled that justice was in abeyance, through the King's fault, and told him that the Londoners, with certain prominent men, prelates and others, wanted to put a stop to it, and had unanimously agreed – this was the reason for his visit – that the Earl ought to return to England, for he was wasting his

1. Froissart: *Hôtel de Vincestre* (Winchester), the modern Bicêtre; but this is on the opposite side of Paris to Saint-Denis. Difficult though it is to credit, most of this detail appears to be sheer invention, as is much of the rest. Thomas Arundel had been deprived of the see of Canterbury and banished from England at the time of his brother's execution in 1397. He joined Bolingbroke in Paris soon after the latter's banishment in the following year. However, the possibility that he returned secretly to England to confer with Bolingbroke's supporters and then carried their offer of the crown back to Bolingbroke in Paris cannot be entirely ruled out and would partly justify Froissart's account.

time in France. He would be made King, since Richard of Bordeaux had done or permitted so many infamous things that the whole population was complaining bitterly and was ready to rise against him.

When Lord Derby had heard all the Archbishop had to say, he did not reply at once but went over to a window which looked on to the gardens and reflected for a while. Many thoughts passed through his mind, and at last he turned and said to the Archbishop: 'Sir, you have given me a great deal to think about. I am reluctant to take this opportunity and reluctant to let it slip. I quite understand that I could not return to England for a long time to come, except by the means you suggest to me, yet I hesitate to agree because the King of France and the French have shown me every courtesy and say they will go on treating me with all honour for as long as I wish to stay. If in fact, taking you and my good friends in London at their word, I have to bind myself to everything they desire, that means that King Richard would be captured and destroyed, and I should have the blame for it. That is not a thing I would undertake willingly, if there is any other form or manner in which it could be done.'

'Sir,' replied the Archbishop, 'I have been sent to you for the good of us all. Call together your council and tell them what I have told you. I will address them, too. I do not believe that they will advise you against it.'

'I agree,' said the Earl. 'Such things require deliberation in council.'

Derby is enthusiastically advised to accept the offer. Faced with the choice of reaching England through Hainault or through Brittany, he chooses the second and leaves Paris on the pretext of a visit to the Duke of Brittany, a relation by marriage. The Duke encourages him in his venture and offers to support him with ships and men.

After these arrangements had been agreed upon, in all good faith and amity, the Earl spent some time with the Duke in pleasure and relaxation, making it appear that he intended to stay on. But meanwhile preparations were going forward at a seaport which I think was Vannes, and to which the Duke and the Earl presently came. When it was time and the wind was favourable, the Earl went on board ship with all his followers and they were accompanied by three vessels manned with men-at-arms and crossbowmen who were to escort them as far as England.

Their fleet raised anchor and put to sea. The farther they sailed towards England, the better wind they had. They made such good progress that after two days and nights they reached Plymouth [1] where they disembarked and entered the town a few at a time. The Bailiff of Plymouth, whose duty was to guard the town and port for the King, was disquieted to see so many men-at-arms and archers, but the Archbishop of Canterbury reassured him, saying that they meant no harm to England, but had been sent by the Duke of Brittany to serve the King and the country. This satisfied the Bailiff and meanwhile the Earl of Derby hid his identity and stayed quietly in his room, so that no one in the town was able to see and recognize him. As soon as they were lodged, the Archbishop had letters written and sent them off to London by one of his men. The man rode so fast, taking fresh horses in each town, that by dawn the next day he reached London and clattered into it. He went straight over London Bridge, for the gates were open, and made for the house of the Lord Mayor, who was still in bed. When the Mayor heard that he came from the Archbishop of Canterbury, he got up, had the man brought into his room, and read the letters. He was overjoyed by the news they contained and, having dressed rapidly, he sent his servants round from house to house to inform those who had played the principal part in inviting the Earl to return – although everyone, in London and elsewhere, was delighted by the news. More than two hundred of the most prominent citizens quickly assembled and after discussing the matter briefly, for there was no need for long deliberation, they said:

1. *Pleumoude*, hardly more than a name for Froissart. In another passage he appears to confuse its whereabouts, placing it near the Isle of Wight. Bolingbroke certainly did skirt the Channel coast, putting in briefly at Pevensey, before sailing on to land definitively at Ravenspur in Yorkshire. It was from there that he rode to London.

'Quick now, let us get ready to go and greet our lord of Derby, since we invited him to come.'

The meeting between the leading citizens and Bolingbroke, who has travelled overland after the messenger, takes place near Guildford, says Froissart. The next day most of the population of London come out to welcome him and escort him to the city.

To make a long story short, it was eventually decided that they would march with all speed towards the King, whom the Londoners and others now called plain Richard of Bordeaux, with no courtesy titles. Indeed, the foul-mouthed ale-swilling populace of London so detested him that they could hardly mention his name without adding, 'Damn and blast the dirty bugger.' The citizens had already covenanted with the Earl of Derby that he should be their lord and king and should act in all matters on their advice. Further to this agreement, the Earl stipulated that he and his heirs should assume responsibility for the government of the kingdom for all future time. This the Londoners swore to him, put it in writing and sealed it. They promised further to have the same undertaking sworn to and sealed by the population of the rest of England in so solemn and binding a way that it would never be in question; and they promised to remain always loyal to him and to help him to attain his ends.

Once these conditions had been agreed to by both parties – and it was done quickly, for they did not want to lose time – it was arranged that twelve hundred London men, all armed and mounted, should set out for Bristol with the Earl of Derby and remain with him until they had captured Richard of Bordeaux and brought him to London. This achieved, it would be decided what to do with him, for he would be brought to trial before the nobles, prelates and commons of England and judged according to his acts. It was also agreed, to avoid possible scandal, that the armed men whom the Duke of Brittany had lent to the Earl as his escort should be sent home, since they would have enough men of their own for the purpose.

THE SURRENDER OF KING RICHARD

News reached King Richard's army of the approach of Lord Derby and the Londoners. Many knights, squires and archers heard of it before the King, but those who knew would never have dared to tell him. As the news spread from mouth to mouth, many, including some nearest to the King, were in a state of great alarm. They saw at once that events were shaping in a way that was dangerous for themselves and the King, for they had many enemies in England and these, who had pretended to smile upon them before, would become open now that the Earl was on this side of the sea. Many knights, squires and archers, who had served the King for the season, hid their intentions and slipped quietly away. Some returned to their homes. Others, by the shortest road they could, made for the Earl of Derby and joined him.

As soon as Humphrey of Gloucester and Richard[1] of Arundel learnt that their cousin of Derby and the Londoners were coming, they called their men together, left King Richard, and did not stop riding until they reached the Earl's force, which had passed Oxford and come to a town called Cicister. The Earl was delighted to see his cousins and they to see him. He asked for news of the King, his forces, his whereabouts, and how they had got away. They answered: 'We did not see him before we left. As soon as we heard you were coming we got on our horses and rode towards you. We wish to serve you and help to avenge our fathers whom Richard of Bordeaux put to death.' 'You are welcome,' the Earl replied. 'You will help me and I will help you. The task is to take our cousin Richard back to London.'

When the facts could no longer be hidden, Richard's counsellors came to him privately and said: 'Sire, you must think what to do. A decision has to be made quickly, for the men of London have risen against you in force and are evidently

1. The name of the Arundel heir was Thomas, like that of his uncle the Archbishop. He had already joined Bolingbroke in France, and returned to England with him. His younger brother was called Richard.

coming to seek you out, accompanied by your cousin the Earl of Derby, whom they have made their leader. And since he has crossed the sea on their invitation, there must be a close understanding between them.'

On hearing this, the King was shaken to the core and could find nothing to say. He realized at once that things would go from bad to worse if he could not take some forceful action. When at last he spoke, it was to say to the knights who had brought him the news: 'Quickly then, alert our men, archers and men-at-arms, and issue a general order for everyone to be ready to march, for I will not flee before my subjects.' 'Before God, sir,' the knights replied, 'things look very black, your men are deserting and slipping away. You have lost quite half of them already and those who are left are utterly dispirited.' 'What do you think I should do, then?' asked the King. 'We will tell you, sire. You cannot hope to face your enemies in the field, but must retire into some castle where you can hold out until your brother, Sir John Holland, comes to your support. He is brave and soldierly enough to do so and he will already have heard the news. Once he is in England[1] he will so manage things, by force of arms or negotiation, that your prospects will be quite different from now. When he is known to be in the field, many who have deserted you will rally to him.' The King accepted this advice unreservedly.

At that time the Earl of Salisbury was not with the King, but in another place some way off. On receiving news of the situation, he at once saw how dangerous it was for himself and the King and those who had so far advised him. So he did nothing until he should hear more. The King's uncle, the Duke of York, had not been with the King's army, but his son the Earl of Rutland was with it for two reasons; first because the King was extremely fond of him, and secondly because he was Constable of England, which made it his duty to take part in the expedition.

More news was brought to the King soon after he had finished supper. He was told: 'Sire, you must decide now what you intend to do. Your army is nothing compared to

1. He had succeeded the Earl Marshal as Governor of Calais.

what is approaching. A battle is out of the question, you could not hope to fight one now. You must get out of this corner by skill and good judgement, appease your enemies if possible, as you did once before, and then punish them in your own time. There is a castle twelve miles from here called Flint[1] which is quite strong. We advise you to make for it and shut yourself inside there until you have further news of the Earl of Huntingdon and your other friends. We will send to Ireland and elsewhere for help. And if your father-in-law, the King of France, hears that you are in difficulties, he will give you support.'

Richard acts on this advice, leaving Rutland at Bristol with the bulk of his forces.

The Earl of Derby and the Londoners had their spies coming and going who reported all the King's movements to them, and there were also the knights and squires who came over to the Earl of their own accord. The Earl thus learnt that the King had withdrawn to Flint Castle and had hardly any men with him, apart from the members of his household; also that he seemed to have no intention of fighting, but only wanted to escape from his predicament, if possible by negotiation. It was immediately decided to follow him to Flint and, once there, to contrive to take him by force or otherwise. When the Earl of Derby's force had come within about five miles of the castle, they found themselves in a large village. Here the Earl halted, took a meal and a drink, and decided solely on his own initiative to ride ahead with two hundred men, leaving all the rest behind. He hoped to induce the King to let him into the castle by peaceful means and, once there, to bring him out by persuasion. He would guarantee him protection against all dangers, except that of going to London, and even there he would promise to preserve him against bodily harm and would mediate between him and the Londoners who were so enraged against him.

1. Froissart: *Flitch, Flinth*. The 'twelve miles' is either a scribal mistake or an example of geographical confusion. Richard in fact went first to Conway Castle, and was either persuaded or tricked into going to Flint by Archbishop Arundel and Northumberland.

When the Earl told those around him of his plan, they approved of it, but said: 'Sir, make quite sure that there is no double-dealing in this matter. Richard of Bordeaux must be taken, dead or alive, with all the traitors who have influenced him, and brought to London and put in the Tower. Nothing else will satisfy the Londoners.' 'Of course,' the Earl replied. 'Everything that has been agreed upon will be done. But if I can persuade him to come out of the castle peaceably I will do so. If I cannot and he refuses to listen to me, I shall let you know at once. You will come and we will start the siege. We will go to work by force, since the place is not impregnable, until we have him dead or alive.'

This last statement was enough for the Londoners, and the Earl of Derby left the main body and rode forward with two hundred men only. They were soon outside the castle, in one of the rooms of which the King was sitting dazed and trembling among his men. The Earl and his troop dismounted before the castle gate, which was naturally shut and barred, and he went and banged loudly on it. Those inside asked who it was. The Earl of Derby answered them: 'I am Henry of Lancaster. I have come to take back my inheritance of the Duchy of Lancaster from the King. Go and tell him so from me.' 'My lord,' they said, 'we will do so willingly.' They went up to the room in the keep where the King was with the men who had so long been his advisers, and told him: 'Sire, it is your cousin the Earl of Derby who has come to reclaim his inheritance of Lancaster from you.' The King looked at his knights and asked them what he should do. 'Sire,' they said, 'there is nothing unreasonable in this demand. You can allow him to come before you, with a dozen followers only, and hear what he has to say. He is your cousin and a great man in this country. If he chooses, he can well make peace for you, for he is much loved in England, particularly among the Londoners who brought him back across the sea and who are supporting him against you so strongly at this moment. You must hide your real intentions until this trouble has blown over and your brother the Earl of Huntingdon is able to join you. It is a great pity that he is at Calais, for those who revolt against you in England would keep quiet and not dare to offend you if they knew he was with you. Also, he is married to the Earl of Derby's sister and through his mediation we hope and believe that you would reach a peaceful understanding with everyone.'

The King agreed to this suggestion, saying: 'Have the gate opened and let him come in, with eleven others only.' Two knights went down to the courtyard and out through the wicket-gate, where they bowed to the Earl of Derby and the knights accompanying him. They greeted them with great courtesy, knowing that they were on the weaker side and that they had done very wrong and were hated by the Londoners. They wished to put things right if they could by flowery politeness, so they said: 'What is your pleasure, my lord? The King is at mass, and he has sent us to inquire on his behalf.' 'This,' said the Earl. 'You know that I have come to claim back the Duchy of Lancaster. I want to talk to the King about that and certain other things.' 'My lord,' they replied, 'you are most welcome. The King will be glad to receive you and listen to you. He said that you should come in with just eleven companions.' 'I am willing,' said the Earl, and entered the castle with his eleven men. The wicket was immediately shut, leaving all the others outside.

Now consider the great risk that the Earl was running, for he could have been killed in there with all his companions as easily as if they had been birds in a cage. But he thought nothing of the danger and went straight forward until he came before the King.

When the King saw him, he changed colour, like a man who felt he had done him a great wrong. Making no attempt to show him honour or respect, Lord Derby asked bluntly: 'Have you breakfasted yet?' 'No,' answered the King. 'It is still quite early. Why do you ask?' 'It is time you did,' said the Earl. 'You have a long journey before you.' 'What journey?' asked the King. 'You have to go to London. I would advise you to eat something now. You will have a more comfortable ride.' Depressed and frightened by these words, the King replied: 'I am not hungry yet. I don't feel I could eat.' But his knights, seeing that things were going badly and wishing to humour the Earl, said: 'Sire, do as my lord of Lancaster asks. He only means it for your good.' 'I will, then,' said the King. 'Have the tables laid.' The tables were prepared quickly. The King washed and sat down. He was served. The Earl was asked if he would eat as well. He said no, he had already breakfasted.

While the King was sitting there trying to eat – but he could swallow almost nothing, his heart was so heavy – the whole country round Flint Castle became covered with men-at-arms and archers. Those inside the castle could see them only too well from the windows. The King caught sight of them when he rose from table after a brief and melancholy meal. He asked his cousin who these people were and received the answer that they were mostly men of London. 'And what do they want?' asked the King. 'They want you,' said the Earl of Derby, 'to take you to London and put you in the Tower. There is no other way for you.' 'No,' said the King, who was terrified to hear this, knowing how the Londoners hated him. He went on: 'You, my cousin, cannot you do something to prevent it? I will never willingly put myself in their hands. I know that they have hated me for a long time, I who am their sovereign.' The Earl replied: 'I can see no way of preventing it, unless you surrender to me. If they know that you are my prisoner they will not harm you. But you must get ready, with all your people, to go to London and be imprisoned in the Tower.'

Seeing himself in this desperate situation and utterly cowed by the fear that the Londoners would kill him, the King surrendered to his cousin of Derby, promising to do whatever he asked. His knights and officers all followed his example, in order to avoid greater perils. The Earl, in the presence of the men he had brought with him, accepted them as his prisoners and ordered them to be taken to the courtyard. Horses were to be saddled and the gates of the castle thrown open. When this was done, large numbers of men-at-arms and archers came crowding in, upon which Lord Derby, whom I will now call Duke of Lancaster, issued strict orders that no

one was to presume to take anything in the castle or lay hands
on man or servant, on pain of hanging and drawing. He led
his cousin King Richard down from the keep to the courtyard, talking to him all the time. He let him keep his whole
household just as it was, without removing or changing any
of his attendants. While the horses were being got ready, the
King and the Duke continued to chat together, closely watched
by some of the Londoners who were present. A thing then
happened which was told to me and which I will relate.

King Richard had a greyhound called Math, a truly magnificent dog, which would follow no one except the King.
Whenever he was about to go riding, the greyhound was
loosed and came bounding up to the King and put his paws on
his shoulders. Now, as the King and the Duke were standing
talking in the middle of the courtyard, with their horses ready
for mounting, this greyhound Math left the King and went
to the Duke of Lancaster, showing him all the marks of
affection which he used to show to the King. He placed his
forepaws on his shoulders and began to lick his face. The
Duke of Lancaster, who had never seen the dog before, asked
the King: 'What does this greyhound want?' 'Cousin,' replied the King, 'it is an excellent omen for you and a bad one
for me.' 'What do you mean?' asked the Duke. 'I mean,' said
the King, 'that the dog is hailing and honouring you today as
the King of England which you will be, while I shall be deposed. The dog knows it by instinct. So keep him with you,
for he will stay with you and leave me.' The Duke of Lancaster understood perfectly and stroked the greyhound, which
henceforth ignored Richard of Bordeaux and followed him.
These things were observed or known by over thirty thousand people.

*The King is escorted under strong guard to the outskirts of London.
According to Froissart, they avoid the large towns, pass near Oxford,
and halt at Windsor, then at Chertsey.*

King Richard of Bordeaux had pleaded movingly with his
cousin of Lancaster not to take him through London, which
was the reason they took that road. Meanwhile, as soon as the
Londoners had got the better of Richard, they sent some

prominent citizens to the young Queen Isabella, who was then at Leeds Castle with her court. They went to the Lady de Courcy, who was the second in importance after the Queen, and said: 'Lady, get ready and have all your things packed. You must clear out of here. And make quite sure not to show the Queen any displeasure when you leave. Say that your husband and your daughter have sent for you. If we see you doing anything else, your life will answer for it. You must ask no questions, that's all you need to know. You will be taken to Dover and given a boat to take you across to Boulogne.'

Very frightened by these threats and knowing how hard and relentless the English were, the Lady de Courcy answered: 'I swear I will do everything you say.' She was soon ready. She was provided with horses and hackneys for herself and her attendants. All of them went; not a single Frenchman or Frenchwoman stayed behind. They set out on the road and were escorted to Dover, where they were well and generously paid, each according to his station. At the first tide they boarded a ship and sailed across to Boulogne.

The young Queen's household was so broken up that neither man, woman nor child was left to her. They were all thrown out, those of French nationality and many of English nationality who favoured King Richard. A new court was formed with other ladies and maids-of-honour, household officers and servants, and all of them were warned in advance never to speak of King Richard as they valued their lives, not even among themselves.

The Duke of Lancaster and his company left Chertsey for Sheen, and from there they took King Richard to the Tower of London by night, with all those of his knights and followers whom they wished to imprison in it. In the morning, when the people of London learnt that the King was in the Tower, they were far from sorry, but there was a great murmur of discontent that he had been taken there in secrecy. They were very angry that he had not been led right through the city – not so that they could applaud and honour him, but to revile him and show their hatred. Consider for a moment what it is like when the people are roused to revolt and get the upper hand of their master, and especially in England. Then there is no stopping it, for they are the most dangerous common people in the world, the most violent and presumptuous. And of all the commons in England the Londoners are the ringleaders. They are indeed very powerful in men and resources. Within the boundaries of London they can raise twenty-four thousand men armed from head to foot and at least thirty thousand archers. That is great strength, for they are tough, sturdy, bold and confident. And the more blood they see flowing, the bolder and fiercer they grow.

The Earl of Rutland and Thomas Despenser, whom Richard had left at Bristol, hear of Richard's surrender and incarceration and disband their army. They go to a castle of Despenser's in the Welsh Marches, to await developments. The Duke of York keeps to his castle and continues to remain passive.

Lancaster (Bolingbroke) recalls Warwick from exile and restores all his rights. He invites the Earl of Northumberland and his son Henry Percy to join him. He lays hands on 'the four Londoners' who had strangled his uncle Gloucester at Calais and puts them in prison. He then turns his attention again to Richard.

The Duke of Lancaster and his counsellors conferred with the Londoners as to what should be done about Richard of Bordeaux, who was confined in the big tower in which King John of France had once been housed, in the days when King Edward was at war with France. It was decided that King Richard should be allowed all his ease and comforts, if he was prepared to enjoy them reasonably, because the news of his imprisonment would soon be known throughout Christendom, and he had reigned for twenty-two years, though now they wished to depose him. As a first step, they examined his reign and put down all the facts in writing under separate heads, of which they found twenty-eight. They then went to the Tower, in company with the Duke of Lancaster and some of his knights, and entered the room where King Richard was. They addressed him without any marks of respect and read out all the charges to him in full, to which he made no reply, for he knew that they were true. He only said that everything that he had done had passed through his council. He was

asked if he was ready to name his principal advisers. He named
them, evidently hoping that this would provide a way out and
that he would be acquitted at the expense of his chief counsellors, as had happened on the former occasion, when those
on whose advice he had misgoverned the realm had been left
to take the punishment. But such was not the intention of his
captors and the Londoners. They said no more for the time
being and left the Tower. The Duke of Lancaster returned to
his palace, leaving the Lord Mayor and the lawyers to meet
together in the town hall, which in London is called the Guild-
hall and is the place where judgements are given on cases concerning the citizens of London. When the city leaders and the
chief lawyers were seen to be going there, a great crowd assembled. It was expected that some sentence would be pronounced, as indeed it was. I will tell you what form it took.

First of all, the facts in the King's disfavour and the charges
which had been read to him in the Tower were now read out
publicly and it was pointed out that the King had denied
none of them. He had said, however, that he had consented to
do all these things principally on the advice of four household
knights of his inner council, and that it was on their recommendation that the Duke of Gloucester, the Earl of Arundel
and Sir Thomas Corbet had been put to death. For a long
time they had been persuading and inducing Richard of Bordeaux to commit these acts, which were unpardonable and demanded punishment. Thanks to them also the court of justice
in the Palace of Westminster had been closed and all the other
royal courts throughout England, which had encouraged
numerous crimes and had incited bands of malefactors to roam
the country robbing merchants and farmers in their own
homes. By permitting such things, they had come near to
ruining the realm of England beyond recovery. Also, it was
impossible not to conclude that they intended to restore
Calais and Guines to their enemy, the French.

When this case had been expounded to the people, many
were amazed and horrified and some began to mutter: 'These
things call for exemplary punishment and for the deposition
of Richard of Bordeaux. He is quite unworthy to wear a

crown. He should be stripped of all his honours and at best be kept in prison on bread and water, to live there as long as he can.' While some were muttering this, many more cried aloud: 'Your Worship the Lord Mayor and you others who hold justice in your hands, pronounce sentence, we demand it! Show no mercy, the cases you have presented require none. And do it quickly, for their own acts condemn them.'

The Lord Mayor and the law lords then withdrew to the judgement chamber and sentenced the four knights to die by being fastened to horses at the foot of the Tower of London, where Richard of Bordeaux could see them from the windows, and from there dragged on their buttocks, each separately, through the city of London until they reached Cheapside, where their heads should be cut off and placed on pikes on London Bridge and their bodies drawn by the shoulders to the gibbet and left there.

As soon as this sentence had been pronounced they prepared to carry it out, for everything was ready. Leaving the Guild-hall among a vast crowd of people, the Mayor and the officers appointed for the task went to the Tower and immediately had the King's four knights brought out. Their names were: Sir Bernard Brocas, Lord Marclois, Master John Derby, receiver of Lincoln, and Lord Stelle, the steward of his household. They were taken into the courtyard and each fastened to two horses in full view of the men who were in the Tower including the King, who were all filled with terror and anguish because they expected the same fate, knowing the ruthlessness of the Londoners. Nothing more was said. The four, one after another, were dragged through the streets of London to Cheapside and there, on a fishmonger's slab, their heads were cut off. They were set up on four pikes at the entrance to London Bridge and the bodies were hauled by the shoulders to the city gibbet and hung up there.

After these executions, the crowds dispersed to their homes. King Richard was in great anguish, feeling trapped and at the mercy of the Londoners. He counted his power for nothing, for it seemed that every man in England was against him; and if there were any who did wish to help him it was beyond their power to do so or to show him the slightest sympathy because the movement against him was so strong. His followers said to him: 'Sire, it now seems that our lives are worth nothing, since when your cousin of Lancaster came to Flint Castle the other day and you surrendered to him in good faith, he accepted your surrender on condition that you and twelve of your knights should be his prisoners and should suffer no harm; but now four of the twelve have gone to an infamous death. The reason is that the Londoners who are supporting him have bound him in such close obligations that he cannot withstand them. God would be showing us great mercy if He allowed us to die a natural death in here – not to suffer that ignominious death which it is horrible to think of.'

At this, King Richard began to weep bitterly and to wring his hands, cursing the hour when he was born if he was to come to such an end as that, until his men were moved to pity and tried to comfort him. 'Sire,' said one of them, 'you must take heart. We know, and you know, that this world is vanity and its chances and changes are unpredictable. Fortune sometimes runs against kings and princes as well as against humble people. The King of France whose daughter you have married cannot aid you at present, he is too far away. But if you could avert this danger by dissembling and so save your life and ours, it would be something achieved. Then in a year or two things might change for the better.' 'What do you think I should do?' asked the King. 'I would do anything to save us.' 'Sire,' said the knight, 'we know for a fact, and all the appearances confirm it, that the Londoners want to make your cousin of Lancaster king. It was with that idea that they sent for him and have been helping him in his cause. But as long as you are alive it would be very difficult to crown him without your absolute and formal consent. So we suggest that the best course for your safety and ours would be, when your cousin comes here to see you – or you might speed the matter up by asking him to come – for you to say in a pleasant and friendly way that you wish to resign the crown of England, with all your rights to it, absolutely and formally into his hands, so making him king. By that means, you will do much to placate him and win him over, and the Londoners at the same time. Then you will beg him to let you go on living here or elsewhere for the term of your natural life; and we with you, or each separately, or outside England as exiles. To lose one's life is to lose everything. Anything is better than that.'

King Richard took these words to heart and said that he would act on them, because he felt that he was in great danger. He gave his guards to understand that he would be glad to talk to the Duke of Lancaster.

RICHARD'S ABDICATION

News was brought to the Duke that Richard of Bordeaux was asking for him and greatly desired to speak to him. He immediately left his palace – it was late afternoon – and went by barge down the Thames, accompanied by his knights. He entered the Tower by the back way and went into the keep where the King was. Richard greeted him with great courtesy, making himself very humble before him, like the frightened man he was, and said:

'Cousin, I have been thinking over my position, and God knows it is weak enough! I see that I should no longer think of wearing a crown and ruling a nation. If God would receive my soul, I could wish I were out of this life by a natural death and that the King of France should have his daughter back, for we have not had much pleasure together; nor, since I brought her to England, have I ever been on the same good terms with my people as before. Having considered it carefully, cousin, I fully see and admit that I have behaved very wrongly towards you and several nobles of my own blood in this country, and I realize that such things have made peace and forgiveness impossible for me. Therefore, I gladly and willingly resign to you the crown of England, and I beg you to accept it as a freely offered gift.'

On hearing this, the Duke of Lancaster answered: 'What you have said makes it necessary to assemble representatives of the three estates of England. Indeed, I have already written to summon the prelates and nobles of the country and the

councillors of the principal towns. Within three days there
will be enough of them here for you to make the resignation
which you desire in due form. By this act, you will do much
to appease the hatred which many of the English feel for you.
It was to end the disorders which had arisen in the country
through the break-down of the judicial system that I was sent
for from beyond the sea, and for that reason that the people
wish to make me king. Strong rumours are going about the
country that I have always had a better claim to the crown
than you. When our grandfather, King Edward of happy
memory, raised you to the throne, this was pointed out to him,
but he had always had such affection for his son the Prince of
Wales that no one could dissuade him from his purpose of
making you king. If you had then followed the example of
the Prince and had heeded good advice, as a true son should
endeavour to do to the best of his ability, you would still be
king and in possession of all your powers. But you have always done the opposite, and now the rumour is, throughout
England and beyond, that you are not the son of the Prince of
Wales, but of some clerk or canon. I have heard from certain
knights who were in the household of my uncle the Prince
that when the Prince felt that his marriage was a failure because your mother was a first cousin of King Edward and he
was beginning to conceive a great dislike for her because she
bore him no children – and also he was godparent with her[1]
on two occasions for children of Sir Thomas Holland – she,
who had won him in marriage by guile and cunning, was
afraid that my uncle the Prince would find some pretext for
divorcing her. So she arranged to become pregnant and gave
birth to you, and to another before you. The first died too
young for any opinion to be formed of him, but about you,
whose habits and character are so different from the warlike
nature of the Prince, it is said in this country and elsewhere
that your father was a clerk or canon. At the time when you
were conceived and born at Bordeaux on the Gironde there
were many young and handsome ones in the Prince's house-

1. Godparents being within the forbidden degrees of affinity, it was
supposed that their union would be unfertile.

hold. That is what people are saying in this country, and you certainly seem to prove it, having always tended to favour the French and to desire peace with them to the prejudice and dishonour of England. Because my uncle of Gloucester and the Earl of Arundel wisely and loyally remonstrated with you and tried to preserve the honour and achievements of their fathers, you treacherously had them killed. For my part, I have taken you under my protection and I will defend you and prolong your life, through human pity, as far as I can. I will plead your cause before the Londoners and the heirs of those whom you unjustly put to death.'

'My deepest thanks,' said the King. 'I have more trust in you than in all the rest of England.'

'Rightly,' said the Duke. 'If I did not go – and had not already gone – against the will of the people, you would have been their prisoner and deposed amid humiliation and mockery, and put to death as your evil deeds deserve.'

King Richard swallowed all these things which the Duke of Lancaster said to him and had nothing to say in reply. He quite saw that neither force nor argument could help him, but only meekness, friendliness and plain dealing. He made himself as humble as he could, continually begging the Duke of Lancaster that his life should be spared.

After spending more than two hours in the Tower of London with King Richard, insisting again and again on the mistakes and abuses of which he was accused and which were undeniable, the Duke took leave of him and went back by the river to his palace. Next day he sent still more urgent summonses throughout the length and breadth of England. There came to London his uncle the Duke of York with his son the Earl of Rutland, the Earl of Northumberland and his brother Sir Thomas Percy, all of whom he made very welcome. There also came a large number of prelates: archbishops, bishops and abbots.

Then the Duke of Lancaster, accompanied by these lords, prelates, dukes, earls, barons and knights and the most prominent citizens of London, went to the Tower, all of them on horseback, and, reaching the open space in front of it, they dismounted and went inside. King Richard was brought down and came into the hall vested and arrayed as a king, wearing an open mantle and with the sceptre in his hand and the crown with which he had been crowned upon his head. No one stood at his side or supported him when he began to speak, uttering these words in the hearing of all:

'I have been Sovereign of England, Duke of Aquitaine and Lord of Ireland for some twenty-two years, and this sovereignty, lordship, sceptre, crown and heritage I resign fully and unreservedly to my cousin Henry of Lancaster, asking him in the presence of you all to take this sceptre in token of possession.'

He held out the sceptre to the Duke of Lancaster, who took it and handed it to the Archbishop of Canterbury. Next King Richard lifted the golden crown from his head, placed it in front of him and said: 'Henry, fair cousin and Duke of Lancaster, I give and deliver to you this crown with which I was crowned King of England, and with it all the rights belonging to it.'

The Duke of Lancaster took it, and again the Archbishop was at hand to receive it from him. These two things done and the King's resignation thereby given and accepted, the Duke of Lancaster called for a public notary and required a record to be made in writing, with the signatures of the prelates and lords who were present. Soon after Richard returned to his room, while the Duke of Lancaster and all the lords who had attended mounted their horses. The two royal jewels mentioned above were put in strong-boxes and taken to the treasury of Westminster Abbey. The lords all went back to their houses to await the day when the parliament was to be held in the Palace of Westminster.

CORONATION OF BOLINGBROKE

In the year of Our Lord 1399, on the last day of September, a Tuesday, Henry, Duke of Lancaster, held a parliament in the Palace of Westminster outside London. In this parliament were assembled the prelates and clergy of most of England, the dukes, earls and nobles of the realm, and also the commons of each town, in numbers proportionate to the size of the towns. Before that assembly Duke Henry made his claim to the throne of England, putting forward three titles to the office of king: first, by right of conquest; secondly, because he said he was the rightful heir; thirdly, because King Richard of Bordeaux had resigned the crown to him of his entire free will in the presence of prelates, dukes and earls in the hall of the Great Tower of London.

Having put forward these three titles to the crown, Henry Duke of Lancaster asked the people of England there assembled to say what their will was. They answered with one voice that their will was that he should be their king and that they would have none other. He put the same question to them twice again, asking if this was truly their will, and all answered with one voice, 'Yes!' Thereupon the Duke took his seat on the throne, which was covered with cloth of gold with a canopy over it. It was raised up high in the middle of the hall, so that all could see him. When he was seated upon it all the people held their hands up towards him, promising him allegiance and showing their great joy. The parliament was then concluded and a day assigned for the coronation, which was to take place on St Edward's day, Monday, the thirteenth of October.

On the Saturday before his coronation, the Duke of Lancaster left Westminster and went to the Tower of London with a large number of followers. That night all the squires who were to be knighted the next day kept vigil. There were forty-six of them and each had his room and his bath in which he bathed that night. The next morning the Duke of Lancaster made them knights while mass was being sung and gave them long green tunics with narrow sleeves trimmed with miniver and large matching hats also trimmed with miniver like those of prelates. Over their left shoulders they wore a double cord of white silk with white hanging tassels. After dinner that Sunday the Duke left the Tower again for Westminster, riding bare-headed and wearing the King of France's emblem round his neck. With him were his son the prince, six dukes, six earls, eighteen barons and a total of eight to nine hundred knights. The King had put on a short doublet of cloth-of-gold in the German style. He was mounted on a white charger and wore the blue garter on his left leg. He rode right through the city of London and was escorted to Westminster by a great number of nobles with their men wearing their various liveries and badges, and all the burgesses, Lombards and merchants of London, and all the grand masters of the guilds, each guild decked out with its particular emblems. Six thousand horses were in the procession. The streets through which the Duke passed were covered and decorated with various kinds of hangings and on that day and the next white and red wine flowed from nine fountains in Cheapside, each with several jets.

That night the Duke of Lancaster was bathed. As soon as he rose the next morning, he made confession[1] and heard three masses, as his custom was. Then all the prelates there assembled, with numerous other clergy, came in procession from Westminster Abbey to the Palace, to take the King back with them. They returned to the Abbey with the King following, and all the nobles with him. The dukes, earls and barons had long scarlet robes and long mantles trimmed with miniver, and large hats lined with the same fur. The dukes and earls had three bars of miniver about a foot long on their left shoulders, and the barons only two. All the others, knights and squires, had robes of scarlet livery-cloth.

All the way from the Palace to the Abbey a canopy of indigo-coloured silk supported on four silver rods and with four jingling golden bells was carried over the Duke's head by four citizens of Dover, as was their right. On one side of him was borne the Sword of the Church and on the other the Sword of Justice. The first was carried by his eldest son the Prince of Wales and the second by Henry Percy, Earl of Northumberland and Constable of England, for the Earl of Rutland had been deprived of that office. The Earl of Westmorland, Marshal of England, carried the sceptre. At about nine o'clock the whole procession entered the Abbey, in the middle of which

1. One manuscript bears the addition: 'for he had great need of it'.

was a throne upholstered in cloth-of-gold standing on a high platform covered with crimson cloth. On this the Duke mounted and took his seat. He was now in royal state, except that he was wearing neither the cap nor the crown. The Archbishop of Canterbury then mounted the platform and at each of the four corners of it in turn explained to the people how God had sent them a man to be their lord and king. He then asked if they were all willing that he should be anointed and crowned king. They unanimously answered yes, stretching out their hands to pledge him their loyalty and obedience.

When this had been done, the Duke came down from the throne and went to the altar to be consecrated. Two archbishops and ten bishops were there to perform the ceremony. Before the altar his royal robes were taken off, leaving him naked to the waist, and he was anointed in six [sic] places, on his head, his chest, on both shoulders, on his back between the shoulders, and on his hands. Then a cap was put on his head and meanwhile the clergy chanted the litany and the office which is used for consecrating a font. The King was then dressed in ecclesiastical robes like a deacon; crimson velvet shoes like those of a prelate were put on his feet and then spurs with points and no rowels. The Sword of Justice was drawn from its sheath, blessed and handed to the King, who re-sheathed it. It was then girded on him by the Archbishop of Canterbury. Next the crown of St Edward, which has three arches, was brought and blessed and placed on the King's head by the Archbishop. After mass had been sung, the King left the Abbey in this regalia and found outside the Constable of England with his lieutenant and the Marshal of England, who together cleared the way for the return to the Palace.

In the centre of the Palace was a fountain from which white and red wine flowed through numerous jets. The King went through the hall to his private room, then came back to the hall for the dinner. The first table was the King's; the second was for the four dukes of England; the third, for the people of London; the fourth, for the newly made knights; the fifth, for those knights and squires of honour who wanted seats. On one side of the King sat the Prince of Wales holding the

Sword of Justice, on the other the Constable of England, holding the Sword of the Church, and opposite him the Marshal holding the sceptre. The only others at the King's table were two archbishops and seventeen bishops. Halfway through the dinner there came in a knight of the name of Dymoke,[1] in full armour and riding a horse, with both of them, horse and rider, covered in mail with crimson trappings. The knight was ready armed to take up a challenge and another knight went before him carrying his lance. He wore a naked sword at one side and a dagger at the other, and he handed the King a parchment saying that if any knight, squire or gentleman cared to say or maintain that King Henry was not the rightful king, he was ready to fight him there and then in the King's presence, or whenever it pleased the King to appoint a day. The King had this challenge cried by a herald-at-arms at six different places in the hall, but no one came forward. After the King had dined, he took wine and spices in the hall, then retired to his private room. Everyone else left and went back to his own house.

PLOTS AGAINST HENRY IV

Henry IV is not yet secure on the throne. The French, disturbed and anxious about the position of the young ex-queen, grow increasingly hostile. At home, some of Richard's supporters plot to murder Henry at a tournament at Oxford and then to raise the country by using a clerk called Magdalen to impersonate Richard. Forewarned, Henry refuses to attend the tournament.

When the Earls of Salisbury, Huntingdon and Kent and Thomas Despenser saw that their plan had miscarried and that they could not kill the King in the way they had supposed, they conferred together and said: 'We must go after him at Windsor and raise the country on the way. We will dress Magdalen as a king and have him ride with us, giving out that he is King Richard who has been set free. Everyone who sees him or hears about him will believe it, and so we shall get the better of our enemies.'

1. The office of King's Champion was hereditary in this family.

They did as they had decided, banding themselves together and collecting a force of at least five hundred men between them. Magdalen was dressed in royal state and taken with them. They came near Windsor where King Henry held his court, but God saved him in time, for he was warned that they were approaching in sufficient strength to storm Windsor Castle. He was told: 'Sire, leave this place at once, and make for London by way of Sheen and Chertsey, for they are coming straight here.' He and his followers quickly saddled their horses and made off down the road I have mentioned. They had hardly gone when the armed force coming to kill him arrived at Windsor. They entered the castle unopposed and went searching for him from room to room and even in the houses of the canons, but found nothing. When they realized that he had escaped them, they left Windsor in fury and quartered for the night at Colnbrook. They made many people join them, by force or persuasion, saying that King Richard was with them. Some believed this, but others did not.

King Henry, who suspected treachery, spurred his horse on and reached the Tower of London by a roundabout way. He went in angrily and said to Richard of Bordeaux: 'I saved your life with great difficulty and now you are trying to have me murdered by your brother, who is my brother-in-law, the Earl of Salisbury, your nephew the Earl of Kent and Thomas Despenser. It is a pity for you that you planned this.'

Richard of Bordeaux insisted that he was innocent and swore, as God was his witness, that he knew nothing whatsoever about it. He said that he was perfectly content with his present state and had no thoughts of anything greater. There things were left for the time being.

The conspirators skirt London, but fail to attract support there. They make for the west and at Cirencester they separate. Salisbury and Thomas Despenser go on towards the Severn in the hope of raising the Welsh Marches. Huntingdon and Kent, remaining in Cirencester, are attacked and killed by the loyal Bailiff of the town.

There and then the men of Cirencester, who were thoroughly roused against them, cut off their heads and put them in two baskets. They were sent to London by a servant on a horse, as though they were a catch of fish, to gladden the King and the Londoners. The Earl of Salisbury and Sir Thomas Despenser met with a similar fate in the place which they had gone to, for knights and squires acting for the King captured them and cut off their heads and sent them to London. In this same rising there were many other executions of knights and squires who had joined or sympathized with it; after which the country remained in a fairly peaceful state.

THE END OF RICHARD OF BORDEAUX

It was said to the King and his advisers: 'Be on your guard, for the French show signs of wanting war and are assembling a large fleet at Harfleur. It is to be led by the Count of Saint-Pol and Sir Charles d'Albret. If the Earls of Huntingdon and Salisbury and the others who have been killed were still alive, it seems likely that the French would have come across already; they had powerful sympathizers in England.'

It was said to the King: 'Sire, as long as Richard of Bordeaux is alive, neither you nor the country will be secure.'

The King replied: 'I think you are right. But for my part I will never put him to death, since I took him under my protection. I will keep my promise to him until it becomes apparent that he is behaving treasonably.'

The King's knights said: 'It would be better for you if he were dead rather than alive. As long as the French know that he is there they will want to make war on you. They will hope to restore him to the throne, because he is married to the King of France's daughter.'

To this the King of England made no reply, but went out of the room and left them talking together. He went to see his falconers and, placing a falcon on his wrist, became absorbed in feeding it.

Not many days afterwards a true report ran through London that Richard of Bordeaux was dead. From what cause and how it happened I did not know at the time when I wrote these chronicles. His body was placed on a hearse with a black canopy over it. Four black horses were harnessed to it, led by two grooms in black, and four black-clad knights followed behind. So he left the Tower of London where he had died[1] and was taken right through London at a walking-pace until they reached Cheapside, the main street of the city. There in the middle of the street the hearse halted, and the grooms and the knights with it, and so remained for two hours. And over twenty thousand people, men and women, came to see King Richard lying there, with his head on a black cushion and his face uncovered. Some were moved to pity to see him in that state, but others not. These said that for a long time past he had well deserved to die.

Now, lords, consider well, kings, dukes, counts, prelates, all men of noble lineage and power, how fickle are the chances of this world. King Richard reigned over England for twenty-two years in great prosperity, holding rich estates and fiefs. No King of England before had come within a hundred thousand florins a year of spending as much as he did on the mere upkeep of his court and the pomp that went with it. For I, Jean Froissart, canon and treasurer of Chimay, saw and observed it at first hand. I spent three months in his household and was treated extremely well, because in my younger days I had been a personal secretary of the noble King Edward, his grandfather, and of my lady Philippa of Hainault, Queen of England, his grandmother. And when I went to take leave of him – that was at Windsor – he gave me through one of his knights, called Sir John Golafre, a goblet of silver gilt, weighing well over a pound, with a hundred nobles inside it, which has made me a richer man for the rest of my life. I have a strong obligation to pray for him and I am grieved to write of his death. But since I have compiled and written this history and have continued it to the best of my knowledge and ability, I have recorded it to make known what became of him.

In my time I heard two things which came true, though in very different ways. I remember that I was in Bordeaux, sitting at table, when King Richard was born. He came into the world on a Wednesday, on the stroke of ten. At that hour

1. Richard II died in Pontefract Castle and his body was brought to London. The cause of death is still obscure.

Sir Richard de Pontchardon, who was Marshal of Aquitaine at the time, entered and said to me: 'Froissart, write down and place on record that her Highness the Princess has been delivered of a fine boy, who has come into the world on Twelfth Day. He is a king's son, for his father is King of Galicia. King Peter has given him that kingdom and he will soon be off to conquer it. So the child comes of royal stock and by right he will yet be a king.'

The gallant knight of Pontchardon was not wrong, since Richard reigned over England for twenty-two years, but when he said this he did not know what the end of his life would be. These are things to reflect upon and I have thought much about them since. For also in the year I first came to England to enter the service of King Edward and his noble queen Philippa, the royal couple with all their children went to Berkhamsted, a manor belonging to the Prince of Wales about thirty miles outside London. Their purpose was to say good-bye to the Prince and Princess, who were about to leave for Aquitaine to hold their court there. That was in the year 1361 and I, who was then about twenty-four, listened to an old knight called Sir Bartholomew Burghersh sitting on a bench and talking to the Queen's maids-of-honour, who were from Hainault. This is what I heard him say: 'We have a book in this country called *The Brut*,[1] which many people believe to be the prophecies of Merlin. Now, according to this book, the crown of England will not pass to the Prince of Wales, nor to the Duke of Clarence, nor to the present Duke of Lancaster, nor to the Duke of York, nor to the Duke of Gloucester, although they are sons of King Edward, but it will return to the House of Lancaster.'

Now I, the author of this history, having reflected on all this, say that those two knights, Sir Richard de Pontchardon

1. No doubt Layamon's *Brut* (c. 1200), the English expansion of Wace's Norman French *Roman de Brut*, based in turn on Geoffrey of Monmouth's *Historia Regum Britanniae*. These works told the story of King Arthur. Froissart recounts this anecdote twice in different passages. The two versions, which are complementary and not conflicting, have been conflated here.

and Sir Bartholomew Burghersh, were both right. For I and everyone else saw Richard of Bordeaux on the throne of England for twenty-two years and, while he was still alive, the crown passing back to the House of Lancaster, when King Henry, in the circumstances I have related, became King of England. He had never thought of the crown nor would have done if Richard had behaved in a kinder and more friendly way towards him; and then it was the Londoners who made him King, to repair the great wrongs done to him and his children, which had aroused their sympathy.

When the hearse, with Richard of Bordeaux on it, had been in Cheapside a full two hours, it moved on. The drivers drove it forward and the four knights walked behind. When they were outside London their servants met them with their horses. They mounted and rode on more rapidly, until they reached a village called Langley thirty miles from London, where there is a manor belonging to the King and Queen. There King Richard of Bordeaux lies buried. May God have mercy on his soul.

Notes in Form of Glossary

(The explanations given bear only on the meanings found in Froissart)

ARTILLERY: Siege-engines of catapult type. See also *Cannon*.

BAILIFF: Chief political officer of a town or district, deriving his authority from the King or other overlord. Of the same order as *sheriff* and (in France) *seneschal*, though these offices were higher.

BANNERET, KNIGHT BANNERET: A high officer who led a considerable body of troops, or was entitled to do so. His square or rectangular banner distinguished him from the ordinary knight, who carried a triangular pennon. These distinguishing signs had great practical importance in battles, particularly when fought by large heterogeneous armies such as the French kings assembled. The men fought in groups, which could only cohere round their leader's banner or, if visibility was poor, his battle-cry.

BASCOT: Soldier of fortune, freebooter, used as part of name (e.g. the Bascot de Mauléon).

BATTALION, DIVISION, BODY OF MEN: These are translations of the single word *bataille*, according to context. A *bataille* was a single formation of men in battle-order, of no specific size. The English army at Crécy was divided into three *batailles*, numbering from 1,700 to 3,800 men, according to Froissart's figures. The Flemings at Roosebeke, computed at 50,000, formed a single large *bataille*. Bodies of men on the move ('column' or 'troop' in translation) are usually called *routes*.

BOMBARD: Type of cannon (q.v.).

BOURC: Gascon title meaning 'bastard', but to which no stigma attached. It was adopted as a matter of course by illegitimate sons of prominent families.

CANNON: With two exceptions (mentioned below) the first mention of cannons in Froissart is at the siege of Romorantin (1356), where they were used to 'cast Greek fire and heavy bolts'. Other references follow in descriptions of sieges, but they are not noted as used in the field until 1382, in the battle between Ghent and Bruges (where cannons and/or *ribalds* are used) and the Battle of Roosebeke (bombards and cannons). The assumption is that before that date gunpowder was little used in field warfare. The debated question of the use of cannons by the English at Crécy

(1346) can be summarized thus: (1) It is mentioned in only two Froissart texts, the Amiens MS, composed after 1376, and the *Chroniques Abrégées*, probably composed in the thirteen-nineties, in each of which it merits one sentence. The final version of 1400 (Rome MS) does not refer to it. Neither does the widely circulated first version, composed 1369-73, though the reference to a thunderstorm might conceivably be held to have a bearing on the matter. Le Bel preserves a similar silence. (2) The contemporary Italian chronicler Villani states that the English used 'bombards shooting small iron balls, with fire, to frighten the horses and throw them into confusion. They made so much noise and reverberation that it was as though God was thundering.' The *Grandes Chroniques de France* also mentions 'three cannons'. (3) An order for the casting of cannons in 1346 has been found in English official records, though this does not necessarily prove that they accompanied the expedition and were carried over the whole route from La Hogue to Crécy. (4) Several cannon-balls believed to be of the correct calibre were unearthed on the battle-field between 1800 and 1850, 450 to 500 years after the battle. (See particularly A. H. Burne, *The Crécy War*, Eyre and Spottis-woode, 1955.)

Everything considered, it would seem that, if cannons were fired at Crécy, they had little influence on the course of the battle and made little impression on eye-witnesses (except perhaps on the Genoese archers, who were probably Villani's informants). Also, their use at that date in field warfare would have been quite exceptional. However, Froissart does say that bombards were mounted on ships to be fired at the French land-forces attempting to relieve Calais (1347). This would be even more exceptional and may have been an experiment which was soon abandoned.

CAPTAL: Gascon title roughly equivalent to Count (e.g. the Captal de Buch).

CHIVALROUS, CHIVALRY: The usual rendering in this translation of *courtois*, *courtoisie*, and sometimes of *gentil*, *gentillesse*. The second two words refer basically to 'gentle (or noble) birth', with an extension to the 'gentlemanly' qualities implied by that. (*Chevalerie*, like *bachelerie*, is normally used by Froissart as a collective noun for 'knights' (*chevaliers*), cognate to 'nobility' and 'gentry', though here again there is some implication of quality, primarily military. A knight is assumed to be 'valiant'.) The wider and more significant word is *courtois*, meaning the opposite to 'harsh', 'brutal' or 'barbarous'. Prisoners are given or refused 'courteous' or 'chivalrous' treatment. *Prison courtoise* is captivity in comfortable conditions. The sense is often entirely materialistic and, though the word occurs very frequently, not much mystique attaches to it. The nearest single modern equivalent is 'civilized'.

COMPANION: A fellow-soldier (cf. the modern American 'buddy') or simply a soldier, considered as one of a unit. The *Companies* were bands of mercenaries who kept together for purposes of plunder or to be hired for a regular war.

CONSTABLE: The effective commander-in-chief, appointed either for a particular battle or campaign, or permanently, as Du Guesclin in 1370.

CROWN, GOLD CROWN: French coin (same as *écu*) worth 3 francs.

ENGLISH, see FRENCH.

FLORIN: Coin first struck in Florence in 1252 and used internationally. Nominal English value: 2*s*.

FRANCE, KINGDOM OF FRANCE: The territory under the immediate jurisdiction of the King of France, as distinct from territories whose first allegiance was to their own dukes and counts, or which were ruled by the English or others. Thus, Montreuil, Calais, Vannes, Poitiers, Bordeaux, Toulouse, Avignon, were not considered to be 'in France'. In its narrowest sense, 'France' was limited to the Île de France. (See map on p. 478.)

FRENCH: Often denotes allegiance, rather than nationality. The Lord of Albret married into the French royal family and 'became French'. The inhabitants of La Rochelle were 'French' only after they had changed sides. *English* is used in the same way. The Captal de Buch, a Gascon lord, was 'English' because he served the Black Prince. The Bascot de Mauléon considered himself a loyal Englishman because, he claimed, he had always fought in the English interest. Since many mercenaries showed their 'English' sympathies by plundering the country for personal profit, the English acquired a rather worse name in France than they objectively deserved.

GREEK FIRE: A combustible material which could be shot from cannons and siege-engines. The exact formula has been lost. It seems to have resembled the modern napalm.

HACKNEY: An all-purpose horse used by merchants and other ordinary people for travelling. Sometimes equivalent to 'pony'.

HELM, HELMET: These words have been preferred throughout to the less familiar but often more correct *bassinet*, which is Froissart's usual word. He speaks of Edward III's bassinet at Crécy, the

Black Prince's at Poitiers, and the bassinets of Étienne Marcel's citizen-soldiers. For the jousting at St Inglevert the contenders wore *helms*. Besides some differences in shape, the main distinction was that the bassinet had a movable vizor, the helm not.

IRREGULARS, LIGHT INFANTRY: The translation of several words, such as *brigands, ribauds, coustillers*. In general, they were undrafted troops, with light or no armour and carrying a *coustille* (long knife or short sword), who accompanied the organized armies for what they could pick up. In the English armies, according to Froissart, they were Welsh, Irish and Cornishmen. At Winchelsea, the Spaniards had *brigands* to hurl stones from the mast-tops.

JACK, JACK GOODMAN: From the name *Jacques Bonhomme* given to peasants in France, whence the *Jacquerie*. The name is thought to derive from *jacque* (a jerkin), considered as the peasants' distinctive wear, though a garment of that name was worn by Edward III at Winchelsea and by Bolingbroke on the eve of his coronation – in the second case made of cloth-of-gold. 'Goodman' is slightly contemptuous, as 'my good man' still is today, and one need not be confused by the fact that in Froissart the 'goodmen' are usually 'bad men'.

JOUST: An encounter, always with lances, between two mounted men, in a tournament or a real battle. As it was the most prized knightly exercise, it was also the form of fighting which Froissart describes with most zest. (For detail, see *Tournament at St Inglevert*, p. 373.) Edward III, fighting a sea-battle as though it were a land-battle, according to the naval tactics of the time, 'has a joust' at a Spanish ship, i.e. rams it.

LANCE: (1) The weapon. (2) Each 'course' or running-together of two mounted combatants in a tournament. The rules might require them to run three, or six, lances. Cp. 'round' in boxing. (3) A section consisting of one fully equipped mounted fighting-man, usually a knight or squire, supported by servants and auxiliary soldiers, such as two archers. A force of forty 'lances' could easily number 200 men in all.

MAN-AT-ARMS: A trained, fully equipped fighting-man, with armour, including the 'knights and squires' but not necessarily restricted to them. Always distinguished from the archers and the irregulars (q.v.).

MARSHAL: As the word implies, his main duty was to marshal armies on the battle-field, or when on the move. Like Constable, this also became a permanent title.

MINSTRELS, MINSTRELSY: Any kind of music-makers and singers, and the art of doing this as entertainment. It applied also to street-bands and to the trumpeters and others who accompanied armies. There were 'minstrels' on board Edward III's ship at Winchelsea. Even the clansmen who blew horns at Otterburn are called 'minstrels'. The people who spent the night banging cymbals and drums and blowing trumpets and cornets to celebrate the victory of Sluys were also practising 'minstrelsy'.

NOBLE: Gold coin first struck by Edward III in 1344, with value of 6s. 8d. It was worth about twice as much as the French franc and *mouton*. Mentions earlier than 1344 are anachronisms.

PALFREY: A well-bred riding-horse, lighter than a rounsey (q.v.). Edward III rode one when inspecting his men before Crécy. The Duchess of Touraine rode one at the official entry into Paris in 1389.

ROUNSEY: A strong horse used for travelling, drawing loads, or riding about, but not, by knights at least, for actual fighting. The latter was a *coursier*, translated in this book as 'horse' or 'charger'.

VILLEIN: Properly, a labourer tied to his overlord's land under the feudal system. By extension, all peasants and the common people of the towns.

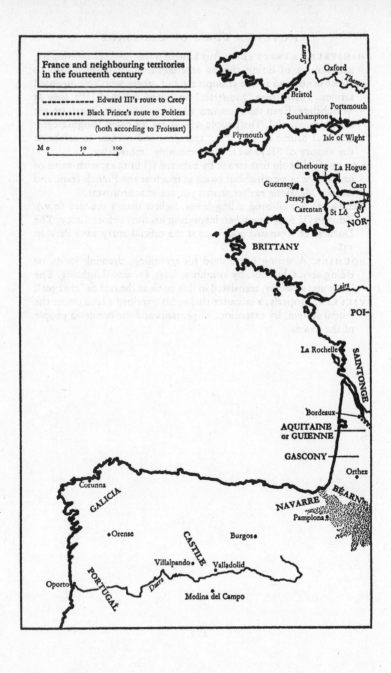

France and neighbouring territories
in the fourteenth century

------------ Edward III's route to Crecy
············ Black Prince's route to Poitiers

(both according to Froissart)

M 0   50   100

Oxford

Thames

Bristol

Portsmouth

Southampton

Plymouth

Isle of Wight

Cherbourg   La Hogue

Guernsey   Caen

Jersey   St Lô
            Carentan

                            NOR-

Ore

BRITTANY

Loire

POI-

La Rochelle

SAINTONGE

Bordeaux

AQUITAINE
or GUIENNE

GASCONY

Orthez

Corunna   BÉARN

GALICIA   NAVARRE

Pamplona

Orense   CASTILE   Burgos

Villalpando   Valladolid

Oporto   Duero

PORTUGAL
            Medina del Campo

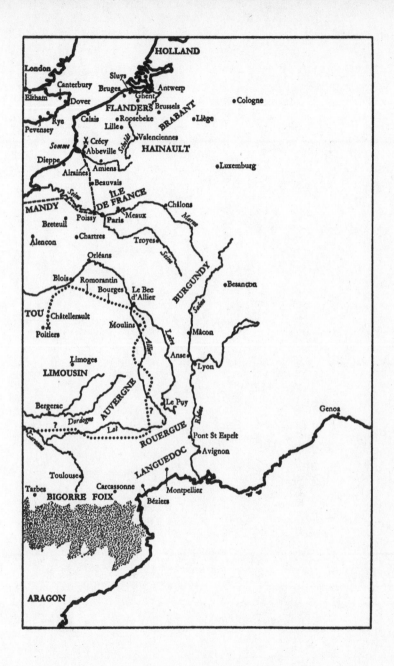

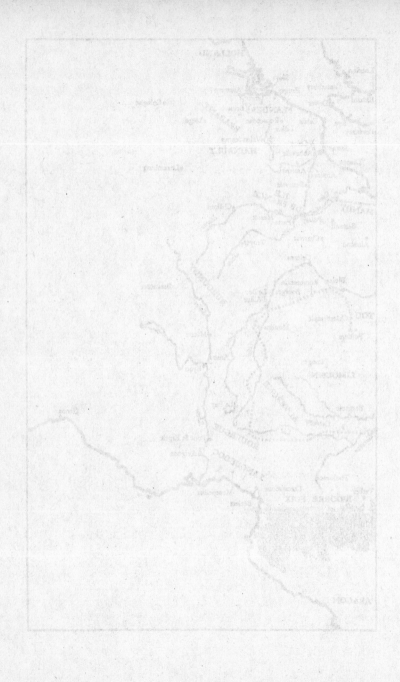

Index of Persons

* Alternately, these references are to Hereford (q.v.). Froissart has *Kenfort*.